the
Serbs

The Peoples of Europe

General Editors: James Campbell and Barry Cunliffe

This series is about the European tribes and peoples from their origins in prehistory to the present day. Drawing upon a wide range of archaeological and historical evidence, each volume presents a fresh and absorbing account of a group's culture, society, and usually turbulent history.

Already published

The Etruscans
Graeme Barker and Thomas Rasmussen

The Normans
Marjorie Chibnall

The Norsemen in the Viking Age
Eric Christiansen

The Lombards†
Neil Christie

The Serbs
Sima M. Ćirković

The Basques*
Roger Collins

The English
Geoffrey Elton

The Gypsies
Second edition
Angus Fraser

The Bretons†
Patrick Galliou and Michael Jones

The Goths
Peter Heather

The Franks*
Edward James

The Russians
Robin Milner-Gulland

The Mongols
David Morgan

The Armenians
A. E. Redgate

The Britons
Christopher A. Snyder

The Huns
E. A. Thompson

The Early Germans
Malcolm Todd

The Illyrians
John Wilkes

In preparation

The Sicilians
David Abulafia

The Irish
Francis John Byrne and Michael Herity

The Byzantines
Averil Cameron

The Spanish
Roger Collins

The Romans
Timothy Cornell

The Scots
Colin Kidd

The Picts
Charles Thomas

*   Denotes title now out of print
†   Print on demand

the
Serbs

Sima M. Ćirković

Translated by Vuk Tošić

350 Main Street, Malden, MA 02148-5020, USA
108 Cowley Road, Oxford OX4 1JF, UK
550 Swanston Street, Carlton, Victoria 3053, Australia

First published 2004 by Blackwell Publishing Ltd
Translated into English by Vuk Tošić

Library of Congress Cataloging-in-Publication Data

Library of Congress data has been applied for.

ISBN 0-631-20471-7 (hardback)

A catalogue record for this title is available from the British Library.

Set in 10 on 12 pt Sabon
by SNP Best-set Typesetter Ltd., Hong Kong

For further information on
Blackwell Publishing, visit our website:
http://www.blackwellpublishing.com

Contents

List of Plates   viii

List of Maps   x

Preface and Acknowledgments   xi

Introduction: Time, Space, and People   xvi

1   Ancient Heritage   1

The Roman Provinces   1

Settlement of the Slavs   7

Sclavinias   10

Christianization   15

The Theme of Serbia and the Principality of Serbia   20

The Coastal Principalities   24

The Town of Ras and Raška Land   29

2   The Dynasty of Sacred Roots   34

Nemanja's Legacy   34

Independent Kingdom   38

The Autocephalous Archbishopric   40

Stability Put to the Test   46

Two Kingdoms   49

Economic Development   52

Dynastic Ideal and Reality   58

The Empire   63
Land of the Emperor and Land of the King   67
Unfinished Society   71
Rift within the Dynasty   75

3   Between the Cross and the Crescent   77
The New Lords and the End of the Dynasty   77
Transfer of the Kingdom to Bosnia   80
The Battle of Kosovo – Reality and Myth   82
The Consequences   85
The Despot and His Land   87
The Restless Littoral   91
Economic Progress   93
Continuity as an Ideal   96
The Burden of Double Vassalage   101
A Chronicle of Demise   105

4   The Sultan's Protected Subjects   111
The Old and the New   111
Flight, Migration, and Settlement   115
The Orientalization of Towns: Varos and Kasaba   120
Economic Life   126
Clans and Clan Society   129
Church in Slavery   133
From Submission to Rebellion   140

5   The Emergence of Modern Christian Society   146
A New State Framework   146
Extending and Reorganizing the Framework   151
Peasants and Citizens, Soldiers and Nobles   157
Christian Education   162
The Beginning of Europeanization   167

6   The Era of Democratic Revolutions   176
    "The Serbian Revolution"   176
    Imposed Revolution   183
    From Prince's Autonomy to Autonomous Principality   190
    The Serbs and Serbia in the Revolution of 1848   196

7   National State: For and Against   204
    Changes in Reality and Changes in Ideas   204
    Ruling Nation   211
    National Minority   217
    In the Center of the Great Eastern Crisis (1875–8)   221
    Diverging Paths of Development   226
    Constitution and Parliament Put to the Test   237
    Times of War   243

8   All the Serbs in One State   252
    Between Unitarian Ideal and Pluralist Reality   252
    Yugoslavia Decreed   261
    Death and Resurrection   269
    Reconstruction and Development   274
    Modernization through Socialism   279
    Epilogue: Breakup of the Federation and the Struggle for a
    National State   288

Select Bibliography   297
Index   301

Plates

1.1 Entrance to Felix Romuliana, palace of Emperor Galerius
(305–11), Gamzigrad, eastern Serbia   6
1.2 A page from the Gospel of Prince Miroslav, late twelfth
century   19
1.3 Tenth-century episcopal church in Ras (Novi Pazar)   21
2.1 Studenica monastery, endowment of Stefan Nemanja,
central Serbia, late twelfth century   36
2.2 Silver coins minted by Serbian rulers, thirteenth to
fifteenth centuries   56
2.3 Kotor, earliest drawing from the end of the sixteenth
century   57
2.4 Family tree of St. Simeon and Stefan Nemanja's
descendants, Dečani monastery (1327–35)   59
2.5 Gračanica episcopal church, endowment of King
Stefan Uroš II Milutin, Kosovo, built 1315–20   60
2.6 Front page of the Prizren codex (sixteenth century),
with translations of Byzantine laws and the Code of
Emperor Stefan Dušan (1349, 1354)   69
2.7 Detail from an early fourteenth-century icon in the
monastery of Chilandar (Mt. Athos)   74
3.1 Manasija (Resava) monastery, the endowment of Despot
Stefan Lazarević, built 1407–17   90
3.2 Early fifteenth-century icon of St. Simeon and St. Sava   98
3.3 Smederevo on the Danube, built 1428–30, Serbian capital
1430–59   99
3.4 Heraldic arms from the fourteenth to fifteenth centuries   100
3.5 Illustrated page from the *Octoechos*, the first book printed
in the Crnojević printing press (1494)   109
4.1 Ottoman buildings in Belgrade before 1688   121

4.2   Mining elders on a sixteenth-century miniature in the codex
      with the Code of Mining Law (1412)   124
4.3   Coat of arms ascribed to Emperor Stefan Uroš (1355–71)   132
4.4   The patriarchate of Peć restored in 1557   136
5.1   Petrovaradin fortress, completed 1716–18   149
5.2   (a) Wirtemberg barracks in Belgrade, 1736; (b) the same
      building seen in 1864   152
5.3   Cathedral of the metropolitans in Sremski Karlovci, built
      1758–62   169
5.4   St. Sava surrounded by Serbian saints; copper engraving,
      Vienna, 1741   170
5.5   Front page of the *Slaveno-serbskija vjedomosti*,
      August 3, 1792   172
6.1   The Great School building (1808–13)   181
6.2   Monastery (1485) and palace (1838), Cetinje   189
6.3   Assignat valued at 5 florins, issued by the Serbian
      authorities in 1848   201
7.1   Residence (*konak*) of Princess Ljubica, wife of Prince Miloš
      Obrenović, in Belgrade, built second half of the nineteenth
      century   206
7.2   Village in western Serbia, mid-nineteenth century   206
7.3   Front page of the first issue of *Beogradske ilustrovane
      novine* (Belgrade Illustrated Newspaper), 1866   210
7.4   Serbian heraldic arms of the nineteenth century   226
7.5   Textile factory in Paraćin, 1880   236
7.6   Idealized portraits of Djordje Petrović Karadjordje and
      Miloš Obrenović   241
7.7   The court of King Nikola of Montenegro in Cetinje   242
7.8   "Hospital train" of the Serbian army   247
8.1   Church of St. George in Oplenac, mausoleum of the royal
      Karadjordjević family, built 1912   254
8.2   The Parliament building in Belgrade   255
8.3   Part of Belgrade after the German bombing of April 6,
      1941   268
8.4   Hydroelectric power station, Djerdap   280
8.5   TV tower on the top of Mt. Avala, built 1965, destroyed
      1999   285

Maps

1.1 Baptized Serbia and its neighbors. ca. 950   13
2.1 The Kingdom of Serbia and the Banate of Bosnia, ca. 1220   39
2.2 The Kingdom of the Nemanjić dynasty, ca. 1300   51
3.1 The despot's state after taking possession of Zeta, ca. 1422   102
4.1 The Serbian patriarchate of Peć, ca. 1640   135
6.1 Serbia under Prince Miloš Obrenović   192
7.1 Serbia and Montenegro after the Congress of Berlin, 1878   227
8.1 Serbia and Montenegro in the Kingdom of Slovenes,
Croats, and Serbs   253

Preface and Acknowledgments

The development of the Serbs, to whom this book is dedicated, has been similar in many respects to the histories of the other nations included in the *The Peoples of Europe* series. As well as the combination of ancient and Slav components analogous to the Roman and Germanic ingredients of Western Europe's development and integration, the Serbs possessed similar cultural and intellectual traits in the development of their group consciousness that kept the group together and provided its identity and longevity.

The Serbs also have a legend about their origin (*origo gentis*), about the separation of the people and their migration from the north under the leadership of the ruler's son. Following their Christianization, the notion that they were a *chosen people*, whose origin was at the very beginning of Genesis, strongly influenced the Serbs. They remained in a direct relationship with the Creator through which all conceptions of divine providence were fulfilled. This idea of a direct relationship with God served many nations in Christian Europe as a way of understanding themselves and their place in the world. The notion of a chosen people was taken from the Hebrews of the Old Testament and transferred to Christians in general, and then to the universal Christian Empire, and later to the individual parts of this Empire. As with other nations, the people who form the subject of this book perceived themselves as God's people, the "New Israel" to whom God Himself had appointed leaders, "some equal to the apostles, others the myrrhobletes and miracle-workers, and yet others great teachers and renowned archpriests." The Serbs did not seek deeper roots or a firmer footing until the eighteenth century.

When secular views became prevalent it was accepted that European and world history had been created by nations formed long ago, each one immutable and possessing a specific spirit. As peoples opposed one another or made alliances, rose to power or fell from grace, became more or less dominant, they themselves were the protagonists of historical events. It took a long time for critical thought to impose a different point of view, under the influence of the social sciences, and question whether history also molds nations, whether historical circumstances and changes affect the conditions for creating and maintaining social groups. This view did not become firmly established among Serbs; even until recently, prevailing opinion held that the nation had been created in distant times and that it had fought for its individual survival and progress.

In the long history of tribes, peoples, nations, and social groups, regardless of what they were called, many facets were transformed along with more permanent elements as the social and economic context within which the group existed experienced change. During the period of the "great migrations" many peoples spread out in an amorphous mass, whose different components overlapped and merged into one another. Greater population density, along with better communications and a higher degree of self-awareness, allowed for something like solidification to occur in which the group achieved durability and took on the shape of the mold that held it at the time. This metaphor might be used to describe what happened during the Middle Ages and focus attention on those frameworks (political, ecclesiastical, and cultural) that acted as the mold. Modern egalitarian societies, with their enormous ability to influence the consciousness of their members through education, propaganda, and the mass media, might be compared to durable and rigid materials that are brittle and break at their weakest point.

When observed in historical perspective, nations lose the complete and integral nature, the secular immutability, which popular opinion has tacitly given them. Closer analysis reveals that the ethnic community brought together different parts and fused them within itself, changing not only its social structure but the culture, beliefs, and symbols that held the nation together and secured its durability. The criteria for distinguishing members of the group and differentiating them from those outside it also changed. The dynamics, even the content, of these changes differ from one nation to the next, depending on the particular circumstances of its development. In any case, the individuality of nations is reflected not only in their position, neighborly relations, struggles, and mutual influences, but also in the specific features of the paths they took in reaching the level of integration that they had achieved by the eighteenth century and the beginning of the modern age.

This book is an attempt to shed light on the development of the Serbs and on the factors pertinent to their creation, development, and preservation as a social group. Since there is no theory to direct such research, these factors are taken from concrete historical circumstances that have already been studied and recognized. The origins of the Serb people are sought not in Pliny and Ptolemy, nor among the ancient Slav or Indo-European community, but among the Serbs and other Slav tribes that migrated to the territories of the northern Roman provinces in the sixth and seventh centuries. This does not imply that the formation of the people was completed during the Dark Ages following their settlement; on the contrary, this book seeks to show the level of integration by carefully tracing its history. It goes without saying that this integration was not completed in the Middle Ages or even in the nineteenth and twentieth centuries.

In addition to the obvious parallels with the development of Western Europe, primarily the role of the classical heritage and the Slavic component as analogous to the Germanic, there is also the type of social and political organization and resistance to the universal claims of the two Christian empires. Furthermore, the nations that developed in the Balkans have a number of particularities that are also manifested in the case of the Serbs. The primary characteristic is certainly the discontinuity with regard to their geographical distribution and political and social structure that resulted from being conquered by the Ottoman Empire in the fifteenth century.

The process of differentiation is also specific, with objective differences between the neighboring populations playing as important a role as the subjective perception of these differences. In the past, differences between nations were mostly attributed to linguistic differences, to the extent that the ethnic community was the equivalent of the community that spoke one language. The people whose history is presented here used the word *jezik* (language) as a synonym for *people*. They were familiar with the legend that 72 nations were created when languages were confused during the construction of the Tower of Babel. However, in the Balkans, among the Serbs and their South Slav neighbors, it was proved that more than one ethnic community may emerge from the basis of a single language, a one-dialectic continuum, and that separation according to other criteria (religious or political) can affect the differentiation and delineation between languages.

The confessional border that separated the Catholic Croats from the Orthodox Serbs turned out to be highly significant, as observed long ago, as was the border between both these Christian groups and their Islamic compatriots, whom for a long time they labeled "Turks." The confessional border was imposed less because of differences in dogma and more because of complex cultural features that formed around a certain religion. A Serb or Croat remaining in the same language community, but accepting Islam, would significantly change his way of life and environment. Differences then were not comparable to confessional differences in modern societies.

A lasting political framework within which life evolved, serving the same ruler or dynasty, unity in loyalty, all created a feeling of connection and led to integration within the state. However, the history of the Serbs shows that this factor cannot be considered decisive. For more than 350 years, from the fifteenth to the nineteenth centuries, the Serbs did not have their own state. They were dispersed over a large area and lived in the empires of foreign rulers and dynasties for centuries. But still they survived.

It was Serbian statesmen and intellectuals who claimed the state played a crucial role during the period of struggle for autonomy and independence. Thus in December 1830, Prince Miloš Obrenović, announcing an act by which the sultan granted him hereditary power in the vassal principality, declared, "Thus, brothers, yesterday we became a nation." It is interesting that two-thirds of the Serbs, with their consciousness, church, and culture, lived across the border, under the rule of the Habsburg emperors. In the next generation, influential politician Ilija Garašanin claimed that "outside of the state a person has no life or history."

Such exaggerated exaltation of the significance and role of the state cannot be justified by facts from Serbian history. They show that the periods without a state and those when parts of the people remained outside the state during its existence were highly significant for the fate of the nation. In both cases the state was the core of historical consciousness that was maintained both through the church, in the form of the cult of native ruler-saints, and through folklore, in the form of epic poetry with heroes and rulers from the distant past.

Due to the discontinuity mentioned above, there was a great discrepancy between the actual course of events and those recited in the episodes that replaced learned history. The significance of portraying history was emphasized because of the continual struggle to reestablish the state, kingdom, empire, and former fame and glory. As has been said many times, the future was envisioned as the restoration of the past. This is why this book pays more attention to notions and depictions of the past.

In an effort to keep in focus the development of the nation as a whole, and given the space limitations of this book, it has been necessary to leave out many details, primarily concerning persons, the institutions of states where the Serbs lived, and especially the foreign policies of those states. Interested readers should consult the extensive and critical literature on Serbian history that deals with periods, events, persons, and phenomena. The bibliography included at the end of the book provides a useful guide.

The bibliography reveals only partially the author's debt to his predecessors who have conducted research in Balkan and Serbian history, since it is limited to European-language works, while the bulk of the scholarly literature is in Serbian and other South Slavic languages. The author is equally indebted to all those who have helped transform the Serbian manuscript into an English book. Alice Coople-Tošić carefully read each page and her assistance is acknowledged by both translator and author. Thanks are also due to the copy-editor, Brigitte Lee, for seeing the book through its final stages.

The author is especially grateful to Professor Bariša Krekić of UCLA for reading the manuscript and suggesting many valuable improvements. His detailed knowledge of the Byzantine, Mediterranean, and Balkan worlds, as well as his immense teaching experience, helped eliminate a number of errors. Of course, any that remain are the author's responsibility.

Introduction: Time, Space, and People

Ever since the loss of belief in a "spirit of the nation," in origin and language as an essential and enduring characteristic of national identity, it has become more difficult to shed light on the creation and destiny of a nation. When the nation is observed as a social group, it is constantly susceptible to change and movement. At no time is it ever so complete that it can neither grow nor decline; its cohesion may increase or contract, the essence of its individuality and difference from others may undergo change, and some of its symbols may be discarded while new ones are adopted.

Changes important for the preservation and development of a group occur over centuries, and thus it is not just the oldest or the most recent period that is significant, as is sometimes thought. There are no privileged spheres of life, such as demographic growth or decline, or linguistic change. Alterations in ecological circumstances, social structure, or culture may have far-reaching consequences for the development of a people. The search for an essential identity has revealed an entangled assortment of numerous historical strands instead of one single factor that can be traced through many centuries.

In the case of the Serbs and other Balkan nations (with the exception of the Greeks), the region of their development was relatively unknown outside their group and their immediate neighbors. This fact has additionally obscured the process of understanding the Serbs' long, complex, changeable, and visibly unfinished history. This introductory chapter is intended to place small, local, and specific phenomena in the context of general and more familiar historical trends. It outlines the major epochs and the dominant powers that long influenced a large region, the geographic space that formed the Serbian historical stage, and the peoples among whom the Serbs developed.

The Epochs of Serbian Development

The name Serb links today's Serb people with the Slav tribe from the time of the ancient Slav community and the period of migrations. During this period, part of the great tribe moved far south, settling in the territory of the Roman Empire. Early Serb traces exist even today in place-names in Poland, and in a vast area that is now Germany, where the *Limes Sorabicus* existed along the Elbe and Saale rivers and where the principalities of the Serbs (Surbi, Sorabi, Zribia) existed up to the twelfth century. Lusatian Serbs (Sorbs), the distant descendants of the Serbs, still live in part of this territory.

No accounts survive from this period about how the Slav tribes differed among themselves or what Serb individuality involved. Does anything apart from their name link the members of these groups who are so far removed in time and space? During the Romantic period it was believed that every nation had a "national spirit," reflected in its language, customs, and folklore. It is difficult to assume that a common "national spirit" existed for the Lusatian Serbs, descendants of the Serbs in the north, and the Balkan Serbs in the south. Serbian linguists have claimed that "within the group of Slav language types, the Lusatian and Štokavian dialects are among the most distant in character" (P. Ivić). Therefore language does not confirm a possible genealogical link between the Serbs from the Balkans and the Serbs from the Elbe River, unless we assume that in the centuries following the migrations, the language changed so fundamentally that even the most stable elements were altered.

In any case, the great distance separating them eventually severed and prevented further ties and mutual influences between the northern Slavs and southern Slavs, whose recollection of their northern origin lingered for some time. In contrast to the great spatial and chronological discontinuity with their northern ancestors, the spatial and chronological continuity of the Serb tribe that migrated to the Balkans and the Serb people who developed in this area in the following centuries is indisputable. Thus a justifiable starting point for the history of this people can be taken to be its migration to the Balkans in the sixth or seventh century AD.

However, such a late and modest beginning failed to satisfy patriotic publicists. Authors emerged in the mid-nineteenth century disputing the migration, and portraying the Serbs as the indigenous population not only of the Balkans, but also of a significant part of Europe and Asia Minor. In the opinion of some authors, it was the Slavs who were the descendants of the Serbs, whose roots in turn could be traced back to the Tower of Babel. Such pseudo-historical literature has not died out; in its recent wave it sought to shift the focus of Serbian history to even more ancient times where there was much scope for unrestrained fantasy.

There is no doubt that the Serbs brought their Slav heritage to the Balkans, including language, material culture, the Slavic pagan religion, and origin legends. There is little information on the earliest material culture because archeological findings are uncharacteristic and difficult to differentiate. Villages of the Slav settlers from the early centuries are archeologically "invisible" and unrecognizable. The names of pagan deities, preserved in present-day toponyms and later literary works, provide clues to religious notions and testify to the link with the religion of other Slavs, but they are not sufficient to differentiate the religious beliefs of individual tribes. Despite scholarly efforts, there is no reliable identification of the supreme Serbian deity.

Legends about their northern origins and migration existed not only among the Serbs but also among their neighbors the Croats, surviving among them until the tenth century. They became widely known due to the scholarly writings of the Byzantine Emperor Constantine Porphyrogenitus. The first few centuries following the Serb migration truly represented the Dark Ages, where no single recognizable element of individuality existed aside from the name and legends of the origin of the ruling clans, and information about them was preserved by outsiders.

The first milestone was Christianization (around 870 AD) and the adoption of the religion of the Book, accompanied by the creation of special alphabets adapted to suit the Slav languages (Glagolitic and Cyrillic). This laid the foundation for the development of culture and literature, which expanded from liturgical books to educational religious subjects, and later to documents and literary works. Christianized Serbs had gained an important instrument for preserving their consciousness and thus also their survival.

Early Christian missionaries suppressed pagan customs, traditions, and beliefs, abolishing and eradicating differences that were rooted in paganism. On the other hand, the advance of Christianization produced new differences, which were imposed by the church centers from which the missions came. Differences in the language of the church service and the alphabet extended to spiritual culture in general, and strongly influenced the process of differentiation and integration of the Balkan ethnic groups.

Christianization also influenced changes in social organization and established a new view of the world and of the people's position within it. The new faith legitimized the ruling class, which was comprised of the ancient ruling families, and included them in the Christian *oikoumene*, embodied in the Roman Empire headed by Christ's emissary on earth. Local rulers were reduced to imperial governors, and the development of political relations shows that they were not always satisfied with this status, that they rebelled and sided with the Empire's enemies.

The period following Christianization, up until the twelfth century, was also the period of absolute domination by the Byzantine Empire. Three hundred years of continuous Byzantine influence left lasting traces on the Slavs in the eastern and central part of the Balkan Peninsula. The Bulgarians and Serbs took on Byzantine traits that would characterize them for centuries. These traits grew and accumulated in subsequent centuries.

Following the rapid decline of the Byzantine Empire (after 1180 AD) and its temporary collapse (1204 AD) came the epoch during which the eastern and central Balkan Slavs gained independence (thirteenth to fifteenth centuries). This period was crucial in establishing important attributes of individuality and identity. Byzantium's withdrawal created space for the development of vast and permanent states, which provided the framework for early and unfinished integration processes. The Bulgarian and Serbian rulers governed their people by "the grace of God," the former using imperial and the latter using royal titles. Their subjects were members of the church, which had local elders and synods. These states were both secular and religious communities, as was the case with Byzantium, and their rulers were appointed by God and directly responsible to Him. The ruling Serbian dynasty included saints, primarily the founder Simeon Nemanja (1166–96) and later his son Sava (1175–1236), the first Serbian archbishop. Their cults offered an opportunity for the development of a specific Serbian tradition as a continuation of the general Christian tradition. Serbian historical personalities were depicted in icons and frescoes and were included in the church calendar and liturgical texts. Since the ruling dynasty was at its source, this was considered to be the beginning of Serbian history and everything prior to it was suppressed and forgotten. Thus the profile of the Serbs was completed and enhanced: the foundation consisting of the Slav language was coated with a layer of eastern Byzantine Christianity, whose particular traits were graven on the collective self-consciousness and passed down through the centuries.

New borders were created, separating the Serbs not only from those who spoke other languages (Greeks, Hungarians, Albanians), but also from those who spoke understandable dialects but whose church services were held in Latin (Slavs in coastal towns and neighboring territories under the jurisdiction of the Catholic bishops). In later epochs Catholic and Orthodox affiliations were crucial for differentiating between the Serbs and the Croats. The unification of the language and

orthography of church books within the Serbian autocephalous archbishopric stressed linguistic differences within the Church Slavonic heritage. Serb copyists complained of the difficulties of translating books
not only from Greek, but also from Bulgarian.

The longer the Serbian state maintained its political independence, the
more its specific history became durable, its society more stable, and its
culture more homogenized. Faced with the Ottoman conquest in the mid-
fourteenth century, the Balkan Christian states began to grow closer
and overcame their former rivalry with the Byzantine Empire. Christian
solidarity developed within the framework of Byzantine Orthodoxy,
without jeopardizing the distinctiveness of the individual peoples.

The epoch of "Turkish slavery" (fifteenth to eighteenth centuries)
interrupted the integration process, and the Serbs as an ethnic group
experienced enormous change with the abolition of their state and their
complex social structures, nobility, and local institutions. Only the
Serbian Orthodox Church, which operated under difficult conditions,
remained a symbol of continuity. The theocratic organization of the
Ottoman state emphasized religious differences through a system of
unequal rights and obligations of its subjects, which in turn resulted in
religious affiliation becoming crucial for identity. Those who left the
Orthodox community were forsaken by the Serb people; they no longer
shared their tradition, they had a different attitude toward the Ottoman
Empire and its authorities, and completely changed their way of life. All
that was left of the Serb people were the dependent peasants (reaya) and
the significantly more autonomous herders. Both groups maintained their
collective consciousness within the home and family, while the Orthodox Church preserved the memory of their rulers, saints, and glorious
past. Heroes and warriors were evoked in epics – an important element
of folk culture.

The early eighteenth century opened a new epoch of modernization
and Europeanization, one that has still not been completed but extends
into the future. It included several important events, two of which were
the beginning of the struggle to establish the Serbian state (1804), which
then became the motherland of the dispersed and divided nation, and
the abolition of feudal privileges and remaining class structures (1848),
which led to the affirmation of the nation based on linguistic unity and
equality and to the tension between religious and secular views as a characteristic of Serbian identity. The epoch of modernization initially
included only that part of the Serbian people in Hungary who were freed
of Ottoman rule. In the beginning Europe was represented in the Balkans
by the Habsburg Empire and Russia, which itself was taking the first
steps toward modernization, and later by the "guarantor" powers and
the entire developed world, which the Serbs joined.

Shifting Serbias

Most European peoples settled in their present territories after significant migrations and frequent struggles over shifting borders. In the case of the Serbs, mobility was so incessant that for centuries people did not establish lasting links with a definite territory, causing their development to be pithily characterized as *shifting Serbias* by St. K. Pavlowitch. This mobility hindered integration of the entire ethnic community, and also made it difficult to trace and understand Serbian history since the settings changed so often. The vastness of the area and diversity of the environments covered become apparent when surveying the territories relevant to Serbian development.

South of the Sava and Danube rivers lay plains, the continuation of the Pannonian Basin, an open space that was suitable for colonizing, communications, and an economy based on agriculture. Even though both rivers formed natural obstacles and served as borders for long periods of time, they were still overcome during state expansions: first from the north (eleventh to thirteenth centuries) when the Hungarian Kingdom established a belt of administrative units south of the rivers in present-day Bosnia and Serbia (as far as Vidin in Bulgaria), and later from the south when the Ottoman army crossed the rivers in the sixteenth century and conquered a large portion of the Pannonian Basin. At that point the territory colonized by the Serbs extended far to the north and the west.

The next region inhabited by the Serbs was the Dinaric Alps, a wide range of mountains extending northwest to southeast, expanding to the east but also becoming lower and more gentle. The mountains separate the interior of the Balkan Peninsula from the Adriatic coast and act as a barrier against the climatic influences of the sea. For centuries they made the passage of people and goods difficult, resulting in significant economic and cultural differences between the coast and the interior. Only a small number of corridors allowed for the movement of people and pack animals, and these caravan routes were replaced by railroads and paved roads in the nineteenth century.

Up until the nineteenth century the Adriatic coast was separated from the hinterland along its entire length, from Istria to Albania: initially the coastal cities were under Byzantine rule until the mid-twelfth century, then they were ruled by Venice from the fifteenth to the eighteenth centuries. Even when the coast was under the control of the states from the hinterland, Hungary in the north and Serbia in the south, their power was always indirect because they had to rely on the town communes, whose autonomy had gradually increased. The coastal region was more urbanized than the interior. There the remains of Roman cities were preserved, where people who had to make their living from the sea through sailing and trade, fishing and salt production found shelter. Karst basins provided a suitable living environment between the coast and the mountains in the hinterland. There was little arable land in the mountains of the continental climate zone, but plenty of pastureland and forests, which provided good conditions for cattle breeding. Semi-nomadic herding, with herds alternating between valleys and mountains, existed for centuries and continued until the modern industrial era.

The main east–west communication lines, as well as those running from north to south, traversed part of the mountain range where the Pannonian plain penetrates furthest to the south along river valleys with rolling hills. Land routes followed the Southern, Western, and Great Morava rivers. The most important route was along the Great and Southern Morava rivers, to the Vardar river valley, which extended to Thessalonika and Thessaly. The route to Sofia and central Bulgaria branched east, up the Nišava River. The mining potential of the land inhabited by the Serbs offered a considerable advantage. Ore was discovered and excavated in three waves: during the Roman period, between the mid-thirteenth and late seventeenth centuries, and during the modern industrial era.

Interest in the little understood original arrangement of Slav tribal territories increased during the struggle for national states and their borders during the nineteenth and twentieth centuries. The "historical rights" of certain nations were based on these tribal territories and the early medieval states, even though objective historical research revealed that these territories had very little in common with the ethnographic maps of the nineteenth century.

According to the earliest layout, the Croats were to the west, from the foothills of the Alps to the Livno and Imota *župas* (regions around the present-day towns of Livno and Imotski in western Herzegovina), and Pliva (around the present-day town of Jajce in western Bosnia). The Serbs were their adjoining neighbors to the east and their territory spanned as far as the town of Ras (present-day Novi Pazar), which was where the Bulgarian state began, covering what is today Serbia. Other tribes were included in the Bulgarian state: Severci (Severjani) between the Danube River and Mt. Balkan, and the Druguviti (Dragoviči) in the Aegean hinterland and Macedonia, who were last mentioned in the early thirteenth century.

The oldest territory bearing the name of the Serbian tribe, "Baptized Serbia," differed considerably from the territory of the later Serbian state. It included much of what is present-day Bosnia but did not incorporate present-day Serbia, which was part of the Bulgarian state at the time. The first significant Serb drift was to the east toward territories that came under direct Byzantine rule after the fall of the Bulgarian Empire (1018). The obvious result of this penetration to the east was the establishment of the Serbian political center in the town of Ras, extending the name to the surrounding territory: Raška land.

A significant part of present-day Serbia including Kosovo and Metohija as far as Mt. Šar, the natural barrier in the south, came under Serbian rule even before the fall of Byzantium in 1204. The northern border of the Serbian state reached the banks of the Sava and Danube rivers only toward the end of the thirteenth century, when Serbs occupied Hungarian territories, which was the cause of many wars during the fourteenth century as the Hungarians refused to renounce their claim.

A second mountain range, extending north–south as a continuation of the Carpathian Mountains, separated the Serbian state from the Bulgarian Empire in the east. The Nemanyid kingdom included what is today Herzegovina and Montenegro, part of the Adriatic coast from the Neretva River to the Bojana River, with the exception of the city of Dubrovnik and its territory. What had been the center of the state during the eleventh and twelfth centuries was now the periphery, since the main direction of expansion of the Serbian Nemanyid kingdom was to the south, toward regions controlled by Byzantium. The seat of the rulers and of the archbishops moved from Ras to courts next to the lake in southern Kosovo, Prizren, and Skopje; and from the border monastery of Žiča to Peć, which was to be the seat of the Serbian patriarchate for centuries to come. This reorientation was brought about by prevailing conditions of development and backwardness. The south was developed, urbanized, and relatively wealthy, while the north was neglected, impoverished, and scarcely populated.

The greatest expansion toward Byzantium was during the reign of Stefan Dušan, "Emperor of the Serbs and the Greeks" (1331–55), when the Serbian state included Epirus and Thessaly as well as Macedonia and Albania. Vast territories began to be lost to breakaway rulers during the rule of Dušan's son, marking the beginning of the pressure on Serbian borders from the south and the east, and the shift to the north. This lasted until the Ottoman conquest, and was continued as Serbs migrated to territories controlled by Christian rulers.

"Baptized Serbia" of the ninth and tenth centuries was replaced by the Nemanyid Serbia of the thirteenth and fourteenth centuries, which included Macedonia and part of Albania, and later in the early fifteenth century by the much smaller Serbia ruled by the despots. It assumed the characteristic shape of a rectangle after the territory of present-day Herzegovina seceded and joined the Kingdom of Bosnia. From 1421 the Serbian state also included most of what is today Montenegro.

After the fall of the Serbian state in 1459, its borders and name disappeared and its people were dispersed throughout a large region without boundaries until the reestablishment of the Peć patriarchate in 1557, which provided the Serbs with a framework for a religious community. Serbia was briefly restored by the Habsburg Empire between 1716 and 1739, with a modest territory between the Western Morava River and the Sava and Danube rivers. A century later (after 1815), this territory became the core of the restored Serbian state, which included an additional four districts in 1878, and part of Macedonia in 1913.

However, the Serbian state encompassed only part of the Serb people, less than half in the beginning, although its population quickly increased, as did its territory, and with it the proportion of the Serb people who lived in their mother country. The Serbs outside of Serbia were divided in several ways: Montenegro had gradually gained independence starting in the eighteenth century and established itself as a separate state. A substantial number of Serbs remained under Ottoman rule. Those who lived in the Habsburg monarchy came under different regimes in Hungary, Croatia, Dalmatia, Bosnia, and Herzegovina (following the occupation of 1878).

Serbia as a whole, along with its ethnic name, again vanished in 1918 when the Kingdom of Serbs, Croats, and Slovenes was formed (renamed the Kingdom of Yugoslavia in 1929). The federal constitution imposed by the Communists in 1944 restored Serbia along borders that were very similar to those of the early fifteenth-century state of the despots, but it was enlarged by the former Hungarian comitats in the north, territories east and north of the Danube that had become part of the Kingdom of Serbs, Croats, and Slovenes following demarcation from Hungary and Romania. The latest Serbia had two autonomous territories, Vojvodina in the north and Kosovo and Metohija in the south. As of 1999, Kosovo has been under international administration, in line with United Nations Security Council Resolution 1244.

The Serbs and Others

There is no single period when the Serbs alone inhabited a large territory, without the presence of other nations. Members of other nations had always lived in border regions and adjacent areas. The Serbs fostered multiple relations and connections with their neighbors, some of whom they accepted and assimilated, while also being absorbed by others.

At the very beginning two components were clearly differentiated: the recently settled Slavs and the native inhabitants they encountered.

Neither group was united or homogenized. The Slavs consisted of several tribes, one of which was the Serbs, and the territory inhabited by one tribe included parts inhabited by other tribes. As has been shown, there is no direct connection between the region where the Serbs settled and the territory where the later Serbian state developed. In the karst valleys in the Adriatic hinterland, the principalities of the Neretljani, Zahumljani, and Travunians later took shape from Serbian foundations. These groups long maintained their individuality and are recognized in the Serbian royal title in the first half of the thirteenth century.

The previous Balkan inhabitants consisted of several different groups. The Roman Empire continued to exist in towns and islands where the government, military, and institutions had been preserved along with the earlier population. During the period of Slav migration, the Hellenic substratum was becoming dominant in the Empire and already being christianized; it became Greek and the Serbs perceived it as the "Greek Empire" for many centuries.

Aside from the remnants of the Roman Empire in the Balkans there were also many enclaves where the original provincial population had lost contact with the capital. The population of various tribal origins had lived under Roman rule for the previous five centuries and was more or less romanized, appearing in a variety of forms.

Roman inhabitants of the towns on the Adriatic coast and islands preserved their own language, which differed from Italian dialects and survived until the nineteenth century. In the interior of the peninsula the Slavs encountered Vlachs, who had also been largely romanized. Over the centuries most of the Vlachs were absorbed by their Slav or Greek surroundings, while others merged with the population on the opposite bank of the Danube where the Romanian nation would later take shape; a Vlach ethnic group still exists today in eastern Serbia, while in Macedonia they are called Tzintzars (Aromani). Albanians who had been little romanized survived in the mountainous regions of what is now northern Albania, which Serbian sources call Arbanasi, maintaining the older form of the name, while the Albanians themselves called it Shqiptarë in later centuries.

Unlike in Italy and the western Roman provinces, the natives and settlers here did not live alongside each other in towns or smaller regions. Accounts from later times (tenth to thirteenth centuries) mention hostilities between the Slavs and Vlachs, and it appears that only later, with Christianization, the creation of durable states, regular trade, and economic cooperation, did contact and intermingling occur.

When the history of the Balkan Peninsula was brought to light between the eighteenth and nineteenth centuries, through the search for national roots, those peoples who had not yet developed into a nation with their own distinct culture and literature were ignored. The role of the Vlachs, as the largest indigenous group, was only brought to the fore through twentieth-century research. Historiographic disputes developed around this issue. Since the name Vlach denoted herders who had taken part in the migrations during the fifteenth and sixteenth centuries, using unquestionably Slavic names and language and belonging to the Orthodox faith, in intranational polemical debates it was disputed that they were Serbs. The Serbian reply was that the term Vlach indicated status and not ethnos, and that the Vlachs did not exist in later centuries as an ethnic group.

However, the maintenance of a special name was the result of different crafts and way of life, with distinct forms of social organization. The name Vlach vanished when these differences lost their meaning. The slavicization process lasted for centuries: as early as the twelfth century there were Vlach groups under leaders with Slav titles; and in the next century Vlach communities, *katuns*, bore Slav names, indicating a certain degree of slavicization. In each century Vlach groups emerged from isolation and mingled and blended with their Slav surroundings.

At the time of its greatest territorial expansion the Serbian state was the "Empire of Serbs and Greeks." Emphasis on the Greek component of the ruler's title was based on governance of Greek territories and justified its imperial claims. However, the Greeks were not the only foreign element – there are charters and legal texts that testify to the ethnic diversity of the medieval Serbian state. A charter from 1300 AD states that potential visitors to the marketplace at Skopje, "whether they are Greek, Bulgarian or Serb, Latin, Albanian, or Vlach, are to pay legal tax." The designation Latin indicated Catholics, merchants from Italy or the coastal towns, as well as settlers from the Serbian hinterland who had converted to Catholicism in the cities. Saxons – German miners – represented a new element from the mid-thirteenth century, and after the end of the fourteenth century Turkish travelers and merchants appeared. Turks later increased in numbers when they conquered the territory.

The Serbian state of that time did not seek to unify or homogenize the diverse parts of its society; on the contrary, it respected the rights of individual ethnic groups just as it did the rights of certain social strata. The state used its authority to maintain the power balance, while harmonizing relations and resolving conflicts between members of groups with special rights.

The general development of the Serbian people was shaken to its foundations by the Turkish conquest in 1459. The Serbian motherland vanished, its ruling class was wiped out, and its institutions were destroyed. The people were dispersed over a vast area as a consequence of many migrations, as far as the Slovene lands, central Hungary, and Transylvania, but thinly and in mutually unconnected enclaves. By 1557, when the Peć patriarchate was restored, the Serbs had no internal links or external boundaries. Under the patriarchs they came together as a religious community linked by the church hierarchy.

The Turkish conquerors added a new ingredient from Asia Minor, as well as islamized subjects from previously conquered European lands. The towns accommodated Armenian, Jewish, Greek, and Tzintzar (Aromani) merchants, while Roma (Gypsies) spread across the land and remained marginalized, rejected, and unrecognized for centuries.

The Ottoman system of privileges and obligations emphasized religious differences, which had also been significant during earlier periods. Islamization was not imposed, but accepting the ruler's religion brought social advantages. Conversion to Islam was not uncommon, especially during certain periods (seventeenth to eighteenth centuries) and in certain regions (Bosnia, Albania). By accepting Islam, the Balkan Christians became detached from their compatriots, who considered them to be Turks, since they had accepted their customs and way of life. On the other hand, within large ecclesiastic communities, such as the Peć patriarchate, differences were eliminated and there was intermingling with the basic mass of the population. The Serbs absorbed not only groups of Vlachs who were later slavicized, but also smaller Greek communities, while the assimilation of the Tzintzars (Aromani) has lasted until modern times.

The war at the end of the seventeenth century (1683–99) represented an important turning point since part of the Serbian people came under Christian rule, developing in significantly different surroundings than under Turkish rule. Their separate existence lasted more than 200 years and represented a serious obstacle to national integration. Religious criteria once more gained importance, since the general position of the Serbs within the Habsburg Empire was determined by imperial promises to observe the faith and church life of its new subjects. An ever more dynamically developing Serbian society was interwoven with the church, a factor that would later prevent the adoption of modern ideas about the nation being a language community and hinder processes of integration. The Serb people were rearranged under Austrian rule. They vanished from the periphery of the regions they had inhabited, and converged on the Military Border and regions along the border with the Ottoman Empire (i.e., the border with Serbia from 1804 to 1815). The intense colonization carried out by the Habsburg authorities during the second half of the eighteenth century directly contributed to this relocation. The Serbs now lived alongside Germans, Hungarians, Romanians, Slovaks, and Ruthenians.

The great turning point in the development of the Serbian people was the creation of the state, first the autonomous principality in 1815, later independent state (1878), and then kingdom (1882). It gradually took over the cultural heritage that had been created in the eighteenth century by the Serbs in Hungary, developing it further and becoming the center of Serbian convergence. The Serbs witnessed crucial European political events (German and Italian unification) or took part in them (the 1848 struggle in the Habsburg monarchy), drawing important conclusions concerning the necessity of struggle for the liberation and unity of the partially enslaved and divided nation.

Serbian struggles, starting with the First Uprising (1804–13), were considered revolutionary and disruptive of relations between states, regardless of whether they were formally associated, for example in the Holy Alliance, or interested only in European balance. At first the main Serbian effort was directed toward the Ottoman Empire, but Austria-Hungary became a persistent competitor following the occupation of Bosnia and Herzegovina in 1878. Clashes with other nations (Greeks, Bulgarians, and later Albanians) were inevitable, since they too sought to free themselves of Ottoman rule and had defined their borders based on "historical rights."

After the long and bloody conflict and huge casualties of the Balkan Wars (1912–13) and World War I (1914–18), the Serbs, having overcome their disunity and division by state borders, found themselves practically all in one state: the Kingdom of Serbs, Croats, and Slovenes (1918–29; Kingdom of Yugoslavia, 1929–41). From this point on it became apparent that the heritage of their previous development imposed other serious problems. It was obviously not only the borders that hindered integration, but also differences that had developed on account of the distinct environments that existed on different sides of the border. Within the context of political and party struggles, in addition to antagonisms that emerged between the nations (Slovenes, Croats, and Serbs), frictions based on regional interests appeared inside those nations themselves. This occurred between Serbs from Serbia and the Serb population from the northern parts who had once been under Austrian-Hungarian rule; while the Montenegrins were dissatisfied with the manner of unification. The population of the territories acquired in 1913 were officially regarded as Serb inhabitants of southern Serbia, but this did not correspond to actuality since a significant portion of them declared themselves to be Bulgarians, and there were also Macedonians.

The difficulty in modifying their historical inheritance was visible also in the spatial distribution and intermingling of Serbs with other Yugoslav nations. In the state created in 1918, a relatively high degree of homogeneity had been achieved only in parts of Serbia and Montenegro that had been liberated early on (including territories acquired in 1878), employing the means commonly used in European states at the time. Serbs accounted for half the ethnically diverse population of Vojvodina; in Croatia their numbers were dense only in the region of the former Military Border, and there were minorities in all the towns. They shared the historical territory of Bosnia and Herzegovina with Muslims and Croats, while the Albanian element had in the meantime grown strong in Kosovo and so-called Old Serbia.

The historical heritage also created indecision as far as distinguishing Serbs from others was concerned. While the Serbian Orthodox Church imposed the notion that only Orthodox Christians were Serbs, secular nationalists, political movements, and parties struggled for the nation to include "Catholic Serbs," and Muslims as Serbs of "Muhammad's faith." No larger group from either of these two confessions integrated into the Serbian nation, but as it later turned out, especially after 1944, large numbers of Serbs could be atheist.

From the present perspective it is clear that the Serbs as a nation were not sufficiently integrated in 1918 when they found themselves in a single state. The political and cultural elites of the time were unaware of the importance of continuing the processes of Serbian integration. This was replaced by the integration of the Serbs, Croats, and Slovenes in the creation of the Yugoslav nation. This project was the highest objective of state policies for the Serbs, resisted only by an intellectual minority, while only a small number of intellectuals in other nations supported it. The "Yugoslav synthesis" was not achieved: contentions between the Yugoslav nations were amplified, and a new division occurred among the Serbs, between those who advocated Yugoslavism and those who wanted to protect Serbian traditions. This division still exists, as the final chapter of this book describes.

1
Ancient Heritage

The Roman Provinces

Parts of the Serbian tribe were among the Slavs who headed south across the borders of the Roman Empire during the sixth and seventh centuries, thus starting a new cycle in their development on its territory. At the time of the Slav migration, an extensively built *limes*, a defensive belt consisting of a series of fortified garrisons, followed the Empire's frontier with the task of preventing barbarian incursions and overseeing the neighboring territory. The defensive strength of the *limes* received additional reinforcement from the Danube River, an immense natural barrier along which the fortresses were located. Construction of the *limes* ended the lengthy process of expanding Roman authority, which gradually spread from the west and the Adriatic coastal region toward the interior of the Balkan Peninsula. A turning point was reached in the early first century AD with the suppression of the Illyrian uprising, resulting in the establishment of a uniform provincial system.

Every Slav who crossed the *limes* was exposed to the lasting influence of the land, shaped by previous centuries of Roman rule. The territories occupied by the Romans were scattered with the remains of Roman cities, crisscrossed by Roman roads, and covered with the traces of earlier inhabitants' efforts to adapt the natural environment to their needs. Serbs and members of other Slav tribes had fundamentally altered their surroundings: from a scarcely populated area, with ephemeral and unstable political entities and without recognizable names and permanent borders, they entered a structured and stable zone. Along with material remnants they found the names of urban settlements, provinces, and regions, all preserved among the sparse and impoverished provincial population.

Some of these names recalled the populations encountered and subdued by the Romans. The name Illyricum, the spacious province that initially included everything the Romans conquered from the Adriatic coast to the Pannonian plain, preserved the common name of the numerous Illyrian groups that inhabited the central and western parts of the Balkan Peninsula. In the first century AD Illyricum was divided into two provinces, Dalmatia and Pannonia. The border that divided them ran parallel to the Sava River (50 to 60 km south of the river). The province of Moesia, which was named after the Pannonian tribe of the Moesi, was divided in 86 AD into Moesia Superior, in the present-day Morava river valley, and Moesia Inferior, in what is now Bulgaria. Later reforms separated Dardania, between the Western and Southern Morava rivers, the Ibar River, and Macedonia. Its name preserved that of the Dardans, a tribe that belonged to either the Illyrian or Thracian tribal groups, an issue that is still being debated. This is also the case for the Triballi, former inhabitants of Moesia, against whom Alexander the Great sent his army.

The newly arrived Slavs had no contacts with these tribes, or rather their distant descendants who had greatly changed under the half-millennium of Roman rule and the influence of Roman civilization. Nonetheless, the names known from toponyms and from the works of classical authors were passed on and later associated with the Serbs; Byzantine writers most often thought they were Triballi, and sometimes Dalmatians. The name Illyrian was used to identify the western wing of the Southern Slavs up to the nineteenth century, although since the Middle Ages it has been used primarily in connection with the Albanians. The artificial continuity of the pre-Roman and Roman period, which was established by means of territorial names and preserved by learned circles, did not affect the Serbs' historical traditions and their understanding of their origin.

The territories of the Balkan Peninsula were not evenly populated prior to the Roman conquest but were for the most part covered by a network of fortified headquarters (*oppidum, teichisma*), from which local tribal rulers governed the surroundings. These centers preserved their function during Roman rule and the tribal communities were governed from here. Often local native settlements formed the core of Roman cities; their role in commerce and in spreading cultural achievements turned them into focal points of romanization.

Dalmatia and other Balkan provinces, especially the interior, were not extensively colonized by emigrants from Italy. Veteran soldiers settled here and were given land and privileges, as was the case in other parts of the Empire. The process of Roman urbanization was spontaneous and depended largely on natural conditions, economic potential, and lines of communication. It was indisputably slower in the Balkans than in the central parts of the Empire, developing gradually, but it also continued at times when other parts of the Empire were engulfed in crisis.

All three provinces under consideration – Dalmatia, Moesia Superior, and Dardania – were renowned for their mineral deposits, and the extraction of precious and other metals played an important role in the economy and in the foundation of cities. Places where gold, silver, copper, or iron were extracted grew in population and maintained close links with their surroundings, from where the supply of miners came. These towns indirectly influenced the development of already existing urban settlements. In the Roman administrative system, mining brought with it certain peculiarities: the presence of local representatives of imperial authority, a greater degree of centralization, the establishment of districts with special local currencies and prices, and increased imperial supervision.

In addition to the littoral, which was the most urbanized and colonized region, highly populated cities arose along major axes, such as the roads running parallel to the Sava, Danube, and Morava rivers, or those connecting Byzantium (Constantinople) with remote border regions to the north (*via militaris*). Cities developed here from different roots and were supplied with everything created by the Roman Empire. Some became centers of provincial authority, such as Viminacium (near present-day Kostolac), while others were even capitals of the co-ruler collegium, such as Sirmium (present-day Sremska Mitrovica). Along the Danube sprouted Bassiana (away from the river, near Putinci, Ruma), Singidunum (Belgrade), Margum (Dubravica near Orašje), and Aquae (near Prahovo). Horreum Margi (Ćuprija), Naissus (Niš), and Remesiana (Bela Palanka) were on the road to Constantinople.

Certain towns were linked to mining, such as Municipium Dardanorum (Sočanica on the Ibar), Ulpiana (Lipljan in southern Kosovo), Municipium Malvesatium (Skelani on the Drina), and Domavia (near Srebrenica close to the Drina River), which was the seat of mining supervisors for the whole of Illyricum. Certain large Roman settlements are known exclusively by their archeological remains, such as Kolovrat near Prijepolje and Visibabe near Požega, whose original names are not known. Certain tombstones have provided text fragments with only the first letter of the name, such as *Aquae S* . . . on Ilidža Hill near Sarajevo or *Municipium S* . . . in Komini near Pljevlja.

Some cities owed their prosperity to their location, a site on an important road or junction, while others owed it to the fact that they were local government seats. In any case, they received forums, temples, waterworks, large public baths, and everything that went along with the status of a city. Numerous structures outlived Roman rule. Abandoned and destroyed remains of cities did not attract Slav settlers. Ancient remains were included in settlements and reused only in regions where Byzantine rule was later established. The Slavs stayed away from ancient ruins swathed in stories that occasionally included the name of an emperor (Dukljanin – Diocletian; Trojan – Trajan).

Some towns influenced the expansion and completion of the Roman road network, which was rational, technically uniform, and subordinated to the needs of the state center. Roman roads also outlived Roman rule and had a powerful influence on the transit routes of people and merchandise in later centuries. Larger towns on the Adriatic coast, which were easily accessible by sea, served as starting points for roads leading inland into the interior of the peninsula. Certain major roads should be noted for their role in later periods: one parallel and close to the Adriatic coast, and the other further inland, parallel to the Sava River. The route along the Morava River valley became increasingly significant as the center of the Empire moved eastward. It was given the name "military road" (*via militaris*) when it connected Belgrade and Constantinople, and was much later the route of military expeditions into Central Europe in one direction, and toward the center of the Ottoman Empire in the other direction.

Initial antagonism between the Romans and the local population was overcome in time, and the province's inhabitants were included not only in local administration, but also in the Roman army. Able-bodied and eager men spent a considerable part of their lives in the military, fighting wars in other parts of the Empire. They became both defenders of the borders and propagators of the Roman way of life. The principles of Roman administrative organization in regions that were conquered allowed room for the remnants of tribal organization in the form of *convents* and *decuries*, which often bore the name of the tribe.

The increasing integration of the local population within the Roman system was reflected by the towns that rose in rank in the administration, with the *municipium* of Roman citizens marking the highest level; on an individual level it was reflected by attaining the rights of Roman citizens. A visible expression of social promotion was the assumption of the name of the emperor who granted citizenship. Numerous tombstones marked *Aelii* speak of the time citizenship was granted. From the beginning of the third century with the Edict of 212, citizenship was extended to all free citizens in the Empire.

Nevertheless some questions remain, such as how romanization influenced people outside the cities and urban regions, how tribal traditions survived, how language and elements of cultural heritage were preserved during the long period of Roman rule, which itself remained on the surface, relying on the cities for its pillars. Different degrees of romanization were found in the descendants of the provincial population with whom the Slavs came into contact upon their arrival. These disparities were caused not only by the difference in tribal background and degree of Roman influence, but also by the fact that Roman administration and civilization expanded in the southern and eastern parts of the Balkan Peninsula using the Greek language, which had not been suppressed in the old Hellenic and hellenized regions. The border between the zones of romanization and hellenization in the Balkan Peninsula can be identified from stone tablets, milestones, public edifices, and headstones. This border started at the Adriatic coast near Kotor and ran towards Niš, then went along the ridge of Mt. Balkan to the shores of the Black Sea. Latin was used to the west and north of this line, while Greek was used south and east of it.

Dalmatia and its neighboring provinces in the central part of the Balkans undoubtedly lagged behind in the processes of urbanization and expanding Roman civilization, but on the other hand showed greater resistance to the crises that shook the Empire in the third and fourth centuries. According to sparse written sources and stone engravings, which are important testimonies from this period, mines were operational even during this time; roads and public facilities were constructed, there was no great depopulation, nor was the economy paralyzed. It is thus understandable that Illyricum gained greater importance in the Empire.

This is evident from incontestable indications, primarily the increased role of warriors from this area who proclaimed emperors from the ranks of their commanders (the "Illyrian emperors"). The administrative units from this area gained in importance, and Illyricum took on new meaning and became one of the Empire's four prefectures; Sirmium became the seat of the *caesar*, one of the four members of the *collegium* governing the Empire. Rulers built their residences in this once underdeveloped part of the Empire, such as Diocletian's palace in the provincial center of Salonae (Aspalaton, Split), while his successor Galerius (305–11) built Felix Romuliana (Gamzigrad near Zaječar). Perhaps these rulers inspired Justinian I three centuries later (527–65) to elevate his birthplace, Justiniana Prima (Caričin Grad, the empress's city, near Leskovac), and grant it privileges so that it might later play a significant role in church history. Finally, the dominance of the eastern part of the Empire was visibly expressed in the founding of the new capital on the Bosphorus in 330, which bore the name of Constantinople and which the Slavs simply called the emperor's city, Carigrad.

The period of crises was followed by changes in the structure of the Empire; at the center, the emperor's power had become almost unlimited, surrounded by a sacred aureole, while at the periphery, military power was separated from civilian rule, with administrative borders frequently shifting. In addition to the already mentioned separation of Dardania from Moesia Superior during Diocletian's reign, the formation

Plate 1.1   Roman heritage: entrance to Felix Romuliana, palace of Emperor Galerius (305–11), Gamzigrad, eastern Serbia. (Photograph by B. Strugar)

of the separate province of Praevalitana in present-day Montenegro and northern Albania was also important.

When the western Roman Empire collapsed in the fifth century under the attacks of barbarian tribes, the eastern Empire continued to exist and attempts were made to revive and restore the unity of the former Empire. The particular characteristics of the eastern part became apparent: it had inherited the entire state tradition, was Christianized, and was based on a Hellenic cultural foundation that included the Christian tradition of Church Fathers. The people were called Romans (Romaioi), and the rulers were Roman emperors. The Serbs, as well as other Slavs, were more observant of Greek cultural identity than imperial pretensions, so they were called Greeks (from the Latin *Graecus*). Learned Byzantines often called the capital Byzantion, recalling the name of the town that had preceded Constantine's capital, and this gave rise to the name of Byzantium and the Byzantine Empire, primarily among humanist authors.

After lengthy resistance, the Balkan provinces also succumbed to crisis. Pressure increased against the *limes* along the Danube and the ramparts did not always hold. They gave way in the eastern part under the Goths, who were turned into federates in 375 and formed a significant part of the Roman army. Their departure for Italy and the capture of Rome in 410 allowed the eastern Empire to recover, but did not relieve it of the

Goths' presence in Pannonia and Dalmatia. The ramparts gave way a second time under the Huns in 448, bringing suffering to the cities and population of what is now Serbia.

In the late fifth and early sixth centuries the Goths ruled the western Balkan provinces. They were a small minority and left no significant traces. Along with archeological remains with identifiable markings, carved rune writing (the Gothic alphabet) was discovered in the ruins of the old Christian church at Breza in central Bosnia. The names of Gacko and the original name Anagastum for Nikšić are associated with the Goths and their language.

Gothic rule ended in 535 in one of the campaigns waged by Emperor Justinian I, who attempted to restore the Empire in Italy, Spain, and Africa. He brought peace to the Balkan provinces and rebuilt fortresses not only along the *limes*, but also in large numbers in the interior. He built the city of Justiniana Prima near his birthplace as the seat of the prefect and archbishop, whose jurisdiction included all the dioceses from Pannonia to Macedonia. The city was later destroyed along with the church organization, but all the imperial legal acts asserting the archbishop's rights were preserved and were to influence the church's organization and its hierarchy four centuries later. Justinian's magnificent city existed less than a century, at a time when a new wave of barbarians was already exerting pressure on the *limes*.

Settlement of the Slavs

The Slavs were included in the final stages of the massive upheavals known as the "great migration." They began at a time when most other peoples and tribes had already settled, primarily on the territory of the Roman Empire. The directions, routes, and flows of Slav migrations are less well known than those of most Germanic and other participants of these mass movements. Spreading out from their debated and hard to identify "ancient homeland," somewhere between the Vistula River and the Pripet Marshes, the Slavs filled the areas left by Germanic tribes moving west to Roman land. Two groups journeyed south toward the Danube *limes*; one arrived at the banks of the lower Danube going east of the Carpathian Mountains, while the other went west of the Carpathians and crossed the Central European and Pannonian plain. Their approach to the Roman border in the middle Danube basin was facilitated by the defeat of the Gepids in clashes with the Lombards (567), and the Lombards' departure for Italy (568).

Both Slav groups encountered other tribes at the borders of the eastern Roman Empire who shared their ambitions of breaking through the barrier. Most important among them were the Avars, who arrived at the banks of the Danube in 558. They established themselves as rulers of the Slavs who inhabited the borders around their centers, and often galvanized Slav groups and led them into Byzantine territory.

In the sixth century the Slavs came within sight of the scholars and authors still in the Empire at this period of crisis and collapse. The rare witnesses to these events focused principally on what affected them most: the destruction of the provinces, looting, and mass deportations. From the information scattered throughout their scripts, it is possible to create an incomplete chronicle of the barbarian raids and to demonstrate that the aim of the assailants was not occupation, but the transfer of loot and slaves across the border. Among the successive waves of attack, some raids can be singled out for their penetration or size, such as that in 550 when the Slavs reached the mouth of the Mesta River, that in 558 when they reached the Thermopylae Pass, or that in 550–1 when they wintered on Byzantine territory "as though on their own land."

During the last decade of the sixth century, the Empire took advantage of a brief truce with Persia and once again forced an offensive. Not only did it recover the border cities of Sirmium and Singidunum, which had been seized by the Avars, but it also pushed the battle to the other side of the Danube and reduced pressure on the border by crushing the attackers that were grouped along it. However, the offensive of 602 had undesirable consequences: a rebellion broke out among the soldiers forced to winter on enemy territory, the belligerent Emperor Mauricius (582–602) was swept from power, and, most important of all, the *limes* was abandoned because the army had set out for Constantinople to secure the reign of the newly proclaimed Emperor Phocas (602–10).

As though a dam had burst, a torrent of Slavs poured over the border and in the years that followed reached the furthest parts of Balkan territory. The stagnant lifestyle of the provincial metropolis of Salona (Solin near Split) ended in around 614; the Slavs attacked and besieged Thessalonika around 617, and in around 625 they put out to sea and attacked the Aegean islands. Under Avar command they threatened the Empire in 626 by besieging Constantinople with the Persians, who attacked from Asia Minor. More or less subordinated to the Avars in the Danube region, the Slavs followed them and provided the forces necessary for large campaigns. Since they were capable of fighting from boats, they attacked solid fortifications from the sea, while the Avar cavalry spearheaded the attack. The Avars returned to their Pannonian home at the end of these campaigns, while the Slavs remained on former Roman soil.

The Byzantine Empire lost all of its land in the interior of the peninsula during these years, retaining only the coastal cities on all four seas and the islands. Constantinople maintained links with them by means of its fleet and naval superiority. After surviving one of its gravest crises in 626, the Empire recovered under Emperor Heraclius (610–41). As a result of internal reforms, and because it had preserved forces in Asia Minor, the remaining parts of the Empire were consolidated and it began the century-long struggle to recover its lost provinces.

The Slavs could not occupy the large and jagged Balkan Peninsula in its entirety. As far as can be ascertained, they followed ancient Roman communications routes and inhabited areas that had previously been cultivated and were suitable for habitation. Variously sized enclaves containing remnants of the old provincial population remained among and around them. The number and distribution of these indigenous "islets" surrounded by a Slavic sea cannot be determined from the subsequent situation. It is highly likely that in the earlier stages the majority remained in mountainous and less accessible areas. The territories of northern Albania, neighboring Macedonia, and Thessaly, also known as Great Vlachia (*Megale Vlachia*) in the early Middle Ages, are known to have been populated to a considerable extent by native inhabitants. There must have been native groups in the Dinaric Alps all the way to Istria in the early Middle Ages, and they were still present in the late Middle Ages.

The Serbs, like most other Slavs, encountered the local population as a variety of groups: first Byzantines, subjects of the Byzantine emperors; then Romans, inhabitants of the Adriatic coastal cities and islands who had preserved their language, a derivative of vulgar Latin, during the Byzantine period; then Vlachs or Morovlachs, who survived in variously sized groups in the interior of the peninsula with no links to Byzantine centers; and finally Albanians, who remained in the Dyrrachium hinterland and whose way of life resembled that of the Vlachs but who still spoke a slightly romanized archaic language.

There is no information regarding early contacts between the Slavs and the remainder of the indigenous peoples. Traditions from much later times speak of hostilities between the local Christians and the newly arrived pagans. A somewhat clearer picture can be formed by studying linguistic contacts and examining traces of mutual influences and loan words. For example, the names of large rivers were taken from the indigenous peoples and the smaller tributaries were given Slavic names. A significant number of mountains, cities, and even the Slavic name for the Hellenes – *Grk, Grci*, derived from the Latin *Graecus* – were taken from the romanized population. At least some Romance and Albanian elements of Serbian cattle-breeding terminology date back to this period, and Slavic elements in Vlach and Albanian agrarian terminology are derived from these early encounters.

Sclavinias

Little is known about the composition and nature of the general Slavic community before it split up into its eastern, southern, and western branches, just as little is known about the site of the Slavs' "ancient homeland." Studies of the most ancient levels of the language reliably conclude that the eastern and western Slavic groups differed from the very beginning. Attempts to reconstruct the earliest layers of the Slavs' religion confirm this conclusion.

Three general names are mentioned for groups present during the migration: Venedi, Sclavinians, and Antae. The first was used by the Slavs' western neighbors, while the other two appeared among those who migrated south. The name Antae was soon forgotten, giving way to the designation Slavs and undoubtedly preceding the names of individual tribes. The Slavs imposed their general name on the peoples with whom they came into contact, and this designation was used among the Albanians, Vlachs, and Byzantines to identify their immediate Slavic neighbors. The name Skje was derived from the Slavic name and was used by the Vlachs and Albanians to denote the Serbian people. The Slavs are referred to as Sclavi or Slavi in Roman writings and the earliest legal documents. The Croats appeared only much later in the north, and the Serbs in the south. Western authors referred to the entire territory of the western Balkan Peninsula as Sclavonia, while fourteenth- and fifteenth-century Venetians and Ragusans (from Ragusa, modern-day Dubrovnik) also called the territory of the Serbian state Sclavonia (Emperor Dušan is *imperator Sclavonie*, and fifteenth-century rulers are *despoti Sclavonie*). A last vestige of this general name for the Slavs is preserved only in the name Slavonia (*regnum Slavonie*, Slovinje), the territory between the Drava and Sava rivers in present-day Croatia.

Before the great migrations that took place within the eastern and western branches of the ancient Slavs, there were certain tribal groups whose names appeared later in different parts of the territory inhabited by the Slavs. Croats, Severci (Severjani), and Duljebi are recorded among the Eastern, Western, and Southern Slavs; Serbs and Obodrites are found among the Western and Southern Slavs; and Druguviti (Dragoviči) are noted among the Eastern and Southern Slavs. No reliable judgment can be made regarding differences between them based on contemporary knowledge. They were most likely genuine social groups, conscious of their links with and differences from others, and having their own traditions concerning their origins, beliefs, and symbols.

Assumptions about who took part in the migrations can be made primarily from later territorial distributions. The names given to more expansive territories testify to the settlement of a significant portion of the tribe. However, even these territories bear witness to the presence of other tribes. Thus parts of the ancient Croatian tribe left traces in the toponyms of Epirus and Kosovo Polje, while the Serbs left traces in Croatian regions (the *župa* of Srb during the Middle Ages), and around Srbica in Thessaly, in the vicinity of Druguviti, who occupied areas in Macedonia and Thrace.

No contemporary records exist of the progress of these migrations; all that has been preserved are much later records of traditions regarding the migration of the Serbs and Croats. The works of Byzantine Emperor Constantine VII Porphyrogenitus (913–59) mention the arrival of the Croats and Serbs during the rule of Byzantine Emperor Heraclius (610–41), when the first wave of Slavic migrations had already swept across the Balkans. They came as allies, at the emperor's invitation, to help defend the Empire. The Serbs came from White Serbia in the north, in the vicinity of the Franks and White or Great Croatia. The ruler's son took "half the people" and joined Emperor Heraclius, who accepted him and installed him in the region called Serblia (Srbica), near Thessalonika. The Serbs did not remain there for long, and eventually wanted to return. They had already crossed the Danube when they had another change of heart and again asked for land upon which to settle. The emperor gave them the deserted lands between the Sava River and the Dinaric Alps, near the Croats, who had also migrated from White Croatia under the leadership of three brothers and two sisters and who had fought for years against the Avars.

The area settled by the migrating tribes had no uniform political organization and tribal territory formed the basis for political groups of various sizes. The predominance of small principalities led contemporary Byzantines to name the Slavs' region Sclaviniai, using the characteristic plural. This name originally denoted land inhabited by the Slavs on the far side of the Danube, and is preserved only in a Byzantine military manual intended for officers fighting the Slavs. The practical purpose of this text is evidenced by the fact that it does not deal in generalities about the barbarians but focuses on the specific enemy. The text incidentally mentions that the Slavs lived near rivers and woods, in villages that were interconnected but at the same time well protected by natural barriers, that they were farmers who had food stores in their houses, and that they also raised cattle. From the Byzantine point of view, they were resolute and cunning warriors who bore light arms and equipment and deployed special tactics.

The area on the far side of the Danube, crisscrossed by rivers, was dotted with numerous small political organizations headed by local princes (*reges, archontes*), who were forced into submission by the

Byzantines or whose support they had gained, fearing the creation of a "monarchy" or strong and unified authority covering a larger area.

After the Slavs had settled on the Balkan Peninsula, the Byzantines mention the "Sclavinias" between Thessalonika and Constantinople in the hinterland of Thessalonika, and later in the hinterland of Dalmatian cities. Occasional reports from the Dark Ages subsequent to the Slavs' migration are in agreement with records from the time when they were still beyond the Empire's borders. Certain tribes included in the "Sclavinias" are recorded in the Thessalonika region ca. 670. Their chieftains (*riges*) fought against, but also negotiated with, the Byzantine authorities. While certain Slavs laid siege to Thessalonika, other Slavs provided the city with supplies.

There is no overview of the Balkan "Sclavinias." A partial map can be reconstructed based on scant contemporary references and traces preserved in the names of later administrative units, dioceses, and geographic regions. Approximately 20 names of former principalities and tribal territories can be chronicled from the Vienna Woods (Wienerwald) to the Black Sea, some bearing ancient general Slavic names such as Croats, Serbs, Severci, Dragoviči, and Duljebi, while new ones were formed on occupied land, sometimes taking the ancient names of rivers, such as the Strymonioi from Strymon and Narentanoi (Neretljani) from Naron, or cities, for example the Carantani from the *civitas* Carantana, and Dukljani from Dioclea.

The regions occupied by the Serbian tribe in karst basins suitable for agriculture between the Dinaric Alps and the Adriatic coast gave rise to the principalities of the Neretljani (between the Cetina and Neretva rivers), Zahumljani (from the Neretva River and the Dubrovnik hinterland), and Travunians (from the Dubrovnik hinterland to the Gulf of Kotor). In their immediate vicinity was the principality of Dukljani in the valleys of the Zeta and Morača rivers, from the Gulf of Kotor to Bojana River. The continental side of the principality bordered on the vast territory where the name of the Serbian tribe was preserved. Continuity was provided by the ruling family, consisting of the descendants of the ruler's son who had brought the Serbs to the Balkans. Emperor Constantine VII Porphyrogenitus called this vast principality "Baptized Serbia," to distinguish it from unbaptized White Serbia to the north. To the west, Baptized Serbia bordered on Croatia, whose farthest *županije* to the east were Pliba (Pliva), Chlebiana (Livno), and Imota (today Imotski). The Ras region in the east (near Novi Pazar) was the Serbian border region toward Bulgaria.

The single structure of this vast principality did not last long. By the middle of the tenth century the shape of the land of Bosnia was clearly evident within it, in the area of the river of the same name. It was later

Map 1.1   Baptized Serbia and its neighbors. ca. 950.

to expand and develop independently. Even later, in the twelfth and thir-teenth centuries, the northern region consisting of the land of Usora extended to between the Vrbas and Drina rivers, while the former border town of Ras became the center of the eastern areas.

The world of the "Sclavinias" was threatened from three sides. The Avars, who imposed themselves as rulers and occasionally led the Slavs on campaigns, have already been mentioned. Their power decreased toward the end of the seventh century and in later centuries their state was toppled by the Franks, who in turn influenced their immediate neigh-bors, primarily the Croats. The Serbs were more directly influenced by two other centers. On one side was the Proto-Bulgarian state, created in 680 when the Proto-Bulgarians conquered seven Slavic tribes (including the Severci) between the Danube River and Mt. Balkan. Installing themselves as the Slavs' rulers, the Proto-Bulgarians used the conquered Slavs to overpower the neighboring Slavs, while maintaining their internal organization and structure.

On the other side the "Sclavinias" were devoured by the Byzantine Empire, which spread from its city strongholds along the coast. The Byzantine emperors transformed the conquered Slavic territories into military-administrative units called *themes*, under the control of a *strategos*, who was appointed by the emperor. The names of certain tribes were thus preserved as themes, such as Vagenetia (facing the island of Corfu) from the Vaiuniti, and the Strymon theme from the principality of Strumljani (Strymonioi). The land was conquered gradually and the breakthrough by Justinian II (685–95) in securing a land route between Constantinople and Thessalonika in 689 was celebrated as a great success.

In imposing their rule over the Slavs, the Proto-Bulgarian state expanded southward and collided with the Byzantine Empire, which was expanding toward the north. Occasionally the Proto-Bulgarians would cause massive Slav migrations, such as that in 762 when, according to contemporary estimates, more than 200,000 people fled to Byzantine territory and were relocated in Asia Minor. The Proto-Bulgarians generally acted with greater caution, appointing their wards to power and making tribal princes their vassals and later local administrators. With their different language, religion, and way of life, the Proto-Bulgarians eventually merged into the Slavic body; they took over the language and handed over their name.

The Byzantine–Bulgarian peace treaty of 764 divided the eastern part of the peninsula. Faced with an obstacle to the south, the Proto-Bulgarians turned west, invaded Pannonia, appointed Slav chieftains on the Drava River (827–9), and reached the Ionian coast of present-day Albania in the second half of the ninth century.

The region inhabited by the Serbs lay in the path of Bulgarian expansion, so it is unsurprising that the first mention of Serbian rulers is made in relation to wars with the Bulgarians. According to a Serbian tradition that made its way into the aforementioned work of the Byzantine emperor, Baptized Serbia was ruled by descendants of the man who had brought the Serbs there and who was still alive when the Bulgarians crossed the Danube and conquered the Slavs in 680. The names of the first descendants are unknown, and there are no details available about the following three (Višeslav, Radoslav, and Prosigoj). One of these must have been on the throne in 822 when Croatian Prince Ljudevit Posavski abandoned Siscia (Sisak) after resisting the Franks for three years, and sought refuge with the Serbs. He used great cunning to kill a local *župan* (*dux*, regional ruler) and take over his region before crossing over to Croatia, where he in turn was assassinated.

Prince Vlastimir, who ruled in the mid-ninth century, was forced to defend himself against Bulgarian attacks. For three years, sometime between 836 and 852, he resisted them successfully. He was succeeded by his three sons, Mutimir, Strojimir, and Gojnik, who divided up the land, an act that was not uncommon among dynasties of this period. During their joint rule, undoubtedly headed by Mutimir, the Serbian princes resisted yet another Bulgarian attack. The Bulgarian ruler, Khan Boris (who later converted to Christianity and took the name Michael, 852–89), sent a large army against Serbia and was heavily defeated. The khan's son Vladimir was taken captive, along with twelve grand boyars. When a truce was negotiated, gifts were exchanged and the prisoners were released and escorted to the border, Ras. This detail reveals the location of the eastern Serbian border in the second half of the ninth century.

The brothers' joint rule was disrupted by internal conflict, which saw Mutimir emerge as victor. He handed his brothers over to the Bulgarian ruler, keeping only his nephew Peter Gojniković, who soon fled to Croatia. From that time on, conflicts within the ruling Serbian family were intertwined with the struggle between Byzantium and Bulgaria for influence over the Serbian principality. Constantinople had greater authority but no direct access and was forced to act through its strongholds on the Adriatic coast, cities united in the theme of Dalmatia. Byzantine influence was most apparent in the neighboring principalities of Zahumlje, Travunia, and Duklja.

Christianization

Christianization of the recently settled barbarians and pagans unintentionally became part of the political struggle for domination of the Balkan Peninsula; Christianization appeared to be a restoration of Byzantine authority. This political aspect of Christianization was also noted by those who were to be converted. When Khan Boris was ready to introduce Christianity to Bulgaria, he asked for priests from the distant Frankish Empire, and in 864 when Bulgaria was nevertheless converted by Byzantine missionaries, Boris-Michael appealed to Rome to avoid the involvement of his rival Byzantium. This caused the first major crisis in relations between Rome and Constantinople.

On the other hand, in 862 the Byzantine emperor responded to the request by Rastislav, prince of Great Moravia, for missionaries who would reinforce the church in his country, which had previously been

Christianized by the Franks. The mission was assigned to the sons of the high Byzantine official Leon, Methodius and Constantine, who were familiar with the Slavic language. They made thorough preparations for the mission, inventing a special alphabet, the Glagolitic, which was adapted to the particularities of the Slavic language, and translated the principal liturgical scripts. The successful missionary work carried out by the brothers from Thessalonika was interrupted by protests from those who had ecclesiastical jurisdiction over Rastislav's state. The brothers traveled to Rome to justify their actions and visited Kocelj, prince of Lower Pannonia, who also sought missionaries to work in his country. The brothers received the pope's dispensation for their missionary work. Constantine took vows in Rome, taking the monastic name of Cyril, and later died there. Methodius continued their work and became archbishop of the restored Sirmium archdiocese. He faced obstructions here too, and the benefits of his labor were only experienced by his pupils, who found refuge in the already Christianized Bulgarian state (885).

The consequences of the Serbs' Christianization can be seen in the Christian names of Vlastimir's grandsons, Peter and Stefan, who were born ca. 870. At this time Constantinople was governed by Basil I, who is credited with Christianizing the Slavs, since their earlier Christianization on arriving in the Balkans had had no lasting effect. The emperor's achievements link Christianization with establishing Byzantine rule and legitimizing the existing ruling clans of the Slav principalities. As the emperor's biographers relate, he did not want to appoint rulers who would provide him with more wealth and burden their subjects, but preferred to let the people be governed by those "whom they themselves have chosen and enthroned accordingly." In this way the emperor ruled the Slav colonizers indirectly, through local princes, a method of exercising supreme power that was not disruptive because it did not introduce foreigners into their surroundings or interfere with their customs and way of life. Their acceptance of imperial authority is confirmed by reports that naval detachments of Croats, Serbs, and others from Zahumlje, Travunia, Konavlje, Duklja, and the principality of Neretljani were sent to southern Italy in 870, where Frankish King Ludwig was fighting against the Arabs.

The adoption of Christianity gradually brought significant changes. In the first instance, people's views about their traditions were forced to undergo fundamental transformation. Each baptized ruler had to face an obligation imposed much earlier, when the Frankish king had been baptized, namely, to honor what had previously been persecuted and persecute what had previously been honored. This did not include their celebrated ancestors, but did include their deities, about which we have little knowledge. The sixth-century Byzantine historian Procopius knew that the Slavs believed "one of their gods, the creator of lightning, is the sole master of the world, and they sacrifice cattle and other sacrificial animals to him." According to Procopius, "they worship rivers and certain other lower deities, offering sacrifices to them and using them for soothsaying." Inferences about the ancient Slavs' religious beliefs can be made only from linguistic traces or from toponyms, rituals, traditions, beliefs, and even the attributes of Christian saints from later times. The Serbs honored the gods Perun, Veles, Vid (Svantovid), Mokoš, and Dabog. Their names were remembered and later included in translations of texts mentioning ancient deities.

The process of acquiring the necessary material for Christian life was painfully slow. The main obstacle was poverty. Much later, in the early thirteenth century, St. Sava is said to have erected a wooden church where one of brick and stone was impossible, and, when a wooden church could not be built, he placed a crucifix. In the ninth and tenth centuries constructions were necessarily more modest. There are no surviving edifices from this period, apart from the church of St. Peter in Ras and a few ruins whose foundations follow closely the model of Constantinople church construction.

There were two opposing trends in the development of the church. One favored continuing the tradition of church centers that had previously had an important role in church organization, while the other favored adjusting bishoprics to the framework of the new states and their capitals. Baptized princes were keen to have a bishop of their own close at hand. In the coastal region, where Christianity had existed without interruption for centuries, every town had its own bishop, but a diocese in the newly Christianized lands would cover an entire country. Thus papal acts mention the bishoprics of Serbia, Zahumlje, and Travunia. All the new bishoprics initially came under the jurisdiction of the old metropolitanate seat in Split, since it had succeeded Salonae. Mihajlo Višević, prince of Zahumlje, which had its bishop's seat in Ston, attended the Split synods in 925 and 927, where discipline and the liturgy in Latin were imposed.

The introduction of Christianity opened the way for Byzantine imperial ideology and the adoption of the idea that the Byzantine emperor was Christ's regent on earth, the father and head of all Christian rulers. Prayers were said for him in church and he was mentioned during the liturgy. Christianization emphasized the lack of equality and the Byzantine view according to which the emperor considered the Slav princes to be his administrators; they were given a position in the hierarchy of the court and granted gifts and symbols of authority by the emperor.

The Christianization of the Bulgarians did not put an end to Byzantine–Bulgarian rivalry, which also involved the Serbian court. Frequent conflicts within the Serbian ruling clan were the excuse for foreign intervention. When Mutimir died in 891 or 892, he was succeeded by his son Pribislav, who ruled for a short while before being overthrown by his first cousin, Peter Gojniković (892–917). The pacification of Byzantine–Bulgarian relations allowed the latter to remain in power for a longer period.

Renewed Byzantine–Bulgarian warfare together with the imperial ambitions of Boris's successor, Simeon (893–927), the tsar of Bulgaria, who was crowned in Constantinople in 913, led to heightened tension, which inevitably affected Serbia. Peter extended his rule to the principality of Neretljani and clashed with Prince Mihajlo Višević of Zahumlje. Mihajlo told Simeon that Peter was plotting with the Magyars against the Bulgarians, so Simeon sent his cousin Pavle Branović (917–20) against Peter and installed him in power. Peter was taken to Bulgaria, and the Byzantine Empire sent Zaharije Pribisavljević against the Bulgarians. He was captured by Pavle, however, who handed him over to the Bulgarians. In the meantime, Pavle had accepted the rule of the Byzantine emperor, so Simeon dispatched Zaharije with Bulgarian reinforcements and he ruled Serbia from 920 to 924. As soon as he had consolidated his power, however, Zaharije betrayed Simeon and crossed over to the Byzantine side.

The repetitive chronicle of conflict and change on the Serbian throne reveals that Bulgarian help was more effective, but Byzantine patronage was preferred. Simeon sent first one army against Zaharije, which was defeated, and then another in 924, with a member of the dynasty, Časlav Klonimirović, acting as bait. Instead of putting him on the throne, Simeon captured all the *župans* (heads of a *županija* or district) and subjugated the entire country. Having become Croatia's neighbor, Simeon soon sent an army against it as well.

Serbia's complete subjugation lasted only until Simeon's death in 927, but it had enduring consequences, especially for the church and culture. The results of Constantine's and Methodius's mission had immense implications for the cultural development of Southeastern and Eastern Europe, which was given full expression in Simeon's empire of the "Bulgarians and Greeks." The Slavic church service developed without impediment and the production of literary works increased. The period of peace under Simeon's successor Peter (927–69), who married into the Byzantine imperial family, helped to reinforce and further expand the church service in the Slavic language (Old Church Slavonic).

Časlav Klonimirović (927–ca. 950), who as a Bulgarian protégé was preordained prince, took advantage of the turmoil that followed Simeon's death. He managed to escape and rebuild the state with the assistance of the Byzantine emperor, with whom he had remained on good terms. The

Plate 1.2 Cyrillic writing and Church Slavonic: a page from the Gospel of Prince Miroslav, late twelfth century. (Photograph by B. Strugar)

peace between Byzantium and Bulgaria also served his purpose. In the meantime, starting in 896, Magyar tribes began settling in the Pannonian Basin, once inhabited by the Avars. For decades their cavalry attacked in every direction, including west and south. Serbia as well as Byzantium felt the terror of their devastation, and even Prince Časlav was slain during one of their raids. Information about the first Serbian dynasty ends with Časlav. It is not known whether it disappeared or whether its descendants lived on in some part of Baptized Serbia. For almost a century there is no information on regions in the interior. During this period the attention of Byzantine writers was focused on the coastal principalities.

The full force of Byzantine–Bulgarian rivalry was renewed during this dark period of early Serbian history, and Serbia was affected by it at least as much as it had been during the first half of the tenth century. An attempt by warmongering circles in Byzantium to overthrow and subdue Bulgaria, with the aid of Russian Prince Svyatoslav (969–71), was successful to the extent that the Empire extended its borders as far as the banks of the Sava and Danube rivers. This situation was shortlived, however; in 976 an uprising that originated in the southern part of Bulgaria aimed to restore the Bulgarian Empire.

Exploiting the Byzantines' internal confusion, the leader of the rebellion, Tsar Samuel (976–1014), quickly extended his power to Attica and Thessaly, as far as the shores of the Ionian Sea, and briefly held the city of Dyrrachium. He marched against Byzantine Dalmatia and conquered the principality of Duklja, where he placed his son-in-law, Prince John Vladimir, in command as his vassal. This breakthrough to Dalmatia implies that Serbia was also subjugated, just as it had been during Simeon's time.

Only after Byzantium had settled its internal conflicts in the late tenth century was it able to embark on an offensive that was to end in complete victory. Samuel suffered defeat after defeat until his death after the battle of Belasica in 1014. He was succeeded first by his son Gavril Radomir, then by his nephew John Vladislav, but they were unable to retain power and the Bulgarian Empire collapsed. This time Byzantium remained on the Sava–Danube frontier for a long time.

The Theme of Serbia and the Principality of Serbia

The Byzantine victory over the Bulgarians is one of the greatest turning points in the development of the Balkan Peninsula. It had long-term consequences not only for Byzantium, which fulfilled its century-long objective to restore control of the Roman provinces, but also for Bulgaria, which remained part of the Byzantine Empire in its entirety for almost two centuries, as well as for the Serbs, who, as next-door neighbors, found themselves in a significantly different position with regard to the Empire. Not only did the Serbs acquire a long frontier with Byzantium, they were also divided by the new borders. The area in which Serbia was to develop in the future was now almost completely under Byzantine control.

The extent of the territory that was under direct Byzantine authority in 1018 can be judged from a list of bishoprics of the autocephalous Ohrid archbishopric. The archbishopric was established in 1020 by Emperor Basil II (976–1025), the conqueror of Bulgaria, to ease the loss

Plate 1.3   Early Christian life: tenth-century episcopal church in Ras (Novi Pazar). (Photograph by B. Strugar)

of the patriarchate that Bulgaria had maintained under its rulers. The westernmost bishops' seats roughly marked both the jurisdiction of the Ohrid archbishopric and the extent of Byzantine authority. The border line had to pass west of the cities of Sirmium (Sremska Mitrovica), Ras (Novi Pazar), and Prizdriana (Prizren). In the north it followed the Drina River, which is explicitly mentioned as the border in the twelfth century, but it cannot be traced precisely elsewhere. The city of Ras, along with its episcopate founded under Bulgarian Emperor Peter, was thus part of Byzantine territory. The city would later play a significant role in Serbia's history.

Some of the descendants of the Serbs who had settled much earlier and been subjects of the Serb princes undoubtedly came under direct Byzantine rule. Emperor Basil II extended the Byzantine administrative system to the conquered territories by establishing themes with much larger territories than those in the coastal regions. He chose the old

Roman cities of Sirmium, Skopje, and Durostorum (Drstar, Silistria) for their seats, appointing governors with the title of *strategos* or *douks*. The governor at Sirmium had the name Serbia in his official title ("strategos Serbias," or "douks of Thessalonika, Bulgaria, and Serbia"), which is an unquestionable indication that at least part of the territory held by the Serb princes was under direct Byzantine rule.

The founding of the Ohrid archbishopric had far-reaching consequences for religious relations in later periods. The territory stretching westward of the three bishoprics of Sirmium, Ras, and Prizren remained under the jurisdiction of coastal church centers, which in turn were under papal authority. Catholicism had not yet started spreading from Hungary; the archbishopric in Kalocsa was established only in the eleventh century and the diocese of Srem much later, in the early thirteenth century. When the final schism between Constantinople and Rome took place in 1054, the border between their jurisdictions passed through Serbian regions. The princes west of this border line remained Byzantine vassals. The ruler of Duklja, who had led an uprising during the change on the throne in Constantinople in 1034, was undoubtedly subjugated. Byzantium did not have extensive access to the coastal principalities and had to rely on the bridgeheads at Dubrovnik and Dyrrachium with their modest territories. From there the emperor's *strategoi* set out to impose supreme rule over the neighbors.

The position of what remained of Baptized Serbia was influenced by neighboring Croatia, which underwent great expansion during the eleventh century and spread from its border regions of Imota, Livno, Pliva, and Pset to adjacent territories. The Magyar tribal state, however, which was baptized ca. 1000 and transformed into a centralized monarchy, had a stronger and more lasting influence. The first king, Stephen I (1000–38), focused on consolidating power within the state, and a period of internal conflict followed his death. It was not until the 1070s that Stephen's descendants, Ladislas and Coloman, were able to reestablish control and provide conditions for expansion. The territory of Slavonia, along with the city of Zagreb, fell under the rule of the Hungarian kings in 1091–5, and through it expansion continued toward the coast. This objective was achieved in 1105, when the Dalmatian cities were conquered, following the conquest of Croatia (1102) by the Hungarian kings.

What remained of Baptized Serbia was now between the hammer and the anvil, the Byzantine Empire and the Hungarian Kingdom, which had already launched its assault in the second half of the eleventh century. The course of events, and the impact of this rivalry on internal relations in Serbia, remain unknown, since there are no sources similar to those that existed during the Byzantine–Bulgarian struggles. Contemporary Byzantine authors concentrated on imperial policies and activities in the hinterland of the coastal cities, and only later reported on the wars with Hungary in the interior of the peninsula.

However, the results of these major upheavals are evident and the visible outcome was a division into spheres of influence. The Serbian *grand župans* (*megazupanos*, *archijupan*) were highly active in the eastern half bordering Byzantium. These local chieftains had a higher status than the *župans* who were expected to recognize the new prince in 924. In the twelfth century, Bosnian bans emerged in western parts of the former Baptized Serbia as vassals to the Hungarian kings. Bosnia, whose individuality had been noted earlier in the writings of Emperor Constantine Porphyrogenitus in the mid-tenth century, became independent and probably exceeded its original borders.

Unlike the northern Byzantine theme of Serbia, the Serbia of the *grand župans* must have been centered in the south. There is no existing description of its area, apart from a report from the mid-twelfth century that the Drina River separated "Bosnia from the remaining Serbia." This could have indicated the northern part, where there were routes going from east to west, while the central region was hampered by mountains. In the upper Drina and Lim regions, however, there were a number of corridors that were used later by merchants and travelers. These were undoubtedly the passages to the east used by Serb rebels against imperial authority during periods of hostility against Byzantium. According to trade routes dating from later periods, the most important passage led from the Lim river valley to Ras (whose name of Novi Pazar first occurs in 1455). The route led across the Pešter plateau to the Ibar river valley, then opened south toward Kosovo and north toward the Morava river valley.

There were other passages farther to the south, where the rule of the *grand župans* also extended. Part of the territory of *grand župan* Vukan in the 1090s was adjacent to the area governed by the emperor's *dux* in Dyrrachium. He is said to have "seized many fortresses under Vukan." The battleground was in Kosovo at the time, in the area between the Zvečan fortress and the governor's seat near Lipljan, which had changed rulers. Vukan had sufficient forces to penetrate deep into Byzantine territory, as far as Vranje and Skopje, where he plundered the outskirts of the towns.

Based on the scant descriptions of these events, it can be concluded that the borders were well established and that treaties were made between local Byzantine officials and Serb rulers. Loyalty was provided by presenting hostages, including the ruler's relatives and *župans*. Vukan would fall into line as soon as the emperor appeared with his army, but otherwise he complained about his neighbors and used their actions against Serbia to justify his raids into Byzantine territory.

Events in the late eleventh century were only a prologue to what was to take place in the twelfth century, during the great struggle between Hungary and Byzantium for domination over this part of Europe.

The Coastal Principalities

The Byzantine emperor's great victory in the early eleventh century indirectly affected the coastal principalities. Emperor Basil II established another theme, Dalmatia (Upper Dalmatia), as part of internal reforms, with the *strategos*'s seat in Dubrovnik. Founded under the name Ragusion or Rausion, the city became the center of Byzantine power, along with Dyrrachium. Byzantine coastal cities did not control the vast hinterlands from which they could attack their neighbors, and could not maintain significant military potential. Certain cities, especially the smaller, more isolated ones, were at greater risk from their neighbors than they were a threat to them. Even though the Empire was disproportionately more powerful than the small principalities, Emperor Basil I introduced a tax of 10 pounds of gold (720 gold coins) that was paid to Croatia's rulers. Only a small portion of this sum was put aside for Dubrovnik (1 pound of gold, 72 gold coins) and was paid to the Zahumlje and Travunia princes, whose territories bordered the town's hinterland.

There is very little information about the principalities themselves. It is certain that in the eleventh century the Neretljani principality was included in the Croatian Kingdom, which was in the process of expanding. The strip between the Cetina and Neretva rivers was called Krajina (the Border), due to its frontier position. The Kačići clan, descendants of one of the old Croatian tribes, played a significant role among the Krajina inhabitants.

It is not clear what changes took place in Zahumlje and Travunia in the mid-tenth century, at which time they had separate dynasties. The Zahumlje dynasty boasted descent from "the inhabitants from the Visla River," and at times came into conflict with the Serbian principality. In contrast, the Travunian dynasty was under the patronage of the Serbian princes and held family ties with them. Konavle was ruled by the Travunian princes in the first half of the tenth century.

The situation had changed drastically by the early eleventh century. The first and only record of an uprising against Byzantine power mentions Vojislav or Stefan Vojislav, who exploited the confusion during a change on the imperial throne in 1034 to turn insurgent. The rebellion was smothered and Vojislav was taken to Constantinople as a prisoner. He managed to regain his freedom and organized another uprising in late 1037 or early 1038, during which he attacked those Serbs who had submitted to the power of the Byzantine emperor.

The difference compared to the tenth century was the extent of the territory under his authority. Vojislav now had control of three previously independent principalities. A well-informed contemporary source states that Vojislav was in Zeta, the core of the Duklja principality, and also in Ston, which was the seat of the Zahumlje bishop and probably that of the princes. His territory therefore extended from the Neretva to the Bojana rivers. It is not clear where he was from, since Byzantine authors refer to him variously as "Stefan Vojislav, Serb archon," "Vojislav the Serb," and "Vojislav the Dukljan." The fact that his successors were later reduced to ruling the southern part of his vast state supports the theory of his Dukljan origins.

During his reign, periods of peace and good relations with neighboring *strategoi* were interspersed with periods of disobedience, such as in 1039 when Vojislav refused to hand over imperial gold from a ship that was wrecked on his coast. Another conflict arose with the Ragusan *strategos* Kekaumenos, who wanted to imprison Vojislav but ended up becoming the wily ruler's prisoner and being taken to Ston. The fact that the rebellion of Petar Odeljan in 1040–2, which aimed to restore the Bulgarian Empire, had taken place in the peninsula's interior worked to Vojislav's advantage. An ambitious Byzantine incursion with a large army from Dyrrachium and the surrounding themes ended in 1042 in the Byzantines' utter defeat.

In the mid-eleventh century Stefan Vojislav was succeeded by his son Mihajlo (after 1050 and before 1055–92?), who was named after one of the Byzantine emperors, Vojislav's supreme rulers. On assuming power he fostered good relations with Byzantium, was "written among the allies and friends of Byzantium," and received the title of *protospatharius*. It is unclear whether he preserved all the territory ruled by his father. There is no record of his activities in Zahumlje; almost everything that is known about him relates to the southern part of the country, and his main Byzantine opponents were located in Dyrrachium. However, the fact that Dubrovnik and its hinterland played a significant role in Mihajlo's church policies cannot be overlooked.

Mihajlo's attempt to extend his authority to the Balkan interior in 1072 testifies to his ambitions. The circumstances were somewhat unusual. Following the Byzantine defeat in the war against the Seljuks in Asia Minor (1071), a conspiracy aimed at instigating an uprising and restoring the Bulgarian Empire was organized in Skopje in an atmosphere of discontent over fiscal policies. The conspirators appealed to Mihajlo for help, and he obliged by sending his son Constantine Bodin as well as a detachment of Italian mercenaries. The young Bodin was pronounced Tsar Peter and, together with the rebel leaders, achieved great success. The army of the emperor's governor was routed near Prizren, and Skopje came under rebel control. Bodin campaigned successfully with half of his army near Niš, while his captain Petrilo advanced toward Ohrid, Devol, and Kastoria, where he was defeated and forced to retreat to Duklja. On his way to Skopje, which had in the meantime been taken by the Byzantines, Bodin was defeated and taken prisoner at Pauni in the southern part of Kosovo. After that he spent some time as a captive in Constantinople and Antioch before being freed by Venetian merchants. The collapse of the rebellion affected Mihajlo's position, since the imperial regent of Dyrrachium launched a military expedition and conquered all the towns in the hinterland, placing them under imperial control. Just how far his focus had shifted toward the coast is evident from the fact that Mihajlo's courts were in Kotor (Dekatera) and Prapratna, the *župa* between Bar and Ulcinj.

The conquest of certain smaller coastal cities and closer ties with Italy and the pope involved the Duklja rulers in church disputes. The vast Split archbishopric with its large number of coastal cities and huge territory in the interior could not meet the practical demands of these new conditions, and competitors soon appeared. Locating the center of the Upper Dalmatia theme in Dubrovnik raised the city's status, and immediately afterwards in 1023 the prelate was promoted to the rank of archbishop. In addition to the city, he now had three states (*tria regna*) in the hinterland under his jurisdiction: Travunia, Zahumlje, and Serbia.

The connection between Split and the coastal towns to the south had been severed. According to Split church tradition, recorded in the thirteenth century, the southern bishoprics had separated from the church metropolitanate (province) because bishops traveling to the provincial synod in 1045 had died when their ship sank off the island of Hvar. According to the same report, the southern bishoprics (Kotor, Bar, Ulcinj, and Svač) were subordinated to the Bar archbishop by papal order.

In reality, establishing the church hierarchy south of the Neretva River was a slow process, and further problems emerged. Papal documents reveal that, during the second half of the eleventh century, there was a formal dispute between the Split and Dubrovnik churches involving Mihajlo Vojisavljević. In early 1077, Pope Gregory VII sent a letter to Mihajlo, as "King of the Slavs," informing him that the papal legate Peter had not yet arrived in Rome, but that he had sent a letter which differed from the royal letter to such a degree that the pope could not resolve "your dispute or that of the Dubrovnik church." An investigation would be necessary to resolve the dispute canonically between the "Split and Dubrovnik archbishops." The dispute was undoubtedly between Split and Dubrovnik, and Mihajlo was the advocate of the Ragusan cause. The church rank (*honor regni*) of his state was tied to the rank and jurisdiction of the Dubrovnik archbishop, which is why the Duklja ruler was closely allied with Dubrovnik, and perhaps even ruled it temporarily.

The papal epistle of 1077 greatly influenced historical views in the nineteenth and twentieth centuries. It was concluded that on this occasion Mihajlo received a crown and royal insignia from the pope. From the form of address, it is apparent that Mihajlo already held the title of king and the papal office used this title. The letter further shows that the king had sought the banner of St. Peter, which is not a royal insignia but a mark of papal patronage, that is, of vassal status. In any case, by receiving the title of king, Duklja's ruler abandoned the Byzantine system of hierarchy, where he held the rank of *protospatharius*, and joined the western system, where the emperor and the pope were engaged in mutual rivalry, bestowing crowns and royal titles and thus allying rulers to themselves.

At the time of the struggle for jurisdiction in Dalmatia, the Normans appeared in the region, having taken southern Italy (Calabria, Apulia, Bari) and driven out Byzantium. They swept through the opposite shore of the Adriatic and were a political weapon in the struggle between the papacy and the Byzantine Empire, as well as between the pope and the antipope. The Normans were extremely ambitious with regard to Byzantium. They attacked Dyrrachium, from which the ancient road, *via Egnatia*, led to Thessalonika.

In the meantime, Byzantine pressure on Duklja had eased not only because of the Byzantine retreat from Italy, but also because of clashes over the throne (1078–81) and the conciliatory attitude of the Dyrrachium governor. Mihajlo established links with the new rulers on the other side of the Adriatic, and his son Bodin married the daughter of one of the Norman allies in Bari (April 1081). Nevertheless, Mihajlo and his son found themselves supporting the new emperor, Alexius I Comnenus (1081–1118), along with the Venetians and Albanians. Bodin attacked and harried the Normans, but during a decisive battle on October 18, 1081, he remained on the sidelines, bringing about the defeat of the imperial army and the fall of Dyrrachium.

The Norman expedition reached Ohrid and Skopje, but was temporarily halted the following year, and ended entirely in 1085. The Byzantine Empire under Emperor Alexius, an energetic and competent warrior, used the opportunity to recover its previous positions. It regained control of Dyrrachium and Dubrovnik, which had surrendered to the Normans in 1081. Meanwhile, Mihajlo had died and Bodin continued to rule single-handed. His neighbor in Dyrrachium was the active and capable governor John Ducas, who was a member of the imperial family. He adopted an aggressive approach to his neighbors and even seized some towns from *grand župan* Vukan. During a confrontation sometime between 1085 and 1090, he defeated and captured Bodin, but kept him in power, undoubtedly with the emperor's approval. There are no accounts of further conflicts with Byzantium.

Bodin was also involved in the cities' struggle for ecclesiastical jurisdiction, but unlike his father, who advocated the rights of the Dubrovnik church, Bodin wholeheartedly supported Bar, which was probably under his control. In 1089 the king addressed Clement III, the protégé of the German emperor, circumventing the heir of Gregory VII, who was to be regarded as the head of the Catholic Church. He received a bull from the antipope granting the Bar bishop the use of symbols pertaining to an archbishop's rank and confirming his jurisdiction over the bishoprics of Duklja, Bar, Kotor, Ulcinj, Svač, Skadar, Drivast, and Pilot, but also of Serbia, Bosnia, and Travunia – three states that had previously been under the jurisdiction of Dubrovnik (Zahumlje, Travunia, and Serbia).

Thus began the long dispute between Dubrovnik and Bar regarding jurisdiction over the southern towns and the hinterland. As the authentic bull of the unrecognized pope had no authority, counterfeit bulls were created in Bar that were attributed to recognized popes, even those from a much earlier period. Dubrovnik was not far behind. Thus both cities produced falsified documentation, making it difficult to make sense of the actual course of events.

Bar claimed its right to the rank of archbishopric as the successor of Duklja, which had been destroyed, and was, it was claimed, a church metropolitanate, like Salonae. The real reason is more likely to have been the position of Bodin's seat, which would also be the source of claims to the deep hinterland. Bar's jurisdiction extended no further than Pilot, a plain north of Lake Skadar. Zahumlje, Travunia, and Bosnia are known to have actually been under the control of the Dubrovnik archbishop. Contemporary papal documents explain that what is described in the documents as Serbia is actually Bosnia (*regnum Servillie quod est Bosna*). The situation in Bosnia in the early thirteenth century reveals just how unsatisfactory church organization was in the states west of the Ohrid archbishopric. Significant changes would take place only in 1219 with the founding of the autocephalous Serbian archbishopric.

The First Crusade brought the European West and the Christian and Muslim East into closer contact. The Crusaders traveled the land route via Belgrade, Braničevo and Niš, while one branch under Raymond of Toulouse traveled south, along the Adriatic coast. The leader of the Crusade visited Bodin. One chronicler described the attitude of Bodin's subjects toward the Crusaders in harsh terms, contrasting this with praise for Bodin's hospitality. This encounter in the winter of 1096–7 is also the last mention of Bodin. He was succeeded by George, who took the royal title, a man known for his seal and for being mentioned in later forged documents.

The Town of Ras and Raška Land

The sparse and fragmented sources on events in the eleventh century reveal that the Byzantine Empire clashed with the Serbs on two separate battlefields. One was in the Dyrrachium and Dubrovnik area, where the Empire was confronted by Vojislav's heirs, while the other was in the Kosovo and Ibar valleys, where its adversary was *grand župan* Vukan. The focus of the struggle shifted at the beginning of the twelfth century, as did the attention of Byzantine authors. The coastal regions were no longer in the spotlight and were replaced instead by the territories in the interior, since a vast battlefield had been established along the Sava and Danube rivers, on the border toward Hungary, which frequently required the emperor's personal involvement at the head of his army.

The two great adversaries on the long frontier, from Dalmatia to the Carpathian massif, were separated by a buffer zone consisting of Bosnia on the Hungarian side and Serbia on the Byzantine side. Prior to 1138, Bosnia was under the rule of the Hungarian kings, who initially appointed dynasty members as their regents, and later bans. John Kinnamos, chronicler of the Byzantine–Hungarian wars in the twelfth century, stated in reference to the events of 1154 that the Drina River "separates Bosnia from the remaining Serbia," but also that "Bosnia is not subjected to the *archižupan* of the Serbs, rather the people in it have a special way of life and government." At that time Bosnia was already pursuing a path of independent development, which it was to continue until the end of the Middle Ages.

The Hungarian–Byzantine wars were fought in several waves during the twelfth century, and in almost all of them the Serbs joined the emperor's enemies. During the first war (1127–9), mostly waged around Belgrade and Braničevo and on the Hungarian side of the Danube, the Serbs conquered and burned the city of Ras, which had been under Byzantine rule.

During this period, especially in the eyes of westerners, the Serbs are associated with Ras, whose earlier history is unclear. The bishopric was founded by Bulgarian Emperor Peter, and under Byzantine rule it was part of the Ohrid archbishopric (1020). For a while the town was the seat of the Ras catepanate, a Byzantine administrative unit. The town of Ras and the territory of its bishopric was the first larger administrative unit seized by the Serbs from Byzantium. Serb rulers made it their seat, which is why Latin texts began to refer to them as the Rasciani and their state as Rascia. The Hungarians, and through them the Germans, used this name up until the nineteenth and twentieth centuries. As with other church seats, the name of the town of Ras was passed on to the region through the bishopric. As with Srem (derived from Sirmium), Braničevo, and Prizren, the name of the land ruled by the Serb *grand župans* became Ras or Raška land. This name appeared in their title along with the name Serbian land, and it was also used by Latin authors, while the Byzantines continued using the name Serbia.

When the Byzantine–Hungarian war of 1127–9 ended in a truce, the Serbs remained alone, facing a stronger adversary, Byzantium, which had devastated the land and deported part of the population to Asia Minor. This was to happen on numerous occasions, yet it did not influence the close ties between the Hungarian and Serbian courts. The appearance of the name Uroš among Serb rulers is attributed to Hungarian influence, and family ties were also strong. Jelena, the daughter of *grand župan* Uroš I, was the wife of one Hungarian king and the mother of another, while her brother Beloš held the highest position in the kingdom (ban, palatine). Through the Hungarians, links were formed with the Normans and the Holy German Empire; they found expression in events in the middle of the century, although they did not significantly improve the position of the Serb rulers, who were Byzantium's closest neighbors and the first to face its superior force.

In the next war (1149–51), *grand župan* Uroš II joined the conflict as a Hungarian and Norman ally, but did not receive the promised help, allowing Emperor Manuel I Comnenus (1143–80) to concentrate his main forces on him. Ras once again was in Byzantine hands. There was fighting around the town of Galič in the Ibar river valley and the Serb ruler was in danger of being captured. The following year (1150), the *grand župan* was supported by Hungarian auxiliary troops, but was nevertheless defeated at the Tara River in western Serbia. The terms of the peace that was consequently signed imposed "twice as large a burden" on the Serb ruler. The size of the auxiliary unit that the *grand župan* was to provide the emperor for battlegrounds in Asia Minor was increased from 300 to 500 warriors, while he provided 2,000 soldiers for the battlefields in Europe.

Even this experience did not prevent the *grand župan* from cooperating with the enemies of Byzantium. However, the consequences were increasingly grave as Emperor Manuel meddled in dynastic conflicts in Hungary and moved the battle zone across the Sava River. In his relations with the Serbs, the Byzantine emperor established himself as their supreme ruler and arbiter, especially since conflicts within the ruling dynasty gave him ample opportunity to intervene. He deposed some rulers, such as Primislav, who succeeded Uroš II, and appointed others, such as Beloš, the brother of the previous *grand župan*. When Beloš moved to Hungary, Manuel appointed Dessa, obliging him to pledge his loyalty and terminate treaties with the Hungarians. This same *grand župan* was formally tried before the emperor in 1163 on charges of forming ties with the Alemanni (Germans) by wanting to marry into them, and also of considering the Hungarian king to be his master. Dessa was imprisoned and sent to Constantinople.

A change that was to have long-term consequences occurred at this time. The emperor promoted to power one Tihomir, the son of Zavida, a relative of the previous *župans*. The new *grand župan* ruled along with his brothers Stracimir, Miroslav, and Nemanja, to whom he assigned *česti*, parts of the state. The youngest brother, Stefan Nemanja, ruled in Toplica, the eastern part of the country. He established special ties with the Byzantine emperor, arousing his brothers' suspicions sufficiently to land him in prison. On his release, Nemanja came into open conflict with his brothers. Tihomir was slain in the battle of Pantino, near Zvečan, and the remaining brothers surrendered to Nemanja, who became *grand župan* (1166–96).

Even though Nemanja came to power at a time of great Byzantine triumphs, when Serbia was not active as it had been previously in the Hungarian–Byzantine conflict, like so many of his forebears he worked with the emperor's enemies. He established links with the Holy Roman Emperor Frederick Barbarossa and with the Venetian Republic, but in 1172 he was left on his own and forced to concede to Emperor Manuel I, who took him to Constantinople to be humiliated before being returned to the throne.

A new turning point arrived with the death of Emperor Manuel in 1180. The difficulties that soon engulfed the Empire provided Nemanja with an opportunity to return to his policy of siding with Hungary. Already by 1183 he was taking part in an expedition led by the Hungarian king into Byzantine territory, which penetrated as far as Sofia. Nemanja was allowed a free hand to expand his authority to the Adriatic coast, where Byzantine influence had weakened but not died out. In 1181 he attacked Kotor and shortly afterwards Bar, which was the stronghold of Grand Prince Mihajlo, a descendant of the Duklja dynasty and Nemanja's nephew. Nemanja and his brothers posed a threat to Korčula and Dubrovnik, where the Normans of southern Italy had replaced Byzantine rule. A truce was signed with Dubrovnik in 1186, revealing that the city was surrounded by territories ruled by Nemanja and his brother Miroslav, prince of Hum, who also controlled the valley of the lower Neretva.

The close associations between towns in the southern Adriatic and the states in their immediate hinterland became apparent during Nemanja's expansion toward the sea. Serbian, Latin, and Greek sources all concur in recounting that a Byzantine territorial entity under the name Kingdom (*regnum*) of Dalmatia and Diocletia had been established, and that it consisted of these towns and their hinterlands. A *dux* (1166) governed the administrative unit of Dalmatia and Diocletia under Byzantine rule. The borders of the Kingdom of Dalmatia and Diocletia were preserved under Nemanja's rule. He assigned "Zeta and its cities" to his eldest son Vukan, who reigned as king. A vestige of the earlier state was preserved in the titles of subsequent rulers and archbishops, in which a distinction was made between "Serbian" or "Raška land" and "coastal land."

A further step in Nemanja's anti-Byzantine policy was the establishment of links with the West; he sent an envoy to Frederick Barbarossa and promised to accept his supreme authority. When the Holy Roman Emperor arrived in Serbia, at the head of the Third Crusade, Nemanja bowed before him in Niš and offered military assistance, which the emperor declined, not wanting to provoke the hostility of the Byzantine Christian ruler. After the Crusaders moved on, Nemanja conquered parts of neighboring Bulgaria on his own account. However, on the death of Frederick Barbarossa, Nemanja was alone against Byzantium, whose power had weakened but was still sufficiently strong to punish a disobedient vassal. Nemanja was defeated in 1190 on the Morava River, near Vranje, and forced to submit to the emperor and relinquish his latest conquests.

Even after this defeat, Nemanja still retained his previous acquisitions in the border region along the Southern Morava, in Kosovo, and in the coastal regions surrounding Byzantine towns. Stefan Nemanja and his family ruled the former territories of Baptized Serbia and the coastal principalities (Zahumlje, Travunia, and Duklja), with the exception of what had now become an independent Bosnia under the supreme rule of the Hungarian king, and with the addition of land seized from Byzantium between the Western and Southern Morava rivers and the Šar Mountains. These territories were not merged into one unified state. Areas with different traditions were in different hands, and the entire formation was thus in danger of breaking apart because of internal conflicts, which is precisely what happened after Nemanja's death.

The marriage between Nemanja's second son Stefan and the niece of the Byzantine Emperor Isaac II Angelus was intended to reinforce

Nemanja's loyalty to Byzantium. This marriage assumed greater importance when Alexius III Angelus overthrew his brother Isaac II Angelus, making Stefan Nemanjić the imperial son-in-law. This status influenced his personal position as well as Byzantium's attitude toward Serbia. As the imperial son-in-law he received the title of *sebastokrator*, and as the husband of a Byzantine princess he gained advantage in the line of succession. To ensure this inheritance, his father, who was then *grand župan*, abdicated in order to spend the rest of his days as a monk, as many Byzantine dignitaries did at the time. At the Ras Assembly of 1196, Nemanja appointed Stefan as his heir and requested everyone, in particular his eldest son Vukan, to submit to the new ruler.

Nemanja took his vows along with his wife and retreated to his endowment of Studenica, which he had built ca. 1183. Abandoning secular life was marked by a change of name, so Stefan Nemanja became the monk Simeon, and his wife Ana the nun Anastasia. Simeon did not remain with the Studenica fraternity for long; in 1198 he went to Mt. Athos to join his younger son Rastko, who had abandoned his position as regent of Hum and traveled in secret to Mt. Athos, where he was ordained as the monk Sava.

Nemanja's sojourn on Mt. Athos had significant long-term consequences; together with his son he founded the Chilandar monastery "to receive men from the Serbian people." Ever since then the Serbs have been represented in the land of Orthodox monasticism, along with Greeks, Bulgarians, Russians, and Georgians. Financial support for the construction of Chilandar was provided by *grand župan* Stefan, while Sava obtained permission from Byzantine imperial relatives in Constantinople. Nemanja died on February 13, 1199 in the newly constructed monastery. He was buried there rather than in Studenica, where according to custom his grave had been prepared.

2
The Dynasty of Sacred Roots

Nemanja's Legacy

The reign of Stefan Nemanja represented an essential turning point in the development of the Serbian state, although this became apparent only after his death. His era had much more in common with the period of his predecessors than with that of his successors, particularly with regard to relations with the Byzantine Empire. During his rule the emperor's supreme power was acknowledged, which resulted in certain real and symbolic obligations; Serbia's ruler was included in the Byzantine hierarchy and was considered as an imperial governor in the province.

By Nemanja's time, however, the balance of power had fundamentally changed. While the Serbian state was increasing in area and strength, the already weakened Byzantine Empire suddenly lost its authority. It was first forced out of peripheral areas along the Sava and Danube. Belgrade and Braničevo were still under imperial rule in 1198, but soon became part of the renewed Bulgarian state (from 1185) and were in later decades the source of discord between Hungary and Bulgaria. The region along the Sava with Sirmium comprised a dynastic territory that would survive as such until the early fourteenth century, first as the dowry of Hungarian princess Margaret (Maria), wife of Isaac II Angelus, and later as the appanage of her heirs.

During the period of Nemanja's first successor Byzantium was forced to defend its borders in Thrace and Macedonia, but its efforts were short-lived since the Empire was temporarily overthrown in 1204 as a result of internal conflicts and the involvement of those who had taken part in the Fourth Crusade, led by the Venetians. Crusader states were founded on the ruins of the former Empire, with seats in Constantinople, Thessalonika, and the Peloponnese, while independent territories were established by members of the previous imperial dynasty or under the command of local rulers in Asia Minor and Epirus.

The Byzantine crisis and the fundamental changes to the political map of the Balkan Peninsula were observed from afar by Serbia, which was itself torn by internal struggles. With the collapse of Byzantium, Stefan Nemanjić, the imperial son-in-law and *sebastokrator*, lost one of the two mainstays of his rule, the other having been lost on the death of his father in February 1199.

By 1202 war broke out between the brothers; Vukan Nemanjić tried to alter the line of succession, which had been established under significantly different circumstances. He found an ally in Hungary, while Stefan Nemanjić sought support from those who opposed the Hungarian king, either temporarily, such as Bosnian Ban Kulin, or permanently, such as the Bulgarian ruler Kalojan (1197–1207). Vukan ousted his brother from power, seized control of the entire country, and became *grand župan*. The Hungarian king included Serbia in the Hungarian royal title, becoming *rex Servie* among others, a title that was subsequently inherited by all Hungarian kings until 1918.

With Bulgarian support, Stefan returned to Serbia and continued the struggle, bringing misery to the country. Hostilities ceased in late 1204 or early 1205, with the conditions of the truce most likely dictated by Stefan Nemanjić. He became *grand župan* and ruler of the country, while Vukan remained in power as grand prince in the part of the country formerly under his control. The renewed peace and unity between the brothers was assumed to be once more confirmed by Nemanja, this time as the country's patron and heavenly protector of his sons. Myrrh had flowed from their father's remains, believed to be a sign of divine compassion and sanctification, and the brothers asked Sava to bring them back to Serbia.

Nemanja's relics were ceremoniously greeted and buried at Studenica, in the tomb that had previously been prepared for them. As further signs of sanctity were observed, the cult of St. Simeon the Myrrhoblete (Mirotočivi) was founded. He became the patron saint of all his descendants, mediator before Christ and the Virgin, and intercessor for his entire people. The *žitija* (hagiographies) to honor the memory of the patron of Studenica and Chilandar were written by his two sons, Sava and Stefan. These works (*The Life of St. Simeon Nemanja* and the *Life of Simeon Nemanja*) mark the beginning of writing among the Serbs.

It was only after the cult was established that the crucial character of Nemanja's rule became clear. He was placed at the beginning of the "sacred dynasty" or "dynasty of sacred roots," which later produced other saints. The aura of sanctity that surrounded some members as well as the entire dynasty enabled the gradual creation of a special Serbian tradition as an extension of general Christian traditions, and placed the

Plate 2.1 Model of piety: Studenica monastery, the endowment of Stefan Nemanja, central Serbia, late twelfth century. (Photograph by B. Strugar)

history of the Serbian people within the common history of salvation. These ideas were nurtured by the church and handed down through the ages, even during periods when there was no dynasty or state. Until modern historical works began to be written in the eighteenth century, Serbian history started with Stefan Nemanja.

Peace between the brothers and the strengthening of the dynasty's authority allowed the heritage of Nemanja's rule to be preserved through difficult times that were full of dramatic changes. The situation was not completely secure, however, even then. Disagreements between the brothers had revealed the danger of partition or confrontation between parts of the state, each with dynamic and strong regional traditions. Still greater was the threat from neighboring states, who took turns in attempting to force their hegemony throughout the Balkan Peninsula.

The triumph of the Crusaders who conquered Constantinople in 1204 was shortlived, as they were checked by the belligerent Bulgarian Tsar Kalojan (1197–1207). Bulgaria encountered trouble of its own after he was killed beneath the walls of Thessalonika in 1207. His death paved the way for the Angelus family, heirs to the previous imperial dynasty, to expand from Epirus to the far north and east in an attempt to reestablish the Byzantine Empire. The unreliability of family ties became apparent in Hum, where the widow of Prince Miroslav and his son Andrija were being pressured by their cousin Peter. Stefan Nemanjić was forced to go to war and secured only part of the principality, the Hum coast and Popovo Polje, for his cousin, Miroslav's heir.

Momentous changes on the Adriatic side of the extended state, where the former key Byzantine strongholds of Dubrovnik and Dyrrachium were located, had meanwhile taken place. Both cities were now under Venetian rule. The elimination of Byzantine power provided space for the promotion of local rulers in Arbanon (Raban), which at the time included Upper and Lower Pilot (Polatum), in the flatlands north of Lake Scutari. The Nemanjić family established ties with an influential Albanian family: Stefan's daughter married *panhypersebastos* Demetrius, son of Progon, whose power was reflected in the treaties that cities all the way to Dubrovnik had signed with him. A serious adversary of both the Nemanjić family and Albanian nobles was Michael I Angelus, despot of Epirus, who waged war against Stefan and seized the city of Skadar, but he died soon after in 1214.

The most powerful inland neighbor of the Serbian state was Bulgaria, where Lord Strez, based in the city of Prosek (Demir Kapija) on the Vardar River, had broken away from the weak Tsar Boril (1207–18). Strez first sought refuge with Stefan Nemanjić, but turned against him after gaining power in Macedonia. A mission led by the king's brother Sava was unsuccessful, but Strez's death ca. 1212 spared the Serbian ruler greater difficulties.

In the space of just one decade, Stefan Nemanjić had witnessed enormous changes. The Empire to which he owed his rise and enthronement had ceased to exist and the lands surrounding him had been fundamentally transformed; instead of one mighty Empire there was a group of small lords, each with his special interests and ambitions. Nevertheless, Stefan coped with all these difficulties and preserved Nemanja's legacy in its entirety. He ruled a territory approximately equal to that governed by his father, and had control over his cousins in Hum and Zeta.

In the Balkan world without Byzantium, the West gained the upper hand, represented less by the victorious Crusaders than by the Venetian Republic, which had become "ruler of a quarter and another half of a quarter" of the Byzantine Empire, and even more by the Holy See, whose universal pretensions seemed to have been realized. In this changed world, the former protégé of the eastern emperors sought the patronage of the leading powers of the West, Venice and the Holy See.

Independent Kingdom

Stefan's western orientation was also shown by his marriage to Anna Dandolo, granddaughter of the Venetian doge who had organized expeditions to Zadar (1202) and Constantinople (1204). This marriage produced sons Uroš, who would later become king, and Predislav (Sava), who became archbishop, while his first marriage to Eudocia had given him Radoslav and Vladislav. Some medieval writers attributed this marriage to Anna as representing the fulfillment of another of the great ambitions of both of Nemanja's sons – the title of king.

Vukan bore the royal title and is mentioned in an inscription dated 1195 in the Church of St. Luke in Kotor, along with his father, who was only *grand župan*. According to the title, Vukan was "King of Diocletia, Dalmatia, Travunia, Toplica, and Hvosno." Yet in 1199 he asked Pope Innocent III for royal insignia! On the same occasion he requested a papal legate for the church synod in Bar and *pallium* (robes, tokens of the rank of archbishop) for the prelate in Bar, which were granted, while the royal symbols were not. Stefan followed his brother Vukan's example before the first conflict broke out between them; he too sought the legate and crown, and according to a papal letter the legate had already been chosen (1201–2) when the pope gave up because of opposition from Hungarian King Emeric. During his short rule of the country, Vukan held the rank of *grand župan* and again sought the crown from the pope. This attempt was unsuccessful for similar reasons.

The Hungarian kings considered Serbia's rulers as their vassals. Serbia was included in their royal title at the time, and being crowned by a universal authority in the person of the pope would make Serbia's rulers their equals. An example visible to all was the Bulgarian ruler Kalojan, who was crowned king by a papal legate in 1204 even though he had enthroned himself as tsar, following the tradition of former Bulgarian tsars Simeon, Peter, and Samuel. The Bulgarian prelate was appointed archbishop on the same occasion but was designated as patriarch, with the Byzantines' later consent. What had failed under Pope Innocent III succeeded under his successor Honorius III, while Hungarian King Andrew II (1205–35) was absent on Crusade. A papal legate brought a crown to Serbia in 1217 and crowned the *grand župan* king, although it is not known where the ceremony took place.

Military intervention by the Hungarian king was belated this time (he returned from Crusade in late 1218), and was probably prevented by the diplomacy of the Serbian king's brother Sava. The Hungarian kings retained the reference to Serbia in their royal title and continued to view

Serbia's rulers as their vassals, imposing this relation whenever they had sufficient power.

In his charters Stefan referred to himself as the "first-crowned king," and his descendants called him Prvovenčani (the "First-Crowned"). The relationship between the title of the Diocletian kings, which Vukan and his first successors had used, is not clear. It is certain that in requesting the crown, Stefan and Sava cited the fact that Diocletia, where their father was born, "had been called a great kingdom from the beginning," and it is also certain that this title was not recognized throughout the country. This is best seen by the fact that when Vukan ruled the country he was called *grand župan*, and later grand prince (1209).

The new title of the Serbian rulers was "crowned king and autocrat of all Serbian and coastal lands." Even though the Byzantine system of hierarchy was abandoned, the term *autokrator* (*samodržac*) was retained, which had been part of the Byzantine emperor's title. This indicated that the ruler was independent and was not subordinated to another authority. Only in later centuries would the term assume dimen-

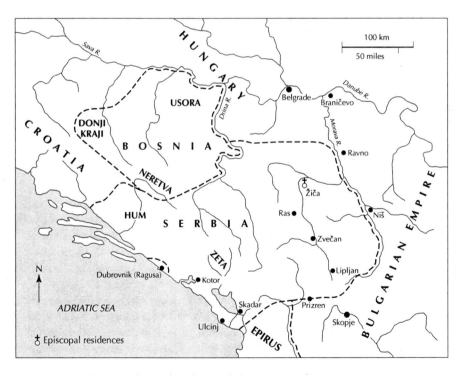

Map 2.1   The Kingdom of Serbia and the Banate of Bosnia, ca. 1220.

sions expressing absolutist tendencies in domestic policy. During the Middle Ages it referred to relations with the outside world and was in accordance with the teaching that power was granted to each ruler directly by God. This was also claimed in the Chilandar charter (1198): "Merciful God made the Greeks emperors, the Hungarians kings, and in His wisdom He set each people apart and gave them laws and established customs, and He appointed lords over them according to the custom and law."

The reference in the title to Serbian and coastal lands, or Raška and coastal lands, which was used until the empire was proclaimed, sums up previous development whereby the inland territories and the coastal lands were perceived as separate entities. The broader version of the title, separating the coastal lands into Diocletia, Travunia, and Zahumlje, as they were during the reign of Constantine VII Porphyrogenitus in the tenth century, was used in parallel with the shorter title up to the reign of King Vladislav I.

Along with the title and coronation came the idea of the crown, more often called *venac* (wreath) or *sveti venac* (*sacra corona*), as a symbol of the ruler's power, independent of the frail and ephemeral person of the individual king. This in turn led to a new perception of the state, stressing its general and public character as well as its indivisibility. From the coronation of the "first-crowned king," there was no more partitioning of the state territory as there had been during the generation of Stefan Nemanja and his children. The independent descendants of the secondary dynasty in Zeta and Hum were ousted during the reign of Stefan's sons.

The Autocephalous Archbishopric

The territory consolidated by Stefan Nemanja and preserved later as a whole by his son, who imposed greater unity and elevated it to royal status, was divided between the church jurisdictions of Rome and Constantinople. The central area, taken from Byzantium in the eleventh and twelfth centuries, was part of the old Ras, Lipljan, and Prizren bishoprics, with the Ras bishopric regarded by the Ohrid seat as "the Serbian bishopric." All three were part of the autocephalous Ohrid archbishopric, which was subordinate to the Constantinople ecumenical patriarchate. Regions where Byzantine rule had not been restored in 1018 remained under the jurisdiction of church centers in coastal cities, under papal rule. By Nemanja's time the Split area had been reduced, leaving Dubrovnik and Bar to fight over jurisdiction of the "three states" (Serbia was equated with Bosnia in papal documents). The division was symbolically expressed through Nemanja, the founder of the dynasty and later saint. According to his son, he was baptized by "Latin priests" in Ribnica, near present-day Podgorica (Montenegro). He was baptized again much later, in Ras, which testifies to the perception of the differences as well as to the reality of the schism, as though an imperfection had been mended by the repeated christening.

The most important difference stemming from the confessional division related to the use of the Old Church Slavonic language in the church service. In the realm of papal jurisdiction, the Old Church Slavonic service and literature were suppressed along with priests who held services in that language. The Split synod of 927 had already prohibited the ordination of priests who did not know Latin, and this attitude was even more strictly enforced as great church reforms spread from the West in the eleventh century. The service in Old Church Slavonic was written in Cyrillic, the basic alphabet inherited from the mission of Constantine and Methodius. Its usage was suppressed in the coastal cities and limited to a narrow stretch of the northern Adriatic coast and adjacent islands.

Prelates from the Constantinopolitan patriarchate were more accepting of the Slavic language, especially in the territory of the Ohrid archbishopric where the tradition of Slavic-language services had been preserved from the Bulgarian period. There was a gulf separating the learned members of the Greek clergy and their Slavic congregation, making them feel like exiles. Slav literacy in Old Church Slavonic spread nonetheless, diffused by the Cyrillic alphabet to the eastern and central parts and taking on the distinctive features of the spoken language. This is confirmed by manuscripts such as Miroslav's Gospel from the late twelfth century (see plate 1.2, p. 19) and Vukan's Gospel from the early thirteenth century. A network of parishes existed in the Byzantine sphere of influence through which believers were brought together, while in the coastal archdiocese there was no corresponding organization of Latin priests. Christian church life was maintained by local brotherhoods of monks, which papal envoys found to be in a poor condition in the early thirteenth century. Even though the bishop of Bosnia was formally subordinate to Dubrovnik and traveled there for his consecration bearing gifts for the archbishop, the condition of his congregation was unsatisfactory, in terms of both discipline and resistance to heresy. Around 1230, papal investigators discovered that the bishop did not know how to perform the rite of baptism, and that he lived in the same village as dualist heretics.

The condition of the church in the coastal cities and their vicinities was also unsatisfactory. This became apparent at a local synod held in Bar in 1199, under Vukan's patronage, with a papal legate in attendance.

The synod addressed general issues of discipline among the clergy and relations with the laity, but also broached individual and specific subjects. Special emphasis was given to curbing simony, buying church titles, and generally eliminating strong secular influences on the church.

The confessional division was visible even among members of the dynasty. Vukan appeared as "a faithful son of the Roman Church," but despite this, when he became ruler of the entire country, in 1203 the pope demanded that he and all his subjects take an oath to confirm them in the "true faith." Stefan Nemanjić also wrote to the pope that "we wish to be called faithful son," but this did not prevent him and his brother from seeking a solution to the church's organization in their kingdom from the opposite side.

After the fall of Constantinople and the great expansion of papal jurisdiction, part of the Greek clergy recognized the pope's supreme authority. They agreed to pledge their loyalty in return for a promise that they could retain their doctrine, rites, and customs. The successors of the Constantinopolitan patriarchs, who did not accept papal supremacy, withdrew to unconquered areas. Thus the city of Nicaea in Asia Minor became the seat of the patriarch of the *oikoumene* (universe). The patriarch in Constantinople gave legitimacy to the self-proclaimed emperors who fought to restore the Byzantine Empire.

The eastern Empire, where the emperor and patriarch performed the duties within their jurisdictions in complete harmony, served as an ideal model of political and church unity for other states and political entities in the East. It was only natural for the state framework to be complemented by an autocephalous church. Domentian, Sava's pupil and biographer, claims that it was Sava who approached the Constantinopolitan patriarch and asked for the archbishopric in his fatherland to be "self-ordained," just as the country was "self-ruled," by the grace of God.

The state seat in Ras was under the jurisdiction of the Eastern Church. Members of the ruling dynasty belonged to it and some were Orthodox monks, which also led them to turn to the East. Practical concerns pointed in the same direction. While the royal crown was sought from the pope, the successors to the Byzantine emperors and the Nicaean patriarch were addressed in order to change circumstances in the church and adjust them to the altered situation.

The mission was entrusted to the brother of the king, archimandrite Sava, who asked the Byzantine emperor and the patriarch in Nicaea to appoint and consecrate one of the monks of his entourage as archbishop. The emperor granted this request, but wanted Sava himself to become archbishop. The patriarch and bishops around him consecrated Sava, thus appointing him as the first archbishop of "Serbian and coastal lands." Sava also asked for a special right in Nicaea: that his successors would not have to come to the patriarch's seat for their consecration, but would be elected and ordained by the local synod. This contained the essence of what it meant to be autocephalous. The country's church synod was now in charge of church life; it could appoint the archbishop and had the potential to modify the way in which the Christian message and principles were spread to suit local conditions and cultural circumstances. Two brothers, one as king heading the country and the other as archbishop at the head of the autocephalous church, seemed to be the incarnation of an ideal harmony.

On his return from this important mission via Mt. Athos and Thessalonika, Archbishop Sava collected people and manuscripts and arranged for the translation of a special version of the collection of ecclesiastical and civil laws regarding church administration and jurisdiction: the *Nomocanon*, later called the rulebook of St. Sava, necessary for those administering the church. Archbishop Sava brought pupils from Mt. Athos and appointed those worthy of becoming bishops to different responsibilities in his archbishopric. The seat of the new archbishopric was in Žiča monastery (near present-day Kraljevo), built by Stefan Nemanjić.

Sava added seven new bishoprics to those existing within the Ohrid archbishopric and placed their seats in different monasteries. The new bishoprics were established west of the former Ohrid bishoprics (Dabar, Budimlja, Moravica), or between the old centers of Ras and Niš (Toplica), and Ras and Prizren (Hvosno). Two of them were in the immediate hinterland of Catholic towns on the coast: the first in rank, the Zeta bishopric, had its seat on the Prevlaka Peninsula in the Bay of Kotor, and the second, the Hum bishopric, had its seat in Ston. The Catholic bishopric was relocated to Korčula, while the Trebinje Catholic bishop retreated to Dubrovnik, where he maintained his Trebinje title and was appointed to the Mrkan Island diocese.

The boundaries of the Orthodox Church had moved all the way to the Bosnian border and the walls of the coastal cities, which remained Catholic and the seats of Catholic prelates, regardless of the king's rule. The expansion of the Orthodox domain with the establishment of the Serbian autocephalous archbishopric did not provoke a Catholic reaction, probably because it was eclipsed by the great shifts that took place after 1204 when papal jurisdiction extended to Constantinople and Mt. Athos.

The reaction of Demetrios Chomatenos, however, was forceful. Consecrated archbishop of Ohrid in 1216, he lost three of his dioceses and bitterly condemned Sava's consecration as a non-canonic act, demanding that the rights of the Ohrid-based church be respected and threatening to expel Sava from the congregation of the faithful. Chomatenos questioned the probity of Sava's life, contrasting the austerity of his youth, when he "abandoned his country and family and all his father's inheritance" and departed for Mt. Athos, "where he became celebrated among monks," with his later life, when "love for his fatherland captivated him and took him away from Mt. Athos, and he again settled in Serbia." Patriotism had turned "the ascetic into the executor and administrator of secular tasks, and made him an envoy to neighboring rulers." Chomatenos's anger contained an element of personal rivalry with the Nicaea-based patriarch and emperor, because his superior was Theodore I Lascaris, whom Chomatenos later crowned emperor. The consequences of Chomatenos's act are not known. What is certain is that Sava did not give up organizing the autocephalous Serbian church, that the earliest record of Serbian bishoprics does not include Lipljan and Prizren, and that after 1220 the Nemanjić family had close ties with the Epirus-based Angelus family. Stefan's successor Radoslav was the son-in-law of Byzantine Emperor Theodore I and he turned to Chomatenos for advice on church issues.

Sava's hagiography discloses what was considered most important in reorganizing the church. The archbishop summoned a synod in Žiča monastery and gave a sermon against heresy, then focused on marital relations, imbuing family life with Christian values and beliefs. Throughout the country couples were married who had established families in accordance with custom, without the participation of the church. "Many churches, small and large," were constructed.

The archbishop and his high priests were responsible for establishing a network of church institutions and training the people who would run them. In many parts of the Serbian state true Christian life began only after the archbishopric was founded. This is why the biographers praise Nemanja and Sava so emphatically for enlightening the country.

The need for liturgical manuscripts encouraged translation and transcription. Modifications to the Old Church Slavonic to adapt it to the specific features of the language spoken among the Serbs were formalized and further standardized within the archbishopric. Just as the kingdom represented a lasting framework in which to regulate the administrative system, laws, and legal institutions, so the archbishopric represented a framework in which cultural uniformity was achieved through the creation and nurturing of specific traditions. The territorial jurisdiction became an area in which writing was standardized, where the clergy received similar training, and where ceremonies became uniform.

Significant cultural differences were bound to arise along the borders with neighboring archbishoprics. This is clear from its relationship toward the coastal cities, whose population remained Latins because of their liturgical language and other associated differences. The Latins included not only the native population of Romans but also people from surrounding areas who had moved to the towns and accepted the Catholic faith. Neighboring Catholic Albanians, who were separated by language and their way of life, were also called Latins, and their priests were known as "Latin priests."

Lasting repercussions were felt along the border with Bosnia, which was part of the Dubrovnik archbishopric at the time of Sava's reforms, even though Slavic-language services were held and it had Eastern-type monasticism. By the end of the twelfth century Bosnia was in turmoil because of accusations of heresy (one coming from Vukan Nemanjić). This had to do with the dualists, who were called Patarins, as in Italy and Dalmatia. Ban Kulin (1180–1204) defended himself against the charges, maintaining that his subjects were true Christians, and invited a papal legate, who arrived in 1203 and obtained guarantees from the local clergy that they would adhere to the customs and rules of the Roman Church. This did not resolve the crisis and the accusations were renewed in 1221, resulting in a Crusade against the heretics that originated in Hungary. The Catholic bishopric was detached from Dubrovnik in 1247 and entrusted to the Kalocsa archbishopric in southern Hungary.

The bishopric based on the Slavic-language service remained active in the country and took the form and name of "the Bosnian Church." It was influenced by the dualists, who in the whole of Europe had managed to survive only there. The Serbian Church condemned members of the Bosnian Church as "thrice-cursed heretics" and worked hard to convert them. Some Serbian rulers, such as King Dragutin (1278–82), used the support of Catholic missionaries in this regard. The religious division proved stronger than the common tribal tradition. While the bans of the thirteenth century, such as Matija Ninoslav, called their subjects Serbs, Ban Stjepan II (1314–53) called them Bosniaks but named the language of his documents Serbian, while he considered Serbia's ruler to be "the tsar of Rasa." The Bosnian state and Bosnian Church set the boundaries of integration at their borders, so the population of this country became primarily known as Bosniaks.

What lay within the boundaries of the Serbian archbishopric was linked to this in a number of ways. First, it formed an entity and, despite the specific features of the different regions, similar traditions and a similar type of piety were passed down within it. This created the conditions for a gradual merging of diverse components. The archbishopric symbolically represented a bond that held believers together. Soon after Sava's death in 1236, the first archbishop became the source of a cult, in addition to that of his father, St. Simeon, in the same way that certain other dynasty members were later worshipped. This cult, which was incorporated in the church calendar and in the founders' portraits in endowed churches, gave the Serbian autocephalous church specific characteristics and later played an important role in preserving continuity.

Stability Put to the Test

The Kingdom of Serbia and its "first-crowned ruler" enjoyed greater respect among other states, but this was no guarantee of security in the constantly changing political situation. The unexpected strengthening of the rulers of Epirus, from the Angelus family under Theodore I, began at about the same time as Stefan's coronation. Theodore conquered Thessalonika in 1224 and adopted the title of emperor. Occupying the vast territory from the Ionian to the Aegean and heading a powerful army, he was closer to Constantinople than his adversaries in Asia Minor, who had a similar goal.

Theodore showed no ambitions toward Serbia, and he had family ties with its rulers. Stefan Nemanjić's eldest son Radoslav was betrothed to Theodore's daughter Anna. This link became even more significant a few years after Stefan's coronation when he fell ill and appointed Radoslav as his regent. Radoslav (1227–33) then became co-ruler with his father. As son-in-law of the mighty Theodore I Angelus, he also represented a shield against threats from other quarters.

The balance shifted markedly in 1230 with the defeat of Theodore I at the hands of Bulgarian Tsar John Asen II (1218–41). The title of most powerful ruler on the Balkan Peninsula was transferred to the Bulgarian, who controlled the territory from the Black Sea to the Ionian Sea. Radoslav's position was severely shaken and in 1233 he was overthrown by disgruntled nobles who placed the son-in-law of the Bulgarian tsar, Vladislav, on the throne. Radoslav retreated to Dubrovnik, issuing the city with a charter, and then went to Dyrrachium. Archbishop Sava blessed this change in ruler and soon withdrew from the archbishop's seat, appointing as his successor his pupil Arsenije, with the help of the synod. He then left on a long pilgrimage to the Holy Land. On his return, he became ill during a stay in Bulgaria and died in Turnovo in 1236. His remains were brought back to Serbia a year later and he was buried in the Mileševa monastery, founded by Vladislav. The reburial of his relics initiated the cult of St. Sava, along with that of St. Simeon.

The arrival of the Tatars (Mongols) in 1241–2 created massive upheavals throughout southeastern Europe. The flat and accessible Hungarian state was plundered almost in its entirety following the defeat of the king's army. King Bela IV (1235–70) saved himself by fleeing to

Dalmatia and the Adriatic islands. The coastal cities of the Serbian state suffered at the hands of the Tatars who made their way to the coast. Kotor and smaller cities in Zeta are particularly mentioned in chronicles. Serbia was raided by a band returning north from the coast in 1242. Bulgaria suffered even greater losses owing to its easier accessibility to the Mongols' Golden Horde state, founded on the shores of the Black Sea.

Fresh conflict arose in Serbia among Stefan Prvovenčani's sons, although the reasons are obscure. Vladislav was overthrown and Uroš I (1243–76) was crowned king. The situation in the Balkans was further complicated by the fact that no state had sufficient authority to impose itself over the others. Power was evenly distributed and the Greeks from Nicaea became increasingly more threatening, conquering territories and securing their authority on European soil.

The position of the Serbian king was affected severely by the restoration of Hungary, which had reinforced its positions in Serbia south of the Sava and Danube rivers, establishing the Mačva and Kučevo-Braničevo banats (districts) as a border defense region. King Bela IV installed his daughter Anna and son-in-law Rostislav Mihajlović, who had been banished from Galicia. Thus the old dynastic territory received a new ruler.

King Uroš I was sought as an ally in the conflicts among the Balkan lords. On one occasion, having abandoned the Nicaean Greeks, he joined the Epirus Greeks and held Skopje for a short time. The border ordinarily lay at Lipljan in southern Kosovo, until the time of Milutin's conquests. When the Nicaean Greeks managed to seize Constantinople in 1261 and restore the Byzantine Empire, Uroš found himself in a similar position to that of Nemanja – he was lodged between two mighty neighbors. The important difference was that he had much greater power than the *grand župans* of the twelfth century.

Using information from scarce sources, it seems that Uroš sought to achieve complete control over the whole of Serbian territory and to remove all traces of autonomy enjoyed by his family members, who were local nobles, and replace them with governors of his own. In Zeta, in the south, where Vukan's son Djordje ruled under the royal title until the mid-thirteenth century, justification was supplied by the old conflict between Bar and Dubrovnik over ecclesiastical jurisdiction over the southern towns. In the meantime, the Adriatic hinterland had been absorbed into the Serbian archbishopric, and in 1247 Bosnia had been placed under the jurisdiction of the Kalocsa archbishopric in Hungary.

The Dubrovnik archbishops aspired to gain jurisdiction over Bar itself, which they claimed had only a bishopric. Formal proceedings were held before the pope, on the one hand, while the two cities, each with its supporters, came into direct conflict, on the other. Bar was backed by Serbian King Uroš and his brother, former King Vladislav, while Dubrovnik sought and found allies among the Bulgarian rulers, the princes of Hum, and the Republic of Venice, which controlled the city. Relations were so hostile that Uroš attacked Dubrovnik on three occasions, while Dubrovnik formed an alliance with Bulgarian Tsar Michael Asen in 1253 with the aim of dethroning the Serbian king.

However, no real change resulted. Proceedings before the pope were drawn out, then suspended, thus forestalling the Dubrovnik archbishops' ambitions. Bar did not obtain jurisdiction over Catholics in the hinterland and they remained under the Kotor bishopric, which during the eleventh century had placed itself under the jurisdiction of the archbishop of the Italian city of Bari, precisely because of the conflict between Dubrovnik and Bar. The Bar archbishop actually became *primas Servie* only in the second half of the fifteenth century.

In this prolonged struggle Djordje, Vukan's son and the king's relative, sided with Dubrovnik, and in the name of the town of Ulcinj accepted the church patronage of the Dubrovnik archbishop. He was probably punished for this action because from that moment on neither he nor his successors appeared in Zeta. Djordje's brother Stefan emerges with the title of prince in his endowment of Morača monastery, while Vukan's third son Dimitrije held the title of *župan*, before becoming a monk.

During Uroš's war with Dubrovnik in 1254, *župan* Radoslav, the son of Prince Andrija, presented himself in Hum as the "sworn liege of the Hungarian king" and promised to wage war as long as Dubrovnik was in conflict with Serbia. There is no later information of his rule in Hum, which was administered by the king's treasurer (*kaznac*). The descendants of Prince Miroslav, the brother of Stefan Nemanja, remained landed lords in Popovo Polje, descending to the level of local nobility and exercising no significant influence.

The iron grip of King Uroš was also felt with regard to the church. His brother, the fourth son of Stefan Prvovenčani, was consecrated as Archbishop Sava II, apparently achieving another ideal harmony of one brother on the royal throne and one in the archbishop's seat.

Finally, Uroš I's attempts to preserve the integrity of the state territory rather than revert to division led to a clash with his eldest son Dragutin and his dethronement. Relations between the Hungarian and Serbian courts had set in train a series of events that led to his downfall. Despite being a vassal of the Hungarian king, some time before 1268 Uroš I attacked Mačva, which was ruled by the grandsons of King Bela IV. The old king's reaction was to send an expedition that defeated and captured Uroš. Relations were restored and later reinforced by the marriage of Uroš's son Dragutin to Bela's granddaughter Katalin (Katarina). According to Hungarian custom, Dragutin became the "young king" and heir to the Serbian throne. In arranging the marriage, Uroš I promised to set aside part of the country and allow his son to rule it independently. He put off his promise despite his son's demands and pressure from Hungary, until Dragutin finally defeated and overthrew his father with the aid of the Hungarian king and Kuman mercenaries in a battle near Gacko in 1276.

None of the sons of Stefan Prvovenčani ended his reign naturally – each was ousted by force. Ambition drove these frequent family quarrels and feelings of family solidarity or Christian morals did nothing to restrain them. A successful takeover required supporters and military power, which meant the active role of the nobility and court circles. Stefan's sons were no exception. Brothers had clashed in their father's and grandfather's generations, and the confrontations were to continue among Uroš's successors.

Two Kingdoms

Unlike his father, who had attempted to hold everything in his grasp, on coming to power Dragutin set aside a special region for his mother centered in Zeta and the coastal cities. Thus the former territory of the Duklja dynasty was restored in a new guise, first as the land of Queen Helen (1276–1308), and later as the province of the "young kings," heirs to the throne. During his short reign (1276–82), Dragutin managed to settle relations with Dubrovnik and sided with the enemies of Byzantium, primarily the Anjous of southern Italy, who were his mother's relatives.

Dragutin had been on the throne for only five years when in 1282 he fell off his horse and broke his leg. According to his biographer, he saw this as God's punishment for his actions against his father. He felt the need to step down from the throne and asked his brother Milutin (1282–1321) to rule in his place. He was later to change his tune, claiming that he had temporarily relinquished the throne to his brother until his recovery. He concentrated on his health, received part of the state's territory in western Serbia, and replaced his mother-in-law, Hungarian Queen Mother Elizabeth, in Mačva and the surrounding territories, which were handed over to female members of the dynasty.

Milutin inherited the animosity toward Byzantium and launched a great campaign soon after taking the throne, conquering northern Macedonia and Skopje. Byzantium embarked on a punitive expedition during which Emperor Michael VIII Palaeologus, who rebuilt Byzantium, died in December 1282. His successor, Andronicus II, sent mercenaries against

Serbia, but they achieved no significant victory. Milutin was presented with an opportunity to renew his expedition in 1283, and he arrived on the shores of the Aegean near the city of Christopolis (Morunac, Kavala). He conquered central Macedonia for good, moving his border to the gorge and city of Prosek (Demir Kapija). The border region toward Byzantium in Macedonia and Albania became the scene of continuous conflicts. The Serbian king even ruled Dyrrachium for a short period prior to 1294.

Dragutin was meanwhile struggling against Bulgarian lords Drman and Kudelin, the rulers of Kučevo and Braničevo (present-day north-eastern Serbia), who were troubling Hungary by crossing the Danube. Milutin came to his brother's aid, an action that had long-term consequences. Sometime before 1290 Dragutin and Milutin defeated and banished Drman and annexed his region to Dragutin's territory. Bulgarian retribution was not lacking; an expedition was sent that devastated Serbia all the way to Hvosno. The seat of the archbishopric in Žiča was set on fire. Milutin counterattacked and again reached the Danube, forcing Vidin Prince Shishman to flee. Later the two were reconciled and established family ties.

In the last decade of the thirteenth century, Dragutin's region thus stretched from Usora and Sol in northern Bosnia to the Djerdap (Iron Gate) Gorge on the Danube River. This was at a time when the Hungarian kingdom was disintegrating as a result of internal strife, and eventually split up into areas governed by oligarchs, independent rulers of large portions of state territory. Former King Dragutin became one of these, governing the territory on the southern periphery of the kingdom.

The regions along the Sava and Danube were now closely linked with the regions to the south, and migratory flows from the south continued. The long period of Hungarian rule did not affect the composition of the population and left no traces in toponyms. After the Byzantines withdrew from the city of Sirmium it lost its significance. Its name, in the form Srem, had already been passed on to the entire region of the former Sirmium bishopric north and south of the Sava. Sirmium's role was taken over by Mačva, a fortress and town on the Sava River, whose precise location is unknown.

Dragutin's territory along the Sava and Danube and Milutin's exploits in Macedonia together doubled the size of Nemanja's state and created the right conditions for shifting the focus eastward. The area included the main north–south routes, including part of the military route from Belgrade to Constantinople. The shift was more apparent to the south at first, symbolized by the transfer of the Serbian archbishops from Žiča to Peć. Ras lost its role as the state capital and was neglected. The rulers attached themselves to a complex of castles (Pauni, Svrčin, Nerodimlja,

The territory of King Stefan Dragutin consisting of parts of the Hungarian Kingdom

Territory lost in 1326

The territory of King Stefan Uroš II Milutin consisting of inherited lands and conquests from the Byzantine Empire

Episcopal residences

Map 2.2   The Kingdom of the Nemanjić dynasty, ca. 1300.

and Štimlja) around a lake in Kosovo (which then existed near what is now Uroševac), Prizren, and Skopje. The focus later shifted toward the Danube region, which became the center of the state in the fifteenth century. Only then, at the turn of the fourteenth century, was the Serbian state constituted in the form known from later periods.

The consequences of division, due to the parallel reign of two rulers who were nevertheless brothers, were felt much earlier than the consequences of the lands' unification. Conflict was already afoot when Milutin forged a truce with Byzantium in 1299 and arranged a marriage with the emperor's 5-year-old daughter Simonis. The exact reason for the estrangement is not known, but it was probably linked to the old

Byzantine condition in forging dynastic alliances whereby the descendants of the Byzantine princess had to have priority of succession.

When the lengthy border wars with Byzantium ended, an internal war erupted and lasted a full decade (1301–11), causing difficulties for both rulers. Dragutin found himself caught in the middle; while fighting against his brother in the south, he clashed with the new Hungarian King Charles Robert (1309–42), since he had previously nominated his son Vladislav for the Hungarian throne. He failed on both sides, but was able to protect his territory. Even though he was abandoned by his supporters, Milutin managed to secure a peace with his brother through the deployment of mercenaries and superior military strength.

A French friar who encountered the two rulers in 1308 left an interesting testimony of the war. He considered Dragutin to be the king of Serbia, and Milutin the king of Raška, having heard Dragutin's claim that he had only temporarily handed over the throne to his brother, until his recovery, but that Milutin had not reinstated him "until this day [1308]." The peace of 1311 preserved previous positions – each brother maintained his own territory, while the thorny issue of succession remained unresolved.

Economic Development

There were enormous differences between the regions comprising the states of the two kings, which would later develop into modern Serbia. The last territories to be conquered in Macedonia, which had been under Byzantine rule the longest, were more heavily populated, economically more developed, and had a greater degree of urbanization. Roman cities in the northern part of the country were also revitalized during the period of Byzantine rule (Sirmium, Belgrade, and Braničevo). During times of peace Byzantine and Hungarian merchants met in these cities. However, they remained in peripheral border regions that were unappealing for colonization. The Byzantines deliberately left these areas undeveloped so that they would be difficult to access. In the twelfth century, when the Crusaders descended the Morava river valley, they spent days walking through the dark "Bulgarian forest." By the fifteenth century the landscape had been completely transformed. French knight Bertrandon de la Broquière took the same route in 1433 and noted that there are "many great forests, hills and valleys, and there are many villages in these valleys and good provisions, especially good wine."

Changes definitely took place during the thirteenth and fourteenth centuries when periods of peace and regular links with southern regions made colonization possible. During their rule the Byzantines settled a group of Armenians in northeastern Serbia, and the Kumans arrived during the Tatar raids of 1241–2. The region was later populated by arrivals from neighboring Serbian and Bulgarian territories, including Vlachs as well as Slavs. Information on settlements from monastery documents dating from the last quarter of the fourteenth century bears witness to a compact network of communities whose lands bordered each other, the sign of a well-established area.

The increase in population necessary for internal colonization and the establishment of non-agricultural settlements was made possible not only by an increase in cultivated land, but also by the development of agricultural technology, which was represented by advanced plows (plows with a coulter, plowshare, and wheels) and in the application of crop rotation (the so-called three-field system), with winter and spring crops and one-third of the land lying fallow. The crops were primarily grains (wheat, oats, barley, and rye, some simultaneously in the same field, such as wheat and barley, or wheat and rye), as well as millet, legumes (broad beans, chickpeas, lentils, and beans, which differed from today's varieties and were more like broad beans), and certain industrial crops (hop, flax, and hemp). The Serbs cultivated the grapevine only after arriving in the Balkans, and its cultivation spread during the course of the Middle Ages, even reaching regions where growing conditions were unsuitable.

Two types of agricultural production are known, one on large monastery lands as mentioned in rulers' charters, and the other on small estates in town districts in the karst land of the coastal regions, where there was a lack of workable soil. Monastery complexes were supplied with everything they needed, following the founder's wishes: fields, vineyards, pastures, hayfields, water mills, hunting grounds, and fisheries. Special attention was paid to establishing a farming estate in the vicinity of the monastery, so that dependent people might serve in the monastery: farmers, fishermen, cattle breeders, honey producers, and craftsmen. The Dečani monastery estate is a good example of this organization. When it was founded in 1330 it included 2,166 farming houses and 266 livestock breeding houses. Dušan's Code (1349) ordered every 1,000 households to support 50 monks.

While large monastery estates were based on the manual labor and duties in kind (*rabota, podanci*) of serfs who went along with the land or colonized it, small personal plots of land in the coastal regions were tended according to a contract system, which implied greater obligations for both sides; the lord provided a house, garden, and part of the seed along with the land, while the peasant (*posadnik, villanus*) handed over part of the crop, gave gifts during the year, and performed certain jobs for the lord.

The basic and certainly the most difficult task was plowing, and it was measured by the area of land that the dependent serfs (*meropah, sokalnik*) were to work. As of the mid-fourteenth century it was measured in days, usually two days a week. The lesser tasks varied. Sometimes they were linked to the trade of a certain family or an entire village; some were appointed to certain houses; some to "anyone who can hold a scythe"; and some tasks were general, such as participating in rabbit hunts, from which only priests were excluded. The duties in kind were mostly tithes (one-tenth of the livestock, bees, etc.), while the duty for leased land was a quarter of the crop. Payments, as with labor, depended on the village specialty or category of the population (whether they were peasants or artisans).

Raising livestock played a vital role in the Serbian economy, and the products (dried meat, cheese, skins, homemade rough wool fabrics – *raša, skjavina, klašnje, pust*) were the first to be included in trade and international exchange. The herdsmen were descendants of the native Balkan inhabitants (Vlachs, Albanians), who took their sheep and horses to the mountains in the spring and remained there with their flocks or herds until the fall, when they returned to sheltered winter lodgings in villages in the valleys. In their search for suitable pastures, the herdsmen ranged throughout the territories bordering the peasant villages. Some communities (*katun, fis, tribe*) had settlements and permanent pastures in the mountains. The main tax on the herdsmen was the tithe, and labor was in the form of transportation, called *ponos* in the old terminology. When the Vlachs were given to a lord, they were obliged to raise the master's horses.

Traded goods included honey, beeswax, and furs, along with the above-mentioned cattle products, while imported merchandise consisted of salt, fabrics, wine, spice, and craftwork brought in by coastal merchants. In the mid-thirteenth century great changes took place in the goods exchanged, as well as in the general development of the economy, when German miners arrived in Serbia, most likely making their way from Hungary. Using their special skills they began silver, copper, and lead production, and in some mines they found silver lined with gold (*argentum glame*), thus expanding the traditional iron production and processing inherited from Slavic culture. They first appeared in Brskovo (near Mojkovac on Mt. Tara, in present-day Montenegro), and soon opened other mines; by the late thirteenth century five were mentioned, and then seven. By the mid-fourteenth century a series of new mines was concentrated in a number of basins. Those that were worked the longest and produced the most included Rudnik (in Šumadija), Trepča (near Kosovska Mitrovica), Janjevo (near Priština), and Novo Brdo (between Priština and Gnjilane), which later developed and became the largest mine in the Balkans.

The Saxons were compelled to include the local population in production, as labor and necessary suppliers. In time the German core dissolved into the Serbian body that surrounded it. The name of the Saxons survived long into the Turkish era and was used for miners and members of mining communities. The Saxons introduced not only mining law and a highly qualified judiciary into Serbia, but also forms of autonomous settlement organization. Their settlements were Catholic oases that increased with the settlement of Dalmatian merchants. Catholic parish churches existed in the Orthodox state's midst, sometimes even two or three of them in mining communities. Their heritage includes German terminology and mining law, which was preserved in later Serbian and Turkish legislature.

Mining inspired numerous economic innovations. The ruler received a significant new source of income from the tax on ore (*urbura*, 10 percent) and smelted metal (10 percent), which was increased by establishing mints where silver coins (dinar, grossus) were produced from the period of Uroš I. Mining brought an income to the surrounding areas: all kinds of supplies were purchased, wages were paid to people who took part in the mining effort, merchants who were attracted by mining products earned a profit and exchanges in kind forced them to bring in trading goods of approximately equal value. Land was cleared in the mining regions to provide plots for farming. Pockets of monetary economic systems and market relations arose amidst an economy based on command and custom.

The opening of mines and the processing of silver was followed by the minting of silver coins. At the height of the Byzantine Empire's power, none of the dependent rulers, not even great opponents such as Bulgarian Tsar Simeon, dared to mint coins. It was only with the temporary fall of Byzantium in 1204 that the imperial monopoly on minting money collapsed. The Serbian hyperper (*yperperi Sclavonie*) is mentioned as early as 1214, but there are no preserved coins. During his reign Radoslav minted copper coins resembling those issued by the Angelus family from Epirus, which were minted in Thessalonika.

The steady issuing of silver money started during the reign of King Uroš I and lasted until the fall of the Serbian state. King Uroš I modeled his coins after the Venetian silver grossus, both in weight (at least at first) and in the representation of the king and St. Stefan, where the Venetian coin had the image of the doge and St. Mark. The Serbian king joined the system that was then becoming established and abandoned units, inherited from the Carolingian system, which were small and limited to the local market. The dominant coins were the larger units of *denarii grossi* in broader use, while gold coins minted in Italian cities (Venice, Florence, Genoa) were used in large-scale trade and linked distant markets.

Plate 2.2 Economic independence: silver coins minted by Serbian rulers, thirteenth to fifteenth centuries. (a) King Stefan Uroš I (1243–76); (b) King Stefan Uroš II Milutin (1282–1321); (c) King Stefan Dušan (1331–45, emperor 1345–55); (d) Prince Lazar (1362–89); (e) Despot Djuradj Branković (1427–56); (f) City of Smederevo, capital 1430–59. (Photographs by B. Strugar)

The names of Serbian coins came partially from the West – dinar, grossus – and partially from the East – hyperper, an attribute of the gold coin from the eleventh century. There were no perpers in circulation, because they were units calculated as 12 dinars. Later the name aspra was introduced, which was used throughout the Byzantine world when gold coins were no longer minted. The amount was determined in relation to copper or small coins (usually 30 or 24 to the grossus), and in the relation of the grossus to the gold coin. From the time it was introduced to the second half of the fourteenth century, one gold coin (ducat, zeccino) was the equivalent of 24 dinars. The rate changed later, not because of the ratio between the precious metals, which remained approximately 1 : 10, but because of a decrease in the weight and silver content of the dinar. The Serbian dinar has been found in hoards not only in neighboring countries (Hungary, Romania, and Bulgaria), but also in far-off places such as Verona (Italy) and Delphi (Greece), which testifies to its circulation.

Mining encouraged urbanization by creating settlements at production sites which drew merchants in far greater numbers than had previously ventured into Serbia; they settled and were included in business undertakings. The creation of a market for precious metals had a direct influence on differentiating the coastal cities. In the twelfth century most were highly praised for their diligent merchants and craftsmen, while the

Plate 2.3 Gateway to the Mediterranean: Kotor, earliest drawing from the end of the sixteenth century. (From the atlas *Viaggio da Venezia a Constantinopoli* by Giuseppe Rosaccio, Venice, 1598, courtesy of Istorijski arhiv Kotor)

rank of a bishop's seat that almost all of them held indirectly evidenced their equality. But by the end of the thirteenth century, the only ones to survive were those in the south with the necessary population and capital for exploiting the opportunities provided by the mines in Serbia and Bosnia.

These cities were Kotor and Dubrovnik, each with its own advantages. Kotor was the city of the Serbian king, while Dubrovnik was under Venetian rule, and at the same time had guarantees from Serbian rulers that its borders would remain inviolable, and that people would have the liberty to move freely and conduct business in their state. Treaties, which were renewed and confirmed over a period of two and a half centuries, provided mechanisms for resolving border disputes, as well as disagreements in trade and the mines. Increased trade in the hinterland affected relations between the coastal cities. Prominent individuals from small cities moved to larger and more thriving ones. Families in Dubrovnik and Kotor became related, and a number of Dubrovnik families arose as offshoots of Kotor families.

The consequences of these economic changes were evident as early as the late thirteenth century, in King Milutin's increased military strength, his ability to maintain mercenary forces in his service, his exceptional building activity, and in the luxury of the court.

Dynastic Ideal and Reality

The Serbian ruling family boasted of its sacrosanct ancestry and of its founders St. Simeon and St. Sava, revealing the importance of solidarity based on family relations. The dynastic ideal was visually represented in the "Nemanjić family tree" that was painted in churches with the clear aim of popularizing the lineage, justifying changes in the line of succession, and verifying the legitimacy of those who commissioned the composition.

The dynasty emphasized its piety by helping and protecting the church, especially by building endowments. The model was set by Stefan Nemanja in constructing Studenica monastery, which was to have served as the mausoleum for his descendants. Nemanja left it to his son Stefan and his descendants for this very purpose. However, a prolonged series of individual endowments followed, starting with Vladislav, the second son of Stefan Prvovenčani, who built Mileševa monastery as his own endowed church while he was still prince. Vladislav later raised Mileševa to second in rank, after Nemanja's endowment. From that moment on, every member of the dynasty built a monastery as his memorial. Uroš I built Sopoćani monastery with its exquisite paintings, his wife Helen

Plate 2.4 Symbolism of dynastic continuity: the family tree of St. Simeon and Stefan Nemanja's descendants, Dečani monastery (1327–35). (Photograph by B. Strugar)

Plate 2.5 Serbian–Byzantine symbiosis: Gračanica episcopal church, the endowment of King Stefan Uroš II Milutin, Kosovo, built 1315–20. (Photograph by B. Strugar)

built Gradac monastery with a strong Gothic influence, and their eldest son Dragutin improved Nemanja's Djurdjevi Stupovi monastery and completed the Arilje monastery when he had already stepped down from the throne. Their youngest son Milutin built a number of churches, including Banjska monastery as his memorial, and Gračanica monastery as the seat of the bishopric. Late medieval historical sources credit him with building 40 churches. The descendants of Nemanja's brothers were not far behind. Vukan's sons were especially active – Stefan built Morača monastery, while Dimitrije built Davidovica monastery on the Lim River.

The endowments were intended to guard the tomb of their founder, and the monastery brotherhood held constant memorial services and prayed for his soul. Aside from this private function associated with the founder and his family, the endowments coincidentally had a more general mission: the number of monks increased and scriptoriums developed, helping to educate new monks and enlightening their surroundings.

In their construction, the Nemanjić family endowments continued the traditions of the Raška school of architecture: churches with a dome over a rectangular foundation, following the models of Romanesque churches on the Adriatic coast. Models from the coast and Italy were also applied to the sculptural elements that decorated church doors and windows. After Milutin's conquests in Macedonia and the incorporation of areas with Byzantine-style churches into the Serbian state, the architectural style turned increasingly to a square foundation with an inscribed cross covered by a number of smaller domes adjoining the central one. Building techniques combined alternating layers of stone blocks and bricks with stonework. This wave of architectural monument spread south of the earliest Raška monuments and bears all the hallmarks of the "Serbian–Byzantine" style (for example, the Virgin of Ljeviška monastery in Prizren, and Staro Nagoričino and Gračanica monasteries).

As the dynasty continued into the new generation, it became apparent that there was discontinuity between the ideals of family love and Christian compassion and the actual relationships between brother, father, and son. Nemanja had already come into conflict with his brothers; Stefan and Vukan engaged in mutual hostilities; Stefan's sons were removed from the throne by force; and Dragutin and Milutin fought a lengthy war against each other over the dynastic succession and whose descendants were to extend the ruling branch.

King Milutin's four marriages, some of which were annulled with inevitable consequences for the descendants, did not help stabilize the dynasty. Milutin even entered into an arrangement with his mother-in-law, Empress Irene Palaeologina, whereby one of her sons, the brother of Milutin's wife Simonis, would succeed him. Two of her brothers even traveled to Serbia, but did not like the country. These plans created hostility between Milutin and his son Stefan Uroš III (later called Dečanski), who in 1308 replaced Queen Helen as the ruler of Zeta and the regions annexed to it.

An uprising broke out and young Stefan Uroš was defeated and blinded on his father's orders, then banished to Constantinople. For seven years from 1314 to 1321 he lived with his wife and children in a monastery in the capital, under the supervision and protection of Emperor Andronicus II Palaeologus. This is where young Dušan spent his childhood and came to know Byzantium and life in the capital. Toward the end of Milutin's life, at the instigation of the Mt. Athos brotherhood and the archbishop, he allowed his son to return and granted him the Budimlje *župa* (present-day Berane and its surroundings) as a means of support.

In the meantime, Milutin appointed as his heir the little-known Constantine, his son from one of his marriages. As Dragutin had died in 1316, he was succeeded by his son Vladislav II, with the approval of the Hungarian king. Milutin soon imprisoned him, thus creating friction with the Hungarian king, who considered Dragutin's lands as part of his kingdom. Milutin embarked on a military campaign, aiding defectors from the Hungarian king and losing part of Dragutin's territory in the process (1317–20). After a long reign he became seriously ill and lost the ability to speak. The struggle for the throne erupted immediately after his death on October 29, 1321.

Vladislav II was released and restored to authority in Dragutin's former lands, but all trace of him is lost from 1325. Half-brothers Constantine and Stefan Uroš collided over their father's throne, with the nobles joining Uroš when he revealed that he was not blind. The act of blinding, which was to prevent Uroš from taking the throne, actually helped him gain it, since the fact that he was not blind was seen as a mark of divine intervention. Constantine was defeated and killed, and Stefan Uroš III was crowned in early 1322 along with his son Dušan, who became the "young king."

Internecine strife provided the opportunity for disorder and raids, and gave border nobles the chance to turn renegade. This had serious consequences in the west, in Hum, where the Branivojević brothers, sons of a local lord, began to handle their own affairs with Venice, neighboring Croatian lords, the Bosnian ban, and Dubrovnik. The Branivojevićs came into conflict with Bosnia and Dubrovnik and disobeyed the Serbian king. They were defeated and removed by 1326, while their territory, the Neretva river basin and the coastal region toward Ston, was controlled by the Bosnian ban and became the focus of discord in relations with the Serbian state over the next decades.

On the other side, Stefan Uroš III continued his father's policies of amity with Byzantium. After being widowed in 1322, he married the emperor's young niece, Mary Palaeologina. She bore him children, which again raised the issue of succession and jeopardized the situation of Dušan, the adult son of his first marriage. Stefan Uroš III was drawn into internal Byzantine struggles, and aided Emperor Andronicus II in his conflicts with his grandson Andronicus III. When the old emperor was overthrown in 1328, the Serbian king remained in dispute with the grandson, who joined Bulgarian Tsar Michael Shishman against him. This alliance brought about a dangerous combined attack on Serbia, the Byzantine emperor from the south, and the Bulgarian tsar from the east. Stefan Uroš III went out to meet the Bulgarian army in battle, defeating it near Velbužd (Kyustendil) on July 28, 1330. Young King Dušan distinguished himself in the combat.

After the victory the Serbian king enthroned his sister, the widow of the defeated tsar, and her son Ivan Stefan, who ruled Bulgaria as tsar for a short while. Andronicus III abandoned his expedition on receiving news of this defeat, thus eliminating external threats, but internal dangers soon emerged in a struggle between the old and young kings. They came into direct conflict between January and April 1331, and a truce was negotiated through the mediation of Dubrovnik. The hard-won peace was shortlived, because the lords surrounding the "young king" continued to incite Dušan to stand up to his father. In the meantime, there was a coup in Bulgaria. In August 1331 Dušan left Zeta, surrounded and captured his father, and imprisoned him in Zvečan castle, where he died on November 11 under mysterious circumstances.

In assuming power Dušan came face to face with the renegade lords in Zeta and northern Albania. He had to yield in the struggle for Hum, and sold Ston and its peninsula to Dubrovnik in 1333 for 8,000 hyperpers and an annual tax of 500 hyperpers. He settled relations with Bulgaria by marrying the sister of the new tsar, Ivan Alexander (1331–71), after having accepted the fall of his cousin Ivan Stefan. He kept on good terms with Bulgaria throughout his dynamic reign.

The first opportunity for involvement in Byzantine struggles and conquests was provided by Syrgiannes Palaeologus, a former close associate and later defector from Emperor Andronicus III. After clashing with the emperor he sought refuge among the Albanians and made his way to Dušan, who lent assistance to Syrgiannes and conquered territories in Macedonia all the way to the walls of Thessalonika. Syrgiannes was assassinated there and Dušan forged a truce with Andronicus III, retaining his earlier conquests and the cities of Prilep, Ohrid, and Strumica. Good relations were maintained with Byzantium as long as Andronicus III was alive. Dušan soon received reinforcements from the emperor for his war against the Hungarian king, who attacked Serbia in early 1335.

The Empire

Serbia's ruling circles drew close to Byzantium in different ways: through marital relations between the dynasties, a practice that was widespread during the rule of Milutin and his son; through appropriating territories with Byzantine institutions and law; and through increased trade and exchanges of people and goods. Finally, there was the fact that hostages spent time in Byzantium, even members of the ruling house such as Stefan Uroš III and his family. The effect of these close relations was to give the

Serbs a more complete understanding of Byzantium and its situation, the discrepancy between its glorious past and grand claims and the grim reality, whereby the once mighty Empire had become a small Balkan state. Starting with Milutin, Serbian rulers consistently showed that they honored the supreme power and higher rank of the Byzantine emperors.

The practice of joint rule, inherited from the Roman period, had been previously associated with the dynasty, especially during the reign of the Palaeologus family. Besides the "grand emperor," who was the only one to be called autokrator, his son, who was expected to inherit from him, would also hold the title of emperor. At one point, ca. 1312, Emperor Andronicus II and his son and grandson were emperors. According to the understanding of Byzantine authors, the emperor's co-rulers had to yield to the supreme emperor. However, this system did not always provide a peaceful transfer of authority, as in the case of the struggle between grandfather and grandson, the old and young Andronicus, and especially when the heir was not of age, as in 1341, when Andronicus III Palaeologus died unexpectedly.

At that time John Cantacuzenus, a friend and close associate of the deceased emperor, imposed himself as co-ruler of the young John V. When he was rejected by the regents, he rebelled and proclaimed himself emperor in the same year. With no support in the capital or among the nobility and lords, he was forced to seek the support of Dušan. After lengthy negotiations, a formal alliance was forged, which provided for a division of the Byzantine lands that were to be conquered. The allies fought together for only a short while; already in the spring of 1343 they went their separate ways and turned against each other, while concurrently conquering cities in Macedonia.

Dušan continued his conquests in Macedonia and Albania, and grew closer to the court in Constantinople, where the dowager empress had the final say. A marriage was arranged between Dušan's heir Uroš (who was 5 years old at the time) and the sister of the young Emperor John V. That is when Dušan started calling himself *česnik Grkom*, which meant that he was a participant of the Greek Empire. In late 1345, after conquering the city of Serres and reaching an agreement with representatives from Mt. Athos, who pledged to recognize him as their ruler and mention him during the liturgy following the Byzantine emperor, Dušan proclaimed himself emperor.

At Easter the following year (April 16, 1346) his coronation took place, attended by Serbian bishops and clergy as well as by the Bulgarian patriarch, the Ohrid archbishop, and representatives from Mt. Athos. Dušan claimed to have the blessing of the Byzantine bishops and the entire synod, but it is not obvious who is implied by that phrase. The

Serbian kingdom was not downgraded by the changes as Dušan had crowned his son Uroš king; and the legality of the young emperor in Constantinople was not disputed. Another empire was created and stood with the Bulgarian Empire (which had been renewed in the late twelfth century) alongside the Byzantine, which aspired to unite the entire Christian universe and last until the end of the world.

The Serbian ruler became "Emperor of the Serbs and the Greeks," and in Greek charters he bore the title of the emperor of "Serbia and 'Romania,'" not the emperor of the Greeks (*Rhomaoi*), as were emperors in Constantinople. However, the situation soon changed. John Cantacuzenus made good progress in the Byzantine civil war and seized control of the capital in February 1347. He set himself up as co-ruler to the young John V Palaeologus, who married his daughter. His hatred for Dušan became part of Byzantine court policy. Dušan could no longer be a participant in the Greek Empire, and instead became its adversary.

Dušan continued his conquests and was facilitated in his task by the plague, which swept through the Balkans in 1347–8. He extended his rule to Epirus (1347) and Thessaly (1348), replacing the former governors with his associates – half-brother Simeon Uroš in Epirus, and his brother-in-law Caesar Preljub in Thessaly. His borders were at their broadest at this time: the Gulf of Corinth to the south, the Christopolis Gorge to the east (east of the city of Kavála), excluding certain large cities such as Thessalonika and Dyrrachium, and a number of small coastal towns. In the north Dušan's state extended to the Danube and Sava, and as far as Drina in the west.

The period of these conquests coincided with certain domestic events, which portray Dušan as a "grand emperor," one in the line that started with Constantine the Great. In particular there was the promulgation of the *Zakonik* (Dušan's Code, 1349), which includes an introduction describing his ascent to the imperial throne as an expression of divine grace. At that time new translations were made of Byzantine world chronicles ("Letovnik," a chronicle by George Hamartolos), while old translations were modified to include Emperor Dušan's reign, and his coronation became a crucial historical event.

Several attempts were made to recover the Hum territory, sometimes with Venetian mediation, but they remained unsuccessful and Dušan decided to take back the disputed territories by force. In October 1350 he launched an expedition that temporarily conquered Hum and continued west, reaching the Krka River, where the people of Trogir and Šibenik were preparing to greet him with gifts. The emperor probably intended to visit and help his sister Jelena, the widow of Croatian nobleman Mladen III Bribirski. When her husband died in 1348, her son was still a child and she was forced to defend the towns of Omiš, Klis, and Skradin on his behalf against the Venetians.

Dušan, however, had to halt the expedition west, since Cantacuzenus had taken advantage of his absence to launch an offensive in Macedonia, with Turkish help, to recover the Byzantine cities of Berrhoia, Edessa/Voden, and smaller surrounding towns. His troops even got as far as Skopje, and some of Dušan's officials were discussing terms of surrender. Dušan covered a great distance in a short time, visiting Dubrovnik on the way, and was in Macedonia by late 1350. Before laying siege to the cities that were to be regained, Dušan entered into negotiations with Cantacuzenus, but they came to nothing.

The split in the Byzantine leadership, which later led to another civil war, was already evident. The Palaeologus family negotiated with Dušan behind Cantacuzenus's back. A charter issued by John V Palaeologus, dated 1350, mentions Dušan as "His Highness the emperor of Serbia and kind uncle kyr Stefan." When armed clashes erupted, the Bulgarian tsar and Dušan found themselves on the side of the young Palaeologus, while Cantacuzenus had as his allies Orhan's Turks, who had only just established their first strongholds on European soil (Tzympe in 1352 and Gallipoli in 1354). Dušan tried to draw Orhan aside and even discussed betrothing his daughter to the Ottoman emir, but the negotiations were abandoned.

In 1352 a great battle took place near Didymoteichos between the young Palaeologus and the insubordinate Cantacuzenus. The former had the support of the reinforcements sent by the Bulgarian and Serbian tsars, while the latter was aided by Emir Orhan's army. This great confrontation between the Palaeologi and Cantacuzeni dynasties highlighted the weakness of the Christian armies, which were heavily defeated. As his grandfather had done in 1308, Dušan began negotiations with the Avignon pope in 1354, holding out the prospect of the recognition of papal primacy and requesting that he be appointed as the captain of Christendom in the struggle against the infidels.

These plans were vehemently opposed by the Hungarian king, who launched an expedition against Serbia in 1354. There was no change in the borders; the cities along the Danube and Sava remained under Hungarian control, while the territories to the south remained under Serbian rule. Internal Byzantine conflicts were sparked off again in 1354 when Cantacuzenus was overthrown and forced to join a monastery. Dušan remained with the Palaeologus family but did not abandon plans to conquer Constantinople, which he discussed with Venice. However, his sudden death on December 20, 1355 while visiting newly conquered Byzantine territories put an end to that particular project.

Land of the Emperor and Land of the King

Byzantine contemporaries understood that Dušan had divided the country at the time of his coronation. He ruled the conquered Byzantine lands, following Byzantine law, and left the lands from Skopje to the Danube in the authority of his son, in accordance with Serbian laws. In charters issued to Dubrovnik in 1349, Dušan himself differentiated between the "emperor's lands" and the "king's lands," but at the same time did not recognize the king as having any true authority, according to his Code. In practice he ruled alone, maintaining and stressing the continuity of the kingdom in relations with Venice and Dubrovnik, with which the Serbian state had long-term treaties.

Sparse documentation hints that Dušan sought to equate his entire state with the Byzantine Empire, so that it was not an empire in name only and an unattainable ideal, but something close to reality. Some things were easily changed or modified, because they depended on the ruler and his cronies. It was easy to assume the title of "Emperor of the Serbs and Greeks" and to raise the emperor's wife to the rank of *augusta*; it was easy to transfer the Byzantine imperial dignities of despot, *sebastokrator*, and *caesar* and assign them to relatives or the husbands of relatives, following the Byzantine model. The emperor's half-brother Simeon Uroš and the empress's brother John Asen were appointed despots; Dejan, husband to the emperor's sister Eudocia, and Branko Mladenović, whose links with the court are not clear, became *sebastokrators*; and the *caesars* were Preljub, husband of the emperor's cousin Irena, Vojihna, and Grgur, of whom little is known, including the degree of their relation. Some were appointed rulers in parts of the empire: Simeon in Epirus, John Asen in southern Albania (Kanina and Valona – present-day Vlorë), *sebastokrator* Dejan was given the Velbužd region, and Branko Mladenović was given Ohrid.

The introduction of Byzantine order and ceremonials was perhaps not swift, but it could be achieved. It was even easier to introduce administrative customs and Byzantine terms adapted to suit the Serbian language (chrysobull, prostagma). Many things, however, changed slowly and with much difficulty, which limited the emperor's ambitions. The most obvious were those regarding the legal system and legislature. The various parts of Dušan's vast state differed greatly. Those who had been conquered last lived according to the Byzantine system, a state of affairs that Dušan approved and endorsed. Territories conquered by Serbian rulers after 1282 were under lengthy and strong Byzantine influence and their institutions and past way of life endured. Even significant parts of Nemanja's state, in the late twelfth-century territories east of the Drina

River, had been under Byzantine rule for two centuries, but Byzantium had been eliminated relatively early, before great economic and social changes took place, thus only certain general structures remained: settlement organization, elements of the fiscal system, weights and measures, and monetary units.

However, the Nemanjić state as part of Dušan's empire also included territories that had never been under direct Byzantine rule and were influenced by Byzantine civilization from outside and from a distance. This is why a division was created, analogous to that in the European West, between countries with both written and common law. The border is difficult to define and in reality it may not have been clear cut. Ever since conversion to Christianity the influence of written ecclesiastical law grew gradually but inexorably, entering the secular domain, primarily in matters regarding marriage, the family, and inheritance.

Written laws arrived in Serbia by way of the church. It has already been mentioned that St. Sava arranged the translation of the *Nomocanon*, a collection of different legal compilations relating to the church as well as to the entire Christian community. It mostly consisted of decrees issued by the ecumenical synods regarding church order and discipline, but the entire *Procherion*, a collection of imperial laws dating from the second half of the ninth century, as well as numerous other regulations, addressed the life of the laity. The *Nomocanon* was an essential book for administrating the church, and every bishop had to have a copy.

In addition to this collection, two significant compilations focusing on the laity were translated into Serbian Church Slavonic from the Greek. These were the *Codex Justinianus*,[1] containing elements of private law, and the *Peasant Law*, which covered relations between lords and peasants and the rules of life in rural communities.

Issuing laws was both the right and duty of the emperor. Dušan's Charter, which accompanied his Code, reveals the emperor's motivation: "It is my desire to enact certain virtues and truest laws of the Orthodox faith to be adhered to and observed." The Code, containing 135 individual articles of law, was promulgated at the Assembly on May 21, 1349. The laws were organized by content at the beginning of the Code, with the first group addressing church issues, followed by those on nobility, and so on down the hierarchy. The second part of the Code was promulgated in 1354. It was half the size and at times cites issues from the first part, referring to it as the "first Code."

---

1 This short compilation should not be confused with the *Codex Justinaneus*, even though it bears the name of the same emperor.

Plate 2.6   Imperial law giving: front page of the Prizren codex (sixteenth century), with translations of Byzantine laws and the Code of Emperor Stefan Dušan (1349, 1354). (From the CD ROM *Dušanov zakonik. The Code of Tsar Dušan. Povodom 650 godina od proglašenja*, Narodna biblioteka Srbije, 1999)

In areas that had been previously regulated by law (such as church organization and discipline), provisions were connected to what was of topical interest: mandatory church marriage, banning conversion to Catholicism, which was taking place in the mining and trade communities, issues of immunity and jurisdiction over church lands, relations between the clergy and village lords, and so on. The Code did not focus on monastic discipline, which was regulated elsewhere, but prohibited residence outside of monasteries and provided the optimal ratio between monastery estates and brotherhood size (50 monks were to be supported by 1,000 households).

Dušan's legislators did not contest or restrict Byzantine law; rather, they continued it and applied it in areas that were difficult or contentious, either because of the resilience of legal customs or the stratification of society. The Code concentrated on issues of criminality, the preservation of public order, and judiciary procedure, and neglected property issues where there was a strong influence of common law (land boundaries, village damages). This is reflected by efforts to expand the area of state regulation that was originally limited to fiscal and defense issues, and only had marginal dealings with the judiciary. Over time state power acquired new tasks, or took them upon itself. In addition to protecting the church and the clergy, widows, and infants, which held a common place in the ruler's duties, the need arose for the care of foreigners, travelers, and merchants, for the population to be protected against attacks and threats, and for their property, which was becoming increasingly diverse, to be secure. Even though each individual *župa*, region, and town retained their collective responsibilities, the state no longer left them to defend themselves alone against thieves and bandits, and took on the task of persecuting criminals and guaranteeing order and security.

The state's endeavors to suppress violence, theft, and banditry permeate both parts of the Code. Aside from the general measures that were to "eliminate theft and banditry" (punishable by hanging upside down, blinding, the destruction of villages, and imprisonment of the village lord who was held liable for damages), responsibility extended to all those who were at the lowest level of government (*knezovi*, *primićuri*, *katunari*, *čelnici*), and a short trial and punishment procedure was prescribed.

The state's ambitions are reflected in the effort to completely control the territory. The emperor's *kefalije* were responsible in the event of robbery or theft for roads where the *župas* or villages did not have a lord. If there was a bare hill between *župas*, the inhabitants of the surrounding villages were required to keep guard and were held responsible for any damage that occurred. Copying the Byzantine administrative system was another expression of this aspiration. The administrative organization of the territory by the early Nemanjić rulers is not known. Documents indicate the jurisdiction of *župans*, *kaznaci*, and *tepčije*. The expansion of the *kefalija* system started before Dušan's time and was encountered in territories seized from Byzantium after 1282. There was already a *kefalija* in Zeta under Milutin. Starting with Dušan's reign, the entire state territory was covered with *kefalije*. The realm of a single *kefalija* became smaller and often covered one *župa* or neighboring *župas*. The *kefalija* was based in a city with the boundaries of its jurisdiction and responsibility clearly demarcated. It represented the emperor, played a role in the judiciary, and was ultimately responsible for ensuring public order. The *krajišnici* (border region soldiers) and *krajiške vojvode* (border commanders), located in border regions, were responsible for defense against foreign attacks, but also against raids. Complete control of the vast state area could only be achieved through great effort, discipline, subordination, and continuous supervision. This was difficult to maintain over an extended period of time, which was confirmed immediately following Dušan's death.

Unfinished Society

Emperor Dušan was unable to establish a single regime throughout the entire state using his Code. This was simply not feasible with the means available at the time. The Code itself contained articles indicating that certain groups or categories of subjects lived according to special norms or according to the dictates of their leaders, who were not part of the emperor's administrative system. Not only church matters were excluded from lay jurisdiction (Art. 12), but church members as well; lay men and women who resided on and managed church lands were tried before entities from their own church (metropolitans, bishops, abbots) or, if they were members of different churches, they were tried by both churches (Art. 33). In a general article of the Code, the emperor confirmed the charters issued to "Greek towns" when he took them under his rule (Art. 124), and in general no one could violate the chrysobulls issued to the cities (Art. 137).

Other sources, which are unfortunately very rare, reveal that groups mentioned in the Code, such as the Saxons and the Vlachs, had separate forms of organization with their own hierarchy and jurisdiction. The Saxons had their own judges and common law in the domain of mining, which was recorded only 50 years later. The situation was similar in the Vlach and Albanian communities. All had their own bodies or individuals who were called to judge their members.

The coastal towns had the most distinct individuality. They passed their own laws, which were collected in statute books (Kotor in the early fourteenth century, Budva in 1350; the Bar and Ulcinj statutes have not been preserved and are known only through references). Citizens continued to be under the jurisdiction of their laws even if they left their towns on business. Town regulations, statutory decisions, prohibited people from summoning their fellow citizens to the royal court or participating in royal judiciary bodies.

The medieval state showed no tendency toward suppressing or abolishing autonomist norms that applied to groups within the population, or toward making them uniform by force. It had to cope with a different type of problem, one that originated from relations among such autonomous groups. The procedure for resolving disputes became increasingly complicated. As economic relations improved and people traveled over greater distances, mixing with others more frequently, disputes resulted between members of social groups that were under different jurisdictions.

A practice from common law was raised to the level of general norm during the reign of King Milutin and was applied at the borders. For example, disputes between royal subjects and the inhabitants of Dubrovnik were resolved by a court consisting of an even number of judges from both sides. This was the so-called *stanak*, and was broadly applied by the coastal cities. Where there was no common border, such as between Dubrovnik and Bosnia, in the thirteenth and first half of the fourteenth centuries disputes were brought before the defendant's court, in line with Roman tradition. A mixed court was explicitly prescribed between the Saxons and Ragusans, and between Ragusans and the king's subjects. Mixed courts remained in force as long as there were states and communities with special rights and individual jurisdictions.

The need for new solutions also originated from increasing social inequality that had to be institutionally reflected. Numerous means for resolving disputes in common law originated from a society of equals, and had equal rights in mind. In traditional common law procedure the jury (*porota*) played a central role. It did not make judgments but aided the suspect or defendant by showing its confidence in his moral qualities. The accused was required to obtain a number of persons (between 1 and 24 depending on the gravity of the accusation), who would swear with him that he was not guilty and thus "justify" him in this respect.

State authorities did not contest this important institution of the people, but sought to formalize its operation. It was stated that jurors were to be sworn in by a priest and in church, that they were not to reconcile conflicted parties, that they could not include relatives or malicious persons (the former practice of choosing jurors from among the accused's circle of relatives and neighbors gave way to the principle that neither relatives nor opponents should be included). This formalization included enforcing the principle that jurors were to be chosen from the accused's own community. Correspondence between the widow of Serbian Prince Lazar and the people of Dubrovnik in 1395 explicitly states that "you may know that not all people are equals, some are nobles and others are serfs, such is it among the Serbs and throughout the world, and it is not the law that the Latin should swear for the Serb nor the

Serb for the Latin, but that the jury for a Ragusan should be his fellow Ragusans." The same principle was applied as of Milutin's time to social stratification. Dušan's Code supported King Milutin's old rule according to which the jurors of a grand lord should be grand lords, those of the middle class should be their fellow freemen, and those of the *sebrdija* (commoners) their peers. In addition to unequal punishment, this was an important instrument in strengthening social inequality.

The legislator had in mind the tripartite division of society, while the terminology of Byzantine legal texts distinguished between two categories: *nobility* and *commoners*. In Serbia these terms included a number of different strata, with one group including *velmože, vlastela*, and *vlasteličići* (the nobility), and the other divided into a number of categories differing in rank, obligations, status within the family, estate, and town. The Code particularly mentions *otroci* (serfs), *meropsi* (sharecroppers), *dvorani* (household servants), *župljani* (*župa* inhabitants), *sirote* (widows), *sokalnici* (servants), *stanici* (travel servants), and *trgovci* (merchants).

The state, personified in the ruler, could not create a single framework through legislature and regulations that would gradually establish a society of equals. On the contrary, individuality was emphasized by creating instruments to resolve disputes among different and unequal structural components of the population. This was understandable since the state carried out its function within these autonomous communities who lived according to their specific laws. This was where individuals came under direct supervision and control; this was where internal disputes were resolved and dues to the state assigned.

Society was on the way to becoming more completely integrated, but not all parts reached the same level. The church with the clergy was integrated on the level of the entire state. Under one hierarchy, following the same rules, carrying out similar tasks, its members were also separated from the laity symbolically by their place of residence, their vestments, and way of life. The upper social class was greatly integrated owing to the fact that they served the ruler and were personally subservient. They were linked by privileges and a corresponding way of life for which they prepared in their youth by serving at the court. This class absorbed and assimilated foreigners into itself, especially during the period of the despots, when commanders (*voivode*) included Turks and Albanians. There were, however, great differences among the nobility, not only in their hierarchical level and wealth, but also in their background, numbers, and the importance of their previous generations and regions of origin, since they included descendants of former dynasties, local lords, and so on. The broad base of the nobility was only differentiated from the unprivileged class in the *župa*, just as the patricians set themselves apart in the coastal cities by closing their ranks and reserving all posts and functions for those whose ancestors sat on the city council.

The remaining and most numerous component of the population was not at all unified within the boundaries of the kingdom or empire. The "serf assembly" mentioned in Dušan's Code (Art. 69) was an ill-intentioned, prohibited congregation, a conspiracy, and not part of the state assembly. Ordinary people were gathered in territorial communities, villages, *katuns*, boroughs with special jurisdiction, and *župa* communities. Ties and uniformity were being established within these boundaries, and this was a precondition for broader integration, the founding of the "third estate." Development in this direction was halted in Serbia when the Turkish invasion destroyed the existing social structure.

Plate 2.7 Artistic maturity: detail from an early fourteenth-century icon in the monastery of Chilandar (Mt. Athos). (Photograph by B. Strugar)

Rift within the Dynasty

On the death of a ruler who is the pivot of a state, the origin of all relations of personal dependence upon which the state's organization is founded, crisis inevitably ensues, especially if his death is abrupt or unexpected. In Dušan's case his son and heir had long been preordained with the title of king, but Uroš was only 17 years old at the time of his father's death in December 1355. Judging by his fate and information from later times, he did not distinguish himself by his abilities. Nonetheless, problems emerged only gradually. In the spring of 1357, Dušan's young heir, Emperor Uroš (ruled 1355–71), issued charters and carried out his duties as ruler in council with his mother and the patriarch. Territories had already been lost in the Christopolis region, in Epirus, and along the northern border.

Despot Simeon, the young emperor's uncle, was driven out of his territories in Epirus by the former ruler. Simeon ruled Kastoria and its vicinity, proclaimed himself emperor, and attempted to seize Skadar from his nephew in 1358. Despot Nicephoros II, who had restored Byzantine rule in Epirus and Thessaly, was killed the following year and this opened the way for Simeon to rule Thessaly, not as governor but as sovereign ruler. He founded a separate empire and new branch of the dynasty, proclaimed himself "Emperor of the Serbs and Greeks," and called himself Simeon Uroš Palaeologue. He was succeeded by John Uroš Palaeologue, who was later ordained, taking the name Ioasaph. Descendants of this branch of the Nemanjić dynasty remained in Thessaly until ca. 1420.

Summarizing events over a longer period, former Byzantine emperor John VI Cantacuzenus described the situation following Dušan's death in the following terms: "the king died, the ruler of the Tribals, and no little confusion broke out among them. Simeon, the king's brother who ruled Acarnania, sought to govern all the Tribals, as though they truly belonged to him, and he won over many respectable Tribals as his supporters in the effort. The King's son Uroš went to war against his uncle, because of his father's power. And Jelena, his mother, trusting neither her son nor her husband's brother, subjugated many towns and surrounded herself with a considerable army, and held onto power without attacking anyone or starting a war. The most powerful of the lords removed the weaker ones from power and each subjugated the nearby towns. Some helped the king in battle, not as subjects, but by sending troops as allies and friends, and others helped his uncle Simeon. Some did not take sides but held onto their troops and looked to the future to join the one that triumphed."

The few details known from contemporary sources fit this general picture. The great empire did not start coming apart along the border between the "emperor's lands" and the "king's lands," nor along the borderline between "Greek land" and "Serbian land," but along the borders of the regions controlled by members of the dynasty or the emperor's close associates, governors, and bearers of "high imperial dignities." John Comnenus Asen, the young emperor's maternal uncle, seceded in Albania around Vlorë, proclaiming independence. Serres was the part of the state where the emperor's mother seceded, and under her was *kesar* (*caesar*) Voihna. Together in 1357 they repelled an attempt by Mathew Cantacuzenus, son of the former Byzantine emperor, to extend Byzantine rule. Uroš's maternal uncle Dejan proclaimed independence north of the empress's territories, and founded the Dragaš dynasty, which ruled until 1395. Prince Vojislav Vojinović was influential in western areas all the way to the coast and Dubrovnik, until he was carried off by the plague in 1363, as were many of his contemporaries.

The young emperor had no heir, and was not even married (he was to marry Anna, daughter of Prince Alexander, ruler of Wallachia, in 1360, but he had no children). There were no conditions for recreating the emperor-king system, but it was not forgotten. The Hungarian king attacked Serbia in 1359 and penetrated deep, almost to the West Morava River; he acquired one of the feuding Serbian lords in the north as his vassal. The fact that the Hungarian king at the same time was also victorious over Venice was of greater importance: the Republic was ousted from Adriatic cities by the Zadar peace of 1358, placing Dubrovnik under Hungarian supreme rule. This change provoked a hostile reaction from Prince Vojislav, who sought to recover Ston and its peninsula. Another significant change took place in Zeta, where Dušan's governors and their descendants were pushed out by the Balšić brothers, minor nobles from the Skadar region, who imposed their rule over towns and tried to subjugate Kotor.

3
Between the Cross and the Crescent

The New Lords and the End of the Dynasty

Indisputable signs that Dušan's young heir was not ruling the inherited empire effectively became evident soon after the Hungarian expedition against Serbia in 1359. Placing Dubrovnik under the supreme authority of the Hungarian king provoked an attack by Prince Vojislav Vojinović, who plundered the Ragusan territory, pillaged merchants, and demanded that Ston and its peninsula be handed over to him. When Emperor Uroš restored guarantees of free movement for the Ragusans in September 1360, he explicitly stated that they could "go to the Zeta of the Balšić, but also to the state [država] of Prince Vojislav."

The division of the Serbian lands became apparent during the new war of 1361–2. Dubrovnik had allies in the Balšić brothers, while Prince Vojislav sided with the city of Kotor, which was suffering more because Dubrovnik had blocked the entrance to the Bay of Kotor and closed the city's access to the sea, while the Balšić brothers pillaged the territory up to the city gates. Merchants from Serbia were treated as enemies in Dubrovnik, but special ties were maintained with representatives of the Serbian patriarch and metropolitan of Zeta. When hostilities ceased the city of Kotor emerged as the heaviest casualty. It never recovered its economic footing or regained its former importance. Peace between Dubrovnik and Serbia was signed in 1362, restoring borders, releasing prisoners, returning plundered goods, and putting an end to destruction and bloodshed. The emperor's charter describes events curiously – "the Ragusans felt threatened by my empire and were in dispute with the empire's brother Prince Vojislav and the empire's city of Kotor" – as though each pursued its own policies, and the emperor sat on the side as mediator. The emperor retained this role in the future.

Lord Vukašin, ruler of vast territories in Macedonia and the city of Prizren, with which the Ragusans then had close ties, is mentioned in connection with the war with Dubrovnik, along with the emperor and the empress. His son-in-law was Djuradj, the most influential of the Balšići clan. The path to Vukašin's rise is not known, nor are the circumstances that led to great changes in Uroš's empire in the second half of 1365. Vukašin became the emperor's co-ruler, bearing the title of king, while his brother Uglješa received the title of despot, becoming the ruler of Serres, which had previously been governed by the widowed empress Jelena. From the outside it seemed that the system dating back to Dušan's time had been restored, according to which there was a king along with the emperor. The important and essential difference was that the co-ruler was not a member of the "sacred dynasty." Folklore had it that Vukašin dethroned Uroš, but in time documents surfaced revealing that Uroš and Vukašin sent envoys to Dubrovnik together, that they minted coins on behalf of both the emperor and the king, and they were portrayed together on the wall of the church in Psača. There is no doubt that they ruled together, for a time at least.

Dušan's successor had willingly chosen a powerful lord, or accepted one forced upon him, one who could provide useful support, but who could also burden him with the problems of his relations with other lords. The political map of the lords' territories changed in the meantime. Prince Vojislav died in 1363, and his widow was not able to retain his inheritance for her sons. She was ousted by Vojislav's nephew Nikola Altomanović, who appears as the ruler of the territories from Mount Rudnik to Dubrovnik. Prince Lazar Hrebeljanović rose parallel with Nikola, north and west of the Dejanović territory, and was centered in the mining town of Novo Brdo, with territories extending from Kruševac in the north to Rudnik in the west.

The young and uncontrolled Nikola Altomanović caused the greatest unrest. He came into conflict with all his neighbors, became involved in conflicts in Bosnia, attacked Dubrovnik and abused the population, and demanded taxes that were supposed to be paid to the ruler. According to information recorded much later, Nikola Altomanović clashed with Vukašin in 1369, when a split between the emperor and the king allegedly occurred. Contemporary sources do not give explicit accounts, but certain details confirm the later version. In early 1370 King Vukašin issued a charter to the Ragusans including the usual guarantees of freedom of passage and safe trade, which validated all earlier charters and did not mention Emperor Uroš at all! Djuradj Balšić also defected from the emperor according to a contemporary report from 1369. Another sign that the emperor was ignored is the fact that Vukašin appointed his son Marko as the "young king" sometime prior to 1371. In early 1370 Nikola Altomanović started demanding the "St. Demetrius tribute" (2,000 hyperpers annually) from Dubrovnik, which belonged to the ruler. A new war between Altomanović and Dubrovnik broke out, with the Balšić brothers and Vukašin siding with Dubrovnik.

While the sovereign rulers in Dušan's former territories bickered among themselves, the Ottoman Turks, under the leadership of Murad I from 1362, were conquering vast territories on the European continent, where they had obtained their first strongholds about ten years earlier. They took Philippopolis (Plovdiv) and Adrianople (Edirne), and in 1366 regions all along the Aegean coast up to the territories of despot John Uglješa. The latter was threatened most by the Turkish expansion, as was Bulgaria, which was still ruled by Dušan's brother-in-law Ivan Alexander.

During a visit to Mt. Athos in 1370 when he offered contributions to the monasteries, despot John Uglješa revealed that he was preparing for war against the "Muslim infidels." He was supported in this enterprise solely by his brother Vukašin, who had been busy aiding the Balšić brothers in their war against Nikola Altomanović only a few months earlier. He was to attack Trebinje in June 1371. This operation was expected to draw some military support from Dubrovnik but was never carried out.

The brothers John and Vukašin launched their expedition against the Ottomans in September 1371, advancing toward the heart of the Ottoman state in Europe. They were attacked in their sleep before reaching the battleground near the Maritsa River and, along with the majority of their army, were massacred on September 26, 1371. Murad's Turks had no cause for concern for some time: their neighbors grew increasingly obedient. The Byzantine emperor became an Ottoman vassal, and the Bulgarian emperor along with the Dragaš brothers, lords from the eastern part of Dušan's former empire, shared a similar fate.

Uglješa's state was not conquered by the Turks at that time but by a weakened Byzantium, which held onto the Serres region for slightly over a decade. The deaths of Uglješa and Vukašin provoked a struggle for their territories. Vukašin was survived by his sons Marko and Andrijaš, who managed to hold onto the territories in Macedonia. Prizren and the territories north of the Šar Mountain came under the rule of the Balšićs and Nikola Altomanović, who laid siege to Prizren in 1372. The sons of *sebastokrator* Branko Mladenović spread out from southern Kosovo. The most important of them was Vuk Branković, who relied on his father-in-law Lazar Hrebeljanović, the lord of Novo Brdo and its vicinity.

Emperor Uroš died almost unnoticed in early December 1371. He had next to no influence and was eclipsed by these developments. Although his death did not change the balance of power, it did have symbolic importance. The "sacred dynasty" died along with him, and the question arose of who would replace it. As later events demonstrated, factually established power legitimated itself by proving genealogical links with the Nemanjićs. The generation of Dušan's associates and relatives left the historical stage, while the new aristocrats made their rise official, not through imperial decrees and titles bestowed by the emperor, but by stressing their origin in the "sacred roots."

Transfer of the Kingdom to Bosnia

When the storm aroused by the struggle over Vukašin's inheritance subsided, the map became stable. Nikola Altomanović was in the western half, up to the border with Bosnia, while Radič Branković, a descendant of Lord Rastislalić from Dušan's period, was in the east. Both were vassals to the Hungarian king, who interfered in and supervised their actions through Nicolas Gorjanski (de Gara), Prince Lazar's other son-in-law. South of them were Prince Lazar and John and Constantine Dragaš (Dejanović) in the border region toward Bulgaria. Velbužd, their seat, would later be named Kyustendil after Constantine. Even more to the south, up to Šar Mountain and Skopje, was the land of Lazar's son-in-law Vuk Branković. At the far south lay the territory of Vukašin's successors, which was divided into that of his widow and that of his sons King Marko and young King Andrijaš, each of whom minted their own coins.

In such a mosaic, it was difficult to maintain a stable balance. The need to avenge some wrong or right a previous injustice constantly arose. Nikola Altomanović and Prince Lazar quarreled over Rudnik. Since Nikola had clashed with Bosnian Ban Tvrtko I (1353–91) and waged war with Dubrovnik (1371–2), a web was woven tightly around him aimed at depriving him of the protection and support of the Hungarian king. This aim was achieved in 1373 when Ban Tvrtko and Prince Lazar went to war against Nikola and defeated, captured, and blinded him. The division of land that followed was to have long-term consequences. Tvrtko obtained the neighboring land up to the Lim River, including the Mileševa monastery and Onogošt. The territories to the east and north were seized by Prince Lazar, while the Balšić brothers took advantage of Nikola's defeat to seize three *župas* between Dubrovnik and the Bay of Kotor (Trebinje, Konavli, Dračevica). They would later be seized by Tvrtko in 1377, increasing the hostility of the Balšićs, with whom Tvrtko had clashed over Kotor.

Tvrtko thus added new territories of the Nemanjić state to the land his uncle Stjepan II (1326, 1330) had seized in the Neretva valley and area toward Ston, becoming one of the rulers of Serb regions. He was reminded that he was a relative of the Nemanjićs, his grandmother having been the daughter of King Dragutin. This relation was shown in one of the Nemanjić lineages (family trees) and served to document that the "double crown" belonged to Ban Tvrtko, one through his ancestors the Serbian lords, who had passed on to the Kingdom of Heaven, and the other inherited from his ancestors the Bosnian lords. It was obvious that Vukašin's heirs and Marko's royal crown were not even considered at the time.

Tvrtko sought to harmonize his *de facto* position with state-legal understandings by having himself crowned Serbian king. As he said in a charter issued to the Ragusans in 1378, "I went to the land of the Serbs desiring and wanting to take the throne of my parents, and received the crown of the kingdom of my ancestors." It is not known where the coronation took place, but it came about on St. Demetrius's Day, October 26, 1377. The ceremony was approved by the Hungarian king, as Tvrtko's supreme ruler and governor of the Serbian lords, among whom Prince Lazar had the greatest power and authority. Tvrtko also adopted the ruler's name of Stefan, which was borne by all later Bosnian kings, and crowned himself "King of the Serbs, Bosnia, Maritime and Western Areas."

Two decades after Dušan's death the empire he left behind had fundamentally changed. The last conquered territories of Epirus and Thessaly were seized first and were not included in the later fate of the Serbian state. The memory of the Serbian state was preserved in the next belt of territories, from Albania to Bulgaria. The Balšićs promised to release Dubrovnik from the annual tribute of 2,000 hyperpers "if anyone becomes emperor, lord of the Serbs and Serbia." Marko was king in Macedonia, as heir to Vukašin's title of co-ruler, but the lords from the central regions did not care for him. Their neighbors to the east, the Dragaši, preserved the designations received from the Serbian emperor: John Dragaš bore the title of despot, while his brother Constantine was identified as the "lord of Serbia" by Greek sources.

The concentration of land was noted in the former Nemanjić territories. On one side the Bosnian ban incorporated the southern regions from the Neretva River to the Bay of Kotor and continued the Serbian monarchy by shifting the kingdom, but without actual power over the territories of the Serbian lords. The border between the Serbian and Bosnian states was settled along the dividing line of Nikola Altomanović's lands.

There was a parallel process of land concentration on the eastern side, shown by the expansion of Prince Lazar's territories and his ascent to the pinnacle among Serbian lords. He was able to subordinate Radič Branković in 1379 after seizing part of Nikola Altomanović's territory and expanded north to the Danube.

Lazar was satisfied with the old title of prince, but added the symbolic attribute of Stefan, calling himself *samodržac* (*autokrator*) and taking the position previously occupied by the emperor with regard to the church. He and Djuradj Balšić, who with his brothers had received the protection of the pope in 1369, convened the synod to appoint the patriarch in 1375. Disputes arose between Chilandar monastery and the lords and those cases that could not be resolved by the patriarch were tried by Prince Lazar. The prince presented himself as the successor of the "sacred founders" who would continue their work.

It was noted some time ago that one of the mainstays of Prince Lazar's strength lay in the "family alliances" he formed by marrying off his daughters. The first was wed to Vuk Branković, lord of Kosovo and its surroundings, the second to Djuradj Stracimirović, who became a leading figure in the Balšić family in 1379, the third to a relative of the Bulgarian emperor, and the fourth to Nicholas de Gara, the ban of Mačva. The fifth and youngest daughter was to play a role in politics only after her father's death when she was bestowed on Ottoman Sultan Bayazid (1389). The concentration of power on two points, Tvrtko and Lazar, was striking, but other lords who had inherited former royal and imperial power in their territories did not decline in importance.

The Battle of Kosovo – Reality and Myth

After the battle of the Maritsa River the Ottomans greatly extended their circle of vassals, who were obliged to contribute to the Empire's further ascent and consolidation by paying annual tributes and joining forces with the sultan in his military expeditions. They placed the urban strip and important routes along the Aegean coast under their direct rule. In 1383 the Ottomans conquered Serres and its vicinity, expanding toward Thessalonika. The monks from Mt. Athos, whose main estates were threatened, then approached them. Through Gallipoli the Turks fostered ties with their territories in Asia Minor and established relations with the major maritime powers, Venice and Genoa, which had for decades been contending bitterly over the remnants of the Byzantine Empire.

The tactics of Ottoman expansion had already been perfected. They would become involved in local conflicts at the invitation of the feuding Christian lords, familiarize themselves with the terrain, take what they wanted, and make those they aided their dependants. They undertook expeditions far from their core territory. While ruling only Thrace they sent troops to Ioánnina and Berat in Albania, and later to the Dubrovnik hinterland. A ruler's death or family clashes were usually used as the grounds for establishing direct rule. Turkish detachments turned up in all parts of the Balkan Peninsula long before the territory of the Ottoman state approached the region.

The Ottomans had already reached Prince Lazar's territory in 1381, when the prince's commander Crep smashed the Turks in the battle of Dubravnica (near present-day Paraćin, in the Morava river valley). The Turkish unit had probably strayed there after some military operation in Bulgaria. A few years later, in 1386, a much more serious attack followed. Sultan Murad himself led the army that penetrated into Serbia, all the way to Pločnik in Toplica. There was no battle at the time. On that occasion, or somewhat later, the Ottomans raided Gračanica monastery, where the tower and its books were set on fire.

On the other side, the inherited hostility between King Tvrtko and the Balšićs triggered a Turkish raid into the Bileća region, where commander Shahin was defeated in August 1388. A buffer zone existed between the territories of Prince Lazar and Vuk Branković on one side, and the Ottomans on the other, consisting of the territories of Turkish vassals (the Dragaši – Dejanovićs in the east, Vukašin's heirs in the south). However, it was obvious that the Ottomans were closing in.

Parallel with these events, the vast Hungarian Kingdom created by Louis I Anjou (1342–82), surrounded by vassal territories on all sides, was crumbling. When King Louis died in 1382, he was succeeded by his daughter Maria, who ruled with her mother, the daughter of Bosnian Ban Stjepan II, but was met by resistance from the nobility. The ruling Anjou dynasty had relatives in southern Italy, where part of the Hungarian aristocracy sought an heir for the deceased king. Charles of Durazzo took the Hungarian throne, but soon became involved in court intrigues and was assassinated at court in 1385. The queens were accused of the assassination and open rebellion followed. The queens were captured in 1386 and their palatine (highest court dignitary), Nicolas de Gara the Elder, was murdered. A large group was formed in support of Ladislas of Naples, while Sigismund of Luxembourg, the young queen's fiancé, tried to rally nobles loyal to the queens.

At first King Tvrtko honored the king's successor, his cousin, and took Kotor with her approval in 1384. However, when internal rebellion erupted in Hungary he openly sided with Ladislas of Naples, along with Prince Lazar, and challenged Sigismund of Luxembourg. Tvrtko provided refuge for the rebellious Croatian noble brothers Ivaniš and Pavao Horvat, Ivaniš Pališna, and others. For a while Ivaniš Horvat ruled Mačva and Belin, Hungarian territories in Serbia south of the Sava River. Starting in 1387, Tvrtko conquered territories in Croatia and subjugated cities in Dalmatia. The city of Split resisted the longest and the deadline for its surrender was set for June 15, 1389.

King Tvrtko I and Prince Lazar were cut off from their Christian surroundings because of the conflict with the Hungarian queen and Sigismund of Luxembourg, and were joined only by the supporters of

Ladislas of Naples and the Croatian rebels. Both sides of the Hungarian feud sought allies. Florence sided with the Anjou, while Sigismund of Luxembourg was supported by Venice and Duke Visconti of Milan, alleged by his contemporaries to have supplied weapons to the Turks.

Sultan Murad headed for Serbia in the early summer of 1389. He assembled an army of vassals and mercenaries, along with his own troops. By way of his vassals' territories he reached Kosovo, from which routes led in different directions. Upon receiving news of his approach, Prince Lazar, Vuk Branković, on whose land the battle was fought, and King Tvrtko, who sent a large unit under the command of *voivoda* Vlatko Vuković, joined forces.

There is reliable information as to where the battle took place: part of the Kosovo Polje (Field of Blackbirds) near Priština, where Murad's *turbe* (burial stone) still stands, was noted in sixteenth-century maps. The date of the battle is indubitable: St. Vitus's Day, June 15, 1389. It is also certain that Sultan Murad was murdered and Prince Lazar was taken prisoner and slain the same day. Some Christian warriors became Turkish prisoners, and Bosnian nobles from Vlatko Vuković's unit were still being sought in 1403 in Constantinople.

Information regarding other important details was at first contradictory. King Tvrtko reported his great victory with some casualties, but "not many," in letters to his city of Trogir and his ally Florence. The death of the Ottoman ruler gave the Byzantines, and others all the way to France, the impression that the Christians had been victorious. According to medieval notions, holding onto the battleground was crucial in rating the outcome. The Turks remained in Kosovo for a short time, then headed east so that their new ruler Bayazid could strengthen his position. Vuk Branković, the lord of the territory, remained in place and in power, and did not immediately yield to the Turks.

Indisputable contemporary witnesses stated that contradictory versions of the battle circulated from the very beginning. Five weeks after the battle, no one in Venice knew who had succeeded Murad, and the Venetian envoy was instructed to tell anyone he found in power that the Republic had been informed, "although not clearly," of the war between Murad and Prince Lazar, "of which different things had been said, but were not to be trusted." Chalcocondyles, a fifteenth-century Byzantine historian, directly compared the Christians' claims with those of the Turks, who maintained that the sultan had been killed after the battle, while inspecting the battlefield.

As time passed the tales unraveled further. The leitmotif of treason emerged on the Christian side, first linked with the Bosnian detachment and a certain Dragoslav, and then becoming focused and remaining on Vuk Branković. In the first decades following the battle, the theme emerged of the slandered knight, who went to the Turkish camp to slay

Sultan Murad. Under the influence of epic tales of chivalry, Murad's assassin and Lazar's traitor were linked together, both becoming the prince's sons-in-law. In the late fifteenth century the topic of the prince's dinner and Lazar's toast was well known. An entire collection of epic poetry was created containing many picturesque details, very far from reality.

The general view of the battle and its consequences was also far from reality. The battle of Kosovo was not a Crusade, nor was it the defense of Christianity, because the hinterland was hostile. At the time of the battle, Sigismund of Luxembourg had started an expedition against the Bosnian ruler. Prince Lazar had managed to achieve peace, with the mediation of his son-in-law Nicolas Gara the Younger, while Tvrtko remained at war with King Sigismund.

The idea that the "fall of the Serbian Empire" took place at the battle of Kosovo is fundamentally wrong, because the state continued to exist for a further seven decades and experienced economic and cultural revival. According to folklore traditions, the battle of Kosovo set off migrations and ruptured the development of clans and families. Of all Serbian historical events, the battle of Kosovo has been the most popular episode, deeply engraved in the national consciousness. It served as an inspiration for courageous deeds and sacrifices up to the twentieth century, and was widely used in condemning and stigmatizing treason.

The Consequences

Turkish domination and superiority achieved in the battle of Kosovo became apparent only in the years that followed. Soon after the battle Bayazid was forced to travel to the central region of the state and Asia Minor, where uprisings had broken out. Murad's death was also followed by rebellions in the European territories. Some Turks were captured in Kastoria when the city was seized from Turkish rule by the Christians. The circle of Ottoman vassals expanded in the first months after the battle when Lazar's successors acknowledged Bayazid's supreme rule. One of the conditions of the agreement was that Lazar's youngest daughter, Olivera, join the sultan's harem. Her brother, Prince Stefan Lazarević, journeyed to Asia Minor himself and urged Sultan Bayazid to grant Serbia sovereignty. "I freed the land and the cities of my homeland," he states in one of his charters.

Trouble from the north followed the death of Prince Lazar. First Ivaniš Horvat took Mačva and Belin, which became a battleground until Lazar's son-in-law Nicolas de Gara the Younger drove him out. In November 1389 King Sigismund headed a campaign aimed at occupying the fortresses in Serbia that belonged to him. The fortresses of Borač

(Gruža) and Čestin (Šumadija) were seized and held by Hungarian garrisons for a while. The Turks carried out raids across the Danube and Sava rivers into Hungary, making their way through the territories of Lazar's successors, and King Sigismund repeated his expeditions in the following years.

A stronger Ottoman presence was noted again in 1392. The Turks captured Skopje at the beginning of the year, and Vuk Branković was subjugated and obliged to pay the tax or *telos* to the Ottomans. Turkish units raided Bosnia where Tvrtko's heir Dabiša confronted them in 1392, after Tvrtko's death in 1391. This was the only sign that Bayazid had returned to the European theater after settling affairs in Asia Minor. In the summer of 1393 he conquered central Bulgaria, including the capital Turnovo. During the winter of 1393/4, he gathered his vassals in Serres, planning to execute them all. He abandoned this intention, but there were consequences as regards his relations with the Christian lords. Some were subjugated completely, while others resolutely rebelled. Thessaly, which had been ruled by one of the Nemanjić successors, was conquered in 1394; in the same year there was a great expedition across the Danube, and a new raid into Wallachia during which the battle of Rovine was fought on May 17, 1395. Ottoman vassals King Marko and Constantine Dragaš were killed in the battle, and Stefan Lazarević fought alongside them.

The defeat of Bulgaria fundamentally changed the political map of the Balkans. Byzantium was reduced to the vicinity of Constantinople and was surrounded by Ottoman territories on all sides, with geographically unconnected remnants in Epirus and in the Peloponnese. Constantinople was subjected to a lengthy siege starting in 1394. Following the deaths of Constantine Dragaš and King Marko, their territories were turned into Ottoman *krajište* (border regions). The Turks had reached the Adriatic and Ionian shores near Skadar.

Ottoman expansion and Constantinople's cries for help revived the desire for a general crusade against the infidels that had never completely been quenched. Even Emperor Dušan had been pondering the idea prior to his death. King Sigismund of Luxembourg, who had in the meantime reclaimed Dalmatia and Croatia, conquered Bosnia in 1394 and regained control of the situation in Hungary with his own resources. He sent out an appeal to Christian rulers, and responses came from warriors from many lands ranging from Rhodes to England.

A mixed Christian army crossed the Danube and collided with Bayazid and his vassals at Nicopolis on September 26, 1396. The Christians were routed, and the king and other commanders barely managed to save themselves. Prince Stefan Lazarević took part in the battle and distinguished himself on the Ottoman side.

The consequences of the defeat were suffered by all those who sided with the Christians. The rulers of Vidin, the remaining part of Bulgaria, were wiped out and Vuk Branković was trapped and imprisoned (he died in captivity the following year, on October 7, 1397). His lands were seized by the Turks (their *kadi* was in Gluhavica, their *kephale* in Zvečan), and a portion was ceded to Prince Stefan. Vuk's widow Mara, Stefan's sister, and her sons remained on part of Vuk's lands.

The area of the former Serbian state that had been joined to Bosnia under Tvrtko I had already taken the path toward becoming the independent territory of the family founded by *voivoda* Vlatko Vuković. As he had died in 1392, he was replaced by his nephew and heir Sandalj Hranić (1392–1435). Tvrtko's successor Stefan Dabiša (1391–5) had inherited hostile relations with King Sigismund along with the lands conquered by Tvrtko I. After Sigismund defeated and captured Dabiša and the Bosnians in 1394, they were forced to succumb and swear that Bosnia would crown Sigismund king after Dabiša's death. When this occurred in 1395, Bosnia avoided the obligation and kept Dabiša's widow Jelena on the throne (1395–8).

The queen had to rely on her principal lords, whom she mentions in her charters: grand *voivoda* Hrvoje Vukčić Hrvatinić, Prince Pavle Radenović and *voivoda* Sandalj Hranić. Sigismund's defeat at Nicopolis and the renewed movement against him in Hungary freed Bosnia of its obligation, and Stefan Ostoja (1398–1404 and 1409–18) was elected king by the Bosnian Diet.

Stefan Lazarević's relations with Bayazid reached a crisis in 1398. In January the young prince led an expedition into Bosnia, which ended in failure: the army suffered during the cold winter and achieved no successes. He clashed with disgruntled lords Nikola Zojić and Novak Belocrkvić, who wanted to be equal to the ruler and become Bayazid's direct vassals. He fell from Bayazid's grace and was accused of plotting with Hungary. His mother, Princess Milica, now nun Eugenia, was forced to go before the Ottoman ruler and plead for her son. According to Stefan's biography, Bayazid allegedly advised the young Stefan to slay the powerful and subdue them to his will, and raise the benevolent and meek and make them great. This was to prepare Stefan for the turmoil that Bayazid predicted would follow his death.

The Despot and His Land

The great Ottoman conquests in the years following the battle of Kosovo were halted by threats in the east. Some of the conquered Turkmen tribal chiefs had tried to secure the support of the Mongol ruler Timur, whom the Europeans called Tamerlane. The diplomacy of the Byzantines, who had been under siege in Constantinople for years, also played a part. In 1400 Bayazid was menaced by the powerful conqueror in the east.

When he decided to test his strength, Bayazid gathered his vassals, including the young heirs of Prince Lazar, Stefan and Vuk, and the sons of Vuk Branković, Djuradj and Lazar, who had recovered part of their father's lands. The encounter between the Ottoman and Mongol forces took place on a battlefield near Angora (present-day Ankara) on July 28, 1402. The victory was Tamerlane's. He captured Bayazid and held him captive until his death in 1403, and released the vassals, thus allowing the young princes to return home.

The state of relations among the Serbian lords while Bayazid was their ruler is not known; their subjugation probably kept them united and disciplined. After Bayazid's fall they undoubtedly feuded. While Stefan Lazarević enjoyed the hospitality of the Byzantine co-emperor John VII Palaeologus, Djuradj Branković was held prisoner in the same city.

During Stefan's stay in Constantinople, a small family episode took place that was to have long-term repercussions. The young Serbian prince was unmarried and his host sought a suitable match from among his wife's relatives. Stefan's biographer says that the choice fell on the empress's sister, who came from the family of Francesco Gatilusio, lord of Mitylene (Lesbos), Italians who had become rulers in the Levant. As an imperial son-in-law Stefan was qualified to receive the Byzantine title of despot, which John VII granted him in 1402, even though his uncle, "grand emperor" Manuel II, was traveling through Europe seeking aid for Constantinople. The wedding was to take place later on Lesbos, where Stefan traveled by sea.

Before being used to indicate an autocratic, cruel, and unlimited rule, the word despot, meaning lord, had positive connotations for a number of centuries. In the twelfth century it became a technical term indicating a high dignitary, second to the emperor. The title was reserved for the emperor's sons, brothers, and sons-in-law. The Serbs were acquainted with the title and Serbian emperors bestowed it, as did Byzantine and Bulgarian emperors. The novelty here consisted in the fact that the title had been awarded to the ruler of a state, so that the designation of despot would become the ruler's title and would continue to be bestowed by the Byzantine emperor.

Emperor Manuel returned from the West in 1403 and a few years later, in 1410, Stefan underwent a new "coronation" as despot. Stefan's successor, Djuradj Branković, who had been a prisoner in the Constantinople dungeon, was a Cantacuzenus son-in-law (he was married to Irene Cantacuzena) and thus qualified to become despot. He was wed by Emperor John VIII's envoy in 1429. His son married one of the emperor's cousins in 1446, thus becoming despot alongside his living father. Prior to the death of despot Stefan in 1427, the title was understood as the equivalent of the title *dux*, which was second to that of king in the West. The "despot of the kingdom of Rascia" was the leading lord in Hungary, second to the king. The title was awarded in Hungary, even after the fall of Constantinople, and between the sixteenth and seventeenth centuries it was borne by pretenders to the throne and adventurers.

By marriage, the Serbian despot formally became a member of the Byzantine imperial family and was subordinated to the Byzantine emperor as father and lord. What the powerful emperors of the eleventh and twelfth centuries had not been able to implement by force now came to pass on its own. The Serbian ruler, who was already acquainted with dual vassal obligations – toward the Hungarian king and the Turkish sultan – chose by himself to be subjected to the weak and distant Byzantine emperor. Neither in 1402 nor at any time later did Serbia have a common border with what remained of Byzantium.

The new despot was still not the lord of the lands he had inherited; Stefan had to fight for them against his close relatives – his sister's sons. He returned by sea after spending some time in Lesbos. In the meantime, Djuradj Branković had freed himself from captivity and set off toward Serbia by land, receiving reinforcements from Bayazid's immediate successor, Suleyman. Stefan and Vuk Lazarević had been expected in Dubrovnik but came ashore in Bar, stopping with their brother-in-law, Djuradj II Stracimirović, and traveled to Serbia with his help. They reached their homeland by November 1402 and clashed with their nephews at Tripolje, near Gračanica.

Stefan was victorious and installed himself as their lord, in the same position held by his father, Prince Lazar. His mother Milica mediated the peace. In the meantime, King Sigismund faced strong opposition in Hungary from a group of lords who attempted to overthrow him and crown Ladislas of Naples, who had arrived in Zadar for the coronation. Sigismund needed allies and made peace with Stefan in 1403 or early 1404, handing over Belgrade and the fortresses south of the Sava and Danube, to which Hungary held rights.

The despot used peace with the Turks to settle affairs in the state, whose center had moved north. The Turks directly ruled the territories south of the Šar Mountain – the Skopje border area (*krajište*) – and they held special privileges and maintained strongholds in the neighboring Branković territory. The shift north is apparent in the fact that the capital was moved to Belgrade. In addition to other important buildings, Despot Stefan built the metropolitanate church in Belgrade. He also endowed his mausoleum church in the northern region, on the Resava River (Resava monastery, or Manasija).

Plate 3.1   The church as fortress: Manasija (Resava) monastery, the endowment of Despot Stefan Lazarević, built 1407–17. (Photograph by B. Strugar)

Hostilities among Bayazid's successors provided the Balkan Christians with a respite. They liberated certain former Byzantine territories, created an opportunity to drive out Turkish rule from Bulgaria, and attenuated or eliminated Turkish supreme rule. On the other hand, the struggles among Bayazid's successors involved Christian lords, emphasizing old conflicts and creating new ones. This became clear in the case of the Serbian lords. After hostilities between Lazar's and Vuk's sons were calmed, conflict broke out among the Lazarevićs, who had been divided previously. Princess Milica used her authority to settle the antagonism between her sons and grandsons, but the moral authority she provided disappeared with her death in 1405.

Bayazid's inheritance was first controlled by Sultan Suleyman, who was initially friendly to the Brankovićs. In 1409 when Vuk Lazarević sought the sultan's support in an attempt to partition the state territory away from his brother, he received the support of the Brankovićs' and Suleyman's auxiliary troops, who devastated parts of Serbia. Despot Stefan was forced to yield southern parts of the state and retreat north. He, on the other hand, sought support from the Hungarian king, and in 1410 Hungarian troops reached Trepča and Priština, where they set fire to the borough.

Stefan backed Suleyman's brother Musa in his conflict with the sultan. Musa sought to rule the European part of the Ottoman Empire. He also brought Vuk Lazarević and the Brankovićs to his side, while the Byzantine emperor remained loyal to Suleyman. Musa and his allies were defeated near Constantinople. Despot Stefan had the opportunity to withdraw to Constantinople, while Suleyman sent Vuk and Lazar Branković to Serbia, just like after the battle of Angora, while keeping Djuradj behind. The two Serbian princes were captured by Musa near Philippopolis and were put to death in 1410.

Stefan and his nephew Djuradj, each remaining alone in their families, came together and forged a lasting peace, most likely mediated by Mara Branković, sister of Stefan and mother of Djuradj. Together they took part in the war against Musa, helping secure the power of Bayazid's son Mehmed I, who would gradually restore the Ottoman Empire.

Another step toward closer relations with Hungary occurred in 1411 when Stefan received the mining town of Srebrenica and territories west of the Drina from King Sigismund, along with territories in Hungary that the king had seized from Bosnian *herzeg* (duke) Hrvoje Vukčić. These territories would later be the source of discord between the Bosnian kings and Serbian despots.

Since Despot Stefan had no offspring, he chose Djuradj as his successor and gave him control of his father's lands, with the capital in Vučitrn. Soon after the peace was forged, Djuradj married Irene Cantacuzena, the cousin of former Emperor John VI. The peace between Stefan and Djuradj had repercussions resulting in the unification of their lands, even though the Brankovićs' territories remained in a less favorable position with the Turks and included certain Turkish enclaves, such as Trepča.

The Restless Littoral

Djuradj helped his uncle and carried out the missions assigned him. This became especially clear during events that followed the death in 1421 of Stefan's nephew, Balša III Balšić, who left his lands to the despot. However, the fulfillment of his wishes came up against difficulties rooted in the recent past.

When the Turks, along with Bosnia, appeared as adversaries, having conquered Skopje and established *krajište*, Djuradj II Stracimirović Balšić sought support and aid from Venice. The Republic welcomed every opportunity to establish its influence, since the conditions of the Zadar Treaty of 1358 prohibited it from holding land between the Gulf of Quarnaro (Kvarner) and Dyrrachium (Durres). Djuradj was held as a Turkish captive from 1392, and was forced to hand over the cities of Skadar and Drivast and the St. Sergius Marketplace on the Bojana River in order to secure his release. In the fall of 1395, he exploited the Turks' absence to recover these cities and cede them to Venice. Along with Dyrrachium, which had been procured in 1392, these were the first Venetian strongholds on the Adriatic coast, and in the future Venice would be an important factor in Zeta. In time Balšić was bothered by Venice, whose authority was rejected by the local population. In addition, local adversaries such as Radič Crnojević and Sandalj Hranić followed in Tvrtko's footsteps, who aspired to conquer Kotor and occasionally ruled Budva.

In the changed situation following the battle of Angora, Djuradj's successor Balša III (1403–21) took control of the family territory, aided by his mother Jelena Lazarević. They would soon turn against Venice and waged a 10-year war with the Republic. At first Venice used its fleet to return the mutinous cities, and even seized Ulcinj, Bar, and Budva (1405). Balša became Suleyman's vassal, like his cousins in the hinterland. The situation changed once again in 1409 when Venice purchased the rights to Dalmatia from Ladislas of Naples and started fighting for control of the Dalmatian cities. After great effort and bloodshed, Balša III seized Bar in 1412 and Venice, pressed by difficulties elsewhere, agreed to return territories it had previously seized.

The old royal city of Kotor suffered a succession of crises. In 1370 it came under the rule of the Hungarian king, and in 1380 there was an uprising by the commoners against the aristocracy, which had returned to power with foreign help. In 1384 it was overpowered by King Tvrtko as he enforced his policy of restoring the Nemanjić state. Bosnian supreme rule continued under *voivoda* Sandalj Hranić, who participated in the revenues from the salt trade. Balša later laid siege to the city and it entered secret negotiations with Venice, its surrender marked by the flying of the Venetian flag in 1420.

Balša III had previously entered a new war with Venice, which was connected to the war with Hungary and the Turks. He laid siege to Skadar, but lost Budva and Luštica with its salt works. When he yielded the territory to his uncle Stefan Lazarević, it was plunged in warfare. Venice took advantage of Balša's death and seized Ulcinj and Bar in 1421. Despot Stefan first demanded that Venice return Balša's cities, then arrived with an army and took control of Balša's lands, excluding Ulcinj and Budva. He continued the siege of Skadar during 1422, but without success. Peace was brokered in 1423. The despot took charge of Budva and the salt works, and returned part of the Kotor district. Remaining disputed issues were settled in later negotiations, in Vučitrn (1426) and Smederevo (1435). Peace between Venice and the despot prevailed during the period of negotiations, and was later ended when the Ottomans conquered the despot's state in 1439.

The Balšić family territory survived during a turbulent six decades, threatening and obstructing the development of the coastal cities, which were often under siege, cut off from the hinterland, and prevented from trading. Even though order and control were in principle better maintained within the territories of the individual lord, this was not the case with the Balšić family dominion; the dynastic rulers continually caused turmoil and unrest. When the territory came under the rule of Despot Stefan, the earlier autonomous position of the cities was confirmed, while the remaining territory was included in the centralized and uniformly organized state. The state that united the lands of Prince Lazar, Vuk Branković, and the first generation of the Balšićs was similar in range and area to the Nemanjić state, prior to the wave of conquests that started with Milutin's military victories in Macedonia.

The greatest difference was in the absence of areas that were included in Bosnia (approximately present-day Herzegovina). The border was near the Lim River, at Onogošt (Nikšić), and Boka (the Gulf of Kotor). The city of Novi (present-day Herceg Novi) was under Bosnian rule, while Kotor was ruled by Venice.

Economic Progress

Political changes were frequent during the period when the territories of the feudal lords were being established, expanded, and merged, but they did not have a serious impact on the economy and were not followed by great destruction. Merchants, however, whose work was hindered by unsafe roads, complained about the situation. "We cannot live unless we trade, and most of our trading was done in the kingdom of Raška (Serbia); because of the poor situation in that state of Raška due to rifts among the barons, we cannot and we dare not trade there to the extent that we traded in the past," complained the Ragusans in 1371. Similar difficulties soon followed in the maritime trade, on account of the war between Venice and Genoa over the island of Tenedos. All together, the wars and insecurity in maritime trade caused a crisis in the entire Mediterranean resulting in a rise in the price of silver, which was needed in the mints belonging to numerous states and rulers with royal minting rights. From a price of 6 ducats for a pound of silver (approx. 330 g) the price rose to 7.5 and 8 ducats, and stayed at that level until Turkish conquests ended free trade and directed all silver to the sultan's treasuries and mints.

The increase in price changed the economics of metal production and merchants were greatly attracted to buying silver mines and even investing in silver mining. This resulted in a number of new mines in different parts of the Serbian state. In addition to those already existing in the basins of Kopaonik and along the Drina River, there was Železnik in Kučevo in the east, Rudište near Belgrade, and mines on Mt. Cer as extensions of the existing Drina river basin (Krupanj, Zajača, and Bohorina). The wave of new mines had an indirect influence on equalizing the level of development. The southern regions, which had been in the lead, lost their advantage even though they were still home to the largest and most important mines (Novo Brdo, Trepča). The northern regions gained all the advantages that accompanied mining, including a new type of settlement, increased trade, market relations, and autonomy.

The routes taken by the silver remained the same, with only the main mediators changing. Kotor was almost completely driven out, and Dubrovnik maintained its leading role, without competition. A significant number of Ragusan merchants financed mines by purchasing parts of pits and melting houses and organizing production, something that mining law allowed them to do.

It is possible to provide a rough estimate of the volume of production during this period of economic growth. The accounting records of a Ragusan company (the Kabužić brothers, Caboga) have been preserved and published. The company specialized in silver and gold trade and shipped the metal to Italy, primarily Venice. Between December 1426 and November 1432, 10,613 lbs of silver passed through their hands, which is approximately 3,480 kg. The same trade company exported 565 kilograms of silver mixed with gold (*argentum deauratum*) during the same period, with gold accounting for a quarter of the amount. Another source for estimating production is the Dubrovnik mint record from 1422, which shows how much silver had been exchanged for coinage during that year. It was mandatory to trade in 6 percent of what was exported, at a set exchange rate. Based on information on the amount of silver that was handed in, the entire quantity may be estimated at 5,672 kg modern weight.

Both these important sources speak of what was shipped to the west. Most likely very little was exported north, since Hungary was also a great exporter of silver and gold. Exports toward Turkish territories remain unknown, as do amounts that remained for handicraft work and

Serbia's mints. A rough estimate can be made of the value of goods imported into Serbian regions in order for trade to be balanced. The estimated value of goods exported by way of Dubrovnik in 1422 was 130,000 ducats, calculated at the average price of 7.5 ducats per lb.

The nature of the mining business, which involved years of work without income until the mineral deposits were reached, stimulated the development of debt and credit operations. Trade had a similar influence, with a vast supply of goods offered in exchange for the expensive silver. The natural consequence was that Serbia's population became greatly indebted. Numerous individual documents and diplomatic complications regarding relations between Dubrovnik and the Serbian despot mention the degree of indebtedness. The records of Ragusan merchant Miho Lukarević from 1432 to 1438 have been preserved, listing 1,200 individuals, half of them from the city of Novo Brdo and half from the surrounding area, who were indebted to him. Money was loaned with guarantees in the form of collateral, property of value greater than the loan, or with the obligation of another person to repay the loan if the debtor was unable. According to an old privilege from charters issued by the rulers, the Ragusans' oath was to be believed regarding the size of the debt. The creditors' interests were also protected by the custom of handing the debtor over to the creditor, who could imprison him until the debt was paid.

The extent of the debts can be deduced by the political and diplomatic negotiations and arguments of the Ragusan government, which supported its citizens and their interests, and of the despot who sought to protect his subjects. The right of the Ragusans to substantiate the amount of their debts by oath alone was disputed and a moratorium on debt payments was introduced in certain regions, and later in the entire country. All real estate except *pronoia* was acceptable as collateral (since the ruler, not the debtor, was the owner of the land), and only the "third dinar" (one-third) of the wage or income could be collected to repay a debt. Despot Djuradj even carried out a monetary reform in 1435 instructing that a payment of 10 new dinars covered a debt of 16 old dinars.

The weight of the Serbian dinar at that time was reduced to approximately 1 g, with about 35 to 40 dinars equivalent to one Venetian ducat. They were called asper, reminiscent of the earlier Byzantine and contemporary and later Turkish coinage (*akca* – the Turkish translation of the word asper – means "white" money). The Dubrovnik government requested that the despot honor old customs and demanded discipline from its own citizens. Inquiries were made into claims that some had collected the same debt twice, and citizens were ordered to use discretion in escorting debtors who were handed into their custody and to treat them humanely. Debts remained a pressing issue until the fall of the Serbian state.

The increase in domestic trade may be judged by the appearance of a new type of settlement, the *trg* (marketplace), whose very name described its economic function. The *trg* usually had the privilege of an annual fair (*panadjur*) taken over from Byzantium. Some cities that became prominent later had already in the fifteenth century obtained the status of *trg* – Zaslon (Šabac), Valjevo, Paraćin, Užice, Čačak – while others emerged only later in the earliest Turkish censuses (*defter*) under the name *bazaar*, with several times the income of the largest villages. Some continued developing even under Turkish rule owing to their privileged position or some other circumstance and survived to develop into modern towns.

During the fifteenth century there was visible progress in mastering the methods and processes of medieval technology. The greatest achievements were in the domain of mining and metallurgy, as described in invitations to miners and experts who came from other countries, even those that were economically more developed. Mention has been preserved of invitations from Sicily (1397), Siena (1437), the court in Naples (1452), Ferrara (1457), and Urbino (1481). Hydrotechnical works were carried out with much skill, harnessing the power of water, which was used either directly in the ore mills and rolling mills or indirectly in the bellows at the smelting works. The technique of manufacturing bells and cannon had been mastered, which was considered a high point in medieval technology. The mention of a Serb from Mt. Athos who installed a clock in Moscow in 1404 that chimed the hours testifies to the skill of manufacturing processes.

The textile industry was on a more modest scale. In the fifteenth century Dubrovnik had a true *arte di lana*, the production of woven woolen cloth, while *herzeg* Stefan Vukčić Kosača only established this craft in 1448 in his city of Novi. It was introduced with the help of an Italian master from Rimini, but the results were not successful and the products had to be completed and dyed in Dubrovnik. The tradition of silk production and manufacturing the cloth called *tella di Prisreno* continued in the Prizren region, passed down from the Byzantine period, as was the case with *tafotta rasciana*, which is mentioned in the fifteenth century.

Continuity as an Ideal

The disappearance of the dynasty, and the state structures and organization associated with it, created an urgent need for those who gained power to legitimize their authority. This was especially marked in the case of the territorial lords of the second generation, who could not boast of high-ranking titles and administrative positions received from the emperor. Available information points to the conclusion that most of these lords retained modest titles, such as *župan* and *knez*, which had ancient origins but which by the mid-fourteenth century had been degraded on account of their widespread use. Others accepted the general attribute of lord or master, which was part of a ruler's title and was used when addressing him.

The most common means of legitimization was establishing a link with the dynasty. This was done in a variety of ways. Ban Tvrtko proved his descent from King Dragutin by lineage; Prince Lazar is said to have descended from Dušan's servant, but more importantly his wife was the descendant of Vukan, Stefan Nemanja's oldest son, which linked their offspring to the Nemanjić family. This also included the Branković lineage, since Mara was the daughter of Prince Lazar and Princess Milica.

The need to emphasize continuity produced literary genres focusing on dynastic history and the events following Dušan's death. Genealogies (*rodoslovi*) illustrated the expansion of Nemanja's descendants, and important Serbian events were described in annals (*letopisi*), created according to the model of the Byzantine short chronicles, continuing the world chronicles translated during Dušan's era.

The biographies (*žitija*) of the kings and archbishops, started by Danilo II, came to a halt with Dušan's reign on the secular side, and continued up to Patriarch Sava III (1375) on the episcopal branch. Dušan's ascent was portrayed in a negative light because he abandoned the "forefathers' royal authority" and reached for an empire. This led to a split and excommunication by the Constantinopolitan patriarch, a wound that had to be healed. Prince Lazar is credited with playing the main role in this regard. He restored unity between the churches and reinstated the old order.

Writings about Prince Lazar offered some kind of substitute for an official biography. They focused on his self-sacrificing death, praised his heroics and martyrdom, and established a cult, thus upholding the continuity of the "sacred rulers." The aspiration toward continuity governed people's behavior and actions. King Tvrtko presented his conquest as the continuation of the restoration of the Serbian Kingdom, thus "the city of our ancestors, Kotor, has fortunately come into our possession for eternity." In negotiations between the Ragusans and hinterland rulers, even the most minor dissent was placed within a long-range perspective by recalling how things were "during the time of the first Serbian lords."

In practical life continuity was particularly stressed in relations with the church, with ruling princes assuming the role of protector and "second patron," continuing the work of the first founders, but also

Plate 3.2 Worship of native saints: early fifteenth-century icon of St. Simeon and St. Sava. (Narodni muzej Beograd, with permission)

following their example in establishing endowments for themselves and their families. Prince Lazar built the exonarthex for Chilandar monastery, with which the Branković family was closely associated, having a family member as a monk in almost every generation. Following the example of his Serbian ancestors, Simeon Uroš founded the Transfiguration on Metéora, a nucleus that was to develop into the well-known monastery complex.

What was new was the fact that lower-level nobles established family endowments, emulating the greater lords who in turn took after earlier rulers. Shifting the state center northward was followed by a wave of new church edifices and monuments of new design. They were modeled after Dušan's buildings and contemporary monuments in Constantinople and Thessalonika. Churches built according to the Morava school of architecture, as the latest style was called, contained significant Byzantine elements that testified to the cultural homogenization of the eastern Christian world under Byzantine influence.

The central dome was accompanied by secondary domes; polychrome effects were achieved by alternating layers of stone and ceramics; sculptural devices were applied to a greater degree; and facades were decorated with paintings. Gothic associations were created by the windows and rosettes on the western facade. Examples were set by members of Lazar's dynasty (Ravanica, Ljubostinja, Manasija with their numerous specific features), and followed by those of the nobles (Kalenić, Drenča, Neupara, Vraćevšnica). These and other monasteries are situated north of the Western Morava River.

Secular construction also maintained continuity. Inherited techniques and materials were used and followed familiar forms, primarily those from the Byzantine capital. The city of Smederevo was completely rebuilt (1427–30) according to a plan and type of fortification modeled after Constantinople. The continual threat of Ottoman expansion prompted the construction of new fortifications and the repair of old ones. Mining and urban settlements were buttressed with external walls and a reinforced inner fortification capable of withstanding prolonged sieges, as shown by Novo Brdo. Ravanica and Resava (Manasija) are examples of monasteries that also served as fortifications.

By the end of the fourteenth century the greater lords and rulers had transferred their seats to towns, which in turn became capitals: Kruševac for Prince Lazar, Belgrade for Stefan Lazarević, Smederevo for Djuradj

Plate 3.3   Transfer of the state center: Smederevo on the Danube, built 1428–30, Serbian capital 1430–59. (Photograph by B. Strugar)

Branković. Customs acquired from the West during the Nemanjić period continued, such as the knighthood represented by orders of chivalry and heraldry, present in Serbian coinage since the time of Stefan Dečanski and Dušan. Heraldic symbolism with its characteristic language was used not only on coins and seals but also on rings, manuscript decorations, and even gravestones.

During the period of the despots there was more intensive work in copying manuscripts and translating texts, thus increasing the old Serbian collection of books. Records show that rulers played a

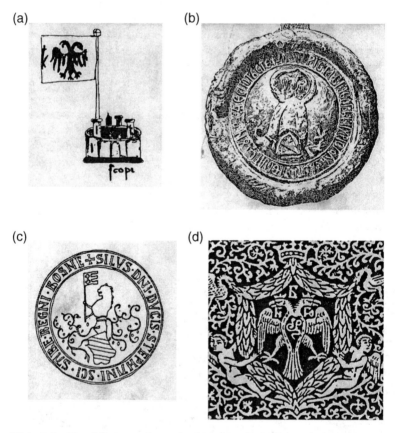

Plate 3.4 Heraldic arms from the fourteenth to fifteenth centuries. (a) Two-headed eagle ascribed to Serbia (*Seruja*) in the Catalan map of 1339; (b) seal of Despot Stefan Lazarević (1426); (c) seal of Stefan Vukčić, *dux sancti Sabe* (before 1466); (d) arms of Djuradj Crnojević, lord of Zeta (1494).

significant role in ordering and inviting monks from Mt. Athos to work on manuscripts. The selection of copied and translated work was broadened to include literary texts (*Aleksandrida, The Tale of Troy, Tristan and Isolde*) in addition to ascetic moral literature and treatises on different areas of knowledge. The tradition of writing biographies of prominent figures also continued. The biography of Jefrem, the first patriarch following those noted in Danilo's collection, was written by Bishop Marko. The biography of Despot Stefan, which has many distinctive aspects, was written by Constantine the Philosopher, at the request of the patriarch and the synod. All that remains concerning Despot Djuradj is the "graveside lament" containing rhetorical praise of his individual deeds. Only later, among refugees in Srem, were writers found to include the last of the Branković family (Despotess Angelina and sons Djordje and Jovan) in the series of sacred rulers.

The Burden of Double Vassalage

The capitals on the banks of the Danube, first Belgrade and then Smederevo, symbolized the position of the despot's state, so different from that of the Nemanjić state. While the earlier state aimed south in order to conquer urbanized and richer areas, the later one expanded north, settling and cultivating once-deserted territories. This served both as a starting point for further migrations northward and as a bridgehead from which the state was restored when it fell under Ottoman rule.

The disputed territories along the Sava and Danube (including those in northeastern Bosnia), which were commonly known as "the land of King Stefan" (meaning Dragutin), ceased to be the subject of discord between Serbia and Hungary and became the link that brought them together. The despots owed vassal obligations, in exchange for which they occupied leading positions in the Hungarian Diet and aristocratic hierarchy. Starting with Stefan Lazarević, they were all second to the king; they had their estates, an obligation to maintain a *banderium* – a detachment of 1,000 cavalrymen – and to take part in expeditions undertaken by the king, with an army of 8,000 soldiers. Stefan obtained Hungary's approval for Djuradj to be enthroned as his heir. There were no wars between the states of Hungary and Serbia, but there were conflicts, such as when the Hungarians interfered in the discord between Stefan and Vuk Lazarević, or when Despot Djuradj became involved in the battle between Hungarian lords.

The Turks' defeat at Angora in 1402 did not free Stefan of his vassal obligations. The treaty between Suleyman and Emperor John VII

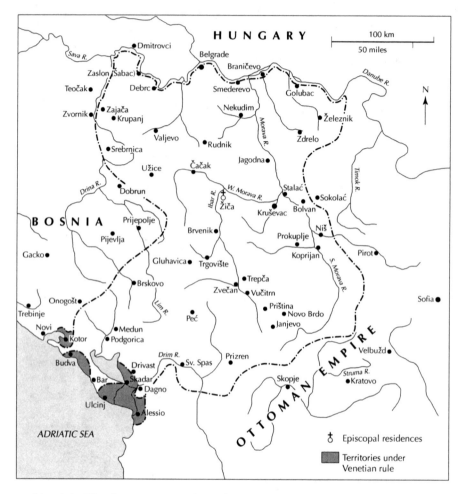

Map 3.1 The despot's state after taking possession of Zeta, ca. 1422.

Palaeologus included the obligation that "Lazar's son" pay taxes and provide support troops, although he did not have to lead them personally. However, during the contention between Bayazid's sons he had to choose whom to support. Stefan remained with the Constantinople emperor and dragged the Hungarian king into the fight between Mehmed and Musa. The alliance's army headed by Djuradj Branković defeated Musa in Bulgaria in 1412 and enabled Mehmed I to restore power throughout the state. The new sultan was loyal to the despot for a time, but soon continued his predecessors' policy of conquest. In 1415 Bosnia was included in the circle of Ottoman vassals, first the kingdom and then its seceded portions ruled by the Pavlovićs and Sandalj Hranić. Soon the sultan was in a position to mediate in disputes between the Christian lords.

The despots still called themselves independent rulers, and Stefan Lazarević's biographer found a unique expression of greatness in the double obligation: "The eastern rulers, with the western as their enemies, seized land and warred against each other, and [the despot] sent his army to the eastern [rulers] against the western, and he himself went to the western for counsel. And all this was done publicly for many years. No one else, verily, created anything similar, only he, great and marvelous in his wisdom and power." In reality the despot was pressured by both sides. Murad II (1421–51), the successor to Mehmed I, punished him for aiding his adversary in the struggle for the Ottoman throne. Serbia was plundered, lost territories, and fell into severe difficulties on the death of Despot Stefan on July 19, 1427.

His successor, Djuradj (prince from 1427, despot from 1429), was immediately harassed from both the Turkish and Christian sides. King Sigismund rushed to take over Djuradj's towns and managed to seize Belgrade. Golubac was handed over to the Turks by the despot's local lord because a debt had not been repaid, while the Serbian ruler maintained control of Mačva. A great battle was fought between Hungarians and Ottomans over Golubac, a siege in which the Hungarian king himself participated, but he was pushed back across the Danube in 1428. Besides Golubac, the Turks also took territories to the south – the Niš region and the city of Kruševac. Along with the reinstatement of previous tributes and military obligations, such was the price Djuradj Branković paid for Turkish recognition.

Djuradj also played an active role within family politics during this time. He married one of his daughters, Cantacuzina, to Count Ulrich of Cilli, a relative of the Hungarian king and one of the most powerful individuals in the monarchy, and presented his other daughter, Mara, to the harem of Sultan Murad II. Her dowry consisted of Toplica and Dubočica, which were recognized as belonging to the sultan. However, even that was not enough to keep relations stable. New demands soon followed: the town of Braničevo (near present-day Kostolac) was handed over to the Turks in 1437, and a raid by the Hungarian king that reached Kruševac and torched Turkish boats near Stalać the same summer provoked retaliatory attacks from Murad against Serbia and Transylvania.

The prospect of aid from Hungary faded with the death of King Sigismund in December 1437 after a lengthy reign. A Turkish expedition attacked Serbia in 1438, seizing the towns of Višeslav and Ždrelo, near the border, and Borač, Ostrovica, and the fortified Ravanica monastery, then in the heart of Serbia. The following year the expedition headed for

Smederevo, which surrendered in August 1439 after a three-month siege. It was not until the summer of 1441 that the Turks succeeded in capturing the mining town of Novo Brdo, which put up fierce resistance under a difficult siege and suffered numerous casualties. During this wave of conquests the Turks did not penetrate the mountainous region of Zeta, where conflicts had erupted between rivals Bosnian Duke Stefan Vukčić Kosača, who seized Upper Zeta, and Venice, to whom Despot Djuradj had entrusted control of the coastal cities.

The Ottoman Turks' great triumphs threatened their neighbors, primarily the Hungarian Kingdom that now bordered Ottoman territories, and rekindled the idea of a Crusade that had faded following defeat at the battle of Nicopolis. The aim was to combine Christian forces from a number of states and drive the Turks out of Europe. However, a serious obstacle to this endeavor was posed by the struggle for the Hungarian throne that succeeded the death of King Albrecht (1437–9). The exiled Serbian despot was also involved in the contest, having nominated his youngest son Lazar as Hungarian king. The Crusade was made possible only after power had been consolidated by the young Polish Prince Wladyslaw III Warnenczyk (1440–4), who was introduced by a group of Hungarian lords. Money provided by Despot Djuradj funded the army's expansion and an important role was played by a detachment of Wallachian warriors under the command of *voivoda* Janos Hunyadi. The combined forces of the king, despot, and *voivoda* crossed into Serbia in the fall of 1443 and defeated Turkish troops along the military route to Niš and Sofia. Freezing weather stalled the allied army at Zlatica in December, forcing it to return to Belgrade and Hungary.

Murad II had difficulties elsewhere and was willing to consider negotiations, which began in the spring of 1444. An agreement was reached by June, with the main articles providing for towns to be returned to Despot Djuradj. "And the despot received the Serbian Land and entered Smederevo on August 22," recorded contemporary Serbian authors. The despot's sons Grgur and Stefan, who had been blinded by Murad II, were released at the same time.

In Hungary the agreement with the sultan was broken under the influence of the papal legate and warmongering circles, and preparations were continued for a fresh assault. An expedition was launched in November 1444, without the despot, and ended in defeat at the battle of Varna and the king's death.

The 1444 agreement as well as later truces and peace treaties confirm that Hungary and the Ottoman Empire had established a system of vassal states that recognized each other's rights and interests, although not to the same extent. The band of states started at Dubrovnik, which was under the Hungarian king, then continued through the territory of the

Kosače and Pavlovići regional lords under Ottoman rule, then to the land of the Bosnian king, whom the Turks considered as ruler only of the portion of his kingdom not governed by vassals, then to the territory of the Serbian despots, then crossed the Danube to the territories of the Wallachian and Moldavian dukes, and ended at the shores of the Black Sea.

The system did not remain evenly balanced for long and power gradually shifted in favor of the Ottomans. The economic inequality between the two blocs also became apparent. The Ottoman sultan was able to raise a cavalry of several tens of thousands of men every year. They were awarded *timar* (grants in lands or revenues) and did not burden the sultan with any additional costs. The sultan also maintained a detachment of footsoldiers (janissaries), who acted as a kind of personal guard and whose numbers increased over time. They were paid annually, regardless of whether there were any expeditions or not. Finally, during campaigns the sultan would employ additional mercenary troops, often consisting of Christians, who were paid for the time they served in the war.

In contrast, the Christian societies had armies consisting of nobles who were obligated to take part in campaigns undertaken by the king, and who could raise an army consisting of serfs (one equipped soldier per 25 to 30 households) and professional mercenaries, who were very expensive – three gold pieces per month. A relatively modest detachment numbering 5,000 mercenaries would require the huge sum of 45,000 pieces of gold for a three-month campaign. When plans were drawn up for the campaign against the Turks in the second half of the fifteenth century, an estimated 200,000 gold pieces were required, exceeding the amount available to a single ruler. The pope's help was increasingly sought and he collected funds for the Crusades from Christian states. A significant portion of the troops on the Christian side came from cattle-breeding regions. This is evidenced by the important role accorded Vlach and Albanian warriors, whose leaders (Hunyadi, Skanderbeg) were capable of raising much greater armies than leaders in crop-growing regions.

A Chronicle of Demise

The state of the Serbian despots was restored after only five years of Ottoman rule (1439–44), which allowed the previous regime to be reestablished since the conquerors had not had time to implement fundamental changes. The Ottomans turned out not to be invincible, but, at the same time, the balance of power had not essentially altered. Internecine strife following the death of the young Hungarian king in

1444 further weakened the Christian powers. At first Murad II did not display greater hostility and even temporarily abdicated in 1446 before returning to power. This provided Despot Djuradj with a respite. He shared his rule with his youngest son Lazar, who married one of the cousins of the Byzantine emperor and was crowned despot in 1446. Djuradj's two older sons, released by Murad II in 1444, had been blinded and were thus unable to rule.

Djuradj was placed in a difficult position by a new attempt at a great offensive against the Turks, organized by Janos Hunyadi, governor of the Hungarian Kingdom. Hunyadi was backed by Alfonso of Aragon, ruler of southern Italy, who had ambitions toward the Hungarian throne. As the rival armies circled around the despot's territory, the site of the upcoming battle, Djuradj tried to remain neutral. When the Christian army was soundly defeated at Kosovo in October 1448, Hunyadi went into hiding and was finally captured by Djuradj, who demanded compensation for the damage caused to his land. He held Hunyadi captive until his son Ladislav was handed over as a hostage.

After Hunyadi's release, battles raged even more intensely in Hungary between the two groups of lords, one assembled around Hunyadi and the other around Count Ulrich of Cilli, Djuradj's son-in-law. The despot, whose property in Hungary had been ravaged, was also involved. The warring continued until the despot's death, and certainly hindered the Christians' defensive capabilities.

The enthronement of young Mehmed II (1451–81) changed the situation in the Ottoman Empire. He was dissatisfied with the former vassal relations, and sought to turn as many vassal states as possible into *sanjaks* (Ottoman military-administrative districts). The conflicts among the Christian nobles aided him in this respect. Djuradj was at war with the Bosnian king (1448) over Srebrenica and territories west of the Drina River. Stefan Vukčić Kosača, who had grown completely independent of the Bosnian king, pronounced himself *herzeg* ("Herzeg of St. Sava"), and attacked Dubrovnik in 1451 in an attempt to seize the Konavli region, which the city had purchased from its neighbors in 1419 and 1426. A coalition was forged against the *herzeg* which planned to purchase his land from the sultan for 50,000 ducats, while taking over his tributes. On the other hand, the Hungarian court, as Dubrovnik's patron, was drawn into the war. Even the *herzeg*'s older son and landed nobility from Hum, a district to the west of his state, rose against him. Peace was reached between the *herzeg* and his son in 1453, and with Dubrovnik in 1454, restoring the situation that existed before the war.

These petty squabbles and disputes, characteristic of earlier Balkan policies, exhausted the Turkish vassals while Mehmed II laid siege to Constantinople, which fell on May 29, 1453. Only fragments of the millennial Byzantine Empire remained in Trebizond and Morea (the Peloponnese), ruled by a minor branch of the Palaeologi family.

The despot's state and Bosnia were the first to meet the fate of Constantinople, and Mehmed II soon proved that he was not about to abandon his intention of conquering the remaining territories. Attacks followed every year. On hearing of the fall of Constantinople, Djuradj transferred all his moveable property to his estate in Hungary (Bečej on the Tisa River). A brief pause in hostilities with Hunyadi allowed him to join the campaign in 1454 when the Turks attacked Serbia and the Christians rose up in neighboring parts of Bulgaria.

An attack on southern Serbia followed in 1455, when Novo Brdo and other towns (Prizren, Peć, and Bihor near the Lim River) were besieged and captured. The land link with territories in Zeta was severed and they were subsequently controlled either by Venice or by its *voivoda* Stefan Crnojević, who founded a new dynasty of Zeta rulers. The following year, the sultan headed another expedition into Serbia: first toward Smederevo and then against Hungarian-ruled Belgrade, which was under siege until 22 July, 1456. Crusaders from European states came to the city's rescue. Reinforcements and supplies arrived by way of the Danube, where the Turkish fleet had previously been defeated in a great river battle. The resistance led by Hunyadi and the fanatic Franciscan friar Giovanni Capistrano thwarted the Turkish attacks. Even the sultan was wounded and withdrew his troops without a victory. The Christian triumph resounded far and wide. Then the plague struck the Christian army and Hunyadi and Capistrano succumbed. By the end of the year, the elderly Djuradj was also gone. In the meantime, fresh struggles erupted among Hunyadi's successors in Hungary.

After only a year, in 1458 another Turkish military expedition set out against Serbia. A succession of towns in the north, including Višeslav, Bela Stena, Resava, and Golubac, were seized. The despot's state was reduced to Smederevo and its vicinity and a belt of land along the Sava River, which could be administered from Belgrade. Despot Lazar died in January 1458, which deepened the crisis in the remaining territory. Two factions were influential in the court. One was in favor of the Turks and proclaimed as despot the commander Mihajlo Andjelović, whose brother was *beylerbeyi* (governor-general) of Rumelia under Mehmed II. The people of Smederevo prevented this coup along with the other faction, supported by Hungary. Andjelović was imprisoned and the blind Stefan Branković became ruler. Under the influence of the Bosnian and Hungarian kings, Stefan Tomašević, the son of Bosnian King Tomaš, was brought to Smederevo to marry the daughter of the late ruler Lazar and be enthroned as despot. The ceremony took place on March 21, 1459 but did little to diminish the threat, since the sultan chose Smederevo as his target that year. The city resisted the siege for a time, but surrendered on June 20, 1459 on condition that the young despot and his escort be allowed to leave the city.

The fall of Smederevo and the Turks' arrival at the Sava–Danube line symbolically represented the fall of the Serbian state, parts of which had been conquered long before (in the late fourteenth century), while some parts still retained a certain degree of independence. With Serbia conquered, the Ottomans were free to continue toward Bosnia and the Adriatic hinterland, which was not then on the main route of Turkish expansion.

There was a respite as expeditions were sent against other lands (Trebizond, Morea, and Wallachia), but in 1463 it was Bosnia's turn. On the one hand the sultan aided the rebel son of *herzeg* Stefan, while on the other he conquered towns ruled by the Pavlovićs and the Bosnian king. Stefan Tomašević, who had become king of Bosnia in 1461 and had previously surrendered Smederevo, was himself captured. On this occasion he was executed after giving the order for the forts to surrender to the Turks.

The fall of Bosnia in the spring of 1463 instigated an alliance between Hungarian King Matthias Corvinus (1458–90) and Venice, whose territories in Dalmatia were directly threatened. In the fall of 1463 Matthias entered Bosnia and by the year's end had conquered Jajce and other towns, including Zvečaj, Zvornik, and Teočak. *Herzeg* Stefan was able to reclaim his territory. Bosnia was seemingly restored with the coronation of Hungarian Lord Nikolaus Ujlaki (1471–7) as king. In 1464 the sultan led a new expedition, which regained control of a greater part of Bosnia. The country remained divided until the great Ottoman offensive of the early sixteenth century.

After these developments only the mountainous region on the coast was not under the control of the Ottomans, with the Albanians providing the greatest resistance under the leadership of George Castriota Skanderbeg. They were bordered by Ivan Crnojević (1465–90) and even *herzeg* Stefan, whose land was divided in a dispute between his sons. An expedition by one of the sultan's commanders in 1465 was enough to conquer most of the *herzeg*'s lands. The sultan's territory completely surrounded Dubrovnik, which had paid an annual tribute to the sultan since 1458. Isolated pockets of territory around the mouth of the Neretva River and the town of Novi remained free, from where attempts were made to extend and restore control of parts of the *herzeg*'s lands.

The greatest change took place in 1479 when the Turks captured the town of Skadar (Shkoder) and briefly controlled the land of Ivan Crnojević. The *voivoda* fled to Italy, but returned after the sultan's death

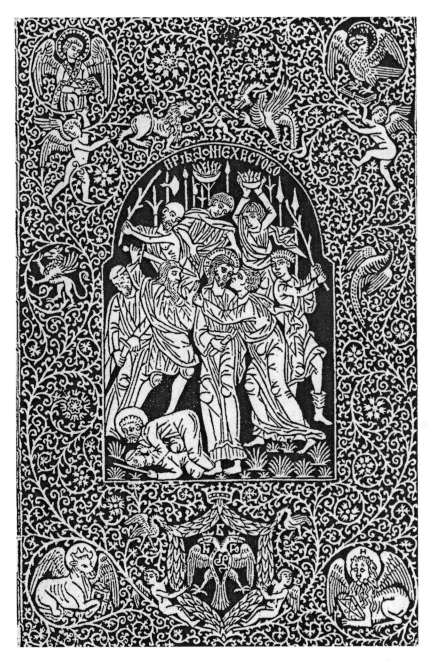

Plate 3.5 Illustrated page from the *Octoechos*, the first book printed in the Crnojević printing press (1494). (From the reprint *Oktoih prvoglasnik Djurdja Crnojevića 1494*, Cetinje, 1987)

in May 1481 and restored the state with the capital in Žabljak (present-day Rijeka Crnojevića), and in Cetinje from 1485. Since the town of Novi had been captured in 1481, the small territory ruled by Crnojević was the only one to remain free, except for Venetian lands. It even experienced a moment of glory in 1493 when Ivan's successor Djuradj (1490–6) obtained a printing press, which was used to print Cyrillic books necessary for the Orthodox Church service.

As was the case for previous rulers, family disputes made Djuradj Crnojević's position increasingly difficult. He was opposed by his brother Stefan, who joined forces with the Turks. When he felt directly threatened in 1496, Djuradj Crnojević abandoned Montenegro. Thus the last free territory of the former Serbian state ceased to exist. The coastal cities remained under Venetian rule: Kotor and Budva permanently, and Bar and Ulcinj until 1571.

4
The Sultan's Protected Subjects

The Old and the New

By the time the Ottomans vanquished the state of the Serbian despots their experience of administering conquered lands was already considerable. First they turned the territories into administrative units or sanjaks, whose names evoked the names of their former lords. Thus the southern part of Serbia, conquered in 1455, was registered as the "*vilayet of Vuk's land.*" The northern part, which was subjugated in 1459, included the territory west of the Drina River, along with Srebrenica, since it had belonged to the previous ruler, the Serbian despot. These administrative units were provisional and were only stabilized after the conquest was completed and the border moved further away. The permanent boundaries of lower-level administrative units – nahias and kazas – were established before those of larger areas and entire countries.

Although the Ottoman administration preserved some of the old names, many others have been forgotten. The name of Herzegovina, taken from the title of Stefan Vukčić Kosača (*herzeg*), only became common during the Turkish era; Bosnia's name was first preserved in the name of the sanjak, and later (1580) the Bosna pashalik. The case of Serbia was different; sanjaks on its territory were named after their towns. The most important was the Smederevo sanjak, even though the seat of the sultan's governor after 1521 was in Belgrade. Only much later, after its governor attained the rank of pasha, did the name of the Belgrade pashalik prevail. The name of Serbia and its borders was better preserved by increasingly active European cartographers than in the Ottoman administrative system.

The former territories of the Serbian despots were divided among the sanjaks of Vučitrn (derived from Vuk Branković's land), Kruševac (Alaça Hissar), and Prizren, in addition to the Smederevo sanjak. Some areas of the former state became part of sanjak seats outside Serbia: the Vidin sanjak in the north, the sanjaks of Sofia and Kyustendil in the east, Zvornik and Bosnia sanjaks in the west, and the Dukagjin sanjak in the south (after the fall of Skadar in 1479).

The Ottomans primarily took control of fortresses, administrative seats, courts, and former centers of power. Fortresses were occupied by Turkish garrisons; towns received appropriate administrative or judiciary officials, with their staff and servants. There were no migrations from Asia Minor, as was the case with the formerly conquered territories close to the Ottoman center. The network of lower-level nahias and kadiluks covered the earlier Serbian administrative units, the former *vlasti* (city territories ruled by a *voivoda* during the period of despots) or the even older *župas*, whose borders had been defined much earlier and with great precision because of the population's collective responsibility. In some cases the new territories corresponded to old ones, although often the names of fortresses or towns were imposed. In the first half of the sixteenth century the kadiluks of the Belgrade pashalik included Smederevo, Belgrade, Užice, Čačak and Niš. There were significantly more nahias, and their number continued to grow. A census taken in 1563 records that there were seventeen nahias in the Smederevo sanjak alone.

Turkish administration did not extend below these units; it did not reach the level of the village, where local chieftains remained. They were called different names: *protoger, knez, kmet, primićur* among the herdsmen, who were ranked beneath the *knez, subasha* (assistant to the sanjak-beg), and *voivoda*. It was their duty to collect taxes and return runaway *reaya* (peasants). This term originally referred to the entire working and dependent population, regardless of their religion, and was only later applied to subjugated Christians in the eighteenth century.

Everything that had been public property or had belonged to the ruler before the Turkish conquest was included in the sultan's *hass*, or source of income. Large estates with important economic resources were also established for sanjak administrators – the sanjak-beg – and were transferred from one official to another, along with the title. The remaining land and resources were distributed as *timars* and *ziamet* to warriors, sipahis, and lower-ranking officials.

During the first few years after the conquest sipahis occasionally included Christian nobles who remained on their land and assumed their usual responsibilities, their obligations matching those of the Muslim sipahis. Censuses (*defteri*), which were carried out immediately after occupation, provide information on the number and distribution of these Christian sipahis. The greatest concentration was in the Smederevo sanjak; in 1476 there were 64 Muslim *timar* holders and 85 Christians. The number varied in other sanjaks but, regardless of their distribution at any given time, Christian sipahis were a passing phenomenon and either died off or converted to Islam and were no longer distinguishable.

When Serbia was conquered, the Ottomans had already acquired and perfected a method of counting and recording everything at their disposal. The different censuses most often recorded revenues and provide a valuable insight into the distribution of the population, agricultural crops, sources of revenue, and so on. The most useful *defteri* contain a detailed count for every village of every head of a family and unmarried male and every widow caring for a household, while records on duties for the entire village are expressed in currency or other units representing payment in kind. Such censuses show the quantity of grain a village provided, how much comprised a tenth of the unfermented grape juice (the Ottoman administration ignored wine), a tenth of the bees, the amount of the swine tax, and so on. All this information has allowed scholars to conjecture the extent of expected production, but what remains unclear is how the duties were set and collected when annual harvests were uneven. It is also hard to explain the large discrepancies in average duties per household in neighboring villages of approximately the same size.

Most of the population, consisting of all those in the communities included in the *hasses* or *timars*, were taxed or provided mandatory labor depending not only on their personal status, but also on the status of the community. In the fifteenth century, peasants' duties were relatively equal throughout the empire: one-tenth of the grain and wine increased by the *salarye*, a 2.5 percent fee for the landlord, so the duties were actually one-eighth. A true tenth was given of other farm and agricultural products (millet, oats, lentils, linen, hemp, vegetables, beehives, and honey). Taxes were also applied on pigs and mills. The sipahi was paid the *ispenja*, amounting to 25 *akçe* per household, while the sultan was paid the *haraç* (*djizja*), a per capita tax, as well as a tax on sheep.

A different system was applied for cattle breeders as long as they enjoyed the status of privileged Vlachs. They paid one gold piece, a *filurya*, per household (thus the term *filuryçi*), and contributed sheep, cheese, tents, and rope. The *katun* was the fiscal unit, numbering 20 houses, and later 50 houses. The Vlachs provided soldiers, one for every five households, and one per household for raids and attacks on enemy territory.

The complex Ottoman military machine required a vast number of support services, such as craftsmen (cannon makers, gun makers, crossbow makers, blacksmiths, carpenters) and guards for roads (*derbendçi*), boats, river crossings, bridges, gorges, and mountain passes. These services were provided by local residents, who in return were exempted from paying some of their duties (usually the *haraç* and *ispenja*), or received the status of *filuryçi*. In garrisons the local population was also included in the temporary semi-military ranks of *akinçi* and *martolos*. In the mid-sixteenth century this privileged status was revoked, and everyone was placed in the same class as the *reaya*, except for the class of chieftains.

Mining towns underwent the least modification and were accepted with their organization and complex division of labor. As they were included in the sultan's *hass*, they were assigned emins or amils, supervisors or representatives, and later kadis, who monitored the accuracy and legality of their operations. Mining centers were badly damaged during wars in the mid-fifteenth century and the skilled population fled. Ottoman authorities sought to revive production and return it to its previous level to maintain the sultan's finances. A series of inspections was ordered by the state in 1488 to determine the condition of the mines and to decide measures to increase production and income.

The greatest novelty imposed by the Ottomans was the ban on gold and silver exports. Everything that was produced was to be delivered to the sultan's closest mint. This cut off trade and indirectly excluded merchants from the circle of mining entrepreneurs. Financiers and creditors disappeared, and the Turkish authorities demanded the introduction of the *saraf* (moneylender). Moneylenders were found among the Jewish people who had been driven out of Spain in the late fifteenth century and arrived in the Ottoman Empire in large numbers.

There were considerable changes in the upper echelons of society. While the lesser nobility could hold onto their property by accepting sipahi obligations, as noted above, dynasty members and high-ranking nobility either fled before the conquerors, such as the family of the last despot, or sought refuge on estates received as a sign of the sultan's grace, a long way away from the land they had once ruled. A special case in Serbia was that of Empress Mara (d. 1487), the daughter of Despot Djuradj Branković and former sultana, who was highly respected and remained on an estate centered in Ježevo (present-day Daphni near Mt. Athos). Her protection included not only relatives, such as her sister Cantacuzina and niece Jelena, but also some of the despot's commanders (Oliver Golemović, Toma Cantacuzinus). Others found sanctuary as monks in some of the Mt. Athos monasteries (Grgur Branković, *čelnik* Radič).

The religious activity of the once wealthy church was tolerated, along with its hierarchy, clergy, monastic life, and numerous institutions, and the faith of its believers was respected. The church was allowed to continue its mission, but under far more difficult circumstances, as will be discussed later. Church buildings were seized immediately after the capture of towns and cities and were adapted to the needs of the Muslim conquerors.

Flight, Migration, and Settlement

The great migrations that had begun earlier continued after the establishment of Ottoman rule in territories that had formerly been part of
the Serbian state. Many of these migrations cannot be traced through
documents, and we know of them only through their long-term consequences. They primarily included migrations northward, which increased
the population of regions furthest away from the direction of Turkish
expansion. Such movements were only rarely noted in documents. This
was the case of Kovin (Keve), the seat of the Hungarian comitat
(županija) on the left bank of the Danube, near Smederevo. Serbs had
reached Kovin earlier when they abandoned Serbian territory. When
Smederevo was besieged in 1439, the Kovin Serbs fled into the Hungarian interior and were allowed to settle on the uninhabited island of
Csepel, to which they gave the name of their previous settlement:
Ráczkeve, Srpski Kovin.

Prior to the final conquest of Serbia, the Turks often took inhabitants
as slaves, frequently to Asia Minor. After the battle of Nicopolis in 1396,
the Turks resettled the population of Szavaszentdemeter (Sremska
Mitrovica) in Brusa. During the great conquests they carried off a
large number of men and women as war booty. According to reports
by Franciscan monks in Constantinople, who kept track of the fate of
Christians transferred to Anatolia, more than 60,000 people were
taken from Serbia during 1438 alone. It is estimated that 160,000 people
were seized from southeastern Europe during two turbulent years of
war (1439–40), and estimates for the seven-year period between 1436
and 1442 total over 400,000. There were great losses during slave
marches: of the 7,000 people driven out of Serbia in 1440, 3,000 died
from cold or from animal attacks. Eastward migrations continued even
after the Balkan land had been conquered. The population of Ohrid was
moved to Constantinople in 1466, and the following year a similar
fate met the inhabitants of Novo Brdo. After the conquest of Belgrade
in 1521, a great mass of the city's population was taken to Constantinople, where the settlers' memory is recalled in the name of the nearby
Belgrade Forest.

When the border of the Ottoman Empire had become firmly established along the Sava and Danube rivers, a contest ensued for control
of the population rather than for territory. The Turks continued to raid
border areas and take people away. Hungarian King Matthias Corvinus
complained in a letter dated 1462 that during the previous three years,
200,000 people had been seized from his country. Realizing the damage
caused by these losses, he tried to reverse the situation following Turkish

methods. Each expedition into Turkish territory included plundering and deporting of the population.

King Matthias invited lords and warriors from Serbia. He granted them land and gave them important positions in his army, mostly in the light cavalry, a force consisting primarily of immigrants. Men who joined his service and later won recognition included Despot Vuk Grgurević, the grandson of Djuradj, brothers Jovan and Dmitar Jakšić, and Miloš Belmužević. After the death of Despot Vuk in 1485, the king summoned Djordje and Jovan, sons of the blind Stefan Branković, from Styria and appointed Djordje despot, a position to which Jovan later succeeded. The Branković estate was in Srem, centered in Kupinik, a town on the banks of the Sava.

The greatest migrations took place in the fall of 1480 and 1481, when the Hungarian king's army, combined with the Serb lords, crossed the Danube east of Smederevo and made its way to Kruševac. The army plundered everything in sight and deported 60,000 people to the Banat and Maros regions during the first expedition, and 50,000 people during the second. Reports mention long processions of wagons laden with families and their belongings, difficulties on the road because of bad weather, and technical problems in crossing the Danube.

Such operations changed the appearance not only of the regions where people settled, but also of those from which they were taken, as great gaps were left that needed to be filled. The population of the eastern Morava river basin that was deported had apparently been settled there several decades earlier to replenish a shortfall created by previous wars.

King Matthias was forced to justify the war migrations and seek forgiveness from the pope, since some of his commanders refused to take people as booty. In an effort to populate the barren border regions, the king requested that settlers be well treated and their faith respected. They had previously been exempt from paying church tithes. He also asked that spouses captured and taken away by the Turks be pronounced dead, so that those left behind could remarry and have children.

Another way to fill the space left behind by mass abductions is evidenced by the greatly increased numbers of Vlach cattle-farming communities reported in the census that surveyed parts of Serbia in the second half of the fifteenth century. They were registered in groups led by their chieftains – knez or primićur, who were supervised by the knez, subasha (assistant to the sanjak-beg), and voivoda. Mountain cattle-farming regions offered an inexhaustible supply of people for settlement or for military expeditions.

The situation observed during the half-century in which the border was maintained along the Sava and Danube rivers also applied to other border areas. Conquests near the Adriatic coast in 1474 and 1479 resulted in migrations overseas to southern Italy and in the enlargement of groups of refugees who had earlier fled hunger and the Turkish threat. Serbs created their own communities and brought their customs with them. The first verse folk epic (*bugarštica*) about Despot Djuradj and Janos Hunyadi was recorded in 1495 among Serbian refugees in the Apulian town of Gioia del Colle.

After the fall of Serbia most migrations were toward Bosnia, whose border became settled for a time in 1464. Bosnia had been divided between the Hungarians, who ruled Srebrenica banate in the northeast until 1512 and Jajce banate in western Bosnia until 1528, and the Ottomans, who controlled the central and mountainous regions inhabited by Vlach herdsmen.

Vlach groups moved within the territories ruled by the Ottoman Empire, filling the gaps created by war. They traveled from the Pavlović region (southeastern Bosnia) to central regions (Maglaj, Tešanj, Žepče), and only spread north of the Sava and northwest (the future Bosnian Krajina) after the fall of the two banates in 1512 and 1528. One family from the Banjani clan, which had spread south of Mt. Durmitor, left traces of its movement, a rare example of documented migration. While on Pavlović land (1485 and earlier) *knez* Šajko headed the family. The *knežina* registered near Maglaj in 1489 was ruled by Nole, the son of *knez* Šajko, and in 1516 his other son Njegovan was in the neighboring Ozren nahia with his group. On the other hand, it is known that the vicinity of the Teočak fortress was inhabited by the Rudinjani, also Vlachs from the herzeg's land.

There had been heavy westward migrations paralleling the coast some time earlier. In 1436, Croats, Vlachs, and Serbs appeared at the same time on part of Count Ivan Frankopan's estate on the Cetina River. The count extended the same privileges that his predecessor had offered to all three groups. Great changes in the Dalmatian hinterland occurred in the early sixteenth century, when in 1537 the Klis sanjak was formed during the Ottoman expansion. The Dalmatian hinterland and regions of Lika and Krbava then came under Turkish rule, and the barren regions were filled with a fresh wave of herdsmen.

Similar events to those that took place along the Sava and Danube were repeated on the new borders. Neighboring Christian lords and commanders of individual border defense regions sought to transfer the population to their side – often by force. The Habsburg commanders brought hundreds if not thousands of families from Bosnia, and later from parts of Croatia and Dalmatia, to the Christian side, and settled them on deserted Slovenian land along the border with Croatia in a great arch from Bela Krajina (the vicinity of Černomelj), across Žumberk and Vinica (west of Varaždin). Colonization continued from 1526 to well into the seventeenth century. Serbian communities were dotted about until the twentieth century, preserving memories of their origin.

These developments recurred when the border of the Ottoman Empire was moved significantly northward in the early sixteenth century with the conquest of Srem and Slavonia (1536). The colonization of herdsmen from southern and eastern regions was more extreme in regions where fighting persisted and where the effects of plundering were more severe. Thus the Požega valley was more heavily colonized than northern Slavonia, where the old population remained.

These migrations removed many of the cultural and religious barriers that had been established during previous centuries and created conditions for establishing new borders over time. Because of these mass movements, populations began to mix or be divided on the basis of religion. Not long after the settlers arrived, there was an explosion in the construction of Christian Orthodox monasteries. A significant proportion of the churches in present-day Herzegovina, which was under Christian rule and formed part of the Orthodox episcopates and metropolitanate, were only built under Ottoman rule. Some are small buildings with buttresses and distaff-shaped church towers, erected on commission by coastal craftsmen and modeled after old Catholic churches. Several larger monasteries were built for the needs of the hierarchy: Tvrdoš near Trebinje, Žitomislić by the Neretva, Zavala in Popovo Polje, and, deeper in the interior, the Holy Trinity in Pljevlja, Piva, and Nikoljac (in Bijelo Polje). The example of Herzegovina reveals that the immigrant Vlach herdsmen had greater religious zeal or economic power than their predecessors who lived there under Christian lords.

There is evidence that the monasteries of Tavna, Vozuća, Gostović (in southeastern Bosnia), Papraća (near Zvornik), Ozren (near Maglaj), Lomnica (in northeastern Bosnia), Moštanica, and Gomionica (near Banja Luka) existed in Bosnia in the first half of the sixteenth century, with Rmanj (Hrmanj) being the farthest to the west at the end of the century. Even though the order in which the monasteries were built cannot be determined from the scattering of early references, it is known that the most distant were built later during the sixteenth century. Serbian liturgical manuscripts were copied in Sarajevo (which was founded after the Turkish conquest) as early as 1520.

The Krka and Krupa monasteries (on rivers of the same name) in Dalmatia were part of the same wave, as was the Dragović monastery, whose monks were driven by famine to move to distant Baranja, where they founded the monastery of Grabovac (in present-day Hungary) in 1578. It is more difficult to distinguish between the monasteries in Srem that were built under Christian rule and those that were erected after the Ottoman conquests, since the earliest documents preserved make no mention of the time of their construction. It is certain that the monasteries of Obeda and St. Luke near Kupinovo were built by the Brankovićs soon after 1485, as was Krušedol (1509–16). It is highly likely that the Fenek monastery (near Zemun) dates back to the fifteenth century. A relatively large number of monasteries were constructed in a small part of Srem, which is why the Fruška Gora hills, with the monasteries of Jazak, Remeta Velika and Mala, Rakovac, Šišatovac, Grgeteg, Kuveždin, Divša, Vrdnik, Pribina Glava, and Karlovci, are compared to Mt. Athos. There is an incomparably smaller number of monasteries in Slavonia and Croatia (Orahovica, Lepavina, Pakra, Marča, Gomirje), all of which were founded after the Ottoman conquests, following the wave of colonization.

The original design can be distinguished in only a small number of churches, whose architecture was modeled after older monuments from the Morava and Raška schools (dating from the Nemanjić dynasty and time of the despots). Some of the new churches served as models for those that were constructed later. Earlier traditions in painting were also adopted as regards iconographic themes and artistic expression. Icon painting in particular was influenced by old monuments as well as by the Creto-Italian school in Orthodox regions that came in contact with Italian painting.

Serbs who were moved to the western side of the border between the Ottoman and the Habsburg empires in Croatia were incorporated in the Vojna Krajina (Military Border), established during the sixteenth century with centers in the recently founded Karlstadt (Karlovac, 1540) and Varaždin. Soldiers were settled on land that they worked, provided that a family member always remained in the military. The fiscal system and military service at the frontier favored the *zadruga* or extended family, which would remain a characteristic of the social structure for a significant portion of the Serbian people.

Northward migrations only became more substantial after 1541, when Buda finally fell and sanjaks, nahias, and kadiluks were founded on Hungarian territories up to the Tisa River. The taking of Banat (1551–2) completed the Empire's territories in the north. The extension to Gyulafehérvár (Alba Iulia) in Transylvania (1566) was crucial for Serbian migrations, since many Serbs who had migrated to the Banat and Moriš regions during the second half of the fifteenth century came under the sultan's rule.

Bačka had been colonized by herdsmen from mountain regions who had been encouraged by the state authorities, as was the case in previously conquered territories in the west. The Ottoman rulers, however, did not approve of colonizing Banat with settlers from the Smederevo sanjak, favoring people from Transylvania and Hungary instead. They believed their subjects crossed over to the Timişoara sanjak because the *haraç* there was paid per household, not per capita, and thus prohibited movement across the Danube.

There is little information about the churches in Bačka from a later period of habitation, the only references being to Bodjani monastery, near the Danube, and to Kovilj, where there was a Franciscan monastery. In Banate, as in Srem, a number of monasteries and churches were constructed during the period of Christian rule. Neither the early sources nor the architectural style is sufficient to distinguish between the two groups. There was Vojlovica monastery on the Danube, Hodoš and Bezdin near Arad, Mesić and Šemljug near Vršac, and the Partoš monastery near the present-day border with Romania.

The multiple migrations that took place from the end of the fourteenth to the end of the sixteenth centuries separated parts of the Serbian population from their regions of origin and dispersed them across a territory much greater than the vast medieval state at the peak of its expansion. Later developments would show that this expansion had been a mixed blessing. From a sparsely colonized territory in which their numbers were unevenly distributed, and where they were often mixed with other peoples, the great changes of the late seventeenth century brought them face to face with both spontaneous and planned colonization. They were thus isolated and marginalized, especially at the periphery. This disproportionate expansion also had much more far-reaching repercussions: the Serbs were unable to integrate their entire ethnic domain. Different parts of the nation found themselves in significantly different circumstances, and their development thus took diverging paths. This became apparent not only after the Ottoman rulers were driven back in the late seventeenth century, but also on several later occasions.

The Orientalization of Towns: Varos and Kasaba

The imposition of a homogeneous organization within the Ottoman Empire in the reign of Mehmed II the Conqueror (1451–81) eliminated many inherited differences, making Serbian regions equal to those territories in Bulgaria and Byzantium that had been conquered earlier. Regional and local differences were to emerge only during the rule of Suleyman I the Magnificent (1520–66). During the sultan's great development of the regulatory system, he laid down *kanuni* (laws) for individual sanjaks. It was then the practice for the population to cite old "laws" and "customs," which were occasionally allowed. Differences mainly applied to taxes and duties. Although this did not significantly

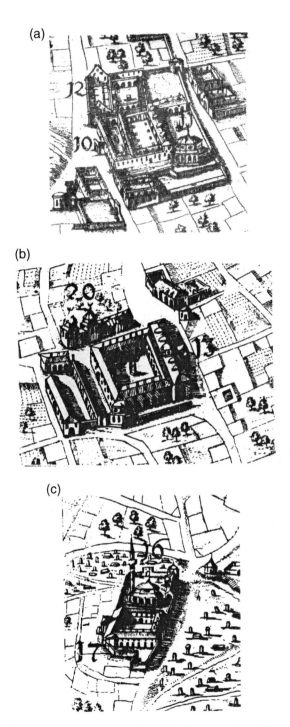

Plate 4.1 Ottoman buildings in Belgrade before 1688. (a) The vezir's palace; (b) karavan-saray and bezistan; (c) mosque with hospital. (From the plan made by Joan Baptist Gumpp, 1688, reprinted in *Beograd na planu iz 1688 godine*, Belgrade, 1978, by Narodna biblioteka Srbije)

influence the general status of the sultan's subjects, the maintenance of the old fiscal system in Hungarian territories induced people to move north, which emphasized some old differences while creating new ones.

Viewed from a distance and over a longer period, the Turkish regime seems unchanging, almost fossilized. Numerous institutions introduced during the conquests were still around in the wake of the first Serbian uprising of 1804. However, changes did occur and the regime showed the greatest interest in urban communities. The larger the town and the higher its rank in the Ottoman administrative and military hierarchy, the faster it changed, in terms of both its population and its urban characteristics. In addition to commanders and military personnel, administrators, judiciary officials, and Muslim holy men, the newly arrived conquerors brought servants and manpower, which made up the various parts of their organization, and were accompanied by the craftsmen needed to fulfill their specific requirements. These included places of worship, which were either quickly constructed or adapted from appropriated church buildings. Minarets began to punctuate the urban skyline, and mosques served to divide the town areas into mahallahs. Alongside the old Christian neighborhoods known as *podgradje* (*suburbium*) or *varos*, there arose mahallahs, which were named after places of worship.

In the first decades following the conquests, especially in the early sixteenth century, high-ranking officials founded pious endowments – *vakfs* – which most often consisted of a mosque and *medrese* (school of theology), *hammam* (public bath), and *imaret* (public kitchen for the poor). These institutions had their own organizational system with novices and reinforced the Islamic component of the community.

It was not only urban communities that changed under the new conquerors; their Christian populations came under the influence of increasing orientalization. Craftsmen were included in the traditional Ottoman system of *esnaf* (guild organizations). This is when the word entered the Serbian language, because there is no mention of guild organizations during the period of Serbian state independence. The Turkish *esnaf* took root in Balkan towns and had similar functions to guild organizations in European countries, being concerned with both working conditions and production and with the needs of the craftsmen and their families.

The urban population was exposed to greater temptation from islamization than others, and it is likely that conversion was more easily achieved in the town environment. This is the only explanation for the changes that occurred during the sixteenth century. What had once been a small Muslim core amid a largely Christian population turned into a small number of Christian mahallahs amid a greater number of Muslim ones. The increase in the Muslim share of the population and decrease in the Christian share are also confirmed by censuses, where families were polled rather than individuals, and by the layout of urban areas, where Muslim mahallahs took the lion's share.

The urban inheritance that the Turks encountered upon their arrival consisted of several types of settlements, primarily old cities from ancient and Byzantine times, whose precedence had already been established (Belgrade, Smederevo, Kruševac, Priština, Niš, Vučitrn, Prizren, Užice, Čačak). These cities were not all the same size and did not develop equally. Their role and significance was reflected in the rank they received: şeher, for large cities, and kasaba for more modest towns. The coastal towns, which had formed an important group of settlements from the previous period, either did not come under direct Ottoman rule, such as Kotor and Budva, or else lost their urban features after 1571 when they were brought under Turkish control, such as Bar and Ulcinj. At the same time they lost their populations, their distinctive social structure, and even their economic function.

Under Ottoman rule, the discrepancies increased between administrative seats, which had been founded early on, and mining markets, which had broken free of the general developmental trend on account of their distinctive features. Since free trade and exports were prohibited, the Ottoman authorities were keen to revive mining production so that silver would flow to the sultan's mints. Efforts to revitalize production are shown by the aforementioned survey of 1488 on the condition of the mines and measures to be taken as well as in regulations that date from the period of Suleyman the Magnificent (1536).

The characteristics of mining and the complexity of the production process required expertise at many levels, ranging from operations in the pits and foundries, to organization and supervision, to dispute resolution. The Ottoman authorities only made appointments at the highest levels: emins or amils, landlords and caretakers, to manage and collect the revenue, and kadis to supervise these authorities and ensure legality. Other workers were found in the places they were required. Mining law and organization, not only at the mine but also within mining communities, were preserved along with the workers' expertise. This is apparent from the Saxon Laws (kanun-i-Sas) that were passed during Suleyman's reign, which are literally based on mining regulations from Despot Stefan's Novo Brdo Code of 1412. Under Turkish rule, the laws were codified for Kratovo, Novo Brdo, and Srebrenica and their regulations were passed on to other mines, regardless of whether they were of old or recent foundation. Mining communities had their own administration headed by a knez and assembly, which resolved difficult cases, while hutmans and urbarars dealt with lesser disputes.

The Ottomans managed to revive work in the larger mines that had not been exhausted, such as Novo Brdo, Trepča, Srebrenica, Rudnik, and

Plate 4.2 Economic continuity: mining elders on a sixteenth-century miniature in the codex with the Code of Mining Law (1412). (From a manuscript in the Arhiv Srpske akademije nauka i umetnosti, Belgrade, with permission)

the Kopaonik complex consisting of Plana, Zaplanina, Belasica, and Koporić. They even founded new mines such as those at Sase, near Srebrenica, and Siderokapsa, near Mt. Athos. During this period mines in eastern Serbia (Kučajna, Majdanpek) began operating, while those in the Drina region lost importance. The growth in mining under Suleyman can be compared to the period of expansion in the first half of the fifteenth century. The extent of the Turkish administration's involvement was to determine which villages should provide charcoal. Sometimes they resettled miners in order to develop mining in locations where ore had been discovered. On one such occasion miners from the Rudnik mine in Šumadija were moved to Kamengrad in the Bosnian Krajina. The Ottoman army's huge need for iron redirected some of the former silver mines to iron production. Many smaller mines were opened and *samokovs* (tilt hammers) were used for forging the metal. Some of the mining towns, such as Rudnik, provided cannonballs for the Turkish army.

The mining towns were not islamized to a great extent. Since they provided steady revenues and employment as well as relative security, dignitaries of the Serbian Orthodox Church sought sanctuary there, although they had avoided them during the period of Christian rule. The following towns are mentioned in Turkish records as forming episcopal seats or parts of bishoprics: Novo Brdo, Janjevo, Rudnik, Belasica, Kratovo, Srebrenica, Zaplana, Majdanpek, and Samokov (in present-day Bulgaria). Modest Catholic parishes also survived in mining communities and came under the jurisdiction of the Bar archbishops, who carried out visitations and left records of the condition of their flock.

Mining towns were not immune from the effects of the great crisis that shook the empire in the late sixteenth century, one of whose striking features was high inflation. In the seventeenth century there was also a change in the relative importance of certain mines: some that had been less lucrative became important sources of income, while old and prominent mines, such as Novo Brdo and Trepča, lost their prominence. Mining communities did not survive the war of 1683–99.

In general, urban communities stood out from their rural surroundings during the period of Turkish rule. Their unequal economies and the different status enjoyed by the population were now joined by the religious context: urban communities were the centers of islamization, which directly influenced the general cultural ambiance. Toward the end of the Ottoman reign, Christians all together are thought to have comprised one-third of the town inhabitants. They were stereotyped as "they [who] wear Turkish clothes and live by Turkish customs," and furthermore "they are not counted among the Serbian people" (Vuk Karadžić).

Those who converted to Islam were even more decisively excluded. They were perceived simply as Turks and Serbs "of the Muslim faith" were considered an impossibility until well into the nineteenth century. The reason for their identification with the Turks derived from the cultural differences that came with conversion. Starting with their birth and the names given them, all the way to their burial ceremonies, their lives differed in terms of their surroundings, clothing, eating habits, moral instruction, and social status. These differences were emphasized by their attitude toward the state and historical tradition. Those who had taken up Islam pledged loyalty to the sultan and could not revere the anti-Turkish traditions inherited from their ancestors.

Economic Life

Changes in land ownership that resulted from Turkish rule had no direct bearing on agriculture as far as agrarian techniques or crops were concerned. However, certain shifts were noted over time, primarily the establishment of livestock breeding and the partial allocation of fields for pasture. These changes were fostered by the settlement of herdsmen in predominantly agricultural regions. This general trend contributed more to reducing the number of vineyards than did the negative view of wine and alcohol held by the Muslim authorities.

Regions populated by Serbs within the vast Ottoman Empire were increasingly exposed to influences from the East, including the influx of previously unknown crops. The conquerors brought with them different eating habits, in which rice played a significant role. Rice growing was introduced in Macedonia, which had been subjugated earlier, and spread from there northward to the Niš region and the Morava river basin, and subsequently to the Banat region, which was marshy and suitable for rice cultivation. The production of rice was extended by *orizari*, a category of skilled farmers who enjoyed privileged status. Nevertheless, rice production did not take hold permanently outside Macedonia. Since local production was small, trade was important, and rice formed a sizable component of cargos transported by boat between Belgrade and Buda in the late sixteenth century. This is the period when "rice for the poor," or *tarana*, appeared, a coarse wheat-flour dough that was used instead of rice.

Commercially valuable plants arrived in Serbia at this time from the East, although they originated from the New World. Innovations were not introduced from the West, as they were to be in the eighteenth century and after, but came via port towns and coastal regions of the Ottoman Empire, which maintained links with Mediterranean ports where boats arrived from America.

Vegetable crops, such as beans, tomatoes, and peppers, would later become highly significant, but at this time they had no economic value outside of households and family sustenance. There may have been greater cultivation of the "Turkish pepper," inherited along with its name *papar* (paprika), in the plains of southern Hungary, where it was to become more important in the eighteenth century and from where it spread to other European countries.

A similar route, from the West by way of the East, was taken by the "Turkish grain" – corn (*kolomboć, carevica*) – a new plant that was grown for ornamental purposes as well as for its healing properties, and which offered great potential for revolutionizing nutrition. This is understandable bearing in mind that, on average, four grains of wheat were harvested for every grain that was sown. Documents from the late Middle Ages reveal that a harvest of 10 to 12 grains was considered good, although it was rarely achieved. Just one ear of corn, however, contained more than a hundred grains, and one plant bore a number of ears. Ottoman authorities exempted the new crop from payment of the tithe, but even this did not help it spread and play a greater role in the nutrition and expansion of the population. This only occurred in the eighteenth century when authorities made additional efforts to extend the crop. Cotton or *bambak*, an old crop grown in Byzantium, arrived in Serbian regions and was used for handmade products. Its cultivation in the European part of the Ottoman Empire began relatively late and did not extend north of Macedonia.

Regions inhabited by Serbs occupied a peripheral position in the Ottoman Empire. Additionally, they had inherited trade relations with regions that remained outside Turkish control. During certain periods before the peak of Turkish expansion, these links were facilitated by Serbs who had migrated across the Empire's borders.

Two main trade routes remained from the Middle Ages: one linked the interior of the Balkan Peninsula to the coastal towns and the Mediterranean, while the other made its way toward Central Europe through Hungary. Both remained active during the period when the whole Balkan Peninsula formed part of the Ottoman Empire. The Mediterranean route was more frequently traveled during the Middle Ages, but it gradually gave way to the Pannonian route to Central Europe, which continued on toward the rest of Europe.

Trade between the interior and the coastal cities, with Dubrovnik still predominant, underwent a structural transformation following the ban on silver and gold exports introduced by the new authorities. The most valuable and profitable commodities had become inaccessible, so all merchants had to return to traditional livestock goods, forestry products, and cottage industry, which some of them had never abandoned.

Dried meat, cheese, and different types of hide (cow, sheep, and goat), either rawhide or processed, were procured in the interior and transported to the coastal regions, from where they were shipped to Italy. The hides were destined for Venice and Ancona. Certain kinds were recognized for their quality and price, such as hides from fine sheep (montonini), lambskin suitable for parchment, and especially cordovan, goatskins tanned and dyed according to a Turkish method Furs – rabbit, marten, fox, squirrel, and lynx – were also exported, but in much smaller quantities. Just as in the Middle Ages, beeswax was a significant export, in both forms – raw yellow and processed white. Salt remained the main import, followed by textiles, primarily Italian, while Flemish cloth was replaced by English, especially the less expensive kersey; craftwork, medicines, and spices arrived by land through Turkish intermediaries.

This vast single market, with free trade guaranteed by the payment of an annual tribute to the Porte by the Republic of Dubrovnik, allowed the Ragusans to expand their business over a much greater area that included Bulgaria along with Bosnia and Serbia, as well as territories conquered in Hungary. There were Ragusan communities not only in Sofia and Belgrade, but also in Timişoara and Buda. During this period merchants from Dubrovnik made their way to smaller settlements, where they linked local people into a network of suppliers and agents.

As early as the second half of the fifteenth century, trading was established along the frontiers between Hungary and the Ottoman Empire during periods of truce and peace. The right to trade across the borders was also confirmed by later treaties. Imports still consisted of craftwork and textiles, while exports went toward Austria and beyond. Livestock reached all the way to Germany and France.

Items produced in Serbian regions joined goods from the central areas of the Ottoman Empire. Serbian merchants formed only one part of those who maintained trade; a greater role was played by Jews, Armenians, and Greeks, and often also by Tzintzars (Aromani), who were considered Greeks. All shared the same *esnafs* with local Muslims, who were considered Turks, until the seventeenth century, when organization began to be differentiated along confessional lines. Belgrade prospered most from trade to the north and west, being at the finishing point of the Constantinople road and at the beginning of the Belgrade–Buda waterway.

Traffic thrived once the middle course of the Danube became an interior Ottoman transport route, but because of the lack of technical progress it quickly became a bottleneck. In mountain regions and along routes to the coast, cargo was still transported by pack animals, joined in caravans. Oxcarts played a greater role in open country. Specialized crafts appeared, such as *rabaçi* (derived from Turkish *araba* = cart), along with *kiriçi*, and sometimes they were grouped into entire settlements. The vast unbroken area in which merchants could move freely, with its efficient authorities and absence of numerous taxes, was certainly an advantage brought by the Ottoman regime. However, this advantage started to fade in the late sixteenth century with the increase in highway robbery and banditry, especially during times of war.

Over time the Ottoman Empire lost another important economic advantage: its monetary system based on the silver *akçe* (called asper in Europe, previously used as Byzantine and Serbian coinage). At the end of the fifteenth century the ducat was worth 45 *akçe*; in the mid-sixteenth century it was worth 60, while in 1585 it went from 110 to 120 *akçe*. In the seventeenth century gold coins were withdrawn from circulation and replaced by large foreign silver currency. Monetary disturbances burdened the population and had serious consequences on all aspects of life, including army provisioning and merchants' trading conditions.

Clans and Clan Society

As well as emphasizing the contrast between towns and rural areas, the Ottoman rulers reinforced the disparity between farming regions and mountainous cattle-breeding areas. The great majority of the farming population had the status of *reaya* and were obliged to serve their lord, while most of the population in cattle-breeding areas enjoyed a privileged position for some time and preserved their traditional internal organization. In the inaccessible mountainous regions, the Turkish system of government developed a distinctive form, primarily due to the absence of sipahi as the direct lords.

Vlachs from cattle-breeding regions were registered and required to pay a ducat as a form of tax and service. Often they were moved in groups under their chieftains, who were recognized by the Turks as lords of their people. Sometimes the chieftains received *timars*; and even when they were not formally recognized as sipahi, they had the greatest power and influence because of the patriarchal obedience they were owed according to the Vlachs' traditional organization. *Voivode, knezovi*, and *primićuri* were on the the lowest, albeit influential, rungs of the Ottoman administrative hierarchy.

From the sparse records available, it is known that the descendants of the native Balkan population, the Vlachs and Albanians, both lived in compact ethnic communities along with Slav peasants on the territory of their *župas*. The need for pasture compelled them to spread out over vast areas. They maintained winter quarters in the valleys and retreated there once the mountain pastures where they spent most of the year with their herds became inaccessible. As they moved away from their native region, their many branches took on the language of the Serbian environment, as shown by the names given to groups and individuals. In some places slavicization took place early on, while in others it happened later or not at all, as evidenced by the present-day Albanians, Vlachs, and Tzintzars (Aromani).

The Paštrović clan (derived from *pastor*, shepherd) settled in the Kučevo *župa* (near Budva) in the second half of the fourteenth century and developed into an aristocratic community that remained there for centuries. This process of settling and integration with the local population was repeated many times over the next century. Indeed, sizable areas of Herzegovina were named Gornji Vlasi (Upper Vlachs) and Donji Vlasi (Lower Vlachs).

Segregation policies were included in royal charters from the fourteenth century declaring that "a Serb shall not marry a Vlach," but they were unsuccessful. The consequences of intermarriage and assimilation were uneven: in some places the Slav side tilted the scale, and in others it was the Romanic or Albanian. The need for warriors, especially horsemen, increased the Vlachs' importance and pulled them out of their marginal position. During the internal struggles in Serbia after the fall of Dušan's state, and especially during the wars against and alongside the Ottomans, Vlach warriors took over the role that had earlier been assumed by the nobility.

During the period of the independent state, some areas, such as Mt. Durmitor, the Jezero region, Sjenice, and the territory along the route to Ras, were considered to be Vlach. According to the Turkish census of Herzegovina from 1477, differentiations still existed and some villages were registered as being "in the possession of Vlachs," while others, mostly deserted, were listed as "Serb settlements." During migrations under Ottoman rule, vast mountainous regions became Vlach territories, controlled by *katun* organizations and their chieftains.

Former *katuns* began to be called clans (*plemena*). In the old Serbian vocabulary, the word *pleme* did not denote a large group or the core of a people, but rather an extended family. References to the Nemanjić clan implied the entire assembly of descendants, while the Kosača clan, which was mentioned in the fifteenth century, included only four houses. The change of terminology, from *katun* to clan, also marks a phase in the slavicization of the native Balkan population and shows a desire to climb the social hierarchy. The ruling class took on the previous titles of *voivoda* and *knez*. An elementary English dictionary compiled in Constantinople explained to sixteenth-century travelers that *knez* denoted an earl, while *katunar* was a lord.

Shifting population groups led to changes in the names of towns and regions. In some places the name of the *župa*, the old territorial unit, was used for the clan, such as the Piva and Morača clans. The more frequent case was to fit the *župa* into the clan's territory or for the *župa* to be covered by it. The *župa* and town of Onogošt is a typical example; it was renamed Nikšić after the Nikšići Vlachs, who only appeared in the mid-fifteenth century.

Clan regions were in constant turmoil. Aside from long-term clans, there were also short-lived tribes, parts of which would sometimes migrate elsewhere, while the remainder died out or became assimilated into another clan. Important testimony about the world of the clans from the late sixteenth century can be found in a letter to the pope sent by Damjan and Pavle, two monks from the Mileševa monastery, explaining "what is Serbia." The clan territories of a dozen chieftains (four *voivode*, one *knez*, and the rest untitled) are cited, extending from the Adriatic coast to the Lim River. In addition to the familiar old *katuns* of the Banjani, Drobnjaci, and Ridjani, and old *župa* names and regions (Dračevica, Trebinje, Rudine, Piva, and Gacko), new clan organizations were included, such as Plana, Nikšići, Kolašinovići, and Vraneši. Neighboring Montenegro had its own clans (Vasojevići, Bjelopavlići, Piperi, Njeguši, etc.), as did Dukagjin, with Albanian tribes. Beyond this zone of clans were monasteries and mines in the interior representing the former core of the state, while northern Serbia also remained outside this general picture.

The actual self-government of clan territories provided room for the development of legal customs previously repressed by state authorities. Numerous suppressed beliefs, superstitions, and rituals of pagan origin came to the fore as the direct influence of the church declined, owing to the small number of clergy, insufficient means for their education, and difficulties in maintaining the parish network. Levels of literacy were also lower than they had been during the period of the medieval state. Scarce documentation left by the clans reveals the mechanism of blood feuds and settlement of disputes operating within families as well as between entire brotherhoods. Old institutions and practices were reestablished, such as the secret witness (*sok*), the ordeal (*mazija*), proof of origin (*svod*), and the jury (*porota*). The attitude toward the legal heritage of the Serbian state is characteristic. While Dušan's Code was maintained and adapted in smaller autonomous communities under Venetian rule where there was a continuity of institutions and legal traditions, for example Grbalj and Paštrovići, there was no trace of Dušan's laws being applied among the clans.

The degree of autonomy of the clan societies enabled them to disassociate themselves from their surroundings and preserve their seclusion, reaffirming a rigid organization based on genuine or fictitious blood relations. Solidarity and reciprocity governed these societies, in which women were forced to submit to their husbands, the young to their elders, and clan members to their chieftains. This behavior was enforced by an unwritten code, and social control in the form of "public opinion" was very effective.

It was also among the clan environment that much of "folk culture" developed, for example handmade products, style of decoration, poems, songs, dances, and different ways of passing on tradition. Efforts to seek the ancient Slav heritage in this patriarchal culture, which also included the ancient Balkan culture, would be futile as centuries of symbiosis preceded its creation.

Plate 4.3 Inventing state tradition: coat of arms ascribed to Emperor Stefan Uroš (1355–71) in the *Illyrian armorial* produced in Bosnia between 1555 and 1595. The copy shown here is dated 1603. (From the Belgrade codex of the *Illyrian armorial*, with permission of the Muzej primenjene umetnosti, Belgrade)

Clan societies energetically fostered views of the past, but in distinctive ways: first through the family, brotherhood, and clan genealogy, then in epics describing the heroic deeds of their contemporaries and ancestors, and finally in the accounts of crucial events. Migrations carried tales of the battle of Kosovo, Kraljević Marko, and other folk heroes far beyond the regions where they originated. Individuals as well as the entire class of chieftains claimed descent from the old nobility. This shaped their relations with the church and they were portrayed as new patrons. In the writings of sixteenth-century humanists on the coast, the *katunari* bestowed their daughters on kings. The coats of arms of certain *katuns* are even included in the great heraldic collection ("Ilirski grbovnik") created in Bosnia in the late sixteenth century.

Church in Slavery

With the fall of the Serbian state, the Serbian Orthodox Church was deprived of the protection and support of the Christian ruler and the nobility. It became impoverished and was forced to adapt to its altered circumstances, continuing its mission with immeasurably smaller means and greatly limited freedom of action. The conditions for its survival were indeed less favorable, but they cannot be described by a short and simple formula. They were neither unbearable nor favorable thanks to the tolerance and indifference of the Ottoman rulers.

Daily church life was not defined solely by the traditional Islamic attitude toward great monotheistic religions; those who advocated tolerance derived their arguments from the same traditions as those who at other times were bent on exterminating Christianity and its places of worship. Tolerance was undoubtedly reflected in the general policy of allowing *zimi* (subjects protected by the sultan) to practice their faith and their holy men and high priests to take care of their spiritual needs, as prescribed by their religions. However, from the very beginning, numerous restrictions were imposed on the life of the Christians, indicating their slavery. All archpriests, who were canonically appointed, had to receive the sultan's decree, the *berat*, allowing them to perform their duties; in addition, they were required to pay the *peshkesh*, a permit tax (in the event of any change in sultan or dignitary), and the *kesim*, an annual levy from congregational proceeds. The *peshkesh* for the Peć patriarchs in the seventeenth century was 100,000 *akçe*, which was equivalent to the annual amount of other levies.

Churches were appropriated and transformed into mosques, especially in larger towns and fortresses. The construction of new churches was not permitted, but dilapidated or crumbling churches could be repaired under certain conditions and with official approval. Church bells could not be rung. Political factors undoubtedly influenced relations toward Christian churches and their hierarchies. Greater leniency was shown during the period of Ottoman expansion and conquest than later on, when the mighty Empire was completed and consolidated. One of the rules of Islamic tradition held that churches would be preserved if a town surrendered, and that they were to be appropriated if it was taken by the sword. Constantinople was defeated after a lengthy siege, yet Sultan Mehmed II spared most of the churches and allowed the ecumenical patriarchate to carry on its duties. One of his successors had to use witnesses to claim that Constantinople had surrendered in order to preserve the Christian churches from attacks by militant Muslim clerics. This inconsistency in central government was even more obvious at the local level, especially in the reconstruction and erection of new churches. Prohibited in principle, dozens of churches were nonetheless built in regions settled by Serbs during Turkish rule.

Certain Serbian eparchies were included in the Ohrid archiepiscopate, whose seat was captured by the Ottomans early on. The fall of Constantinople in 1453 was a significant turning point in the lives of the Balkan Christians. As well as allowing the ecumenical patriarchate to function, Mehmed II the Conqueror installed Gennadios Scholarios as patriarch, appointing him head of all Christians in the Empire.

The Serbian patriarch's flock soon joined the ranks of the sultan's "protected ones," between 1455 and 1459. The demise of the Serbian despots' state brought an end to the autocephalous framework, and after the death of Patriarch Arsenije II in 1463, the issue of the composition of the synod that appointed the head of the Serbian Church was inevitably raised. There were no longer any state borders and parts of the church had previously been separated and joined to the Ohrid archiepiscopate. The Serbian patriarchate had undeniably ceased to exist. This is evidenced both by the lists of Serbian patriarchs and by the designation of Patriarch Makarije after 1557 as *restorer* of the Serbian Church throne. However, because of the scanty sources, it is impossible to determine when the patriarchate collapsed; according to some, it happened soon after the Ottoman conquest ca. 1463, while others claim that it took place in the first half of the sixteenth century. Some say that the territory of the patriarchate of Peć was subordinate to the Ohrid center, while others maintain that they were all subordinate to Constantinople.

Around 1525, citing the charters and traditions of his church, Ohrid Archbishop Prohor renewed the autocephalous archiepiscopate, which included the entire Serbian Church. The Serbian priests objected to this. Pavle, the metropolitan of Smederevo, pronounced himself patriarch and was able to thwart the Ohrid archbishop's pretensions. However, Prohor was released from imprisonment and assembled the synod in 1540; Pavle was defeated and forced to adhere to the synod's decisions.

Troubles dating from this period demonstrate that the unity of the Orthodox Christians within the Constantinople patriarchate was not maintained; autocephaly was restored even under the sultan's rule. The next step occurred in 1557 when the Herzegovina metropolitan became the patriarch of the renewed Peć patriarchate, owing to the fact that he

Map 4.1   The Serbian patriarchate of Peć, ca. 1640.

Plate 4.4   Ecclesiastical continuity: the patriarchate of Peć restored in 1557. (Photograph by B. Strugar)

was a relative of the grand vizier. Large portions of the former Hungarian kingdom had been captured by this time and were difficult to rule from Constantinople, especially as they were mostly inhabited by Serbs.

The renewed patriarchate immediately adapted its system of eparchies to the changed distribution of the Serb population. By this time the greatest wave of migration was coming to an end. In forming its new eparchies the patriarchate followed administrative borders within the Ottoman Empire. This is apparent in the episcopates named after Hungarian towns and those that match the names of the sanjaks. Eparchial seats in the new territories in the north did not have the permanence that characterized the old eparchies. Contemporaries claimed that the patriarchate had 42 eparchies, and that during the time of Patriarch Pajsije (1614–47) the number dropped to 33. The vast area under the patriarch's jurisdiction included three Bulgarian eparchies and spread to Transylvania in the north, Buda and Pécs in the northwest, and almost to Zagreb[1] and Dalmatia in the west.

Ottoman authorities adopted a stricter attitude toward the Catholic Christians here as well as in the Holy Land, Constantinople, and on the Greek islands. The pope was the head of the sultan's enemies; Catholic prelates were obedient to him and thus were not allowed to work in the Ottoman Empire. Catholics were regarded as parishioners of the Orthodox priests, who paid taxes to the sultan on their behalf, thus enabling them to maintain their spiritual life. The Bosnian Franciscans had the largest congregation, regarded by the Porte as members of the "Church of Latin holy men in the sanjaks of Bosnia, Klis, and Herzegovina." There were also Catholics in mining parishes and in regions settled by Albanians, who were under the jurisdiction of the archbishop of Bar.

Catholic priests were not persecuted in principle, nor were they prevented from performing their religious services, but they were not granted the sultan's decree and formal permission to work, and even the usual tax was not collected from them directly. The role of mediator played by the Serbian archpriests led to complaints and disputes over the collection of taxes from Catholics, over whom the Serbian clerics had no spiritual authority, a fact that was confirmed by rulings of the Turkish judiciary. It is certain that there were cases of abuse, but not a single source mentions an "immense conversion of Catholics to the Orthodox faith." Similar problems occurred on the Aegean islands and in Constantinople itself, in fact, wherever there were Catholics.

The church suffered great material losses. Some monasteries initially retained part of their property, while some had to perform falconry duties in order to keep them. The estates of others were seized immediately after occupation and handed over to warriors. The census of the *timars* in the Skadar sanjak, conducted in 1485, includes not only villages mentioned in the charters of Dečani, Holy Archangels, and Žiča, but also churches and small monasteries that had once been included in the patriarchate's estate. Church property also suffered greatly in the general confiscation that took place at the beginning of the reign of Selim II (1568–9). Monks were granted priority in the purchase of confiscated

---

1   In the seventeenth century this westernmost eparchy (based in the Marča monastery near Ivanićgrad) bore the unusual name of Vretania, after Britain, which was included in the title of the Serbian patriarch.

property. However, this required large sums of money that had to be borrowed, and the church struggled for decades to repay its debts.

Monasteries and churches were forced to change their financial structure completely. Instead of relying on a small number of immensely wealthy sponsors and patrons, they turned to a large number of smaller benefactors and donors. This was achieved by the diligent collection of church taxes and charity, known as collecting for later prayers. Followers were registered in *pomenici* (necrologies) so that prayers would be said for their souls during monastery liturgies. Large-scale exploitation of vast church estates came to an end and was replaced by rational economizing on the small pieces of land that remained.

Despite the loss of church property and other difficulties, archpriests and priests continued to make endowments and invest in building, renovating, painting, and maintaining churches and monasteries, probably with the help of lay relatives from their locality. Powerful and wealthy patrons were sought among the remaining Christian nobility in Wallachia, Moldavia, and increasingly in Russia. Russian rulers made donations to Chilandar and other monasteries, just as the Serbian despots had earlier presented gifts of silver or land to the Greek monasteries on Mt. Athos. Monks took some of their treasures and sacred objects to foreign courts. However, the greatest support and aid came from their compatriots. References to contributions and donations are included in inscriptions regarding church construction and repairs, in notes on the financing of paintings, and on commissions for manuscripts and holy items. There is also mention of clan chiefs and sipahi, warriors in the sultan's service. After the restoration of the patriarchate, major benefactors came from clans and clan societies, who were also members of the hierarchy.

Contemporary sources reveal that the Serbian Orthodox Church continued its mission regardless of its unfavorable position. The greatest expansion of monasteries was observed in newly colonized regions in Bosnia, Slavonia, Dalmatia, and Banat, as has already been mentioned. It was not only individual monasteries that were founded but entire groups, or small "holy mountains," such as the Ovčar-Kablar monasteries in the gorges of the Western Morava, the Fruška Gora monasteries in Srem, and the Jašunje monasteries near Leskovac.

An important part of the church mission depended on holy books, which were inherited but whose stocks had to be constantly replenished. This task was facilitated by the introduction of printing, which arrived in Montenegro via Venice on the initiative of *voivoda* Djuradj Crnojević. The Crnojević printshop had a brief period of activity between 1493 and 1496, when it published five church service books (Oktoih I and II, a Psalter, a Book of Gospels, and a prayer book). Its work was continued in Venice by merchant *voivoda* Božidar Vuković, who published a number of editions between 1519 and 1538. His repertoire was broader and included educational works as well as liturgical books. A number of printing presses operated within monasteries – Goražde, Rujno, Gračanica, Mileševa, Mrkšina Crkva, and one in Belgrade owned by a merchant from Dubrovnik – but all were short-lived and only published one or two books. Widespread poverty restricted the market and provided unsuitable conditions for efficient printing.

Manuscripts that were written in this period reveal that the level of literacy was maintained. The number of places where copying work was carried out was on the increase. Most of this work involved liturgical books, but a large number of miscellaneous codices appeared on assorted subjects, along with older literary works. Some very important medieval works were preserved because of copies from this period. The manuscript heritage contained newer translations from the Greek, as well as the adaptation of texts from other Slav literatures.

The continuity of native genres is apparent in biographical writings, whose subjects were drawn from the last members of the Branković family (Angelina, Maksim, Jovan) as well as local martyrs (Djordje of Kratovo) from the early sixteenth century. After a long intermission, in his *Life of Emperor Uroš* Patriarch Pajsije (1614–49) sought to connect this ruler to the uninterrupted line of Serbian history. Pajsije's work started with the Nemanjić ancestry and continued to the author's time, with Uroš's life representing only one episode. The author himself reveals his larger ambition: "it was my desire to understand and learn this: whence the Serbs originated, and for what purpose."

Preoccupation with historical themes was accentuated in the further development of genealogies (*rodoslovi*) and chronicles (*letopisi*), and their incorporation into texts that historically linked Nemanja's time to that of the compiler or his continuators. Chronicles were translated into Greek, and in the eighteenth century into Latin. The *Chronograph* arrived from Russia, with a survey of general history including the Russians, Bulgarians, and Serbs, and was continued and revised to include events from Serbian history.

As time passed, copying work declined. In the seventeenth century Patriarch Pajsije made great efforts to save older manuscripts, which he himself rebound and placed in safer monasteries or returned to their owners. What was preserved of their heritage did not influence the Serbs during the next century, however, for they turned to Russian printed books.

From Submission to Rebellion

The Ottomans ruled the Serbs and other Balkan Christians for different periods of time, depending on the region: for over 250 years in the Pannonian Basin, almost 400 years for those liberated during the uprisings of the nineteenth century (1815, 1833, and 1878), and 450 years for those liberated in the First Balkan War (1912). During these periods of occupation numerous generations changed, and almost every one left testimony showing that they were loyal to the sultan, took part in campaigns, filled entire branches of the army, and performed lower-level administrative functions. But there is parallel testimony that they also intended to rise up against Turkish rule and restore the Serbian state. The shift in emphasis is noticeable: during the first period of Ottoman rule there is much more about servility and participation in conquests, while during the War of the Holy League (1683–99) reports mention only defections, uprisings, and joining battle alongside the Turks' enemies. The least frequent reports of resistance against Turkish rule come from the first decades following the conquest, when only those Serbs who had settled in Hungary were fighting the Turks. The great majority of Serbs were under Ottoman rule by the mid-sixteenth century, and only those who had crossed the border as *prebezi* and *uskoci*, and thus came under the Venetian and Habsburg defense systems, remained beyond their reach.

Efforts to renew the Serbian state were made as early as the reign of Hungarian King Matthias Corvinus, who set the return of Serbian towns and territories as a condition for negotiations with the Turks in 1473–5. Shortly afterwards, in 1482, Sultan Bayazid II hinted to Despot Vuk Grgurević that he "would hand over land and towns, and that we might be between the emperor and the glorious king, as our ancestors had once been." This did not happen, but the Branković family did not give up hope. When Despot Jovan made endowments to the Athonite monasteries of Chilandar, St. Paul, and Esphigmenou in 1499, he promised to grant them all that Djuradj had promised, if God and the Virgin were benevolent and "make me lord of the Serbs."

After the dynasty died out, local people in the sultan's territories, often with outside influence, made plans to rise up against Ottoman rule. Renowned merchant and printer *voivoda* Božidar Vuković, an agent of Holy Roman Emperor Charles V, traveled as a merchant throughout the Turkish Empire. He negotiated a plan to land a Christian army on the Adriatic coast, somewhere near Skadar, counting on a general uprising of the population. In 1538 Božidar proposed that the emperor appoint him despot so that the venture would be more successful. He spoke with the Serbian patriarch in person and was informed of the slaughter of 80 Serbs from the border region at the hands of the Turks. The city of Novi (Herceg Novi) was seized in the war of 1537–8 that was led by Spain and Venice against Turkey. A Spanish garrison entered the city, but there was no response from the defeated population. The allies parted and peace was concluded without any change having been achieved.

Some Serbs expressed their views against Turkish rule in contacts with Christian travelers and envoys of European rulers, as is evidenced in the envoys' letters. During a visit to Mileševa monastery in 1533, imperial envoy Cornelius Duplicius Sheperus noted the influence on the population of old prophecies of a Turkish downfall. Earlier prophecies were transferred to the Ottomans: God had allowed Ishmael to subjugate the Christians, stamping out church service, but God would send a ruler who would do away with the infidels and hand over the crown to God, indicating the second coming of Christ. Manuscripts on such prophecies were widespread among the Serbs, and in Mileševa monastery they were attributed to St. Sava. The influence of prophecies on views of political events was apparent up until the twentieth century.

Each Ottoman war against Christian forces was a cause for hope and gave an opportunity for groups of all sizes to side with the Christians. The 1593–1606 war between the Ottoman and Habsburg empires had far greater repercussions among the conquered Christians than any previous conflict. There were open Serb uprisings against Turkish rule in two separate regions: in Banat among Serbs on the border with Transylvania and Wallachia, and in the heart of the clan region, among the chieftains of the Herzegovina clans. In both cases the Serbs assisted the enemies of the Turks and worked toward restoring their state. The renewed Serbian patriarchate made contact with Christian courts and the Holy See, for which Patriarch Jovan II (1592–1614) was imprisoned in 1612 and most probably put to death.

In the border region of Banat, where the Serb population had existed for more than a century and had been under Turkish rule for only four decades, ethnic leaders had maintained ties with the Transylvanian prince. Although an Ottoman vassal, he played a duplicitous game and incited mutiny while presenting himself as loyal in communications with the Turks. In the spring of 1594, when the Turkish army was dispatched to a distant battleground near Esztergom, there were several uprisings against Ottoman rule: *hajduk* (outlaw) incursions evicted Turkish garrisons from Vršac and its vicinity, from the Bečkerek area, and around Pančevo. In 1594 around 5,000 rebels attacked and seized the fortresses of Bečkerek, Bečej, and Titel and destroyed Turkish boats on the Danube that were supplying forts further north. The rebels demanded help from the Austrian imperial army and the Transylvanian prince, whom they regarded as their lord, and Bishop Theodore and local chieftains received oaths of allegiance from fellow fighters in the Vršac area. When the Austrian army abandoned its siege of Turkish fortresses in the north and the Transylvanian prince withdrew his help, the Turks turned on Banat and shortly after defeated the rebels near Bečkerek and Timişoara. Contemporaries linked this movement with the burning of the remains of St. Sava on the hill of Vračar, near Belgrade, in the spring of 1595.

While rebels in Banat turned to Transylvania and the Habsburgs, clan chiefs in Herzegovina cooperated with Italian counts, and particularly with the Spanish viceroy, who was established in Naples. Individuals from coastal towns, soldiers, even priests served as mediators. There is a good deal of evidence about these negotiations, meetings, travels, and plans, but very little concerning concrete actions. Documents reveal the main participants in negotiations with Naples under their leader *voivoda* Grdan of Nikšić, who was expected to assemble the chiefs from Montenegro and Dukagjin (the Skadar sanjak that extended deep into the interior as far as Metohia). They also include descriptions of their views of operations against the Ottoman Empire and their predictions for the future should Turkish rule be overthrown. For years they persisted with the same plan – the Christian army was to disembark at Novi and Risan and march on Onogošt, where it was predicted that they would be joined by 100,000 local fighters.

The chieftains' demands were that the entire population be freed from all taxes and contributions for three years; that the monasteries retain their revenues and be given back everything the Turks had seized; and that their religion be untouched. The chieftains presented themselves as nobles (*condes*, *voeuodas*, *barones*), and most of their demands regarded their own interests. Above all they wanted the return of their estates, the maintenance of their privileges, immunities, and titles, and appointments to positions in the army and administration in accordance with their abilities. The plan was for power to reside in the hands of local people, except for the Napolitan viceroy's governor. The unusual demand presented in 1602, whereby Turks who voluntarily accepted Spanish rule would remain free and keep their estates, was never again repeated.

There is no confirmation that these plans were ever carried out. It was not until the Venetian–Turkish war over Crete of 1645–69 that the Serb population along the Venetian–Turkish border from northern Dalmatia to the Bay of Kotor was caught up in warfare. In addition to settlers on Venetian territory, *uskoks* (defectors) as well as numerous *hajduk* groups based on Ottoman territory fought alongside Venice. The Montenegrin clans came to Kotor's aid. This was the first time a border shift occurred to the Ottomans' detriment, and a narrow strip of land in central Dalmatia and on the Montenegrin coast came under Christian rule.

The war that started in 1683 with the Ottoman siege of Viennese city walls was of crucial importance, as indicated by the extent of Serb participation in the fighting and its consequences on their further development. The long and unrelenting struggle to push back the Turks began with their defeat beneath the city walls. Buda was recovered in 1686, and the following year the battle moved southward, passing to territories inhabited by Serbs. Austrian imperial troops were joined by detachments of "Rascian militias" in the conflicts of 1687. The Ottomans were driven out of Slavonia at this time, and by 1688 the front reached the Sava River. The fall of Belgrade in 1688 was decisive.

Complete chaos erupted within Ottoman ranks after the seizure of Belgrade. The emperor's army proceeded south in two columns, through western Serbia and the Morava river valley. The fall of Čačak, Užice, Niš, and Skopje denoted their swift progress, and the imperial army's numbers were swelled by Serbs who joined during its advance. The borders in the Adriatic hinterland shifted after Venice joined the effort in 1684. The Serbian patriarch at the time, Arsenije III Čarnojević, openly cooperated with commanders of the Habsburg and Venetian armies. After Kosovo and northern Macedonia were defeated, plague broke out in the army. This was followed by France's attack against Habsburg territories in Germany and the Turks' counterattack against imperial forces, which quickly changed the situation.

Following the defeat at Kačanik on January 3, 1690, Austrian troops began to withdraw northward and the population, fearing Ottoman reprisals, retreated with them. The train moved toward Belgrade for weeks and months, growing larger as it was joined by new groups of refugees. In an effort to prevent unfavorable consequences, the emperor, in his capacity as king of Hungary, delivered a manifest to the Balkan Christians, calling on them not to abandon their homes but to take up arms and join the imperial army. He promised to observe all the old privileges, primarily that of appointing chieftains – *voivode* – and exemption from paying taxes and duties, except for those that had existed before the Turkish conquest. All of this implied the liberation of Serbia, which was once again being subjugated by the Ottomans and whose population was preparing to leave the country.

The decision to leave was clear in June 1690, when the assembly of Serb chieftains along with the patriarch in Belgrade sent Bishop Isaija Djaković to Vienna to request church autonomy and jurisdiction for the patriarch similar to the situation he had held in the Ottoman Empire. In August, when the Serbs started crossing the Sava River, the emperor issued the first of a series of "privileges" that were to greatly influence the position of the Serbian people in the monarchy. The Serbs were granted freedom of religion, allowed to keep the Julian calendar, and permitted freely to appoint archbishops to govern the church and to appoint bishops and priests. The difference between these demands and those emanating from the circle around *voivoda* Grdan in the early seventeenth century is striking. Secular elements of Serbian society do not appear at all, even though they took part in both the war and the migration. A contributing factor was undoubtedly the absence of the class of elders such as that found in clan society, in addition to the huge efforts by the Habsburg authorities to prevent the emergence of rivals for control over the Serbs.

An episode involving the self-proclaimed Despot Djordje II Branković, alleged descendant of the medieval dynasty, bears this out. A Serb from Transylvania, he claimed to have been anointed despot by the patriarch and was able to obtain the titles of baron and count through diplomatic activities at the Transylvanian and Wallachian courts. He did not participate in military operations, but sought the appointments of despot and assistant commander in the imperial army. The Vienna court made use of him before abandoning and imprisoning him in the summer of 1689, although he was not prevented from influencing Serbian leaders from gaol.

Before the Turkish recaptured Belgrade in 1690, the last group of Serbs had crossed the Sava and was making its way north. Along the way, sections of the population remained in Srem, Bačka, and Baranja, while others continued north to Buda and Szentendre. Patriarch Arsenije III claimed that 30,000 people had followed him (on another occasion the figure was 40,000), undoubtedly an exaggeration, although there are no testimonies that might provide a more reliable estimate. The settlement of refugees was accompanied by conflict with the local population and authorities, especially in towns.

For this reason, the emperor issued a "protective patent" in December 1690 through the Hungarian court confirming prior promises and obliging lower-level authorities to observe them. Liberties and immunity extended to all the Serbs and their property. Tension rose around the issue of secular leader at the assembly in Buda in 1691, since the Serbian chieftains favored the imprisoned Djordje Branković, who was declared despot. The court did not agree and sought an accommodation in promoting imperial officer Jovan Monasterlija to the rank of "vice-voivoda." At first he was received with distrust. However, since the struggle against the Turks was still ongoing, the military command was willing to meet the Serbs halfway. The battles of Slankamen (1691) and Senta (1697) showed how desperately needed they were.

The Serbs' "privileges," of which increasing mention was made, actually consisted of guarantees of their basic human right to live unmolested and to practice their faith. The promised liberties and immunity were not territorially limited but were linked to ethnicity and religion. The personal nature of such rights, broadly applied during the Middle Ages, is not easily accommodated with the intentions of a modern state to create a single legislation within its borders.

Since the "privileges" had been granted under different conditions, both before peace was concluded in 1699 and after it, between 1718 and 1739, when part of Serbia was under Habsburg control, their application was unequal. From the very beginning the "privileges" were a disputed issue, first in daily politics regarding relations between Hungarian authorities and the ruler, the Serbian metropolitanate, the assembly, and the court, and later as a controversial topic in historiography.

5

The Emergence of Modern Christian Society

A New State Framework

A significant portion of the Serbian population was freed from Ottoman rule forever when the outcome of the 15-year Austrian–Ottoman war was sealed by the Treaty of Karlowitz in 1699. The descendants of those who had arrived in the Pannonian Basin some 150 or 200 years earlier were joined by those who took part in the Great Migration of 1690. Both groups found themselves in territories from which the ruling Ottomans had been driven out, and both were uncertain of their future.

First and foremost, there was no agreement on the status and organization of the liberated territories. The aim of the remnants of the Hungarian Diet, which by 1687 had been reduced to ruling a fragment of the former state, was to renew the kingdom in all its aspects. This included the system of government, institutions, laws, and above all the rights of the nobility, who were to reclaim their lost estates. The first steps were to restore both the comitats, with their autonomy, assemblies, and judges of the local nobility, and aristocratic estates. However, these plans encountered several difficulties, primarily because of the changed general circumstances in which there was insufficient authority to carry them out. In addition, there were the opposing efforts of the Vienna court, which based its plans along the lines of an absolutist policy that sought to transform the heterogeneous monarchy into a unified state. The court needed solutions that would simultaneously provide troops for the unfinished struggle against the Ottomans, give the central authorities direct power, and facilitate the influx of resources from the newly acquired regions, including manpower for defense and future conflicts. The opposition between Austrian and Hungarian ideas continued for decades, both in public and in private, with varying degrees of intensity, and would have a permanent influence on the Serbs' position.

During the short period between the ousting of the Turks in 1686–7 and the arrival of Patriarch Arsenije III in 1690, it became increasingly clear what destiny awaited the Serbs from the experience of regions where the ideal of restoration was carried out, particularly Slavonia, Srem, and Baranja: they were to be turned into villeins on the restored estates and "unified" (joined with the Catholic Church), a fate experienced not only by parishioners but also by priests and monastery elders in Slavonia in 1690. The expulsion of the Turks raised the Catholic Church's hopes that it might make up for its losses due to the Turkish invasion and expansion of Protestantism in Hungary and Bohemia.

The descendants of the earlier Serbian settlers lacked significant defenses, since they were dispersed throughout a large and sparsely populated area, with no leader higher than village chieftain, lower-level military commander, and a few bishops, linked by the distant patriarch. The laws of the kingdom had not touched them since the fifteenth century, when they were exempted from paying the church tithe, and they were later mentioned only in reference to tax-related Diet decrees. The situation changed with the Great Migration of 1690, not so much because of the increase in the Serb population as the fact that those who arrived with Patriarch Arsenije III were protected by the "privileges" and decree of 1690, which was related to the freedom of religion of the settlers – i.e., the Orthodox Church and its hierarchy. The thinly scattered populace thus achieved some kind of internal structure and was held together by a loose framework that linked its diverse elements.

The succeeding course of events reveals the importance of chance, since the Migration had not been planned but was forced by reversals on the battlefield and the fear of Ottoman reprisals. The fact that the patriarch led the people turned out to be crucial, since it enabled a connection and unification with the part of the Serbian Church that already existed under Christian rule. In the first decade following the Migration it was apparent that districts with disparate regimes were developing simultaneously on the liberated territories, some under the rule of military authorities, others under the Court Chamber, and still others under comitat authorities or estate lords. The differences between them only increased over time. Serbs lived under all of these regimes, in different numbers, but because of their connection through the church organization, Sabor (assembly of ecclesiastical dignitaries), and "privileges," these boundaries did not divide them.

The Habsburg authorities persisted in their efforts to hamper unification because it increased resistance to conversion, which took place especially in the western regions at the same time as the restoration of the Catholic dioceses. The court limited the patriarch's activities for a time, prohibiting visitations and even the use of the title, and later, in 1707, bishops from the western eparchies were prevented from attending the assembly. Efforts by those Serbs who sought to settle in a separate territory acted against unification of the diverse elements. Their aim was hardly achievable even by those who had only just arrived, and wholly unrealistic for the entire people, perceived by contemporaries as being dispersed throughout a large area: "Some are around Buda, others on the Arad side . . . while a third part is across the Sava to the Lika and Krbava rivers."

During the war years between 1687 and 1699, Serbs primarily achieved personal freedom and protected themselves from becoming serfs by joining a military organization. This is why they sought to preserve the military wherever possible and grouped into *šanci*, settlements divided into military units under the command of the local chieftains. The aspirations of the Serb warriors matched the needs and policies of the court in Vienna: to extend the region of the Military Border, regardless of opposition from the Hungarian Diet, and adapt it to the new situation. When Ottoman expansion was at its peak, the border extended from the Adriatic coast to Lake Balaton, running southwest to northeast. After the siege of Vienna, the part north of the Sava River was completely out of the frame, far from the Ottoman frontier.

Now the border was much longer, following the Sava River and cutting diagonally across Srem, then following the Tisa River to the Mures, then along this river to Transylvania. Plans were drafted during the war years, but the new border was only realized in 1702–3. Petrovaradin became the center of the new section of the border and the location of a large fortress, while lesser military settlements (*šanac*) were located in a broad band following the Sava, Tisa, and Mures rivers. The position of a great many Serbs depended on the fate of the Military Border, and it was understandable that they fought vigorously to maintain it.

The arbitrary application of the promises contained in the rulers' decrees ended in 1703 when the simmering tension between the Hungarian nobility and Viennese court boiled over into open rebellion headed by Ferenc II Rákóczy (1703–11), whose supporters were called *kurucz* (crusaders), the old name used for participants in the Dózsa Rebellion of 1514. Faced with a serious threat and heavily engaged in the War of the Spanish Succession, the Viennese court became more lenient toward the patriarch, lifting previous sanctions and prohibitions and finally granting him the estate he had been promised. After first being offered Sirač near Daruvar before it was taken back, and similarly in 1697 with the town and castle of Dunaszekcső, he finally received Dalj near Osjek, together with five villages. The patriarch had a pension of 3,000 forints and took care of his family, obtaining the recognition of his brother's title and his descendants' nobility. In keeping with his

Plate 5.1   The new center of power: Petrovaradin fortress, completed 1716–18. In its shadow across the Danube emerged Novi Sad, the cultural capital of the Serbs in Hungary. (Photograph by B. Strugar)

pretensions to the lineage of the Crnojević family, he himself probably suggested the title of "prince of Albania."

The leniency shown by the Viennese court during the Rákóczy uprising was understood as a means of separating the Serbs from the emperor's enemies. The Serbian leadership was linked to the emperor and his court through the development of relations and promises included in the "privileges," even though they had already discovered that laying claims based on the promised "privileges" worked only when the Serbs had power that could be of use to the court.

Because of his distrust of the Serbs under arms, representing military power similar to his own, Rákóczy tried to attract the Serbs to his side. First, he issued a proclamation promising them everything that the other side had already given them if they were to join him, but also seriously threatening if they opposed him. Later he used negotiations and offered money (the patriarch was promised 20,000 forints), and even used the influence of Russia, toward whom the Serbs had already turned. As far as can be concluded from preserved documents, there was no great Serb participation in the *kurucz*; indeed, several clashes with them are revealed, as well as evidence that Serbs joined the imperial detachments that put down the *kurucz*. The war was waged in the same manner as a border war – units were sent to plunder and devastate the opponent's territory. *Kurucz* units penetrated as far as Austria, even though they were based in the north and east of the country. The Serbs in the Mures river basin, Bačka, and particularly on the right bank of the Danube suffered most from such incursions. Rákóczy's rebellion marked the beginning of the disappearance of settlements along the edge of the Serbian ethnic area and a retreat toward more compactly populated regions, a situation that would endure until the twentieth century. People sought refuge from the slaughter by fleeing toward Slavonia, Srem, and Banat, the last-named of which was still in Ottoman hands.

While the war continued, there were changes on the imperial throne as well as on the archpriest's throne. In 1706 the new Emperor Joseph I confirmed the Serbs' former "privileges" and Patriarch Arsenije died that same year. During the previous few years he had tried to resolve the delicate issue of relations with the Peć patriarchate, where the Ottoman authorities had appointed Kallinikos I as patriarch, with the mediation of the Constantinopolitan patriarchate. Constantinople and the eastern patriarchs advised that all archpriests should be equal and subordinate to the Peć archbishop.

There were two tendencies among the bishops: one favored full acceptance of the jurisdiction of the Peć patriarch, and the other favored complete autonomy. Stevan of Metohija was the first to be chosen, but he was not recognized. The next choice was Isaija Djaković, who had the backing of the court after he pledged allegiance to the Peć patriarch. When he died soon after, in 1708, Sofronije of Podgorica (1710–11) was selected as his successor. He was prevented from taking his oath, but received the blessing of Peć, and an appeal was made to the archpriests to yield to him. Thus the bishops and metropolitans under Christian rule were only indirectly linked with the Peć throne by means of the "first metropolitan," who was seated in Krušedol. When Krušedol monastery, the endowment of the Branković family, was destroyed in the 1716–18 war, the seat of the metropolitan was moved to Karlovci, which was closer and more accessible to Petrovaradin. The Orthodox Church organization under the Habsburg emperors was thus commonly known as the Karlovci metropolitanate. This church structure was to play an important role in Serb development for more than two hundred years.

In 1713 the next metropolitan, Vićentije Popović (d. 1725), was elected. During his administration new bishoprics came under Christian rule, along with new territories. The election of metropolitans was an occasion for the Sabor to meet. In order to restrict the archpriests' influence, imperial authorities introduced laymen into the Sabor, giving the gatherings a secular flavor. After the clergy came military representatives, followed by other "classes." German documents called this gathering a Congress or National Congress. The scope of the Sabor's activities became more stable over time: aside from appointing archbishops, it also discussed church construction, the opening of schools, church administration and property, complaints of improper conduct by the authorities or Catholic prelates, and any form of threat. The Sabor could meet only with the ruler's permission and in the presence of his officer.

Extending and Reorganizing the Framework

The war between the Ottoman Empire and Venice in 1714, which was joined by Austria in 1716, brought about significant change. Despite initial successes, there were major defeats, and the monasteries in Srem were devastated by Turkish forces. A crucial event in the war was the Austrian siege of Belgrade that ended with the fall of the city in 1717. A truce was negotiated in 1718 at Passarowitz (Požarevac) which gave the Austrian Empire Banat, the remaining part of Srem, a narrow belt in Bosnia south of the Sava, and northern areas of Serbia up to the West Morava River and east to the confluence of the Timok River with the Danube. Thus the core of the state that had existed under the former despots, as well as a sizable proportion of Serbs from part of Bosnia and the marshy and sparsely populated Banat, were rescued from Ottoman rule.

In dealing with the newly acquired territory, the Habsburg authorities chose to disregard Hungary's demands that the previous system of organization be observed. There was nothing in Serbia that could embody continuity, such as the Diet in Hungary. The Habsburg administration reinstated the name of Serbia (*Königtum Serbien*) and installed a similar regime to the Turkish one: all high-level positions and administrative authorities came under the control of their own people, and lesser positions were ceded to the local population. Belgrade was the center of the Belgrade Administration, which included 14 districts, while seven districts to the east came under the Timişoara Administration. The Administration was headed by a governor, seated in Belgrade, and comprised a mixed military–civilian institution, with military strongholds – the *šanac* and the *čardak* (border post) – along the border. The lower-ranking

(a)

(b)

Plate 5.2 Precursors of the West: (a) The Wirtemberg barracks in Belgrade, 1736, built during Austrian rule; (b) the same building seen in 1864 as Pirinç-han (rice storehouse). Drawing by Felix Kanitz. ((a) From the plan of Nicola de Spar, 1736, reprinted on the CD ROM *Stare karte, gravire i fotografije iz zbirke Muzeja grada Beograda*, courtesy of the Muzej grada Beograda)

administrative bodies and judicial authorities were the local chieftains, *ober-knez*, who governed between 20 and 30 villages (*knežine*), and some villages were ruled by a *knez*, called a judge by the new authorities.

Experience from the Military Border was used in the military organization. The land was divided into captainships, with military commanders from among the local chieftains. Some of the villages near the border had military obligations and were referred to as *hajduk* villages, while others were known as state villages. The new administration found the country in a state of ruin. Almost a third of the villages had been abandoned: 386 were deserted compared to 644 inhabited. Villages were principally colonized by refugees from territories still under Ottoman rule, while German colonists settled in the towns. A "German borough" was created on the Danube side of Belgrade. In an attempt to revive the economy, the new authorities encouraged mining operations near Belgrade and in Majdanpek, but their efforts were brought to an end by the Turkish invasion of 1739. The Austrian administration was corrupt and lacked authority. It neither understood nor respected the population that it was to rule and burdened them with enormous levies. Belgrade changed its image in a short time, for the largest number of foreigners was concentrated there.

The establishment of imperial rule in Serbia increased the number of the emperor's Serb subjects and raised the issue of their position and organization. In 1720 the "privileges" were extended to all Serbs on the annexed territories, but the authorities were reluctant for them to be linked together. The greatest distrust was shown in relations toward the church. After the death of the metropolitan of Karlovci, Vićentije Popović, in 1725, the Serbs requested an assembly of the Sabor to elect another metropolitan for all the bishoprics. The Austrian authorities refused to grant their request, preferring two Sabors and two metropolitans. Finally, a compromise was reached whereby the metropolitan of Karlovci became the administrator of the Belgrade metropolitanate. This situation continued until the Belgrade metropolitan once again came under Turkish rule in 1739.

From their territory in Serbia, the Austrians began secret negotiations during the peace with the patriarch in Peć, Arsenije IV, and with Serbian and Albanian clan chiefs. This time the approach to the clan region, which was ready to rise up against Ottoman rule, was planned by land via Novi Pazar and the Lim river valley. In the summer of 1737, Austria formally launched hostilities against Turkey, which had been at war with Russia since 1735. With great optimism, it undertook simultaneous operations in the direction of Bosnia, Serbia, and Bulgaria. In the central region the army advanced and captured a number of towns, including Niš and Novi Pazar. The patriarch succeeded in raising part of the

Kuči, Vasojevići, Bratonožići, and Piper clans, as well as the Catholic Albanian clans of Klimente, Hoti, Kastrati, and Grude. Imperial troops, reinforced by the rebels, seized Niš and penetrated into Kosovo (Banjska monastery). However, losses in Bosnia and western Serbia undermined their position and the population started to move out. The great defeat near Grocka in 1739 forced the monarchy to sign the unfavorable Treaty of Belgrade, which provided for all territories south of the Sava and Danube to be returned to the Ottoman Empire. This territory did not change hands in later wars. Thus parts of the Serbian population were separated for more than 150 years and prevented from integration.

Failures on the battlefield were succeeded by a second, smaller migration under Arsenije IV Jovanović. Besides the Serbs, this migration included Catholic Albanians, the Klimente, who settled in three villages by the Sava River in Srem. Christian institutions were suspended in Serbia, as was colonization by Germans, who had sought refuge across the Danube from Petrovaradin and created a settlement that would later become Novi Sad.

Serbs who lived far from the theater of war were indirectly affected. After the capture of Banat by the monarchy, areas along the lower Tisa and the Mures rivers that had comprised the Military Border remained far in the interior. This resulted in the Hungarian Diet and neighboring comitats, which were burdened with supporting the Military Border, increasing their demands for it to be "incorporated," i.e. included within the comitats and made subordinate to their administrative bodies. Their demands were supported by serious albeit unjust and offensive accusations against the population of the military settlement.

The Serbian population within this part of the border perceived "demilitarization" as the greatest threat to their religion, ethnic background, and freedom. The border militia did not wish to be placed "under the Hungarians," that is, under comitat rule, nor did they wish to become dependent peasants or serfs. They refused to countenance any change, threatened to move away, and criticized the imperial authorities for their ingratitude and disrespect for Serbian military prowess. Demands to preserve the "military" status were relayed from this part of the border to the Sabor by the metropolitan and became a general issue for the entire people.

The enthronement of Maria Theresa (1740–80) gave the Hungarian Diet the opportunity it needed to legally secure the "incorporation" of the remaining territories in 1741, some immediately and others when circumstances permitted. The monarch was forced to accede to the "incorporation," but implemented it gradually, seeking to find solutions to diminish the resistance of the Serb warriors, who were very important to her. Officers were offered noble titles and estates; soldiers were offered the opportunity to move to regions where the border regime was still in place. An interim administrative unit was set up along the Tisa River in 1751. Land sales were prohibited within it, and guarantees were given that the Court Chamber would remain in charge, with reduced levies and no corvée. The most resistance was in the Mures river basin, where relocation and the offer of citizen status were refused.

Demilitarization coincided with renewed appeals from Russia (the first had been in 1723–4), which was seeking settlers and soldiers for its newly conquered and unpopulated territories in southern Russia. People were assembled by Serb officers who were promised the rank of general and command of the settlers. Austrian authorities initially supported the initiative, while the church and metropolitan persistently opposed Serbian emigration. Later the Austrian authorities strictly prohibited migration to Russia. Those who departed between 1751 and 1753 formed two regiments on two separate territories: one was called Nova Srbija (New Serbia) on the banks of the Dnepr River, and the other was called Slavjanoserbija, on the Donets River. Serb settlers had to overcome serious initial difficulties and in time developed advanced settlements, which were named after places in the old country. From the outset they took part in Russia's many wars. Over the course of one century they were absorbed into the Russian environment without influencing Serbian development either politically or culturally.

Some of the Serbs from the region around the Mures River joined the settlers in Russia, and some (more than 2,200 families) moved to Banat, from where they were pushed by the authorities toward the Srem part of the border. Despite these efforts they remained in Banat, so that the Serbs' presence in the Banat territory was strengthened just before the great wave of western colonization. The establishment of privileged districts (Potisje in 1751, Šajkaš Battalion in 1764, Kikinda district in 1774), the incorporation of Banat (1779), and the distribution of the new Military Border along the Danube (Serbian in 1764, German and Romanian regiments in 1768–9) completed what would long remain the territorial division between the jurisdictions of high-ranking authorities in the monarchy. Regardless of the regime they were under, on the border or in the *provinciale* (comitats in the Hungarian administration), on estates or in the free cities, the Serbs remained tightly connected and united in preserving their individuality under their Sabor and metropolitan.

This became all the more important when the Hungarian Diet took advantage of the empress's difficulties during the War of Austrian Succession to challenge the Serbs' "privileges," which had then been in effect for half a century. The Croatian Diet (Sabor) demanded that the Hungarian Diet abolish the "schismatic" (Orthodox) bishoprics in the "Triune Kingdom" (Croatia, Slavonia, and Dalmatia) and place their congregations under the Uniate bishops. The monarch's promises and legal article 46 in 1741 confirmed the validity of the "statute" passed in the Croatian Sabor, but this did not prevent Maria Theresa from confirming the Serbs' "privileges" in 1743, by means of both the Court War Council and the Hungarian Chancellery. The Serbs, for their part, demanded that the Sabor be convened in order to "proclaim" this confirmation.

This occurred at the Sabor held in Karlovci (Karlowitz) in 1744, where Patriarch Arsenije IV was sworn in, having become the head of the metropolitanate. Numerous complaints and demands aimed at preserving the position guaranteed by the "privileges" were presented to two commissioners, one of whom was from the Hungarian Diet. Most were rejected by the commissioners and the Hungarian Chancellery, and the Serbs were criticized for attempting to create "a state within a state." From that time on, jurisdiction over the Serbs, whether they were part of the heritage of the "House of Austria" or considered an internal Hungarian matter, was increasingly disputed.

One of the Serbs' demands concerned the formation of a body consisting of 12 members from the ranks of the "nation," which would supervise any address to the court on the subject of the "privileges." Three members would be permanently seated in Vienna (the metropolitans also had their authorized agents for communications with the court). The empress issued a protective decree in 1745 according to which the Serbs' "privileges" were not to be jeopardized in the incorporated regions, and founded the Illyrian Court Commission, which displeased the patriarch and Serbian hierarchy as well as the Hungarian Chancellery. The Commission, which consisted of high-ranking court officers and representatives, was to serve the monarch as an impartial advisory body, since the Court War Council and Hungarian Chancellery were often in disagreement. Conflicts with Hungarian authorities increased in 1747 when the Commission was transformed into the Illyrian Court Deputation and put on an even footing with other court offices.

The Deputation functioned for 30 years as a kind of ministry for Serbian affairs, and over time served increasingly as a mediator in the implementation of reforms in Serbian society, even in the Serbian Church's work among the people. It was unpopular with both the episcopate and the Serb masses because of its innovations, which were received with distrust. Even though its formal jurisdiction covered Banat and Transylvanian affairs, the Deputation primarily addressed Serbian concerns, hence the name Illyrian. Apart from the designation Rasciani, which had been used since the Middle Ages in Latin texts (never in Serbian or Greek texts), the term Illyrian, derived from the region's ancient name, began to be used by the Habsburg administration in the late seventeenth century. The Serbs' name for themselves was seldom used (*die serbische Nation*), and the term Illyrian or Rascian prevailed (*die illyrische oder raizische Nation*), especially in official documents. Serbs accepted these designations in official institutional names, but preferred the forms *slavenosrbski* or *srbski*. Official language did not accept the term "Orthodox" for the church (*orthodoxa* was reserved for the Roman Catholic Church) – Orthodox Christians were deemed non-united Christians of Greek rites (*graeci ritus non uniti*).

Peasants and Citizens, Soldiers and Nobles

The territories that had been ruled by the Ottomans were initially in disarray, and only the supreme ruler and those who used the land and facilities directly were known. This situation was relatively quickly rectified. The Court Chamber, the supreme body that managed state property, took charge of administering the territories on the emperor's behalf. In fact it managed only part of the vast area, delegating to others responsibility for land it had been assigned.

Only a handful of the heirs of the territories' medieval owners came forward. In the lands populated by the Serbs, the Kalocsa archbishopric and the heirs of one aristocrat family in Bačka alone claimed their rights. The old lords' role was taken by new nobles, to whom the Court Chamber either sold estates or awarded them on merit. This early land privatization was implemented especially in Slavonia and Srem. Large estates were formed and included dozens of villages surrounding a larger settlement. These estates were placed in the hands of the most influential individuals, who had close ties to the court and state institutions. Thus, for example, in 1699 Prince Eugene of Savoy acquired the Belje estate (30 villages and wasteland, with more than 2,300 families) and the pope's nephew, Livius Odescalchi, came into the Ilok estate with 35 villages. The estates were formed around Zemun (21 villages), Mitrovica (14 villages), Vukovar (31 villages), Pakrac (26 villages), and Karlovci (8 villages). Most estates changed owners over time, and remained intact until the agrarian reforms of the twentieth century.

The restoration of estates had a momentous impact on the Serbian population, since those who lived in villages that came into private hands had to work the land as dependent peasants, in keeping with medieval tradition, which included taxes and forced labor. The basic dues were the so-called "great tithe" of wheat, barley, oat, millet, and wine, while the "small tithe" consisted of livestock (lambs, kids, poultry, and bees). Since the owners lived far from their new estates, the peasants dealt with their caretakers and intermediaries (*provisores, ispani*), who were often stubborn and greedy. The most frequent complaints concerned illegal appraisal and demands for additional labor, known by the distorted Slavic term *robot* (from *rabota*). The state intervened to pacify discontent by passing general regulations called *urbaria*. These prescribed the maximum taxes allowed, which could be reduced by contracts; a series of taxes was prohibited; and supervisory bodies were introduced as well as courts for *urbaria* matters. During Maria Theresa's reign, *urbaria* were drafted for every village and set in print. State intervention did not stop at the taxes of the nobility but included those of the church. This allowed subjects to afford to pay state dues, which were increased on account of the wars.

While the number of Serb subjects on estates increased, there were far fewer Serb lords. In Hungary only the nobility could have estates, while in the Triune Kingdom (Croatia, Slavonia, and Dalmatia) until the mid-eighteenth century, the landowner had to be Catholic. Of the approximately 200 Serbian noble families, there were only a handful of large landowners (the Čarnojević and Stratimirović families in Bačka, and the Servijski, Nako, Nikolić, and Djurković families in Banat). Serbian nobles mostly descended from high-ranking officers and state clerks, while only very few descended from citizens and merchants. A noble title could be obtained by purchasing an estate, especially in Banat after 1779, when the Court Chamber began selling off land.

A fairly sizable proportion of the Serb population lived in territory that remained under the administration of the Court Chamber and was owned by the monarch. Here as well, Chamber officials were the source of the people's discontent, especially the land leasers (*arendatores*) who rented land from the Chamber, since it was not able to work the land itself. Chamber lands were also ceded to military authorities where the border had been organized, and conversely, land in the demilitarized regions was returned to the Chamber.

Larger towns with craftsmen and merchants that previously had a military status sought to buy their freedom from the Chamber. This required large sums of money and the population took out loans which took decades to repay. By buying their liberty, the towns gained the status of "free royal townships," which brought a large degree of autonomy and representation in the Diet of the kingdom. Citizens no longer paid customs duties or road and trade taxes throughout the state, and they also were able to elect administrative bodies (*magistrat, obštestvo*); contributions were the obligation of the entire town and were divided up among the population. The towns covered large areas, since they were also given wasteland. Free towns were islands surrounded by comitats (*županija*) and estates, up to the time of state centralization. During the period in which the Serb territories were demilitarized, Petrovaradin *šanac* was purchased (1748) and renamed Novi Sad (Neoplanta, Neusatz, or Ujvidek). Sombor followed in 1749, and later Subotica in 1779, and Bečkerek ("free community") in 1769. The free towns provided settings for the development of crafts, which included guild organizations established according to trade and confession. The crafts that were colonized in 1690 quickly adapted to the European type of guild organization. Merchants also settled in the towns, growing wealthy and obtaining property on town-owned land on account of their role as mediators between the Ottoman Empire and Christian states. A kind of patriciate was formed in the free towns, which used its power to its own advantage. Descendants of powerful families were educated in the so-called "free professions" (medicine, law, etc.) and civic administration, and Serbian intellectuals of the eighteenth century primarily came from these urban environments.

Large non-agrarian towns developed in the Military Border and, along with the "free royal townships," became an important source of urbanization and expansion of the Serbian citizenry. The larger settlements, former *šanac* and command headquarters, were given the status of "free military communities." Their inhabitants were under no military obligations and had autonomous magistrates who were directly subordinate to the high command. There were about 20 such towns in Serb-populated regions, including the most important: Zemun, Mitrovica, Karlovci, Pančevo, Vršac, Bela Crkva, Irig, Vukovar, and Vinkovci. While towns increased and gained autonomy in the border regions, the Serbian element was disappearing in cities on the boundaries of the ethnic area. The most extreme examples are those of Szentendre, where seven Serbian churches remain from the eighteenth century, Buda, where there was a great "Rascian suburb" with its own magistrate, and Timişoara, where Serbian and German magistrates functioned in parallel for a long time. Pécs, Szeged, and Arad had Serbian populations, but their number and significance declined.

The Court Chamber policy of colonization, which was carried on methodically and consistently from the mid-eighteenth century, was important for Serbian development. The distribution of the population was insufficient to exploit the obvious economic potential of certain regions, especially after the completion of major work on draining marshes and regulating the Tamiš River in Banat by 1766.[1] In planning settlements (a colonization patent had been issued in 1763), the Chamber and other high-level authorities kept political aims firmly in mind. German strongholds were to be established in the border regions as

---

1   River regulation and the construction of canals in Bačka came after colonization, at the end of the eighteenth century.

support for defending and ruling the territories. This policy was put to the test during the rule of northern Serbia. Banat, where the main wave of settlement took place in 1770, was colonized in a highly systematic fashion. Smaller groups of French settlers were included along with Germans and became assimilated into their German surroundings; they were accompanied by Italians and Spanish, who did not put down roots. A large number of villages were established in Banat, with a total of 11,000 families comprising 42,000 individuals. Most were from southern Germany, which is why the term *Švaba*, derived from *Schwaben*, was extended to all Germans, as the term Saxon had been in the Middle Ages. The colonization of Germans started in Bačka in 1750, but the main wave followed a decade later. They principally settled the banks of the Danube and the central Bačka region, where Serbian villages were occasionally relocated, even though the policy emphasized that colonization was not to be to the "detriment of the Rascians." The Chamber gave the colonists land, imposed village and house plans, and provided carts, plows, and tools, which the settlers later repaid.

Large landowners followed the example of the Chamber and colonized people from their other estates with a greater population density. The distribution of estates was such that in Bačka, Hungarians were colonized along the Danube and Tisa rivers, while they appeared only in a small number of villages in Banat toward the end of the century. Movements within Hungary included Slovaks from the northern territories and Ruthenians from the Carpathian region who were settled in a few villages in Bačka. Slovaks were also present in Banat and later in Srem and constituted isolated islands that developed along with their surroundings.

In parallel with this planned colonization, spontaneous migration and settlement occurred: Romanians came down to Banat from mountain regions, while Serbs and Bulgars came from the south, with an especially large wave of emigrants from Serbia who settled in Srem during the war of 1788–91. Trade brought Armenians, Jews, and Tzintzars (Aromani). The Armenians moved from Belgrade to the Petrovaradin *šanac*, while the Tzintzars joined Serb citizens and were absorbed into the greater Serbian surroundings of the same faith.

The process of transforming agriculture, which had been abandoned during the Ottoman period, accompanied colonization. The cultivation of corn spread and became common (potatoes were introduced only in the early nineteenth century to eliminate the threat of famine); wine-growing was renewed; and the authorities encouraged the production of tobacco and mulberries to feed silkworms. Some new vegetable crops were introduced, and the colonists brought with them knowledge of rational farming methods which gradually became widespread.

This spontaneous and planned colonization created a unique ethnic diversity in southern Hungary which later had cultural and political repercussions. Lasting coexistence with neighbors of other tongues, faith, and customs offered an opportunity for exchange, especially in the material sphere, which can be attributed to the common "Pannonian" traits shared by the communities of the region. Tolerance and mutual respect were developed, which is why there were no migrations, even during severe political clashes and border shifts, until 1944. One of the consequences of colonization was that the ethnic Serbian core was crosscut by foreign ethnic elements. While villages remained ethnically homogeneous, towns took on a Hungarian dimension, especially in the comitat seats, and a German dimension, because colonists left their villages for the towns.

The Serbs believed that they were safe only as part of the militia, in territories that were set up as the Military Border, excluded from local authorities, and subordinate only to their commanders and, through them, the emperor. However, despite its attractions, this border was not the "promised land"; it was difficult for those who worked the land, and dangerous and uncertain for those under arms who often lived far from their villages and families. There were no serf-style obligations, no "contributions" to pay, but there were obligations to the command, garrisons, military facilities, and so on. Transport and firewood collection were especially perilous. Some officers demanded to be served as if they were landlords, and there were public works that included the entire able-bodied population. Disturbances, occasional revolts, and actual rebellions occurred because of these burdens and were calmed by the authorities only through the passage of numerous reforms, rules, and regulations concerning the duties of the border militia and their commanders. The general aim of these regulations was to even out conditions and to raise the level of discipline, armaments, uniforms, and so on to that of a regular army. An important provision from a 1752 patent required the border militia to join every theater of war. Although there was no conflict with the Turks for almost half a century (from 1739 to 1788), the border militia suffered casualties on battlegrounds in Bavaria, Bohemia, Silesia, Italy, Holland, and France. Their numbers increased from 45,615 in 1740 to 120,000 in 1796, and in some wars the border militia (not all of whom were Serbs) comprised a third of the imperial troops.

The Military Border offered greater opportunities for moving up the social hierarchy than in other regions and allowed greater social mobility. At the beginning Serbs held only lower-level command posts. However, by the second generation, after receiving an education and because of inherited titles, their prominence and individual merits allowed them to achieve higher ranks, even those of colonel and general.

Some 32 Serbs are known to have held the rank of general or colonel in the eighteenth century. Officers formed an influential part of the Serbian Assembly and were models of the social and cultural life of the monarchy's high society. Border militia officers were the main pool from which the Serbian nobility was recruited.

The Serbian Christian population was dispersed over a large area and was partitioned by borders separating the jurisdictions of civil and military authorities, the Chamber, estates, and autonomous towns. Increasingly it began to diverge according to profession, wealth, position, and education, and this complexity became apparent in the Assembly's composition; in 1749, in addition to 25 bishops and clergymen, it included 25 officers from the Military Border and 25 citizens. The Timişoara Assembly of 1790 also included 25 nobles.

Women were not as invisible as they were in the clan populations or in the *reaya* under Ottoman rule, but even in Christian society, regardless of social status, their lives and activities were set within the family framework. Among the higher classes of nobles and officers, wives and daughters did not share the fate of the thousands of women of lower status who were worn down by poverty and the burden of heavy labor. They could enjoy the advantages of material wealth and prosperity, with servants, comfortable surroundings, the possibility of receiving an education, and opportunities for socializing. From the mid-century, balls were a frequent occurrence in Serb society and were even held by the metropolitans. Females from middle-class families had an equal share in inheritance and women could run estates and workshops, but they were compelled to rely on men for expert assistance. Efforts to develop schools in some towns provided buildings or facilities for female students.

Christian Education

After it was liberated from Ottoman rule, the Serbian Orthodox Church faced highly different surroundings. No longer did it shrink from the rule of the "infidels," nor was it obliged to yield to their demands; now Christian rulers promised to respect its individuality and allow it to work in freedom. These rulers, however, were members of the Catholic Church, which claimed a spiritual monopoly on the land of "apostolic majesty." Reconversion to Catholicism, which had previously been practiced in Bohemia and Moravia, was vigorously implemented throughout the territories reclaimed from the Turks, where the opportunity arose to reclaim long-lost lands and congregations. In its attempts to restore church relations, the Catholic Church showed the same energy and commitment that the Hungarian Diet had done when it set about restoring the organization of comitats and the rule of the nobility.

Encountering resistance from those who were certain to be "united," the Catholic hierarchy relied on the support of the secular authorities in its efforts to convert Orthodox Christians released from Ottoman rule, who were perceived as "non-united Christians of Greek rites." Court and military circles did not withhold their support, but they bore their own interests in mind. The rulers were bound by their promises and guarantees, and by the "privileges," and were also forced to consider the fact that the "non-united" population constituted a growing proportion of their military forces, especially when troops from the Military Border were incorporated into the monarchy's army. The Habsburgs' absolutism increasingly became "enlightened," in the sense that they recognized the need to reform the official state Catholic Church. State authorities felt compelled to direct it, and especially to oversee its work with the laity. They imposed reforms on the Serbian Orthodox Church with equal vigor, observing its canons and traditional organization. The two churches approached an equivalent status during the reign of Emperor Joseph II (1780–90), when the "tolerance patent" was issued.

Ever since Patriarch Arsenije III had crossed over to the monarchy and the first ecclesiastical assemblies, the hierarchy of the Serbian Church had shown that it was only too aware of its difficult position in the face of a powerful rival. It became apparent to the patriarch and to the archpriests from the surrounding areas and their successors that the identity and traditions of their church could only be preserved through education and increasing its members' self-awareness. For this task they would require a better-educated clergy capable of suppressing attempts at conversion and of convincing believers of the value of their faith and traditions. Consequently, a school and a printing press, the most important tools of education, were requested at the Assembly of 1706. The authorities initially turned a deaf ear to these demands, and the Serbs were directed to Catholic schools and printers in Trnava. However, in 1727, the establishment of "higher and lower" schools was permitted. Only then did the obstacle of poverty and ignorance reveal its true scale.

During the first two decades of the eighteenth century modest schools existed only in a small number of larger towns. The gravity of the situation became obvious when northern Serbia was freed of Ottoman rule in 1718. It was therefore only natural for the metropolitans of Karlovci and Belgrade, Mojsije Petrović (1726–30) and Vićentije Jovanović (1731–7), to put all their weight behind the establishment of schools. The first in a series of "pronouncements" was made in 1726 requesting bishops to found schools and supply them with teachers. The archpriests' understanding of the importance of education for their faith had a vital impact on the development not only of schooling and schools, but also of the entire nation. They did not introduce any theological innovations, but returned to old models whereby priests and archbishops simply acted as "teachers." Visitations in 1733 revealed an astonishingly low level of literacy among village priests, which was incompatible with the clergy's educational mission.

Financial resources too were lacking. In 1730 the Assembly refused to introduce school surtaxes, and the state authorities prohibited the establishment of necessary funds. Schools had to be supported by contributions collected in churches and payments made by the parents of students. Teachers also were in short supply. There were no educated Serbs among contemporaries of those who had migrated in 1690, and the metropolitans were forced to hire foreigners as clerks and representatives in Vienna. The only alternative was to seek teachers from Russia, where Orthodox Christianity had been constantly developing. Tsar Peter the Great and the Russian synod accommodated the metropolitans' requests and sent the Serbs books and teachers. Although they were few in number, and some worked for only a short time, the teachers made a great impression. The most important among them was Emanuel Kozachinsky, who worked with four friends in Belgrade and Karlovci until 1736.

As well as resources and teachers, educational models were inadequate. Medieval methods of reading scriptures letter by letter, and copying and reading the Psalter or breviary, were sufficient for the "small schools" where reading and writing (occasionally arithmetic) were taught, but there was no curriculum for further work. In the Slavo-Latin School in the metropolitanate seat, Russian teachers adapted the model of contemporary European schools, which taught liberal arts from grammar to rhetoric, to the Serbian context. The Karlovci Slavo-Latin School developed to the sixth grade when rhetoric was taught.

Russian teachers and their pupils exerted a stronger influence on the development of literacy and education than did Russian liturgical works, which became mandatory in the Serbian Church. The language of old Serbian manuscripts (the Serbian variant of Church Slavonic) was abandoned and replaced by the Russian variant of Church Slavonic, with a constant influx of elements from contemporary literary language. The language of Serbian literature became interlaced with Russian elements (Slavo-Serbian) to such an extent that it became incomprehensible to laymen. Significant differences were noticeable among different authors, and as the aim for "high style" increased, so the clarity of the text declined. Toward the end of the century, Dositej Obradović, one of the most influential authors, wrote using a language close to that used by the people and recommended its adoption.

The death of Metropolitan Vićentije Jovanović and the departure of Kozachinsky and his friends ended the Slavo-Latin School. Educational institutions continued to depend on the personality and inclinations of the archbishop and their public welfare role was still not considered genuinely important within the church. This attitude changed during the administration of Metropolitan Pavle Nenadović (1749–68), himself a student of Serbian schools. He was experienced in administration and put all his energies into reviving the work of his predecessors. Most importantly, he created a firm financial base by founding a national schooling fund (1748), which played a crucial role in the development of Serbian culture.

Metropolitan Nenadović exhorted his congregation to send their children to school, stressing that it was both a religious obligation and an act of piety. He impressed on them the notion that without education, there could be no advancement in the military or civil services, and he encouraged peasants to educate their children and to raise them in the spirit of Christianity. He believed that elementary education was a prerequisite for true piety, and made the completion of grammar school a precondition for admission to the priesthood. State authorities later imposed stricter requirements and candidates had to pass an exam before a special committee.

A school of higher education was founded at the metropolitan's court in Sremski Karlovci with the double task of training clergymen and offering general education for secular service. The metropolitan assembled competent professors (including foreigners) and the school was modeled after the contemporary *gymnasium* (secondary school), being called a *gymnasium publicum*. Bishops founded clerical schools where active priests completed their education and future priests prepared for their calling. Military authorities in the Military Border gave financial support for the founding of German-language schools. Serbian Church circles wanted pupils to become literate and receive religious education in Serbian schools first, and this was later provided in state regulations.

Efforts by the 1769 Assembly and the church hierarchy to improve Serbian schools coincided with reforms carried out by the empress, following Prussia's example. Schools became a state concern and were financed by state authorities, with qualified teachers following a single method and curriculum. The "Normal" school that trained teachers and supervisors of the reformed schools was founded in Vienna. Among Serbs, innovations were first implemented in Banat, which was under the direct control of the Viennese authorities, and by 1777 were extended to the entire state and to Serbs in other regions. School districts were also formed. Three such districts for Serb schools were headed by prominent intellectuals and writers of the time: in Banat, Teodor Janković Mirijevski, who later reformed schools in Russia; Avram Mrazović in Bačka; and Stefan Vujanovski in Slavonia and Srem. They held classes in the seats of their school districts and passed on new methods to teachers, who were supported by each parish after it had provided a school building.

Textbooks were needed to run the schools, primarily primers for learning the alphabet and later more ambitious books. Since they had no printing press of their own, the Serbs had recourse to foreign printing houses that were interested in selling them books. They used the monastery press in Rimnicu (Romania), and the printing press of the Greek family of Theodossi in Venice, which published Serbian books for decades. After the import of Russian books was prohibited in order to decrease Russian influence and prevent money from leaving the country, Viennese printer Joseph Kurtzbeck was allowed in 1770 to obtain Cyrillic letters and was granted a monopoly in printing and selling Serbian books within the monarchy. He printed official decrees and regulations, textbooks and liturgical books, and later literary works. Despite its important role in spreading the printed word among Serbs, this printing house remained unpopular because of its propensity for technical errors and its tendentious changes in certain editions. In addition, the parallel printing of texts in Serbian and German was suspected as an attempt to convert Serbs to the Uniate Catholic Church.

The schooling reform was also viewed with suspicion because it took place on the back of reforms carried out by the Illyrian Court Deputation through the so-called *Regulamentum* of 1770 and 1777. Discontent with the church's situation and with the Deputation's ambitions to regulate the Serbs' "privileges" through a "permanent and lasting system" had given rise to debate in the Assembly of 1769 and led to the issuing of a statute regarding the Serbian community in matters of religion and church life. This *Regulamentum* contained articles on the metropolitan, bishops, priests, monks and monasteries, and certain aspects of religious life, both in the original version of 1770 and in the amended version of 1777.

Even though the *Regulamentum* was the product of many difficult debates between the episcopate and the Deputation, and it was claimed that the synod had approved each article, the document was greeted with hostility and the second version even provoked violent uprisings in Novi Sad and Vršac in 1779. The *Regulamentum* contained provisions on church supervision, accountability, ecclesiastical courts (consistories), and the curbing of individual self-will and thus brought it much closer to the ancient ideal of *sobornost* (collective rule). The fiercest opposition was to the sanitary regulations on burial rites, which were contradictory to custom, and to the reduction in holy days, especially those of Serbian saints (only St. Sava's Day remained as the principal holy day). The number of Catholic holy days was also reduced, since there were too many nonworking days in the year. There were also general protests such as those against the monastic rules, based on the old medieval regulations and thus too strict, or those against the *Catechesis* for Serbian schools compiled by Jovan Rajić, the most prominent theologian of the time.

Despite these disputes and calls for Serbian "privileges" to be abolished, the schooling system developed in both breadth and quality. The new method was adapted to Serbian conditions and approved by the synod's commission. Demands were made by the assemblies for Orthodox students to be accepted for further education, which was supported by the authorities. Biographies from the late eighteenth century indicate that education was also continued at foreign universities. Besides studying in Vienna and Pest, Serbs attended the Kiev Theological Academy as well as German universities, often in Halle. The first printed doctoral theses in Latin date back to the middle of the century (by 1848 there were 59 doctorates in medicine and eight in law).

Toward the end of the century the idea of establishing higher schools of learning was being elaborated. A seminary to educate priests in Timişoara was planned but never carried out. In the metropolitan seat, which had a long tradition of schooling, a school of theology was established and, in 1792, a full secondary school thanks to the legacy of Dimitrije Anastasijević Sabov and other beneficiaries. This was soon followed by a secondary school in Novi Sad in 1810. Secondary schools of the time were much more important than those that followed, offering more than just a foundation for further education. In 1812, a further advance in offering seasonal courses was made when a school for Serbian teachers was founded in Szentendre. A shift in population distribution caused this school to move south to Sombor in 1816, where it worked tirelessly to educate Serbian teachers from all regions. Serbian schooling, perhaps the greatest achievement of the eighteenth century, was to be crowned with the founding of a Serbian university. Metropolitan Stefan Stratimirović (1790–1836) did much to further this intention, even attempting to purchase a building jointly with Protestants that would serve as the university premises.

The Beginning of Europeanization

The first century under Christian rule was characterized for the Serbs by great dynamism. This can best be seen by comparing the devastated wasteland on which they initially settled to the situation at the end of the century, when this same land had become relatively well populated and urbanized, economically active and prosperous. The Serb population had grown to between 650,000 and 680,000 people before 1791, certainly on a par with other populations of the monarchy.

During this period, living conditions for every social class had been transformed under all rulers: from housing and environment, clothing and eating habits, to festivities and other forms of socializing. Changes began to accelerate during this century, and even the Serbs were not bypassed by this trend. The impetus for change came from different sides: from above, from the ruling circles and high society; from the side, from other ethnic groups; and from below, under the influence of inherited customs that had to be modified. Judging from preserved documents, Serbs were open to innovation, while avoiding anything they believed to be a threat to their faith and ethnicity. The example of schooling and education shows how foreign models were accepted, adjusted, and implemented toward ethnic development. Serbs were firmly rooted in the vernacular language, their Orthodox faith, and awareness of their traditions and would rely on this foundation when attending the "German schools," such as those in the Military Border, or when continuing their education in Latin grammar schools and universities. Contemporary skills and teaching techniques could also be used to educate and train priests in religious schools and spread religious morals among the population.

Just as schooling had been accepted and used for national development, so many other innovations that were unknown in previous centuries were adopted. The hierarchical structure and institutions previously known only within the ecclesiastical sphere now permeated the whole of church life, as well as secular society, introducing order and form in relations between people and institutions. Bureaucratization, which undeniably took over the monarchy during the eighteenth century, did not inhibit the development of Serbian society and even enhanced it, enabling the needs and interests of its constituent parts to be articulated and encouraging people to resolve their problems within small communities, such as *obšestva* (city magistrates), or in parishes and school funding authorities. The work of institutions and social bodies developed a feeling of community and public-mindedness that transcended individuals' personal interests. The Serbs now began to perceive themselves as a nation, no longer an indeterminate mass of believers and warriors but a complex entity with numerous elements held together by an extended awareness of themselves as distinct from others.

When conditions improved to such an extent that members of the congregation could afford to construct and furnish churches themselves, they were no longer modeled on distant medieval Serbian monuments. After the period of modest half-timbered or log churches such as those under Ottoman rule, there was a change toward large baroque edifices. Large bell towers were built on the western side of the rectangular-based church with an apse, and symbolic substitutes for domes, reminiscent of Byzantine tradition, were in the center. Northern settlements were the first to accept the new style, apparently in those places where the civic element had taken root (Szentendre, Buda, Szeged, and Dunaszekcsö). The metropolitanate itself made the new style official by constructing two churches in Karlovci. Their example was followed by larger cities

Plate 5.3   Serbian baroque: cathedral of the metropolitans in Sremski Karlovci, built 1758–62, facade remodeled in the nineteenth century. (Photograph by Dušan Tasić, Legacy of D. Tasić, Institut istorije umetnosti, Filozofski fakultet, Belgrade, with permission)

and later by villages. There is a surprisingly large number of eighteenth-century churches in the vast region from Trieste and Fiume (Rijeka) to Szekesfehervar, Szentendre, Arad, and Timişoara.

Older monasteries in Srem received baroque features. The new style was not limited to church architecture but was extended to church decoration, icon painting, iconostases, church vessels, furnishings, and so on. Graphic art also gained importance and produced such masters as Hristifor Žefarović (ca. 1700–53) and Zaharije Orfelin. Several painters of varying levels of skill and talent were engaged in icon and portrait painting. The fact that Serbs also commissioned foreigners, ranging from architects to graphic and applied artists, speaks of their increased cultural needs.

The abrupt change in the language of literacy and education and in the religious ambiance implied a not inconsiderable discontinuity. The old language of manuscripts was abandoned at almost the same time as medieval forms of architecture and church decoration. Although they

Plate 5.4   History revived: St. Sava surrounded by Serbian saints; copper engraving by H. Žefarović and Th. Messmer, Vienna, 1741. (From D. Davidov, *Spska grafika XVIII veka*, Novi Sad, 1978, with permission of the author)

had left behind the poverty and crudeness of the Ottoman period, Serbs under the monarchy did not sever all ties with their past; abandoning old ways on the everyday practical level, they zealously returned to their roots, saints and rulers, church and state, which had been destroyed by the Ottoman conquest.

Even before books on Serbian history appeared, church elders used images and symbols to emphasize the Serbs' descent from famous and sacrosanct predecessors: St. Simeon and St. Sava, the holy martyr St. Lazar, and other saintly rulers, who were petitioners with Christ and the Virgin Mary. Numerous prints, engravings, and panoramic paintings in monasteries and churches depict the Serbs' patron saints. Since Russian ceremonial books embraced Russian not Serbian saints, the metropolitanate recalled its own by publishing collections of church service books and hagiographies (*Srbljak*, 1761, 1765), painting Serbian saints on iconostases, and introducing obligatory holidays to honor their memories. This occurred at precisely the time the authorities were reducing the number of holidays. According to contemporary customs, the metropolitanate had its own heraldic symbols, which it chose from those that were believed to be the symbols of the Serbian Empire, including crowns, fire steels, and the two-headed eagle.

Knowledge of history served a practical purpose since it was often necessary to call on historical arguments to defend the nation's individuality. Neither epic oral history nor the fragmented hagiographic tradition fostered by the church was sufficient, so clergymen went abroad beginning in 1728 to seek authors of Serbian history. Their efforts yielded nothing until 1765, when the first condensed history, entitled *A Short Introduction to the History of the Slavo-Serbian People* and written by Pavle Julinac, was printed in Venice. When it was published, another prominent Serbian author, Jovan Rajić (1726–1801), was finishing a much larger and more ambitious work entitled *The History of Different Slavic Peoples, especially the Bulgars, Croats and Serbs*, which was published in four volumes in 1794–5. This learned and documented work, written in the spirit of contemporary historiography, linked the history of the Serbs with antiquity and the migration of peoples, and placed it in the context of European development. Up until the 1870s it provided the main source of information on Serbian history.[2]

This shift from hagiographic legends and epic motifs to scholastic historiography originating in written sources reveals how modern Serbian

2   Commissioned by Metropolitan Stefan Stratimirović, Rajić translated from the German *A Brief History of the Kingdoms of Serbia, Raška, Bosnia and Rama* (Vienna, 1793), part of the work on world history begun in England.

culture was formed through the combined influence of educated authors, printing houses, and the interests of a literate public, whose profile may be sketched from lists of subscribers to certain books. Starting in the 1760s, the wider reading public was offered calendars with useful and entertaining contents, practical lessons, and information. Periodicals offered a continuation of this at a higher level, first the *Slaveno-serbskij magazin* (1768, only one issue, printed in Venice), then the *Serbskija (povsednevnija) novini* (1791–2, Vienna), and the weekly *Slaveno-serbskija vjedomosti* (1792–4, Vienna).

СЛАВЕННО - СЕРБСКІЯ ВѢДОМОСТИ

Nᵣₒ. I.

Съ Цесаро - Кралевскимъ благоутробнымъ дозволеніемъ.

Въ ВТОРНИКЪ дне 3. АУГУСТА 1792.

ЦЕСАРО- КРАЛЕВСКІЯ ДЕРЖАВИ.

Аустрія.

Изъ Віенни : По извѣстію Фелд-цайгмайстра Кнaзa отъ Хохенлое подъ 4. Аугуста данному , войска Цесаро-Кралевскa противу Француза опредѣ-ленна, отъ 19. Баталліона ПѢшака, и 13. Дивизіона Кавалеріе состоящаcя изъ Лагера при Швецнигу бывшегъ, 1. Аугуста у 10. сахати ноѣи креку-лассе, и на три тала раздѣленна , рѣ-ку Рэннъ подъ нѣговимъ Предводи-тельствомъ безбѣдно прешла,и противъ Непріятела храбро ополчилассе есть.

Повседневно искуство доказало е, да онъ лѣта 1784. како с свакомъ допу-щенно съ Дерви терговати, цѢна ве-сма скочила е, и тако намѢреніе, кое е ова спасителна Нареdба имала, ніесе достигло ; зато по всевысочаишему повелѢнію отъ 26. истекшаго Месеца дижесе она Нареdба , и за будуще, са-мо онимъ Ладромъ, консу отъ ста-рине допущеніе имали съ Дерви терго-вати , и то осведочити могу, или на ново Допущенъ изпросе , съ Дерви терговати допущдалассе, кое за вѢдо-ностЬ и управленіе , онимъ , консе тиѣ: авлассе.

По резолуцім отъ 4. Іоліа сего лѣ-та у становлассе, да между Терговци,

Plate 5.5 Early periodicals: front page of the *Slaveno-serbskija vjedomosti*, August 3, 1792. (From the reprint of the same periodical)

Owing to the complementary interests of printers and authors, the Serbian community obtained important intellectual tools such as grammar books and foreign language dictionaries (Latin, 1765, 1766; German, 1772, 1774, 1780, 1791, 1793; Hungarian, 1795; French, 1805), guides to Slavic grammar, orthography, correct speech (1793, 1794), and calligraphy (1776, 1778, 1795). Manuals for different purposes and professions were printed in Slavo-Serbian: guidebooks for priests (1747, 1787), teachers (1776, 1782, 1787), for writing applications and petitions (1785, 1796), and even for etiquette (1794) and cooking (1805). Guides for practical life were also published: a guidebook for peasant youths (1772) and directions for planting tobacco (1790). *The Experienced Wine-Maker* (1783) was written by the great scholar Zaharije Orfelin.

The role of the printed word among Serbs in the second half of the eighteenth century may be assessed by its increased use for official public notification on the one hand, and by the share of non-utilitarian literature on the other. Official printed documents included not only the ruler's "privileges" but also laws and numerous regulations for the entire state, as well as regulations for the Military Border, the *Regulamentum*, monastic regulations, *urbaria* for certain villages, and so on. Material was sometimes in Slavo-Serbian, but often in bilingual editions in Slavo-Serbian and German. Printed matter even included invitations for public exams in schools.

On the other hand, entertaining literature was printed, a sure sign that a shift could be made from what had been an essential tool to what was a luxury. Novels came to the Serbs in the second half of the eighteenth century: Marmontel's *Bélisaire* (1776), Defoe's *Robinson Crusoe* (1799), and *Candor or the Discovery of Egyptian Secrets* (1800), which launched a series of romantic novels in the following decades. Special literature for children was also developed, including four volumes of Marie Beaumont's *Edifying Magazine for Children* (1787, 1793). Theatrical works were printed, including Carlo Goldoni's *Merchants* (1787), followed by the *Tragedy of Uroš V*, which had been written by Kozachinsky as a school play and later adapted by Jovan Rajić in 1798. Over 400 titles were printed during the century, including gospels, psalters, prayer-books, Christian morals, and even poetry in different meters by Serbian poets.

Such a variety of publications, including a significant portion of translations and adaptations, could not be imagined without translators and authors who emerged from the Serbian environment and were interested in influencing it. These intellectual mediators, as well as other educated Serbs, were familiar with the current of ideas of the period, even those that challenged the ruling hierarchy and called for change and revolution. In the last decade of the century the French revolutionaries' rebellious cries of liberty, equality, and fraternity reached the Serbs by way of officers and soldiers. But the edifying ideas made popular by Serbian authors had a far greater impact. Radical works, those by Voltaire and Pierre Bayle, remained within the circle of educated individuals, even bishops, while the works of Zaharije Orfelin (1726–85), Dositej Obradović (ca. 1740–1811), Aleksije Vezilić (1743–92), Jovan Muškatirović (1743–1809), Atanasije Stojković (1773–1832), and others achieved greater popularity.

These authors brought the German version of the Enlightenment to the Serbs, whose aim was not revolution but improvement of the world through moral perfection and the education of individuals. The Serbian authors of the age of Enlightenment, especially Dositej, merged reason and virtue with a critical view not only of individuals, but also of institutions, customs, and superstition. Criticism was aimed at monasteries, greedy clerics, and uneducated monks but did not approach the foundations of the faith: rational piety and enlightened virtue remained an ideal. This is why enlightenment could be promoted by bishops and orthodox theologians such as Jovan Rajić.

Before the turn of the century, however, there was a split within the Serbian elite not only over the absolutist authorities' reforms, but also over daily political issues. Cultural maturity and growing self-awareness were manifested in the presentations and discussions at the Timişoara Assembly of 1790. During the great revolt against absolutism following the death of Joseph II in 1790, the Serbs refused to be the object of disputes and settlements between the Viennese court and Hungarian Diet. In their efforts to be an independent entity, they were divided between two poles: some demanded Banat as their territory, based on the "privileges," while others demanded that the "privileges" become the law of the Hungarian Kingdom and the Serbs have representatives in the Hungarian Diet. In assessing their situation, some concluded that they were a nation "only in idea" because they lacked territorial organization, while others believed that what was lacking was nobility, a ruling class. The balance of power, however, had not changed. This is best illustrated in the episode of the Illyrian Court Chancellery, which was founded in early 1791 in accordance with the Serbs' wishes, but abolished in June 1792 under pressure from the Hungarian Diet.

Responding to the challenges that faced them in the Christian world, Serbs during the eighteenth century gradually created an extensive and comprehensive culture, with multiple layers and dimensions, which was passed on to later generations. Serbs in the Habsburg monarchy were able to accept and further develop this heritage, in terms of both their numbers and their institutional organization and level of education. It gradually became accepted as well by society in Serbia, whose liberation began in 1804.

6
The Era of Democratic Revolutions

"The Serbian Revolution"

There had been great changes in the structure and functioning of the Ottoman Empire at the time when Turkish rule was restored in Serbia following the Treaty of Belgrade in 1739. In parallel with the revival of sanjaks and nahias, a military-ruled region (*krajina*) was established under the direct control of the Porte. It was headed by a *muhafiz* (governor), who held the rank of vizier and was seated in Belgrade (the term Belgrade pashalik had already become customary by that time).

The sipahis returned to their *timars* but were no longer the main military force, numbering about 900 in the region. Defenses were based on fortresses and garrisons in towns. In addition to garrison troops, whose numbers were falling, there were janissaries, whose numbers were on the increase. They had long since ceased to be the sultan's guard and no longer lived in the capital; instead, they moved to different towns, engaging in crafts, trade, and various activities during times of peace. Their service was hereditary and was well paid. Janissaries made great efforts to become landowners and imposed themselves as *chiftlik* owners on Christian Turkish subjects (*reaya*). Their tyranny often led to violence and forestalled imperial policies toward the *reaya*.

The Ottoman Empire had become a shadow of the once-praised state where the rule of law had been strictly obeyed. The sultan's officers fought among themselves and squabbled over money, using the army as their personal guard. The Porte could do nothing to control renegades in certain parts of the Empire. These and other weaknesses were all too apparent in the Belgrade pashalik during the lengthy period of peace with Austria (1739–88), and even more so after the war of 1788–91.

The land had been severely depopulated. According to Turkish censuses of the pashalik in 1741, only 592 out of 1,546 villages were inhabited, while 721 were registered as abandoned and 233 as long deserted.

The land was gradually resettled, primarily from mountainous regions and without extensive colonization. Livestock breeding became more important, owing to the greater demand for exports to Austria, with pigs being raised predominantly in the vast oak forests.

Serbs under Ottoman rule were dealt a severe blow by the abolition of the Peć patriarchate in 1766. After Arsenije IV left to spend a decade administering the church in the Habsburg monarchy, the Ottoman authorities appointed a new patriarch, thus severing ties between the parts of the Serbian Church. They were later restored, but this did not help the Peć patriarchate, which had fallen heavily into debt. The ecumenical patriarchate had assumed responsibility for repaying the debt but brought the part of the Serbian Church in the Ottoman Empire under its jurisdiction. Greek bishops and priests were appointed from Istanbul and needed an interpreter in order to receive confession from their congregation, according to contemporary accounts. The worst consequence was the loss of the single church framework that had held the Serbs together for centuries. A proportion of the Serbian population lived under the ecumenical patriarchate, another under the Karlovci metropolitanate, and another under the Greek metropolitanate in Venice, while the metropolitans of Zeta, who later became secular rulers in Montenegro, were sometimes associated with Russia, and sometimes with the Karlovci metropolitanate.

The war between Austria and Turkey in 1788 provided an opportunity for the Serbs to rise up against Ottoman rule. Rebels and volunteer units (*Freikorps*) from the Military Border bore the heaviest burden. In eastern Serbia Koča Andjelković, a merchant and soldier, liberated a considerable amount of territory and, with his detachment of rebels and *Freikorps*, prevented Turkish forces in Niš from reaching the besieged Belgrade fortress. He defeated the Turks in a number of confrontations, but was captured and executed. In western Serbia, too, operations against the Turkish army were led by *Freikorps*, along with local rebels, and prevented a Turkish attack from Bosnia. Austrian troops conquered Belgrade in October 1789, but held it only briefly. Many towns were captured in Serbia, including Smederevo, Požarevac, Ćuprija, Jagodina, Karanovac, and Kruševac, but defeats on other fronts, as well as the death of Emperor Joseph II in February 1790, forced his heir to negotiate a peace, concluded in 1791, agreeing to restore the status quo ante. Belgrade was once more under Turkish rule, and the border returned to the Sava and Danube rivers. This development had drastic consequences for those Serbs who had been encouraged to rise up against the Turks, and whose efforts had proved futile. Fresh waves of migration followed.

Their suffering was partially alleviated by reforms introduced by Sultan Selim III (1789–1807) that were aimed at improving conditions in the Belgrade pashalik. The janissaries were forbidden from returning to the pashalik, their *chiftliks* were confiscated, and the old dues to the state and sipahis were restored. The embittered janissaries found support in the renegade Pasvanoglu, who drove the pasha out of Vidin and ruled the town, while the sultan's vizier in Belgrade sought assistance from the Serbs.

Some of the sultan's firmans transformed the situation in the pashalik. The people were able to choose *voivode* and *oborknez*, subject to the pasha's final approval. Starting in 1796, the community's elders distributed and collected taxes. A 15-*guruş* tax was imposed along with the regular imperial and sipahi dues, but nothing more. Turks were prohibited from settling in Serb villages. Permission was given for the repair and construction of churches and monasteries. The Serbs were also obliged to defend the pashalik against the janissaries. A detachment of between 15,000 and 16,000 men was called upon in the conflicts with Pasvanoglu.

Trade with Austria was restored in the decade following the war, bringing many benefits for the towns, especially Belgrade. Serbs grew wealthy through trading in livestock and defended their improved position by force of arms, along with the sultan's Turks. The war against the janissaries went through changing fortunes. In late 1797 the janissaries reached Belgrade, and the following year they were besieged in Vidin. The turning point came at the beginning of 1799, when the Porte, facing threats in Egypt and Syria, withdrew the prohibition on the janissaries entering the Belgrade pashalik.

Once they were back in Belgrade, the janissary leaders (*dahiyas*) temporarily held the Belgrade vizier hostage before executing him and assuming authority. Four *dahiyas* took control of the pashalik. Old *chiftliks* were restored and new ones were created, which led to arbitrary increases in taxes and forced labor. In opposition to the wishes of the Serb *reaya*, who preferred to remain separate from the Turks with only the *voivoda* contacting the pasha, the janissaries appointed their own governors in smaller towns and established *hans* (barracks), from where soldiers directly supervised and coerced the population.

The janissary regime affected not only the Serb *reaya*, but also the sipahis. In 1802 the latter made an unsuccessful attempt to restore power in the pashalik, supported by the Serbs. Afterwards, left to fend for themselves, Serb leaders started preparing for an armed uprising. They provisioned their men with weapons and ammunition, and established links between different groups. The *dahiyas* responded with the "Felling of *Knezes*," when about 70 Serbian leaders and distinguished people were executed. This only hastened the general uprising. The decision was made at a meeting of the most important people from the nahias of

Belgrade and Šumadija on February 2, 1804 (Candlemas), in the village of Orašac near Topola. Their chosen leader was Djordje Petrović – Karadjordje (Black George) (1762–1817) – an experienced soldier and former *Freikorps* fighter and *hajduk*. Owing to the links between local leaders, the rebellion took root in 9 of the 12 nahias of the pashalik. First to be attacked were the *hans*, whose crews were massacred, then larger rebel groups were formed and besieged towns including Rudnik, Valjevo, Šabac, Požarevac, and Smederevo. Even Belgrade was surrounded.

The Serbs' fight for liberation in the Belgrade pashalik began without the backing of the Great Powers, at a time when the Ottoman Empire was not at war. The uprising sparked off numerous other rebellions by the Christian *reaya* and helped unify different constituents of the Serbian population. It lasted less than a decade, from 1804 to 1813, and went through several phases. The first was between 1804 and 1805, when the Serbs rebelled not against the sultan but against his opponents, even receiving support from the imperial authorities in some places. The rebels' moderate demands were aimed at removing the janissaries and restoring the system of self-government that had existed earlier. They were without allies and sent a delegation to Russia, asking for Austria to back negotiations with the Turks, which the Turks decisively rejected. The flight of the *dahiyas* and their execution in late 1804 achieved one of the goals of the rebellion, but the regime did not change and a former assistant of the *dahiyas* remained in power in Belgrade.

In the second phase between 1805 and 1806, the uprising turned into a rebellion against the sultan, after the rebels' deputation to Istanbul had returned empty-handed. Serb demands in the Pećani Assembly in May 1805 were expanded to include calls for Serbia to be ruled by elected chieftains headed by a *voivoda*, with authorization to collect their own taxes and hand them over to the sultan. They also demanded that Turkish officials and sipahis leave the pashalik and that border defenses be entrusted to them.

The Turkish offensive failed and the sultan's army was defeated at Ivankovac (near Ćuprija) in August 1805, although some towns, including Šabac, Užice, and Smederevo, were temporarily seized by the Turks. Starting in 1806, the rebels invaded territories outside the pashalik, taking control of Poreč and Krajina in the east, Jadar and Radjevina in the west, and penetrating as far as Prokuplje, Kuršumlija, Novi Pazar, Nova Varoš, and Višegrad. Efforts were made to extend the rebellion to the clan regions. Strong ties were fostered with Montenegrin bishop Petar I, but Russia restrained Montenegro and the clans in Herzegovina. Two large Turkish armies were defeated: one in the reinforced trenches north of Aleksinac (Deligrad, June 16, 1806) and the other one from Bosnia at Mišar, a field near Šabac (August 12, 1806). The rebels' success was topped by the fall of Belgrade in late 1806.

During this period, authorities superior to the local commander or *voivoda* were established along with courts in villages, *knežinas*, and nahias. The supreme leader (*Vrhovni predvoditelj*) was Karadjordje, who convened the other leaders for assemblies when required, while another permanent body, the *Praviteljstvujušči sovjet naroda srpskog* (Administrative Council of the Serbian People), was introduced and retained its functions during the uprising.

Negotiations were renewed after the lengthy test of the rebels' strength, and Karadjordje entrusted them to Petar Ičko, a merchant from Belgrade. The Serbs' demands became more moderate: a Turkish representative would remain in Belgrade, but the offices would be controlled by Serbs; dues would be paid in a lump sum, and only "evil Turks" would be banished. An agreement was reached on the main points: the sultan's governor was allowed into Belgrade and all that remained was for the sultan to issue a firman, when a reversal occurred that foiled this settlement.

Russia went to war against Turkey in late 1806 and radically revised its view of the rebels. The Serbs broke off their negotiations, thus beginning the short-lived Serbo-Russian military alliance. Having conquered Moldavia and Wallachia, the Russian army reached the Danube and a detachment crossed the river to take part in operations in Serbia. The Russians later had garrisons in Belgrade and Šabac. The uprising gained new momentum with victories in fierce battles near Štubik and Malajnica; Niš was surrounded while Leskovac and regions along the Nišava River were raided. Peasant rebellions erupted and Priboj, Rudo, and Višegrad were temporarily controlled by the Serbs. However, international affairs once again influenced the development of the uprising. Russia signed the Treaty of Tilsit with Napoleon in 1807, which affected Russian relations with the Ottoman Empire and led to the truce of Slobozia in August 1807. This provided the Serbs with Russian protection until the expiration of the treaty in the spring of 1809.

The period of peace between 1807 and 1809 was used to heal wounds, rebuild war-damaged lands, and strengthen the state organization. The *Praviteljstvujušči sovjet* became the highest judicial authority; it was reorganized in 1811 and became a government with six *popečitelji* (ministers) for the main departments. Magistrates or administrative courts were formed in the nahia seats in 1808 and became the local civil authority. The Great Court of the Land was also established. In the same year Karadjordje was granted the right of succession, and in 1811 he received the title of *vožd* (leader), which is mentioned most often with his name. This was all the more crucial because opposition to Karadjordje had begun to emerge, headed by Milenko Stojković and Petar Dobrnjac. They were banished from Serbia in 1811, thus ending domestic quarrels.

The military and state finances were reformed, and education received special attention. About 50 new elementary schools were opened, adding to the traditional schools in monasteries, and the Great School (the embryo of the Gymnasium) was established in Belgrade in 1808. Serbs from Hungary made an enormous contribution and came to teach. Among them was the writer Dositej Obradović, who became Minister of Education and remained in Serbia until his death. The rebels came across symbols in learned works of the eighteenth century and placed them on their state seals and flags.

Renewed Russian–Turkish hostility in the spring of 1809 initiated the next phase of the uprising and reestablished the Serbo-Russian alliance, which lasted until 1812. The rebels advanced in several directions (Vidin, Niš, Bosnia, Stari Vlah) in the expectation of a Russian offensive, which was late in coming. Karadjordje reached the Lim River region, where he was joined by the mountain clans, but news of Turkish advances and the

Plate 6.1   Oriental heritage: the Great School building (1808–13). (Photograph by Dušan Tasić, Legacy of D. Tasić, Institut istorije umetnosti, Filozofski fakultet, Belgrade, with permission)

Serb defeat near Kamenica (not far from Niš) forced him to beat a hasty retreat. The Turks then formed a corridor along the Morava River, which extended to the Danube. Karadjordje successfully halted their progress, but at the cost of heavy casualties. The Russian crossing of the Danube in September 1809 and clashes in northern Bulgaria alleviated the Serbs' position, and they reclaimed all territories except Krajina and the Timok valley. The trenches in Deligrad were once again under Serbian control. Krajina and Crna Reka were conquered by a joint offensive in the spring of 1810, and victories at Varvarin in September 1810 and Tičar (near Loznica) in October 1810 obstructed the Turkish onslaught. After years of warfare, however, the rebels were exhausted, and disagreements among the leaders and opposition to Karadjordje increased.

The representative of the Russian command interfered in these internal disputes, which led Karadjordje to seek help from Austria and even from Napoleon, who had incited the Turks against the Serbs at the beginning of the uprising. The year 1811 passed by in border skirmishes, without any greater activity, until European politics once again affected the course of the uprising – this time fatally. Threatened by Napoleon's attack, Russia signed the Treaty of Bucharest with Turkey in 1812. Article 8 guaranteed amnesty for the Serbs, but they were to surrender their arms and allow the Turks to enter their towns. Autonomy was also provided, but it had to be jointly agreed by the Porte and the rebels. This last phase of the uprising (1812–13) was characterized by desperate resistance, since Serb leaders refused to accept the conditions provided in the Treaty of Bucharest. In the summer of 1813, heavily armed Turkish troops advanced along the thinly extended line of defense, breaking through in several places and forcing the leaders of the uprising to flee the country.

The bulk of the Serbian population sought salvation in flight, while others surrendered, including former leaders, hoping for amnesty despite the Turkish side's failure to observe the peace treaty. Some degree of moderation was exercised, inducing people to return from the refugee camps. The earlier pashalik administration was restored, and property was returned to the Turks. The administration resembled the regime of the *dahiyas*, with its increased dues and taxes, violence, and intimidation, although there were no janissaries. The people and remaining *voivode* soon began to resist. By 1814 Haçi-Prodan's rebellion had erupted in the Požega nahia, but it was isolated and put down with heavy loss of life. The timing was highly unfavorable for the Serbs, since the Holy Alliance formed by the Congress of Vienna after Napoleon's defeat was opposed to uprisings and rebellions and in favor of preserving Turkey.

Despite this, in Takovo on April 23, 1815 (Palm Sunday), the remaining Serb leaders decided to start a rebellion under Miloš Obrenović, *voivoda* of the Rudnik nahia, who had taken a less prominent role during the first uprising. This was not an uprising against the sultan, and towns were targeted because there were no Turks in the villages. After successive battles around Čačak, Valjevo, and Požarevac, the Turks were chased out of the territory of the Belgrade pashalik. This situation was unacceptable to the Porte and two armies were dispatched against the rebels, one from Bosnia and the other from the capital. Miloš Obrenović entered into negotiations with both commanders and eventually yielded to Marashli Ali-Pasha, with whom he reached a verbal agreement in August 1815. This provided for dues to be collected by Serb elders, for trials of Serbs to be attended by Serb *knezes*, for the establishment of a National Office in Belgrade consisting of 12 *knezes*, and for villages to remain inaccessible to sipahis except for the collection of the tithe. This restricted and informal autonomy gave Prince Miloš stability while he negotiated with the Porte and extended his authority in different ways. Fifteen years later, an edict (*hatt-i-sherif*) of the sultan made Miloš's position as hereditary prince official and he achieved internationally recognized autonomy.

Contemporaries and their descendants called the 1804 rebellion an uprising against the *dahiyas*. From a later perspective, it is clear that the struggle was a long and complex one, with clear differences separating the first uprising – Karadjordje's – from the second – Miloš's. Depending on which dynasty was in power in Serbia at a given moment, either one uprising or the other was held in greater respect. Observing events at close hand from a world-historical perspective, Leopold von Ranke called the Serbs' struggle in the Belgrade pashalik the "Serbian revolution," in his book published in 1829. This term was justified by the twin achievements of national liberation, in the form of a lasting but limited autonomy, and personal liberation, with the abolition of dependency and serfdom. However, these achievements were only attained through a continuous effort that lasted 30 years; therefore, the revolution is best seen not as a single event but as a chain of events, from the epic heroics and self-sacrifice of Karadjordje's period to the prosaic years of Miloš's despotic rule, which will be discussed later.

Imposed Revolution

In the late seventeenth century, territories in the Dalmatian hinterland that were suitable for the development of Christian society were also liberated through uprisings and war. Here too, conflicts were followed by migration to Venetian territories, where the Serbian population joined their compatriots who had settled earlier. Here, however, they found themselves under a regime that had been maintained and developed since the Middle Ages. The pillars of the Venetian colonial empire were the coastal cities – the communes of Zadar, Šibenik, Trogir, and Split, from where the patriciate ruled the modest town districts. The old order was preserved through statutes; each town was directly subordinate and economically linked to Venice, while those in the deeper hinterland were cut off by the inaccessible Dinaric Alps.

There were far fewer Serbs here than in the Pannonian Basin. Mid-eighteenth-century estimates place their numbers at around 40,000. They were still called Morovlachs, but this name gradually fell into disuse. Some strayed into the towns, where there were several Serbian merchants and officers from Bosnia, but the majority remained in the outer territories where they had been settled by the Venetian Republic and where they were subject to the tithe and military service. An organization similar to that of the Military Border was created, with divisions into military units ruled by a commander (*serdar, harambasha*). Outstanding soldiers and officers received hereditary land, while the rest agreed to work the land under the established colonate.

The settlers, who were mostly herders, adjusted to the local conditions and moved into farming. Instructions, or rather orders, aimed at rationalizing agriculture were issued by the towns. Venetian towns, with the exception of Split and Zadar, did not play as important a role as Dubrovnik in acting as intermediaries in trade with the hinterland. Venice was clearly in general decline, and world trade shifted to the Atlantic. Dalmatia, which had been a highly developed region during the Middle Ages, became impoverished and the center of development moved northward, with Trieste and Fiume (Rijeka) reaping the benefits.

Serbs were dispersed throughout the Venetian territories, with a larger concentration to be found only in Gornji Kotari. They were conspicuous by their faith and were regarded as "Slavo-Serbian people following the Greek rites of the Eastern Church." There were no "privileges" here, and decisions of the supreme Venetian authorities dating back to the sixteenth century continued to hold sway. These prohibited interference in the church life of Orthodox subjects, but this was not sufficient to protect them from the fervor of local Catholic prelates and priests, who persistently sought to convert Orthodox believers to the Uniate Church. Orthodox clergy were obstructed and the Peć patriarch was not allowed to visit the Orthodox congregation living under Venetian rule. Orthodox believers came under the jurisdiction of the Greek archpriest, the titular metropolitan of Philadelphia, seated in Venice, until he accepted the Uniate Church. Archpriests from neighboring regions were denied permission to work and local clerics could not be ordained.

The situation was more favorable in the south, where the whole of Boka was under Venetian rule following the capture of Novi (Herceg Novi). Waves of immigration were much greater here and the Serbian component was much more dominant. While Dalmatia had 50 Orthodox churches and three monasteries, there were 138 churches and four monasteries in Boka. In the city of Kotor itself, some renowned town churches were turned over to the Orthodox Church. Starting in the mid-eighteenth century, new churches were erected in Serbian villages and schools were founded, with the local population being responsible for finding and supporting teachers.

The Gulf of Kotor found itself in a similar situation with regard to the hinterland as that it had experienced during the time of the Crnojević family, except that instead of a large number of *katuns*, the Venetian authorities were bordered by a small number of clans, and the might of the *voivoda* was replaced by the moral authority of the Zeta metropolitans seated in the Cetinje monastery. The focus of the clans' political life, which had been centered in Herzegovina in the early seventeenth century, now moved to Montenegro. At the time, Montenegro was limited to four nahias and, instead of an outlet to the sea, it had a narrow stretch of shoreline on Lake Skadar. Adjoining it was Brda, the territory of seven large clans: the Bjelopavlići, Piperi, Bratonožići, Kuči, Rovci, Morača, and Vasojevići. The fortified towns of Podgorica, Nikšić, Spuž, Riječki Grad, Medun, Žabljak, Bar, and Ulcinj were under Turkish control. Sipahis and *timars* existed only in the flatlands along the rivers. The Ottoman authorities demanded military service of the clansmen during times of war, but were otherwise satisfied with the *harač*, which they often seized by force. Raiding was prohibited, and the clans were in frequent conflict over territory, looting, and vendettas.

Montenegro's main supporter was Venice, with which it established alliances during times of war and economic cooperation in times of peace. This situation continued until the early eighteenth century, when Metropolitan Danilo (1697–1735) found a protector in far-off Russia, from which aid and liberation were expected. Both came as Russia developed as a European power, reviving its old ties with the Serbian Church probably through the influence of Serbs at the Russian court, including Sava Vladislavić and Mihailo Miloradović.

Balkan Christians were called to arms when Tsar Peter I went to war with Turkey in 1710. Colonel Mihailo Miloradović appeared among the Montenegrin and neighboring clans, and together with the metropolitan launched an unsuccessful attack on Turkish towns. A retaliatory Turkish expedition on Cetinje followed in 1712, when the monastery was torched, and then another expedition in 1714 that brought great destruction. Venice clashed with Turkey between 1714 and 1718 over Montenegrin refugees, whom it did not wish to hand over, and links with the Montenegrins were revived, resulting in the acceptance of Venetian protectorate status in 1717. The Republic pledged to provide help, respect Montenegrin autonomy, and pay a certain number of chieftains, but it also imposed its right to appoint a *guvernadur* (governor) from among Montenegrin ranks. This title became hereditary in the Radonjić family and represented a counterbalance to the metropolitanate for a full century. Following the Treaty of Passarowitz in 1718, the narrow belt in the hinterland between Kotor and Budva that included Grbalj, Pobori, Maine, and Brajići came under Venetian rule. Since this area included the Stanjević monastery, the bishop obtained a secondary residence in Venetian territory.

From this time until its demise, Venice did not wage war against the Ottoman Empire. Consequently, Montenegrin policies turned increasingly to Russia, and occasionally to Austria in the second half of the century. Links with Russia were especially strengthened during the office of Metropolitan Sava Petrović (1735–81) and that of his relative and assistant, and occasional adversary, Vasilije Petrović (bishop from 1750 to 1766). Both visited the Russian court on several occasions and obtained aid for themselves and for their country. Vasilije in particular made bold and unrealistic plans. In his desire to inform the Russian public about the Montenegrin struggle, he published *The History of Montenegro* in Moscow in 1754, in which he glorified the centuries of struggle, proclaimed the Montenegrins' superiority, and emphasized the important role of the metropolitan and his family.

A cult of Russia began to emerge in the meantime, enabling an adventurer named Šćepan the Little (1766–73) to rule Montenegro on the basis of his claim to be the murdered Tsar Peter III. He imposed his rule with the help of monks and a group of chieftains, made peace between the clans, and prohibited vendettas and banditry. Using a detachment of a few dozen soldiers, he paved the way for the establishment of central authority. After his assassination, fighting resumed between the clans and continued even when the Ottoman threat increased with the installation of the Bushatli family as pashas of Skadar. Mahmud pasha set his goal as the conquest of Montenegro and first devastated the land in 1785, when Cetinje monastery was destroyed for the last time. In the allied war against Turkey (Russia 1787–92, Austria 1788–91), Montenegro was involved more as a theater of operations than as a warring side. Even though the ensuing peace treaty provided amnesty for the Montenegrins, Mahmud pasha renewed his offensive in 1792. In the summer of 1796, he led a great army against Brda but was defeated in the battle of Martinići. A fresh expedition against Montenegro in the fall of that year also ended in defeat and the death of the pasha. The struggle with the Bushatli family not only drew Brda and Montenegro closer together, it also rein-forced and increased the authority of Metropolitan Petar I Petrović Njegoš (1784–1830).

A crucial event for Montenegro's development took place at this time. The medieval world, which had been preserved under the Venetian lion, was shaken when French revolutionary troops entered Venice in the spring of 1797. Fighting broke out in some Dalmatian towns, where French supporters were quickly crushed. After the fall of the Venetian Republic, the Montenegrins seized Pobori, Brajići, and Maine, the last remaining Venetian land, but when the Treaty of Campo Formio ceded Venetian territories to Austria, Bishop Petar I himself handed over the keys of Budva to the Austrian governor.

Under the influence of great changes in the region and the unity forged in the struggle against the Turks, an attempt was made to establish state institutions in Montenegro. The *Praviteljstvo suda crnogorskog i brdskog* (Court Council of Montenegro and Brda) was installed by the assemblies of 1797 and 1798, with the task of making peace between clans and resolving other disputes. Legislative reforms were begun at the same time, with the adoption in 1798 and 1803 of the *Zakonik obšči crnogorski i brdski* (General Law for Montenegro and Brda), based entirely on common law.

The existence of a new ruler of the Adriatic coast, Austria, did not alter local circumstances. There was no time for more extensive reforms, because by December 1805 Austria was forced to cede the former Venet-ian territories to Napoleon, in accordance with the Treaty of Pressburg. The takeover was made difficult because Russia, which had strongholds on the Ionian islands, was allowed into Kotor and seized Korčula in the meantime. The age-old Republic of Dubrovnik also fell victim during these battles. The city was conquered by the French army in May 1806, in an effort to forestall the Russians. The Republic of Dubrovnik was abolished in 1808 and its territories were absorbed by Napoleon's Kingdom of Italy, along with the Venetian holdings. French rule was introduced in Boka, and in 1809 it was expanded to include Slovenian lands and parts of Croatia and the Military Border. These territories were extracted from the Kingdom of Italy and joined into the Illyrian Provinces. French rule did not last long, but brought changes that would outlive it. Serfdom and its associated taxes and duties were abolished, as were aristocratic institutions, and equality before the law and courts was introduced. Roads were built systematically and the economy was devel-oped, but the sea blockade stranded the formerly active Dubrovnik and Kotor fleets.

The French authorities' efforts to culturally unite the entire region under their control, by giving it the learned name of Illyria, conflicted with the reality of its numerous religious, linguistic, dialectic, and other differences. They therefore adapted administration and schooling to the "language of the land" or the "language of the surroundings." Belonging to the Orthodox Church, attributed with "Greek rites," was of crucial importance to the Serbs and their individuality. The legalization of religious tolerance and equality of religions in 1808 allowed the church to develop freely. An Orthodox metropolitanate was established in Šibenik and included 40 parishes. What characterized French rule was the separation of this eparchy from other Orthodox churches.

Relations between Montenegro and the French authorities in Dubrovnik and Kotor were permanently tense, and an attack was planned in 1811 because of Montenegro's damaging influence on imperial subjects in the coastal region. However, the following year the Montenegrins established ties with England, whose fleet entered the Adriatic and seized Budva in the fall of 1813 (the English took Herceg Novi at that time and Kotor in early 1814). It seemed a propitious moment to declare the unification of Montenegro and Boka (November 1813, January 1814), including a pledge that they would not separate in the future. A joint administration was established on the basis of parity. However, Austria was anxious to reclaim Dalmatia and its other territories in the Adriatic. Confronting Austrian troops in the spring of 1814, the Montenegrins only briefly postponed the inevitable, since Russia had already agreed for the establishment of Austrian rule.

In abolishing the republic and communes, French revolutionaries actually paved the way for extended Austrian sovereignty, which did not abandon the achievements of the previous regime. Dalmatia and Boka remained a separate administrative unit directly subjugated to the crown. It was ruled by a governor but did not have an assembly, and there was no military recruitment for a long time. Importantly for the Serbs, the regulations on religious equality remained in effect, even though pressure to convert to the Uniate Church would continue for decades.

The changes that occurred after the fall of the Venetian Republic encouraged the Serbs' social development in Dalmatia. The urban element became more visible, the number of educated people increased, and a specific cultural atmosphere was created that supported schools (in 1847 there were 52 Serbian schools with 3,838 students – one-third of them girls). Local publications appeared, such as the *Ljubitelj prosvješćenija – Srbsko dalmatinski almanah* (Serbian Dalmatian Almanac, 1836), which later became the *Srpsko-dalmatinski magazin* (Serbo-Dalmatian Magazine). In 1855 publication began of the *Dalmatinski glasnik* (Dalmatian Herald), and the Matica Dalmatinska cultural society was founded in 1861.

The clans' territory was not directly influenced by French ideas and organization. Montenegro had the greatest contact with the French, having been included in the French regime after its brief unification with Boka. French influence is apparent from efforts to create state institutions and bring about peace between the clans. Before Montenegro could address these issues, however, it had to focus on the struggle against famine and protect itself from the plague. Montenegro also had to settle relations with its new neighbor, Austria, with which it had border disputes that were formally resolved in 1828 and 1841, without the participation of the Ottoman authorities. During the years of hardship, mass migrations took place, primarily to Serbia, but plans for migrations to Russia fell through. Even though it was still tied to Russia and in need of its aid, Montenegro remained passive during the 1828–9 war between Russia and the Ottoman Empire.

A change on the Montenegrin throne reinvigorated relations with Russia as well as the development of foreign and domestic policy. According to custom, Petar I had appointed as his successor his nephew Rade Tomov, who became Petar II and ruled as archimandrite until 1833,

Plate 6.2   Birth of a capital: monastery (1485) and palace (1838), the nuclei of Cetinje as the political and cultural center of Montenegro. (Photograph by B. Strugar)

when he was ordained bishop in Russia. Before his voyage, Russian advisers helped him continue the development of state bodies. The *Praviteljstvujušči senat crnogorski i brdski* (Administrative Senate of Montenegro and Brda) was established and was accompanied in the clans by *gvardije* (guards), who had judiciary, law enforcement, and defensive functions. The bishop was escorted by bodyguards (*perjanici*). Taxes were introduced in 1833 and allowed for a state budget that no longer relied entirely on Russian aid. The greatest cultural advance took place during the reign of Petar II Njegoš, who was celebrated by his contemporaries as a poet. A school and printing press were founded in Cetinje in 1834, where the first Montenegrin periodical, *Grlica* (Turtledove), was printed from 1836 to 1839. Montenegro freed itself of its former isolation thanks to the authority of Bishop Petar II and became an influential force among the South Slavs.

From Prince's Autonomy to Autonomous Principality

Miloš personally carried out and maintained the terms he had negotiated with Marashli Ali-Pasha in 1815, as he negotiated with the Porte and developed unlimited power in the country. He put the National Office under his control and replaced local elders with his own people, thus abolishing the remnants of local self-government that had been left over from the Ottoman period. He convened the Assembly only to announce his orders, obtain approval for taxation, and, in 1817, to have himself elected supreme prince with hereditary rights. He dealt ruthlessly with disobedient chieftains and did not refrain from executing prominent leaders who challenged him. His victims included not just leaders from the uprising, such as Petar Moler, Sima Marković, Pavle Cukić, and Melentije Nikšić, but even Karadjordje, who was killed in 1817 on his return to Serbia.

Miloš's regime did not differ much from that of the Turks, especially because of the tribute and *kuluk* (forced labor), which aroused discontent among the population. He brutally crushed uprisings in 1817, 1821, 1825, and 1826 and intimidated the people and rebels. Miloš acted as both legislator and judge, using his unlimited power for personal gain, and farmed the Turkish customs duties and taxes that were due to the sultan. He provided himself and his partners with a trade monopoly, ruling the land as though it were his estate. At the same time, he drove the Turks out of the nahia seats and towns, limiting their presence to the fortified towns and their movement to the main roads.

Prince Miloš did not leave any room for doubt as to his loyalty to the sultan: he thwarted secret societies and refused to help the Greek uprising of 1821 and smaller rebellions against Turkish rule. He also took every opportunity to exploit the difficult situation in the Ottoman Empire for his own personal ends, obtaining permission for the *haraç* to be paid in an annual lump sum and making his title hereditary. After Russia had imposed obligations on Turkey in peace negotiations of 1826 and 1829, he was also able to recover six nahias that had been liberated during the first uprising.

The autonomy envisaged in 1812 was finally reached through the sultan's *hatt-i sherifs* of 1829, 1830, and 1833. The first two granted Serbia religious freedom, an administration headed by a prince,[1] with the title being handed down through Miloš's family, and the right to maintain its own army and institutions such as hospitals, printing houses, a postal service, and independent judiciary. It was decreed that the Turks would not interfere in domestic affairs and would leave Serbia, except for garrisons in the old imperial fortified towns of Belgrade, Šabac, Smederevo, Užice, Soko, and Kladovo. The third *hatt-i sherif* returned the six nahias to the Serbs and provided a lump sum for all rights and estates of the sultan and sipahis. The takeover of the nahias was hastened by uprisings in 1832 (1833 in eastern Serbia), at a time when the Empire was greatly troubled by unrest in the provinces. Prince Miloš sent his army and the sultan could only acknowledge the fact and include the six nahias within the annual *haraç* of 2,300,000 Turkish guruš. Miloš prohibited forced labor in 1831, bringing to an end all links between the Serbian peasant and the Turkish sipahi. However, in transforming the tribute into a state tax, the prince included the sipahi tithe within it, leaving a remnant of the feudal duties that was abolished only in 1835.

The eviction of the Turks provided the conditions for peasants to become owners of the land that they worked. This process occurred in stages. Ownership was acknowledged only for those holding the *tapu* (deed), which served as a basis on which they worked the land. Some peasants did not have deeds, so it was decided that their land should be surveyed and entered in the land registry. However, this could not be carried out for lack of able personnel. The Turks left behind vast complexes of abandoned villages with land in between. This land became state property and was leased to the villages and often used to house new settlers in the principality.

At this time the question arose as to whether there should be a noble class in Serbia and estates owned by Serbian nobles. This was the aspiration of the elders, many officials, and even the prince's relatives. Russia

---

1 The title was formally *knjaz*. From 1827, the title of *knez*, the vernacular form of the same title, was prohibited for elders of lower rank.

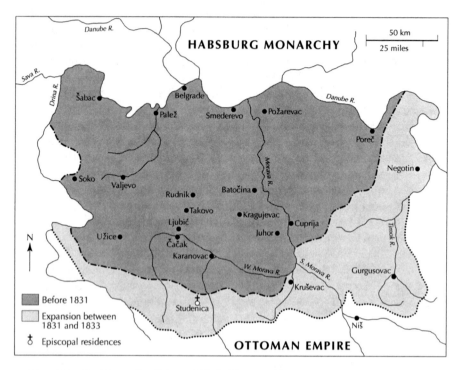

Map 6.1   Serbia under Prince Miloš Obrenović.

and the Serbs from Hungary also supported the idea, pointing to the example of Wallachia and Moldavia. The prince opposed it, although he refused to commit himself explicitly for a long time. However, the constitution of 1838 unequivocally prohibited the restitution of a feudal society.

Autonomy brought church issues to the forefront. After the fall of the medieval state, the church continued to flourish under Christian rulers during the eighteenth century, successfully carrying on its religious and educational mission without relying on state authorities. On the other hand, the struggle to revive the state was fought without the church after 1804. The Greek bishops were at variance with the leaders of the first uprising, and an attempt to ordain a Serbian metropolitan in Russia was unsuccessful for canonical reasons. There were two bishops in the liberated principality, the metropolitan in Belgrade and the bishop of Užice and Valjevo, both under the ecumenical patriarchate in Istanbul.

Like the "first-crowned" king six centuries earlier, Prince Miloš had to obtain ecclesiastical autocephaly for his country. He succeeded in 1831 when Milentije Pavlović (1831–3) was ordained metropolitan of Belgrade and the whole of Serbia, with all Serbian bishops subordinated to him. The bishoprics of Valjevo and Užice were separated, with the Valjevo seat being moved to Šabac. Soon afterwards a fourth bishop was ordained, the bishop of Timok, seated in Zaječar, who covered the eastern part of the new six nahias. The second metropolitan was Petar Jovanović (1833–59, d. 1864), a former clerk of the Karlovci metropolitan and then of Prince Miloš, who was ordained in Istanbul after first taking his vows. Subsequent metropolitans were chosen and ordained in Serbia.

Metropolitan Petar was very active and did much to settle church affairs. The problems he encountered were those of discipline and an uneducated clergy, disorganized marital relations within the congregation, and interference from laymen in church matters. He founded a theological school in 1836, passed regulations on the organization of the church, established the synod and consistories in the bishoprics, and introduced registers of births, marriages, and deaths in the parishes.

The prince's great personal power had another side, reflected in his ceaseless efforts to better the lot of his subjects, do away with bad habits, and introduce innovations that would improve the economy and living conditions. Although he was illiterate, Miloš was well informed and was always accompanied by an educated Serb from Hungary. He acted as a role model, introducing improvements on his estates and giving advice and directions; in the second period of his rule, these were given by means of regulations and Assembly decisions.

Miloš ordered the establishment of food reserves in villages in an effort to suppress famine. Food was taken during periods of want and replenished when conditions improved. He ordered the cultivation of potatoes, and the crop became widespread after 1818. Field watchmen were introduced to reduce damage and prevent conflicts, but the educators (*ekonomi*) appointed to instruct the peasants, improve the level of agriculture, and increase the number of livestock did not remain. The prince urged the cultivation of vineyards and the introduction of new crops such as tobacco, mulberry, and sugar beet. He brought the mining expert, Baron Siegmund Herder, to Serbia in 1835 to visit mining sites, assess the deposits, and analyze the content of mineral springs. Coal mining was introduced in 1837 but did not fare well. The first industrial facilities – breweries, brickworks, mills, and leather processing – were established during Miloš's reign.

Ordinary people's way of life was affected the most by the prince's *ušoravanje* (from *šor*, Hungarian for street). This was a settlement regulation that transformed scattered habitations into compact towns with streets. The project started in western Serbia in 1830 and was extended to the entire country in 1837. This regulation was intended to place settlements in the most favorable locations, increase their size by joining two or more villages (according to the 1834 census, the average was 43 houses per village), and bring together and link the population. There was resistance to the plan, and some people even fled further into the hills, but on the whole the population distribution was altered, especially in large and small towns and large villages, where a preliminary layout was drafted by engineers. Prince Miloš increased the population and area of agricultural land through a general policy of settlement, land allocation, and temporary tax exemption, which in turn brought fundamental change – a shift from herding to agriculture as the economic foundation.

In 1815 the population is estimated to have numbered about 473,000 people; in 1834, when an unreliable census was taken, the figure had increased to 578,192, which implies a density of 17.9 people per km². According to the 1841 census, the population had increased to 828,845, with a density of 21.9 people per km². By the middle of the century, the population was almost a million (956,863; i.e., 25.3 per km²). Growth was the consequence not only of a high birthrate, but also of the influx of people from territories that remained under Turkish rule. Food production could not keep pace with demographic growth, condemning a proportion of the population to a life of poverty. On the other hand, population growth facilitated urbanization, with towns coming under Serb control. Virtually all of the larger towns had medieval origins and continued to exist as modern urban communities, while smaller towns were of less certain foundation and some were reduced to villages.

It is difficult to judge how public health care influenced demographic growth. Already in 1820, there were educated European doctors in the prince's entourage. Within two decades their number increased to 18, and they were to be found in most towns. The first hospital opened in 1826 in Šabac, a city that was the gateway to western influences. It was followed by hospitals in Požarevac and Belgrade (1833, 1836), and then in several other towns. Pharmacies were opened alongside hospitals and a separate pharmacy was established in Belgrade in 1830. Since Serbia was engulfed by epidemics of cholera (1831, 1836) and the plague (1837), Miloš organized a sanitary cordon with quarantined meeting places at times when the border was closed. Syphilis was systematically suppressed throughout the country through compulsory treatment using every available means.

Formal recognition of autonomy under foreign guarantees inevitably influenced the prince's rule. Public authority was emphasized, and rule through personal dependency was to be replaced by rule through institutions, inevitably leading to a restriction of personal power. Miloš was reluctant to hasten this on and persistently held up reforms of the central administration following the model of European states, as his predecessors from the First Serbian Uprising had done. The class of elders that owed their rise to the prince's patronage were increasingly discontented with his autocracy. The basis for disputing his absolutism lay in the provisions of the 1830 *hatt-i sherif*, according to which the prince was required to rule in accordance with a Council of the People's Elders. Instead of forming the Council, which would curb his power, Miloš introduced administrative bodies – five ministers (*popečitelji*, in 1836) and *serdarstvo*, large administrative units. He renamed nahias *okružje* (district) and introduced a guard to accompany him on his travels through the country.

In early 1835 the opposition took up arms under the leadership of Mileta Radojković, governor of Rasina, who had the support of many disgruntled people, including the prince's own wife and brother. The rebels entered Kragujevac, where negotiations were held, and the rebellion ended without bloodshed or damage to property. The prince agreed to adopt an *Ustav* at the Assembly that was to take place at Candlemas (*Sretenje*, February 15, 1835). *Ustav* is an old church term for order, rule, or regulation, and was used on this occasion in an attempt to bypass the prohibition imposed by Ottoman authorities on vassal states.

The task of drafting the document fell to Dimitrije Davidović (1789–1838), an educated Serb from Hungary who had published the *Novine srpske* in Vienna from 1813 to 1821, and then moved to Serbia where he became secretary of the prince's cabinet. The *Sretenje Ustav* (Candlemas Constitution) was liberal for its time, but was more important for proclaiming civil rights and the principle of separation of powers than for the degree to which it restricted the prince. It also established the state symbols of coat of arms and flag. The *Ustav* was in force for only two weeks since it met with universal opposition: from the Porte because a vassal principality was not authorized to adopt a constitution; from Russia and Austria because of its liberal principles; and from Prince Miloš because it limited his power.

However, the obligation of writing a *konštitucija* (constitution) remained and was especially demanded by Russia, who supported the prince's opposition, the Defenders of the Constitution. The prince sought to free himself of Russian patronage by fostering close ties with British consul George Lloyd Hodges (Austrian, British, and Russian consulates were opened in Belgrade between 1836 and 1838). The writing of the constitution was held up because of persistent conflicts, so the drafting process was shifted to Istanbul, where it was completed by Serbian representatives, Turkish officials, and Russian diplomats in late 1838. That constitution was adopted as the sultan's *hatt-i sherif*, which was announced to the Assembly on Kalemegdan (Belgrade) in early 1839.

Prince Miloš was affected by the stipulation on the separation of powers. He had to share power with members of the *Sovjet* (Council), whom he could not dismiss, and he dubbed the document the Turkish Constitution. However, he did appoint ministers and 17 Council members, who took over legislative power in April 1839, leading him to abdicate in June and leave the country. Miloš was succeeded by his sickly son Milan, who died a month later. Authority rested in the hands of the constitutionalists' regency, since several months passed before Miloš's other son, Mihailo (1839–42), arrived in Serbia. Some of the Defenders of the Constitution, headed by Toma Vučić-Perišić and Avram Petronijević, rose against the Obrenović dynasty. They convinced the Porte to regard Miloš's son as an elected prince and not as his father's heir. The short first reign of Miloš's young son was filled with struggles between the Defenders of the Constitution and Obrenović family supporters, who were directed by Miloš from afar. The Porte benefited the most, assuming the position of arbiter and curbing the degree of autonomy attained. It backed an attempt, led by Vučić-Perišić, to dethrone the young prince. The open rebellion forced the prince to leave Serbia in September 1842.

The following month the Defenders of the Constitution elected Karadjordje's son Alexander (1842–58) as prince. His 15-year reign was marked by the influence of the constitutionalists, which is why this period is named after them. They sought to create institutions and state organizations, especially a bureaucratic apparatus. The adoption of the *Zakonik gradjanski* (Civil Code, 1844) was their great achievement. It was created by attorney and writer Jovan Hadžić (1799–1869) and was modeled after its Austrian counterpart. The development of the legislature and state institutions built on the solid foundation that had been laid during the rule of Prince Miloš.

The Serbs and Serbia in the Revolution of 1848

The Hungarian nobility won an important battle in the general reaction against Habsburg absolutism in the last decade of the eighteenth century. It secured the abolition of the Illyrian Court Deputation, which had existed for only 16 months, and all its jurisdictions were transferred to the Hungarian Court Deputation. The Hungarian government regained jurisdiction over all regions excluding the Military Border, and the Serbs once again found themselves under the control of the Hungarian Diet. Their rights were articulated and enshrined in legal form by the Diet (Legislative Act 27, dated 1791), and were no longer founded on the absolutist "privileges." The heritage of the "privileges" was established in the *Declatoria* (1779), which was an amended version of the second *Regulamentum*. Orthodox bishops, headed by the metropolitan, joined the Upper House of the Hungarian Diet as a mark of equality with other subjects. Only the Serbian Church hierarchy was included in mechanisms of state government.

With the shift of the political center, the Serbs' cultural life also changed emphasis. Serbian books were now mainly printed in Buda and Pest, and later in Novi Sad. Serbian intellectuals were concentrated in Pest and founded the *Matica Srpska* (Central Serbian Cultural and Publishing Society) in 1826. Its magazine *Letopis* (initially *Srpski letopisi*, annals) was launched in Pest, where it was published until 1864, as were the *Serbski Narodni List* (1835–47) and *Serbska pčela* (1830–41). The influence of the press increased around 1840 when reading rooms started opening in many towns. Other forms of social activity (theatrical performances, balls, and salons) also acquired a national character.

The Serbian population in Hungary increased, as shown by available data (in 1797 it numbered 667,247; by 1821 it had risen to 750,379; and in 1847 the figure was 896,902). The Serbian population of the Military Border increased its share of the total: from 48.38 percent in 1797 (vs. 51.62 percent in the provinces) to 48.9 percent in 1821, and 53.6 percent in 1847. Geographical movements were also apparent, with the Serbian population migrating southward. In some places precise figures, and in others contemporary observations, reflected the diminishing number of Serbs in larger towns in the north. By 1843 the Serbian population in Szentendre had decreased by one-third. There were only 50 Serbs in Esztregom in 1839, with similar situations in Györ and Komarom, while there is only anecdotal evidence that the number of Serbs had decreased in Eger and Székesfehérvár. The Serbian population in Baja perished in flooding and fires, but those in Szeged and Mohács were unaffected.

Life in the early decades of the nineteenth century continued at its previous pace. The *urbaria* had been adopted earlier, guild laws were passed in 1805 and 1813, and in 1807 the Basic Border Militia Law replaced the previous cantonal system. The end of the Napoleonic Wars marked the beginning of a period of peace and stability, providing conditions for economic revival. There were far fewer "grand policies" in the Serbian community than in the eighteenth century, with assemblies limited to appointing metropolitans (1837, 1842). There was much more focus on events in Serbia. Aid was provided in different forms during the uprisings, and after the defeat of 1813 a wave of refugees was taken in. During Miloš's reign this was followed by the transfer of educated people into Serbia who were appointed to important positions, primarily in schools, state administration, and cultural institutions.

During the first decade of Miloš's rule there were 16 town schools in Serbia; in 1836 there were already 62, equipped with 70 teachers, 50 of whom had come from the monarchy. The first secondary school was opened in Kragujevac in 1835 and another opened in Belgrade in 1838. The Lyceum (Great School) started operations in 1838. The Seminary (the aforementioned school of theology) was established in 1836, and in the following year the Military Academy was founded.

An important advance was made in the literary arena when the prince's printing shop, *Knjažeska tipografija*, was purchased from Russia and set up in 1831. It was active in Belgrade, with a pause between 1833 and 1835 when the capital was moved to Kragujevac. Aside from official publications, primarily the *Novine srbske* (called *Srbske novine* from 1843) and school books, it also published literary works, Bulgarian books, and some publications in foreign languages. The official newspaper also had its feuilleton – *Podunavka* (1843–8) – and before that other almanacs began publication, amongst them *Zabavnik* (1834–6), *Uranija* (1837–8), and *Golubica s cvetom knjižestva srpskog* (1839–44).

After several attempts, the *Društvo srpske slovesnosti* (Society of Serbian Letters), which fostered study in language and science, was founded in 1841 and began work only after the change in dynasties. All these activities and institutions were headed by people from the Habsburg monarchy; all the Lyceum professors and members of the Society were Serbs "from the other side of the border." These included prominent authors such as Jovan Sterija Popović (1806–56), Dimitrije Tirol (1793–1857), Atanasije Nikolić (1803–82), Dr. Jovan Stejić (1803–53), and Sima Milutinović-Sarajlija (1791–1841). The beginnings of Serbian theater were also nurtured in this period thanks to the tireless efforts of the traveler and versatile author Joakim Vujić (1772–1847), who organized the first Serbian theatrical production in Pest in 1813 and became the director of the *Knjaževsko-srpski teatar* in 1834.

The endeavors of educated Serbs from Austria strengthened ties between the disparate components of the Serbian population, but they had their disadvantages as well. For example, there were many Serbs from Hungary among the numerous unpopular civil servants of the constitutionalist regime, and this created antagonism toward the "krauts," as the newcomers from the Austrian Empire were called.

The transfer of cultural achievements from one environment to the other was not mechanical but selective, involving adjustments on both sides. In the Serbian case this was apparent in the language of literature and education. Along with the people and books, the Slavo-Serbian language (Russian Church Slavonic) arrived in the principality with no centuries-old tradition behind it. Discussions and disputes were raised by the official language, becoming louder over time. There were appeals in the last decades of the eighteenth century for a language that would be understood by everyone, not just by the educated upper class. Alternative projects emerged, most from the outskirts of the Serbian area. The most significant was that advocated by Sava Mrkalj (1792–1833), who criticized the alphabet in a booklet published in 1810 and proposed that it be amended in line with phonetic principles. This view was supported by Vuk Stefanović Karadžić (1787–1864), who emerged from a background of uprisings in western Serbia. He was familiar with the people's customs, language, and folklore and devoted all his energies to promoting language reforms. Under the influence of European philologists, especially Vienna-based Slav linguist Bartholomeus Kopitar (1780–1844), he compiled a grammar book and dictionary of vernacular speech and persistently criticized the language situation of the Serbian people in polemical writings. He was opposed by the church, educated people, and contemporary writers (with a few exceptions), and also by principality authorities, but received support from learned European mentors and young Serbs, who recognized the democratic potential of the Serbian folk language as a universal means of communication.

The political dimension of these linguistic disputes was rooted in the belief that language determined ethnicity, which was applied not only in determining ethnic background but also in changing it. Resisting the absolutism of Viennese court authorities, the Hungarian ruling class increasingly sought to make the kingdom an ethnic Hungarian state, even though it was as multiethnic as the Empire. This became apparent in 1830 with the adoption of the so-called language laws, which fixed Hungarian as the official language of public life and schools – even church registry books had to be kept in Hungarian (with consequences on given names). These measures were strongly opposed by all non-Hungarian ethnic groups; one of the responses was the formation of the Illyrian Movement in Croatia, which included Serbs from both Croatia and southern Hungary.

There were other aspects to the Serbs' language problem. It was obvious that language acquired through education could easily be suppressed by eliminating the sources of education, while the language spoken by the people was that of a population of 2 million. However, according to general beliefs inherited from the eighteenth century, ethnicity was protected by the "privileges" granted to the church and applied to the religious congregation. This is why conservatives claimed that abandoning the church alphabet and the language of church literature would be tantamount to treason, and they consequently branded the reformers as traitors, especially for adopting the letter *j* from the Latin alphabet. Abandoning Russian Church Slavonic was perceived as moving away from Orthodox Russia, and this was also believed to be fraught with danger.

On the other hand, accepting the vernacular for elementary education and literature made it easier to communicate with and influence that part of the population remaining under Ottoman rule. It allowed closer links with the Croatian people and opened the door to broader southern Slav integration. These political implications were rarely raised in the language disputes, but they affected the underlying motivation of all those involved. The emergence of young authors such as poet Branko Radičević (1824–53) and philologist Djura Daničić (1825–82), who used Vuk's orthography and vernacular in their influential works, heralded the victory of Vuk's reformist aims. Books were printed with the amended alphabet and orthography, even though they would not be officially approved until after Vuk's death.

Linguistic disputes among the Serbs were in full swing when Europe's revolutionary whirlwind engulfed the imperial capital and quickly spread throughout the country. Hungary's 12-point revolutionary program was published on March 15, 1848 in Pest, and included demands for civil liberties and the abolition of serfdom and feudal duties. Support echoed from all quarters. Since the Serbs in the monarchy had no capital, the revolutionary impulse found an outlet in various places, but not at the same time and not with the same force. At first social issues prevailed – Serbian peasants rose against monastic authority and in some towns, such as Zemun and Pančevo, there was looting and violence as hated officials were ousted. Specific Serb demands were put forward in many places, the most important in Pest and Novi Sad; they were moderate at the time and focused on providing what the Serbs already had – civic equality, religious freedom, unrestricted use of their language, and independence in school administration. They had reason to fear the slogan of one political people and one Hungarian "diplomatic" language.

On the Hungarian side, any separation, particularly territorial autonomy, was dreaded, especially by the radical nationalist wing headed by Lajos Kossuth (1802–94). Although territorial autonomy was not sought at first, distrust was evident in negotiations between Serbian representatives and the revolutionary authorities, and deepened even further. During talks with a deputation of Serbs from Novi Sad in early April, Kossuth, faced with signs that the Serbs might seek autonomy in other quarters, stated: "in that case we shall cross swords."

Rumors of misunderstandings and experience with Hungarian as the compulsory language created bitter opposition. Hungarian-language records and documents were burned in a number of towns, including Novi Sad, Kikinda, Bečej, Bečkerek, and Vršac. Vociferous demands were made for the Serbs' own territory and *voivoda*. The angry mass was

Plate 6.3   Revolutionary economy: assignat valued at 5 florins, issued by the Serbian authorities in 1848. (From the review *Dinar*, no. 19, 2002, with permission of the editor)

directed by students and young people, reinforced by colleagues from the principality. The metropolitan was coerced into holding an Assembly in Karlovci, while the authorities allowed a Serbian Assembly to be held in Timişoara in the presence of a royal commissioner.

At the Assembly in Karlovci, which was actually a large gathering, held on May 12–14, 1848 (May 1–3, according to the Julian calendar), far-reaching decisions were made in proclaiming the Serbian Vojvodina in the territory of Srem, Baranja, Bačka and Banat, including corresponding parts of the Military Border and districts. This newly formed Vojvodina joined in "a political union . . . based on liberty and perfect equality with the Triune Kingdom of Croatia, Slavonia, and Dalmatia." A People's Committee was established as an assembly body. The ethnic individuality of the local Romanian people was recognized, thus preventing resistance from the sizable Romanian population within the Karlovci metropolitanate. Metropolitan Josif Rajačić (1785–1861) was proclaimed patriarch, and Colonel Stevan Šupljikac (1786–1848), who was fighting in Italy at the time, was elected *voivoda*.

The May Assembly's decisions had a revolutionary character with their grassroots demand for change in the monarchy. A new unit had been established within the complicated system of the beleaguered Empire, without the approval of legislative bodies. Since the Viennese court agreed with the Hungarian government in all matters at the time, the May Assembly's decisions were not recognized in either Innsbruck or Pest.

The Serbian leadership could expect support only from Croatia, which had resisted Hungary in a similar manner. Patriarch Rajačić took part in the inauguration of the governor of Croatia, Ban Josif Jelačić, who was elected without the approval of the Hungarian government and was not recognized by Vienna either. The Serbian principality as a vassal state had its hands tied, but its government was actively involved in affairs among the Serbs and urged Serbian leaders in southern Hungary to cooperate with the Croats. It did this both for reasons of principle, in order to enable the "Serbian peoples" to join together as provided in the political program of the *Načertanije* from 1844, and to further its own narrow dynastic interests, since it wished to maintain control of the movement and eliminate the Obrenović family and their supporters.

District and local people's committees were established in late May 1848 as new governmental bodies. The "people's army" was organized and military camps were set up in expectation of conflict. In early June, when the border was ceded to the Hungarian government, Serbian forces were reinforced by a fresh influx of border militia troops and officers who refused to accept that decision.

The first armed skirmish took place on June 12 before Karlovci, when the army dispatched from Petrovaradin to disperse the "rebels" was defeated. The Hungarian government sent Count Petar Čarnojević, a descendant of the patriarch, as its royal commissioner. He succeeded in calming the turmoil in Novi Sad and a 10-day ceasefire was negotiated during the Hungarian elections. However, in early July, fighting erupted and lasted a full year, until the Hungarians capitulated before Russian troops in August 1849. The main battlegrounds were in Banat and Šajkaška, between the Tisa and Danube rivers, and some towns changed hands more than once. It took 20 years for the Serbian population in Bačka and Banat to restore their numbers to their pre-1848 level. The support received from Serbia in terms of volunteers and war matériel gave a significant boost to those fighting for Vojvodina. While luck varied on the battlefield, the leadership of the Serbian movement was preoccupied by the struggle between Patriarch Rajačić and Djordje Stratimirović (1822–1908), who had made a name for himself as commander and leader of the liberal faction in the movement.

The general situation changed in early fall 1848, when the Viennese court, having settled issues in Italy and Bohemia, turned against the Hungarian government. Duties and honors were restored to Ban Jelačić, and he marched with an army on Vienna, which was engulfed in a new wave of revolution, and then on Buda. *Voivoda* Šupljikac was then able to return from Italy to resume his duties, which quelled internal unrest for a short while. The court had hinted at the possibility of recognizing the May Assembly decisions and confirmed the patriarch and *voivoda*, together with their titles. At the same time, the Viennese court embraced the Serbian movement. The army was dubbed the Imperial Royal Austrian-Serbian Corps, even though there were no regular imperial troops among the Serbian soldiers until the spring of 1849. The patriarch paved the way for silent restoration of Habsburg authority by eliminating democratic elements from the movement and putting his trust in Colonel Mayerhofer, the former Austrian consul in Serbia, who took over command of the army after Šupljikac's sudden death.

The constitution conceded from March 1849 provided the Duchy of Serbia (*Voivodstvo Srbija*) with a state system that "would affirm its church and ethnicity, based on the old privileges and imperial orders." Past "privileges" and protective decrees were therefore set down for the future. During the final period of war, from the declaration of Hungarian independence and dethronement of the Habsburgs in April 1849 until the collapse of Hungarian forces in August 1849, the Serbs suffered great tribulation. They were driven out of territories in Bačka and Banat and pleaded once again for help from Serbia (since the volunteer detachment had returned to Serbia in March 1849). In June, military officers loyal to the Hungarian government bombarded Novi Sad from the Petrovaradin fortress and destroyed the town. The difficulties encountered by the Hungarian government did not diminish the military force used against Serb positions. Fierce battles took place in Šajkaška and Banat even as Russian troops entered Hungary.

In the meantime, what remained of the Serbs' leadership came under the control of the Viennese court. In April 1849, the territory of Vojvodina, for which much blood had been shed, was subjugated to imperial military authorities. Prominent leaders of the democratic faction were removed and people's bodies were gradually dissolved. When an imperial patent dated November 18, 1849 set up the special territory of *Vojvodstvo Srbija i Tamiški Banat* (Duchy of Serbia and Banate of Timişoara), there was little celebration.

7

National State: For and Against

Changes in Reality and Changes in Ideas

The first half of the nineteenth century was full of a new vitality. What had seemed a stable world for centuries was changing and being reorganized from its very foundations. In the late eighteenth century the highest authorities had been questioned and kings brought before judicial courts; states were abolished and others created; and ruling classes lost power. Even the church was superseded by secular cults, and what had been considered sacred was declared to be superstition. However, closer inspection reveals that all these dramatic changes remained confined to the sphere of relations between ruler and subject, between social classes, lord and serf, between church and congregation, and between states and nations. The reality for most was essentially a short, insecure life, tormented by poverty and prey to epidemics, a world of poor communications where the horse was still the fastest means of transportation.

Contemporaries recognized the French Revolution, as well as the events that preceded and followed it, as being the origin of change. Viewed from a greater distance, another source of transformation is apparent – the English industrial revolution, which took place at approximately the same time. Unlike the political forces that spread relatively quickly even in that slow world, the new forces originating in the steam engine, mines and foundries, and early factories spread slowly and in small steps. This was because much more than interest, courage, and willpower were needed for their acceptance; considerable funds and new knowledge were required.

By 1850, not one of the industrial revolution's achievements had reached the part of Europe under discussion. There were no steam engines, no mechanized mass production, and no means of transportation relying on the new energy source. Actually, this observation should be limited to land transportation, since the citizens of Belgrade saw their first steamboat in 1827. Belgrade's pier was included in the Danube steamboat line (1834), and later the Sava line (1844) operated by an Austrian steamboat company. For Serbs living along navigable rivers and canals, both on the Habsburg side and in the principality, this early influx of modern technology was crucial for the transfer of people and goods, and for strengthening ties within the area.

Improvement in land transportation was reflected on the one hand by development of the road network with the establishment of a hierarchy differentiating between state, district, and local roads and, on the other hand, by an increase in the number of four-wheel carts having greater carrying capacity pulled by horses instead of oxen. At the beginning of the second half of the nineteenth century, Serbia had about 1,000 kilometers of cobbled roads. A great change in transportation with far-reaching consequences for the entire economy came with the introduction of the railway, which was first made available to Serbs living in the Habsburg monarchy (in Croatia and Bačka during the 1860s). Construction of a railway began in Serbia in 1881 with the implementation of obligations imposed by the Treaty of Berlin. The completion of the Belgrade–Niš section in 1884 incurred great financial difficulties and debts; it was extended to the Bulgarian and Turkish borders in 1888.

The steam engine first reached Serbs living in Hungary: the mechanized loom in Novi Sad (1842), a steam-operated mill in Pančevo (1843), then in 1863 steam-operated threshing machines and plows. In the principality, the state cannon foundry and later the Military-Technical Institute in Kragujevac led the way. In the 1880s the achievements of the industrial revolution spread to different branches of the economy – textiles, food, glass, lumber, and brick-making – but there was no commensurate continuation of the great medieval mining industry. Relatively early attempts to resuscitate former mining regions, for example Majdanpek, Kučajna, Zajača, and Šuplja Stena, did not yield commercial success, and they failed to produce a profit even when they were run by foreign mining specialists. The industry was to achieve success only much later with the introduction of new mining techniques and, in the second half of the nineteenth century, with the increase in demand for coal.

The telegraph reached Serbia in 1855 and at the time was already a public service among the Serbs in Hungary. It traversed large distances, providing quicker communication and more efficient methods of government. It was followed by the telephone in 1883. Electricity arrived after 1890, producing lighting and the electric streetcar. Toward the end of the nineteenth century, the time between the appearance of a technical invention and its implementation in Serbia was shortened. Its application, however, was primarily restricted to the capital, since this was

Plate 7.1 Urban architecture in transition: residence (*konak*) of Princess Ljubica, wife of Prince Miloš Obrenović, in Belgrade, built second half of the nineteenth century, restored 1974. (Photograph by B. Strugar)

Plate 7.2 Village in western Serbia, mid-nineteenth century. Drawing by Felix Kanitz, 1864. (From F. Kanitz, *Serbien: Historisch-etnographische Reisestudien aus den Jahren 1859–1868*, Leipzig, 1868)

the only town with sufficient financial, social, and intellectual resources to embrace technical and scientific innovations. Consequently, the contrast between the capital and other towns increased.

While the material framework of life changed relatively slowly and the consequences of change were only apparent over time, there was great intellectual vitality in Serbia. Generations of young people who had been educated at foreign universities arrived in waves, bringing ideas that inspired educated young Serbs (the Great School opened its doors in 1864). This led to the creation of new political programs and influenced the activities of individuals and groups. Starting in 1839, the Serbian government annually granted 20 scholarships to students for study abroad, at a substantial cost. The idea was to provide people with different specialties for public service; some returned with new insights and a critical view of the regime and the situation in the country.

The idea of a secular society and its separation from the church was not widely accepted by Serbs in the Habsburg Empire or in the principality. In the late eighteenth century, voices could be heard among Serbs in Hungary supporting an autonomous lay culture, but they were not aiming at fundamental change. Along with other inherited ideas, the nineteenth century saw the church in the monarchy naturally assume the leading role in education, which it supported financially through school funds and defended with its authority.

In the principality, starting from the time of Prince Miloš, secular authorities were influential in transforming the church and religious life because of the alienation of the hierarchy and neglect of the congregation that characterized the period of the Greek bishops. State rules regulated religious life and the life of the faithful. The system of education was secular from the outset, with religious instruction given by the clergy under the symbolic supervision of the metropolitan and priests. While the Orthodox Church was completely unrelated to the state in Hungary, the church in the principality merged with the state. The 1883 Church Synod prohibited priests from becoming members of political parties and participating in gatherings.

The ideas of liberalism were introduced by the first generation of students returning from study abroad. When applied to Serbian surroundings, they prompted a struggle against autocratic rule, favored constitutionality and legality, and proposed a greater role for the people's representatives in political life. They revealed their true colors when Prince Alexander Karadjordjević was ousted, when the regime of Prince Mihailo was questioned, and especially when power was consolidated after his assassination in 1868. Liberal ideals were modified after being adopted and were grafted onto allegedly ancient Serb institutions: the Assemblies (Sabor, *Skupština*) and extended families. It was claimed at the time that a democratic system was part of the nature and culture of Serbian society. The "Serbianization" of liberal values was especially advocated by Vladimir Jovanović (1833–1922), an apostle of liberalism. Liberal ideas fostered nationalism, urged the struggle for national liberty, and extolled the national spirit. The liberal vision had already gone far. Vladimir Jovanović dreamt of a United States of Europe and also believed that a "federation of representatives" would be the only "form in which the southern Slav tribes might come together in a strong and lasting state" (1885). The ideal of a federation remained vibrant among the early socialist and other political movements, thus representing a lasting alternative to the real politics of expansion and annexation.

In addition to the issues of liberty and the state system, educated Serbs also contemplated the question of nationality and ethnicity. In the eighteenth century the word *nation* echoed the medieval dimension of a special legal status. In the case of the Serbs, it was founded on the "privileges" that were granted to the Serbian Orthodox Church, which seemed to imply that ethnicity could not be separated from faith. The basis for ethnicity, however, was increasingly recognized as being the spoken language, representing a significant characteristic of ethnic individuality that expressed the "spirit of a nation," for example in folklore. Vuk Karadžić joined the European process of "discovering the people" with his publication of Serbian folk poems, starting in 1814. Serbian poems were translated and became popular, and through them interest in the Serbs increased. Scholars then and later tried to answer questions regarding the origin of the *Iliad* and the *Odyssey* by researching Serbian folklore singers (who used the *gusla*, a single-stringed fiddle) and their audience. The European literati's admiration for Serbian folk poems became an incessant source of pride among the Serbs.

It was more important, however, for the romantics' model of the nation as a union of language and spirit to be fitted easily into the classification and genealogies that were used to explain the development of Indo-European languages. Even though the language situation on the ground was not known, and no hierarchy had been set up of the differences between dialects and languages, the founding fathers of Slavic linguistic studies (J. Dobrovski, P. J. Šafarik, and B. Kopitar) boldly claimed that the regions where the *štokavski* dialect, the most widespread of the southern Slavic dialects, was spoken were inhabited by Serbs. Based on this claim, Vuk Karadžić founded a conviction in 1825 that there were 5 million Serbs, 3 million of whom were Orthodox Christians, 1.2 million were Muslims, and the rest were Catholics in Dalmatia, Croatia, Slavonia, and Bosnia. He also noted that the Muslim population called themselves Turks and that the Catholics used provincial names. Reality was thus not in line with the European model. An opposing view was expressed by the realist author Jakov Ignjatović (1824–89): "a Serb without his religious rites and customs is not considered a Serb. The religious apostate is popularly considered a lost son who has lost his Serbian character. Religious rites still shield ethnicity" (1879). The Serbs' definition of themselves varied between these two extremes. Even during the period of extreme secularization, between 1947 and 1990, the Orthodox faith remained one of the fundamental marks of Serbian national feelings.

A secular orientation, the ideals of liberty, constitutionality, and ethnic sovereignty, and notions about their own and other nations remained at the heart of the Serbs' cultural and political dynamics throughout the nineteenth and twentieth centuries. In the late 1860s these guiding ideas were expanded by a young generation to include faith in scientific ideas, positive knowledge as a means to understand the world and a precondition for progress. The idea was accepted that laws govern social and intellectual development. On the one hand this orientation promoted natural and exact sciences, and, on the other, imposed "realism" and a critical attitude toward tradition and the past. During the last quarter of the nineteenth century, there was a revision of traditional views of history, which in the case of Serbia were founded on folklore. The result was a great debate between traditionalist patriotic historians and critical historians, and the emergence of a critical school of thinking whose influence would remain limited to educated circles.

At approximately the same time, socialist ideas found their way to Serbia, long before industry and the working class (proletariat) were developed. They were introduced by the young intelligentsia, primarily students, and were disseminated by journalists and writers, thus gaining popularity relatively quickly. This led to the first organizations and demonstrations (the red banner was flown in Kragujevac in 1876). A foreign diplomat, who had lived in Belgrade for some time, noticed in 1870 that students of the Great School were "all communists." As was the case with liberal ideas, there were attempts to link Serbian socialist ideas with local institutions that would allegedly have a social character. According to these ideas, industrialization and the capitalist path adopted by Europe could be avoided. Farming cooperatives and village communes were what they had in mind. Radicalism, the strongest political movement that was to play a crucial role in the development of Serbia in the late nineteenth and early twentieth centuries, emerged from socialist roots.

From the liberals to the socialists, all reformers promoted the idea of educating the people. Education stepped outside the framework of schools and was advanced through different forms of information via the press, reading rooms, public lectures, and so on. In the 1880s one educational movement was recognized as having a great, albeit silent, influence on people's way of life. This was health education, which was promoted in the form of lectures, books, brochures, and magazines. Many people were involved, although Dr. Milan Jovanović Batut (1847–1940) was especially prominent for his expertise and method. Even though contemporaries paid little attention to this work, it was more important for the people's development than many political activities. In conditions of poverty, where the network of medical institutions was underdeveloped and there was a shortage of doctors, positive knowledge about hygiene, better nutrition, protection from contagious diseases, and childrearing was an important preventive factor.

Methods of communication changed slowly; until the 1930s newspapers were the only significant means of informing and influencing the public. Printing presses arrived in most towns. Newspapers and other publications became so numerous that they could no longer be listed individually; they ranged from daily newspapers to humorous papers and newspapers for children. Freedom of the press became a measure of the level of democracy that had been achieved.

Technical advances that gained momentum as the century progressed also changed the conditions of government. The state acquired previously unimagined possibilities for supervising and influencing the public. Compulsory elementary education (introduced in 1882 and extended to girls in 1900) included an increasing percentage of children. Compulsory military service (introduced in 1883) subjected the male population to a brief but strong dose of dynastic ideology and patriotic rhetoric, inculcating a sense of duty to serve king and country. The modernized country

Plate 7.3   Innovation in the media: front page of the first issue of *Beogradske ilustrovane novine* (Belgrade Illustrated Newspaper), 1866, with panorama of Belgrade.

of the second half of the nineteenth century acted as a melting-pot that formed the modern nation. From the beginning of the twentieth century, Serbia not only grew in numbers but also became increasingly more *Serbian*, meaning that the once numerous foreign elements were gradually absorbed and assimilated (Aromanians, Greeks), driven out (Turks, and those who identified with them), or ignored (Roma).

This process included barely half of the Serbs. There was parallel development in Montenegro, but it was limited to a different framework and created a different awareness that included the idea of Montenegro as the fatherland side by side with feelings for Serbian nationality. The remaining Serbs, primarily those in Austria, became part of the processes of creating a single Hungarian "political nation." There were hints of this in 1848, but it only became apparent after 1867 when the establishment of the dual monarchy created conditions for the Hungarian part to develop as the Magyar national state. All of the Serbs' energy and political activity were directed toward preserving their ethnicity and resisting Magyarization. While one part of the Serbian nation sought to develop and increase the national state, the other part fiercely resisted assimilation policies and maintained the institutions of a civic society. These different attitudes toward the state and civic society later became part of the Serb mentality and remained active long after the state borders separating parts of the nation ceased to exist.

Ruling Nation

Society in the Serbian principality was not sufficiently polarized to instigate revolutionary activities against the government following events in neighboring countries in 1848, although it did so a decade later and without any foreign encouragement. In 1848 all politically active forces ready to fight were focused on the fate of their compatriots north of the Sava and Danube rivers. The total number of volunteers is not known, but at times there were up to 15,000 men. The ruling oligarchy was not unanimous on the degree of engagement. While Toma Vučić-Perišić claimed that "we have no business across the marsh," another member of the Council, Stevan Petrović-Knićanin, handed in his resignation as a civil servant so that he could fight with the volunteers. He played a significant role as their commander in battles in Bačka and Banat.

Prince Alexander Karadjordjević and the Council, however, were criticized because Serbia was not involved enough. There was even greater criticism that the principality had remained passive in the Crimean War (1853–6), fought by Russia against Turkey, France, and Great Britain.

The consequences of the Russian defeat and the signing of the Paris Treaty in 1856 were that Russia ceased to be the only protector of the Christians in the Ottoman Empire. It was joined by Austria, Britain, France, Sardinia, and Prussia (the latter two gave rise to Italy and Germany).

Guided by the Council members, primarily Ilija Garašanin, the prince pursued a policy of evading conflict over everyday policy issues so as not to endanger the long-term goals formulated in the *Načertanije* (1844)[1] that were influenced by active Polish immigrants who were antagonistic to Russia and Austria. It included directives for Serbian policies in the future and counted on the downfall of the Ottoman Empire. Serbia was to gather "all the Serbian peoples that surround it" and create "a new Serbian state . . . on the good old foundation of the old Serbian Empire." In order to carry out this policy, secret ties were fostered with regions under Ottoman rule, agents were recruited, secret organizations were founded and supported, and were used to disseminate propaganda. The priority region was Bosnia, where there was an important stronghold among the Franciscans. When Austria undertook similar activity in Bosnia, the Franciscans were prohibited from supporting the Serbs' cause.

The Defenders of the Constitution, who were fighting for a constitutional status and against the prince's autocracy, were satisfied with sharing power with the monarch and worked with him to establish state authority. Relying heavily on foundations laid down during Miloš's era, they were able to continue setting up important institutions, primarily courts and the police. The Supreme Court (later the Appellate Court) was established in 1846. Other laws were adopted following the Civic Code (1844) and remained in force for a long time, with uneven effects. The Farmstead Act was renewed and protected small estates from sequestration or confiscation, but not from heritage partitioning, which created dwarf estates. The Guild Decree of 1847 limited competition and trade, but did not resolve the issue of training young artisans and allowed young people to be exploited.

The regime of the Defenders of the Constitution lost authority following disagreements between the prince and members of the Council (there was even a plot to assassinate the prince), and also because of Turkish interference. Young people sent abroad to be educated at foreign universities became advocates of liberal and democratic reforms and

---

1   The draft *Načertanije* was elaborated by František Zah and mentioned a gathering of the southern Slavs. In creating the final text Garašanin left out certain parts that spoke of the southern Slavs and replaced them with the Serbs or "Serbian peoples." The *Načertanije* was a secret document until the early twentieth century.

critics of the regime. Popular discontent with Prince Alexander was fueled by supporters of the Obrenović dynasty. In late 1858 there was a forced convocation of the National Assembly. According to the "Turkish Constitution" it had only an advisory function, but it also contributed to the election of the ruler. Young liberals and Obrenović supporters seized the main role in the organization of the Assembly while the Council members dithered, and the prince's abdication was demanded. He was forced to retreat to the pasha's fortress and later crossed over to Austria. Miloš Obrenović was proclaimed prince (1858–60), even though he was then 75 years old.

Ascending the throne for the second time, Prince Miloš cared little for the new laws and changes that had taken place since his abdication and ruled as he had before, relying on dependable administrators and meddling in everything. He turned against those who had brought him to power and forced them into the opposition. He was succeeded by Prince Mihailo (1860–8), who was recognized by the Porte as the elected prince, as his father had been. Taking the throne at a mature age, with experience and knowledge of the world, Prince Mihailo tried to govern alone, relying only on experienced and influential politicians he had inherited from the previous regime. During his rule a distinction was drawn between the former Defenders of the Constitution, who were now called conservatives, and the liberals, primarily young and educated people. The prince shared the conviction of members of the former Council, such as Ilija Garašanin, that the people should be ruled by a powerful and educated government.

The Porte's interference in internal affairs and their refusal to recognize succession despite the law on inheriting the throne passed the year before led Prince Mihailo to invalidate the "Turkish Constitution" through special legislation: the Law on the State Council, which excluded the role of the Porte because Council members were accountable to the court; the Law on the National Assembly, which remained an advisory body; and the Law on the National Militia, which included military service for men between the ages of 20 and 50 who were trained locally. All these laws were adopted in 1861, while the Law on State Administration (1862) introduced the Council of Ministers as the prince's cabinet.

Prince Mihailo pursued active policies toward Turkey from the beginning of his rule. In 1862 he used the incident of a military conflict followed by the bombardment of the center of Belgrade to demand complete Turkish withdrawal. The guarantor-states forced two Turkish fortresses to close down and reductions of the garrison in those that remained, reiterating the Turks' obligation to leave Serbia. The prince received the firman handing over administration of the remaining fortresses during a visit to Istanbul in 1867. In June 1867 the last Turkish units were ceremoniously dispatched. However, the annual tribute remained in effect as a sign of vassal duties, as did the sultan's flag on the Belgrade fortress.

The long-term goals of Serbian policies included preparations for a general uprising, in parallel with negotiations with the Porte. Significant advances were made during the brief rule of Prince Mihailo in establishing links with Ottoman enemies, and formal alliances were created with Montenegro (1866), Greece (1867), and Wallachia (1868). Negotiations were held with leaders of the Bulgarian emigration, following their proposal for the creation of a common Serbian–Bulgarian state under Prince Mihailo. It was agreed with the leadership of the National Party in Croatia that Bosnia would be absorbed into Serbia as the first step toward a future southern Slav state. The plan to create an uprising in Bosnia in 1867 was later abandoned.

Neither the diminishing of Ottoman authority nor positive changes in state organization were sufficient to raise the prince's popularity with Serbian youth, who were becoming increasingly self-aware and anxious for all Serbs to unite, regardless of the borders that separated them. Student, literary, and choral societies later joined together to form the United Serbian Youth organization (see p. 219), which held its founding assembly in Novi Sad in 1866. Even though it was established as a cultural society, its members were heavily involved in politics, urging war against Turkey and promoting liberal domestic policies. The society's criticism of the prince's regime angered the authorities to such an extent that the second Assembly in Belgrade, due to be held in 1867, was unable to take place.

Despite advocating reconciliation between supporters of the two feuding dynasties from the beginning of his rule, Prince Mihailo was assassinated by a group of Karadjordjević supporters in June 1868. His death shook Serbia to its foundations, because the mainstay of the dynasty had disappeared and there was no heir or replacement. Institutions nonetheless proved that they could work. A regency was formed and the National Assembly was convened, but it was the military minister, Milivoje Blaznavac, who ended speculation and declared Milan Obrenović (1852–1901), the grandson of Miloš's brother Jevrem, as heir. Milan was then 14 years old and a student in Paris. The Assembly could do nothing other than confirm Milan as the legal heir. A new regency was appointed and included Milivoje Blaznavac, Jovan Ristić, and Jovan Gavrilović.

The regents were members of the circle that had been close to Prince Mihailo, but they made efforts to win over the liberals in order to strengthen the regime. A constitution was passed in 1869 disregarding the sultan's supreme authority and the existing laws. The guarantor-states and the Porte were informed, but no complaints were forthcoming. The constitution was disputed at home, however, both by supporters of a strong monarchy and by those who advocated democracy. Yet the fact that it had been adopted was crucial and some of the institutions it introduced represented a progressive step toward the development of parliamentarianism.

The regency held the reins of power and its foreign policy closely adhered to guidelines set by Garašanin and Prince Mihailo until 1872, when the prince came of age. The regency was labeled a police regime, because society had become more sensitive to limitations placed on freedom of the press and on public assembly and political organization. The main target was the socialists, whose development had gained momentum and who had even started their own publications, for example *Radenik* and *Javnost*. The regents followed a balanced budget policy so the country was not indebted, but there was no considerable investment either. They carried out reforms in the national militia but did not eliminate its fundamental weaknesses.

Unlike the principality, which despite several decades without war experienced dynamic internal development (including changes of dynasties and rulers and the introduction of European institutions), Montenegro was involved in a few wars during the same period but saw only one truly great internal development – the introduction of secular rulers. The reputation and authority of Metropolitan (Vladika) Petar II, the poet-author of "Mountain Wreath," were not enough to secure the smooth execution of his last will. He had appointed his first cousin's son, Danilo Stankov Petrović, as his heir. Danilo was opposed by the metropolitan's brother, who was president of the Senate at the time. Ultimately the young Danilo (1852–60) prevailed, but he refused to take holy orders. His supporters pronounced Montenegro "a secular and hereditary principality" with Russian backing, and Danilo I became the "prince and ruler of Montenegro and Brda." A monk from the Boka, who had been ordained in Russia in 1853, became head of the metropolitanate and was limited to church affairs, as were his successors.

The changes on the throne were unacceptable to the Porte, since the metropolitan's authority could to some degree be included in the system of religious leaders under the sultan's rule, but secular rulers would have to become the sultan's vassal. There was a clash of diametrically opposing views: according to one, Montenegro had been undefeated for centuries, while the other maintained that it had been part of the Ottoman Empire all that time.

In aiding an uprising in neighboring Herzegovina, the Montenegrin prince chose armed rebellion against the sultan, even though his military force was inadequate. The sultan's commander, Omer-Pasha, headed an army of 25,000 men, while Montenegro could assemble only 9,000. The Ottoman attack came from a number of directions. The Bjelopavlić and Piper clans were defeated, and in 1853 the Turks turned toward Cetinje. Russia and Austria successfully pressured the Ottomans into leaving Montenegro.

Prince Danilo reorganized the national militia, in spite of resistance and rebellions, and introduced formations and commanders in place of the clan detachments. The prince's guard was also formed, numbering 1,000 troops. The land was divided into administrative units ruled by captains, pushing the previous organization by clans into the background. The General Territorial Law (*Opšti zemaljski zakon*) of 1855 included legislation previously passed by Petar I and Danilo. Some of its articles were fundamental constitutional provisions, but most were part of the penal code. Foreigners were considered equal "even though in this land there is no other ethnic community except for the Serbs and no other faith except for the Eastern Orthodox." Montenegro played a leading role in preserving Serbian traditions owing to its centuries-old defense of freedom, and this paved the way for the development of a cult of Montenegro and its heroes in other parts of the Serbian nation, especially in the late nineteenth century among Serbs in Hungary.

During the Crimean War Montenegro remained neutral, on the advice of Russia, but Prince Danilo wanted to use the peace talks to gain recognition for Montenegro's independence. He was unsuccessful, however, and his support of the uprising in Herzegovina in 1858 brought decisive action from the Porte. A battle was fought on the border near Grahovo on May 7, 1858, and the superior Turkish troops were outmaneuvered and defeated. The guarantor-states stepped in once more and hostilities ceased under pressure from them. Prince Danilo succeeded in getting a boundary demarcation, which was completed only in 1860. Although the practical gain was very small, it influenced Montenegro's international position and reputation among the subjugated Christians. Prince Danilo's rule ended violently in 1860 in a privately motivated revenge assassination.

Danilo was succeeded by his nephew Nikola Petrović Njegoš (1860–1918). The young prince was aided by his father, *voivoda* Mirko, whose assistance was necessary because of the prince's youth and the Ottoman threat. The aid given by Montenegro to the Herzegovina rebellion gave the sultan grounds to declare war in 1862. Following a plan similar to one that had been formulated 10 years earlier, Montenegro was attacked from all sides and offered courageous resistance on all fronts. Once again Omer Pasha threatened Cetinje, and once again hostilities ended with Russia's intervention. This time, however,

Montenegro was forced to agree to the terms of the peace treaty: not to aid rebels and to allow the Turks to build posts along the Nikšić–Spuž road. The Porte waived this right the following year.

Prince Nikola reorganized the military, as his predecessor had done, but went much further. Officers were brought in from Serbia to train the Montenegrin commanders, and modern arms were purchased from Serbia. The alliance with Serbia of 1866, which collapsed after the death of Prince Mihailo, was part of the preparations for the inevitable war. The years of peace were used to develop the educational system, with the founding of the Theology School and Girl's Institute along with 40 elementary schools. A newspaper, *Glas Crnogoraca* (Voice of the Montenegrins), was launched soon after. Even though work on educating the population started later than in Serbia, it yielded significant results, and by the outbreak of World War I, half of the Montenegrin population was literate.

National Minority

There was a belief among the Serbs that their contribution to the revolutionary developments of 1848–9 had been a tragic failure, that nothing had been achieved despite heavy loss of life. Their deep sorrow was expressed in a number of memoirs and literary works. The most embittered were those who had advocated the idea of the "privileges" as a reward for Serbian military achievements for the monarchy and the Habsburg dynasty. In criticizing the ingratitude of the Viennese court, they portrayed themselves as tools of the Habsburgs, which only intensified the negative position of those gathered around the idea of democracy and revolution. The Serbs found themselves among the group of European reactionaries who wished to smother the revolution. Condemnation by the dogmatic advocates of revolution, the most influential of whom was Karl Marx, was directed at the Serbs as much as it was against the Russian tsar.

Their situation was not so unfavorable as regards their initial "demands": recognition of ethnic individuality, freedom to use the Serbian language and the Cyrillic script, freedom of religion, and the right to manage schools and hold assemblies; these were all derived from the Serbs' daily reality and genuine needs. On the other hand, the ecstatic youth who played a crucial role at the May 1848 Assembly were guided by history. The demand for a *voivoda* (who would replace the medieval despot) dated back to 1691, and the demand for special territory was a repetition of the one put forward by Habsburg supporters at the Timişoara Assembly of 1790.

When the *Wojwodschaft Serbien und des Tamiser Banats* (Voivodstvo of Serbia and Tamiš Banat) was formed in 1849, it was obvious that the world had changed in the meantime. The nominally Serbian territory was smaller than what had been sought, since it did not include parts of the Military Border and privileged districts, which had been returned to military rule. The Serbs were not the majority in the Voivodstvo; they were not even the largest ethnic group. According to the 1850–1 census, the Voivodstvo's population consisted of 347,459 Romanians, 335,080 Germans, 321,110 Serbs, 221,845 Hungarians, and 200,727 members of other nations.[2] The Serbs had good reason to comment that the situation would have been more favorable if parts of the Military Border had been included in the Voivodstvo. In fact, after colonization and other changes in the population, there was no larger region where one nation represented a clear-cut majority.

The Voivodstvo was detached from Hungary and placed under a ministry in Vienna, but it was not declared a special "land of the Crown" (*Kronland*). The dignity of the title of *voivoda* was reserved for the emperor, and an Austrian general was appointed vice-*voivoda*. Later the governor, appointed by the ruler, was the military and civilian administrator. The old Hungarian comitats were abolished and two districts (later five) were established, which were then divided into counties and municipalities. The administrative language was German but administrative offices could be addressed in native languages. The Voivodstvo seat (the name Vojvodina was already in use and later prevailed) was in Timișoara, and not as expected in Novi Sad, where the Serbs had a majority. It was important to heal the wounds created by the 1848–9 revolution, during which over 17,000 houses had been destroyed or damaged. Two-thirds were rebuilt and property that had been seized was returned through the courts. The war was followed by years of hunger and contributions were needed to save the poor.

Some of the aims of the revolution were accomplished during the years of reaction: the remnants of feudalism were abolished; there was equality before the law; and the General Civic Code and the Law on Judiciary Procedure were applied to the entire population. Measures were carried out by means of supervision and force, and the neo-absolutist regime earned the nickname "Bach's absolutism" after the minister in charge. The Serbs were not specially targeted. They received a larger number of positions in the civil service than before (second only to the Germans), and public schools remained under the control of Serb supervisors.

---

2   Other nations included 65,796 Bunjevci and Šokci, or Catholic Slavs speaking the Serbo-Croatian language (this figure includes about 3,000 Croats); 22,780 Bulgarians; 25,607 Slovaks; 15,507 Jews; 11,440 Roma; and 2,820 Greeks and Aromanians.

According to contemporary testimonies, this was a "deaf period," although a number of Serbian-language periodicals were launched: *Srbski dnevnik* (Serbian Journal, 1852), *Sedmica* (Hebdomadary, 1852), the first literary publication, *Podunavka* (1856), *Školski list* (School Bulletin, 1858), and *Ratar* (Plowman, 1855–6).

Following the Austrian defeat in the war against France and Sardinia in 1859, there was a need to settle relations with the Hungarian part of the state, and that was only possible at the price of restoring the constitutionality and integrity of the Hungarian Kingdom. One of the first victims was Vojvodina, formally abolished in 1860. The organs of the Serbian Voivodstvo handed over their authority to the restored comitats in May 1861. When confronted with the abolition of the Voivodstvo, with which they had been so displeased, Serb leaders vigorously rose to its defense. An assembly in the spirit of the "discussion assemblies" of the eighteenth century was granted to ease the tension. The Annunciation Assembly in Sremski Karlovci in April 1861 spoke in favor of a smaller Serb territory, but nothing came of it. The rifts that had been apparent at the Timişoara Assembly of 1790 between those who wanted to side with Vienna and those oriented toward Buda were again visible. There was evident discord between the church hierarchy, which had lost part of its authority, and civic-liberal politicians who sought cooperation with the Hungarians. The leaders who were to head Serbian politics in the following decades were already making their mark: Svetozar Miletić (1826–1901) and Mihailo Polit-Desančić (1833–1920). Groups that would later develop into political parties were distinguished by their attitude toward the expected but unattainable reorganization of the Empire on a federal basis. The political organization of the Serbian masses became all the more important: in elections held in 1860 for both the Serbian Assembly and the Hungarian state Diet, there were few Serbs among the electorate owing to the very high property requirement in order to vote. A few years of more liberal political expression and organization passed between the restoration of constitutionality in 1860 and the Compromise (*Ausgleich*) of 1867, which established the dual Austro-Hungarian monarchy and allowed for the Hungarian part to develop as the Magyar national state.

Novi Sad, which became the seat of the Matica Srpska in 1864, was increasingly singled out as the capital, the "Serbian Athens." This was especially true during the time of the United Serbian Youth organization, formed from student, cultural, and choral societies from all the lands inhabited by Serbs. The generations that had been raised in Serbian schools and fed on a diet of nationalism were convinced that the hour of liberation had arrived and demanded action. Displeased with the absolutist rule of Prince Mihailo, they glorified Montenegro, waging a ceaseless battle against the Turks. Progressive political ideas found expression in the United Youth organization. Liberal elements were the most influential, but the socialists were also vociferous. Indeed, the socialist leader, Svetozar Marković, was forced to leave the principality and emigrate to Novi Sad. Although the United Serbian Youth did not significantly influence daily politics, it left behind an important cultural heritage. Almost all Serbian intellectuals from the second half of the century rose from its ranks. It provided a common bond linking the intellectual elite together, despite their geographical separation.

Persecuted by both Serbian and Austrian authorities, the United Youth organization gradually died out and was eclipsed by greater events – the change of ruler in the principality, and the adoption of the Nationalities Law in the Hungarian part of the monarchy, both in 1868. Reforms that affected the Serbian Church and school autonomy were carried out after the introduction of constitutionality. A long-standing dispute was resolved between the newly self-affirmed Romanian intelligentsia and the clergy, who were embittered because they had been pushed into the background and wanted to acquire their own hierarchy. The eastern bishoprics were detached from the Karlovci metropolitanate in 1864 and placed under the authority of the Sibiu metropolitanate. The Serbian Church parishes remained linked to the Timişoara and Vršac bishops, as protopresbyterate. In the same year an Assembly was held, and its conclusions were included in the royal rescript of 1868, which amended the provisions from the 1779 *Declaratorium* and included regulations on the clergy, monasteries, church parishes, schools, consistories, and the management of communal property. Along with the clergy, there were secular representatives in all bodies, from the Serbian Assembly and Assembly Committees to the National School Council and parish administrations. The Assembly included 25 members of the clergy and 50 secular members. Elections revived political life among the Serbs, because political parties were fighting for seats not only in the Hungarian state Diet, but also in autonomous ecclesiastical and school bodies.

The Nationalities Law was adopted in the state Diet despite opposition from representatives of the minority ethnic groups. It principally regulated the right to use minority languages in churches and church bodies and in the schools that they organized and supported. The freedom to use native languages applied to cultural, artistic, and economic associations, which any citizen was allowed to found. State elementary and secondary schools were to be held in native languages in places where larger ethnic groups lived together. The requirements were immediately increased with respect to the equipment and the level of the schools that were supported by the parishes, while practically all the schools in the Military Border became municipal and operated according to state programs and with students of all confessions.

Aside from in Parliament, where the rhetorical flamboyance of the Serbian deputies had no concrete results, the struggle to maintain ethnicity was also carried out in places where Serbs lived with no special political or judicial framework. During the last decades of the nineteenth century the state was unable to fulfill important social and cultural functions, leaving free space for various charitable, cultural, and later sports associations. These organizations, in addition to the church, offered the Serbs and other ethnic groups a solid foundation for preserving their individuality.

There was an unspoken competition between ethnic and religious groups living in mixed societies as to who would show greater solidarity in aiding, supporting, employing, and educating their compatriots. Private foundations and endowments, which existed not only as part of the Karlovci metropolitanate and certain bishoprics but also in larger towns, played an important role in this process. While the state favored unification, homogenization, and absorption into a single mass, society gave expression to the different interests of the population through numerous civic associations and organizations. The capacity of Serbian environments, primarily urban, to develop and maintain their separate social characteristics helped the Serbs in the monarchy to retain their ethnicity at least as much as their political parties did.

In the Center of the Great Eastern Crisis (1875–8)

By the mid-nineteenth century Greece, Montenegro, and Serbia had cast off direct rule by the sultan's governors and officers. However, a large number of Balkan Christians were still the sultan's "protected subjects" and worked other people's land. The Ottoman Empire attempted to modernize, carry out reforms, and adjust to the changed international situation, partially under pressure from rival powers and partially with the aim of attaining internal peace. It was precisely these efforts, however, that revealed how far the state had strayed from the earlier Empire of great conquests, when there had been one central organization and strict laws.

The position of the Christian population ruled by the Turks, including part of the Serbian nation, can only be understood with respect to the backdrop of perpetual chaos and turmoil caused by the inability of the central authorities to provide law and order. The Gyulhane *hatt-i sherif* of 1839 was to provide personal and property security to all, regardless of their religious or ethnic background, and was especially significant for Christian subjects. This document was passed by the sultan and became the foundation for further reforms, which were better conceived than carried out. Only the modernization of the military was relatively successful, even though the introduction of compulsory military service met with strong resistance.

The great majority of the Christian population consisted of peasants, who were primarily interested in the regime that dealt with the land as well as the destination of their products. In 1833 the sipahis were abolished in regions bordering the autonomous principality. This was also attempted in Bosnia in 1836 and 1843, and finally succeeded in 1851. However, the peasants did not become landowners, as in Serbia, because the *chiftlik* system was introduced and new landowners were imposed. The new masters did not feel obliged to adhere to the customs and rules that applied to the sipahis. They increased dues severalfold and enforced unpaid labor – the *kuluk*. A relationship was created that could be compared to the "second serfdom" in the countries of Eastern Europe. Only a third of the former sipahis became part of the new class of landowners. Most of the new owners either purchased the former *timar* or imposed their rule over the peasants.

The new "nobility" of begs and agas in Bosnia cruelly exploited the peasants and the state imposed high taxes instead of the *haraç*, which had been abolished. The dues varied; in some regions one-third of the crop was taken, in others peasants retained only one-third, after the lord and state had taken their share. This was at a time of rudimentary farming techniques. Driven to the edge of existence, abused and humiliated, the peasants rose against their masters and tax collectors and sought justice from higher authorities; in the best cases they sent deputations to the sultan. The rebels sought assistance from the Serbian princes, but they held back and usually only intervened with the Turkish authorities.

The central authorities' efforts to achieve social harmony through general regulations or local decrees and court rulings were heavily resisted by the begs, agas, and Muslim clergy, who mistrusted change and novelty. Reforms had to be imposed by arms. The begs and other "nobles" from Bosnia, who were Muslims of Slavic origin and language, were especially energetic in their resistance, and the imperial army was sent against them on a number of occasions. In the operations of 1850–1, Omer Pasha Latas (1806–71), a Serb officer from the Austrian border militia who converted to Islam and became a high-ranking Turkish military leader, smashed the resistance, conquered the land, and banished 1,500 Bosnian agas and begs to Istanbul.

Waves of rebellions by Christian peasants were interspersed with uprisings by Muslim conservatives against the central authorities. Once the central authorities were consolidated, new decrees followed, testifying both to the changed distribution of power and to the ineffectiveness of previous regulations. Thus the *hatt-i* Hümayun of 1856 repeated the regulations of 1839 and more effectively confirmed the Christians' equality. Christians could no longer be called offensive names (*reaya*), they were allowed to become civil servants, and the testimony of a Christian in public trials had the same weight as that of a Muslim. Equality was introduced in the payment of taxes and tax-farming was prohibited. Christians had equal obligations with regard to military service, but they could buy their way out. Special laws introduced different categories of land ownership, and through reforms of the state administration Christian administrative bodies were introduced into the Council. The work of the church was facilitated and its educational system was tolerated.

Rebel movements did not remain regionally isolated or limit themselves to social demands: they were increasingly included in general political plans. Russia and Austria-Hungary had turned toward more active involvement in the Balkans: Russia because in 1871 it was freed of the obligations stipulated by the Treaty of Paris, and Austria-Hungary because it had been pushed out of the struggle for domination in the German Empire.

Rebellions in Bosnia and Herzegovina had been intended long before, yet what sparked off the Nevesinje rebellion in Herzegovina on July 9, 1875 was the harvest on the eve of the collection of the tithe. The revolt spread without any central organization and soon the Turkish garrisons were isolated and communications were severed. In mid-August the uprising shifted to Bosnia, where the rebel strongholds remained close to the Austro-Hungarian border. The struggle caused population movements and migrations across the border. It is estimated that 200,000 people fled the country. Aside from the uprisings in Herzegovina and Bosnia, there were also rebellions in Bulgaria in the fall of 1875 and spring of 1876, which were put down with great violence and bloodshed. Events in the European part of Turkey became the center of international attention.

Russia and Austria-Hungary were directly interested and signed a secret treaty that divided their spheres of interest. The Austro-Hungarian monarchy made it clear that it opposed Serbian expansion into Bosnia, to which Russia agreed, thus giving it a free hand over Bulgaria and Constantinople. After a brief hesitation, Montenegrin Prince Nikola enthusiastically supported the rebellion in Herzegovina, placing it under his control and providing it with a unified leadership. News of the uprising caused agitation in Serbia: the public demanded that the state intervene, while the prince and responsible politicians were anxious to avoid getting involved. Serbs in Serbia, Hungary, and Croatia formed committees to aid the rebels and the wounded.

In June 1876 Serbia and Montenegro entered the war, having previously forged an alliance. The national militia was put to the test: they had not fought in battle for half a century, and in addition the troops were poorly armed and without proper leadership. Russian volunteers made up for the lack of officers, and military operations were headed by General Chernyaev. Despite some successes (such as the defense of Šumatovac), the situation took a turn for the worse. The prince accepted the diplomatic mediation of the Great Powers and there was a 10-day ceasefire in September. However, General Chernyaev wanted to bring Russia into the war and convinced the prince and Serbian ministers to renew fighting. The Turks seized the strategically important location of Djunis overlooking the road to the center of Serbia, at which time Russia obtained a two-month ceasefire from November 1, 1876.

Montenegro was equally ill prepared for war, but led its campaign successfully. Operations in Herzegovina were prevented by neutral Austria-Hungary, so the Montenegrin army stayed within its borders. It achieved significant successes against the Ottoman army at Fundina (August 14, 1876) and Vučiji Dol (August 28, 1876). Montenegro was included in the ceasefire, but later peace negotiations were held separately for each warring side. Thus Serbia signed a truce on February 28, 1877, while negotiations with Montenegro continued and were suspended in April, before Russia entered the war. Montenegro thus continued its war campaign. In the second part of the war it was threatened by a 65,000-strong Turkish army that attacked from two directions and managed to link up near Podgorica, despite the heroic resistance of the Montenegrins. The capital of Cetinje was threatened, but a significant proportion of the troops were withdrawn because the Russians had entered Bulgaria in early July 1877. After that the Montenegrin army achieved several successes: it took over Nikšić and the fortifications along the road to Bileća, and then followed the Austrian warning not to expand toward Herzegovina. Bar, Ulcinj, and fortresses on Lake Skadar were captured in January 1878. Operations ceased when news arrived that Russia and Turkey had signed a treaty in Edirne.

Unlike the previous war, when Russia had held Serbia back from joining in the hostilities, in the fall of 1877 it urged Serbia's involvement, since the Russian army had encountered fierce resistance near Pleven in Bulgaria. The Serbian campaign started on December 15, 1877 with a march on Niš, which was surrounded. The seizure of Kuršumlija cut off the possibility of help reaching the Turks. Bela Palanka and later Pirot were taken in the southeast incursion. The main troops were sent toward Niš and the city fell on January 12, 1878. This was followed by the capture of Vranje and Gnjilane. News of a truce stopped the Serbian troops near Gračanica in Kosovo.

While this second, more successful war was under way, the Serbian government aspired to the "Old Serbia," which under the Ottomans meant the Kosovo vilayet with the four sanjaks of Niš, Prizren, Skopje, and Novi Pazar. They also had their eye on Vidin. The Treaty of Edirne (January 31) mentions only Serbian independence and correction of the borders. The Treaty of San Stefano (March 3, 1878), between Russia and the Ottoman Empire, was even worse news for Serbia. Serbia gained independence and an additional 150 km^2 of territory, Montenegro gained a significantly larger territory, but Bulgaria stretched from the Danube to the Aegean coast and the mountains of Albania. Russian politicians did not conceal the fact that Bulgarian interests were more important to them than Serbian interests. This instigated a change in public opinion and a redefinition of Serbian policies toward Russia.

Since England and Austria had applied pressure for revision of the treaty, an international conference was called in Berlin (Congress of Berlin 1878). During the preparations, Serbia was obliged to turn to Austria to protect its interests, at the price of promising trade agreements, linking the Serbian railway to Hungary within three years, and regulating the Danube River in the Djerdap Gorge, which would be carried out by Austria-Hungary. The voices of Serbian and Montenegrin representatives went unheard. After considerable wrangling, Serbia gained control of Niš, Pirot, Vranje, Leskovac, and Prokuplje. Despite its dissatisfaction with the expansion to just four districts, this arrangement was grudgingly accepted.

International recognition of Serbian independence was linked to the legalization of religious freedoms and equality. This involved the Jewish community and extended to Muslims and their property. Serbia promised to change nothing in its trade agreements with other countries and to construct transit railways through its newly acquired territories, which had previously been the obligation of the Ottoman Empire. The Assembly held on August 5, 1878 approved the decision of the Congress of Berlin. Montenegro's expansion doubled its size, even though it was smaller than what had been included in the Russian–Turkish treaty. It acquired the important cities of Podgorica, Nikšić, Kolašin, Spuž, Žabljak, Plav, and Gusinje. In 1880 the cities of Plav and Gusinje were returned to Ottoman rule following fierce resistance from the local Albanian population, while Montenegro gained Ulcinj and the territory stretching to the Bojana River.

The Serbs considered the outcome of the eastern crisis and the decisions of the Congress of Berlin to be a national tragedy, not because they had gained less than expected, but because it allowed Austria-Hungary

(a)   (b)

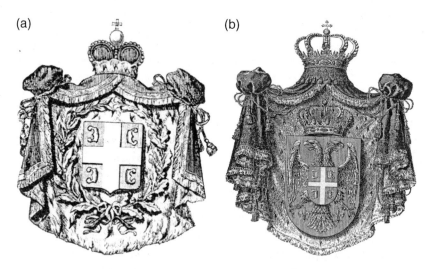

Plate 7.4   Serbian heraldic arms of the nineteenth century. (a) Arms of the principality, 1862; (b) arms of the kingdom, 1882. (From title pages of official publications)

to occupy Bosnia and Herzegovina, ending the possibility of expansion into that territory whose Serb population was yet to be liberated. Austrian rule was considered worse than Turkish, and Serbs and Muslims resisted it for some time.

Diverging Paths of Development

Both Serbia and Montenegro were expanded at the Congress of Berlin, as was Austria-Hungary through its occupation of Bosnia and Herzegovina. This balanced the number of Serbs under Habsburg rule and those in the independent states, with about half on either side of the border.[3] As in the eighteenth century, the Serbs in the Habsburg monarchy were divided, not into different regimes (comitats, estates, the Military Border) but into territories with different state-legal status and organization. The position of the individual was no longer the central issue – subjects had become equal before the law and courts. Rather, the

3   This was the situation ca. 1880. By 1910 the population of the independent states had increased by a million.

position of the national collective was what really mattered. In the modern state, everything that was not part of the ruling nation, individually or collectively, was directed toward assimilation into the "political nation." Groups that had undergone an "awakening" or "revival" and become aware of their individuality fiercely resisted this fate. Given the existence of a Serbian principality and their large numbers, not to mention their eighteenth-century heritage and their experiences of 1848–9, the Serbs were unsuitable material for assimilation. The masses as well as the political and cultural elite recognized and sometimes inflated the threat, defending themselves as far as circumstances allowed.

The organization of the monarchy set by the Compromise of 1867 was dualistic, but the Serbs were divided into not two but four separate groups. Within historical Hungarian territory, the second Compromise of 1868 recognized Croatian autonomy in the domains of interior

Map 7.1   Serbia and Montenegro after the Congress of Berlin, 1878.

organization, the judiciary, and education, and the Hungarian Nationalities Law of 1868 did not apply. Serbs in Croatia came under the jurisdiction of the Ban and Diet. Even though the decision of the 1867 Diet
established in principle that "the Triune Kingdom recognizes the Serbian
people who live in it as a people identical and equal to the Croatian
[people]," equality was hard to attain and sustain, and the term "identical" concealed the threat of assimilation. Given the fact that the
language of the Serbs was the same as that of the Croats, the ruling
"political people," greater importance was given to the name of the
nation and its language, the Cyrillic alphabet, and Orthodox confession
in order to preserve the Serbs' identity.

The number of Serbs in Croatia significantly increased when the jurisdiction of the Croatian authorities extended to the Military Border in
1881. There were 497,746 Serbs comprising 26.3 percent of the population. They were concentrated in certain parts of the former Military
Border, but did not constitute a majority in any town except Karlovci,
the seat of the patriarchate. They had a proportional part in the narrow
population of voters (2 percent of the entire population, 8.8 percent in
1910), and occasionally held as much as a third of the elected seats in
the Sabor.

During the period of disrupted relations following the Austro-
Hungarian occupation of Bosnia and Herzegovina, the Serbs in Croatia
founded an independent Serbian party, which fought for the recognition
of the Serbian name, the Cyrillic alphabet, the independence of the
Serbian educational system, and equal treatment in the state's support of
education and cultural activities. The National Party, which accepted the
Compromise and cooperated with the government in Budapest, showed
greater understanding of Serbian needs than the opposition headed by
Ante Starčević's Rights Party, which denied the existence of the Serbs in
Croatia.

Ban Karoly Khuen-Héderváry (1883–1903), who was unpopular
because of the forced implementation of Hungarian government policies,
made small concessions to the Serb deputies in order to gain their votes.
The "Serbian Law" of 1887 was one significant item. Adopted after
lengthy wrangling, it used the name of the Serbs, confirmed the autonomy of the Serbian Orthodox Church in educational and endowment
issues, and approved the use of the Cyrillic alphabet. It also promised
state support for educational and cultural needs, and approved participation in the Assemblies and independent church and educational bodies.
The law thus extended to Serbs in Croatia what had been in effect in
Hungary since the eighteenth century.

The Serbs supported Croatia's independence and its expansion (after
the Military Border, Dalmatia became an issue). Some Serbian groups,

however, opposed Khuen's regime, but the opposition, which was supported by clerical circles, denied their existence and created a hostile atmosphere, which led to anti-Serb demonstrations in 1895, 1899, and 1902. Because of the nature of their position, the Serbian population had to turn to business and free trade, and by the end of the nineteenth century had made significant advances. The Serbian Bank was established in Zagreb in 1895, and later became the largest financial institution among the Serbs, with investments in Bosnia and Montenegro and branch offices in other regions. The Alliance of Serbian Agricultural Cooperatives, established in 1897, became increasingly active and consisted of 141 cooperatives at the beginning of 1905. The *Privrednik* association was formed at this time with responsibility for the training and employment of young Serbian craftsmen and merchants.

Changes on both Serbian and Croatian sides seemed inevitable once their youth united in 1896 and continued to nurture ties. Relations toward the ruling dynasty became critical ("the new course"), and a Croat–Serb coalition was formed whose leading politicians would later play important roles in the creation of the Yugoslav state: Franjo Supilo (1870–1917), Ante Trumbić (1864–1938), and Svetozar Pribićević (1875–1936). The coalition won elections and hampered the actions of the ban, who was appointed by the Hungarian government. A new crisis was sparked off by the annexation of Bosnia and Herzegovina by Austria-Hungary. In 1909, 53 Serbian politicians were accused of planning a revolution in Croatia, in collusion with the Serbian government. The staged trial for high treason had the opposite effect of what was intended, since Croatian lawyers and politicians came to the Serbs' defense. A subsequent trial for libel resulting from an article by Dr. Friedjung determined that the documents involved had been forged.

At this period Dalmatia was outside Croatia, in the Austrian part of the empire. It was represented in the Imperial Council and had a separate assembly from 1861. The executive authorities consisted of a Territorial Committee and a governor. Serbs comprised 17 percent of the population in Dalmatia and their numbers increased despite unfavorable economic conditions, from 80,000 in 1870 to 105,000 in the 1910 census. The great majority were farmers with small plots of land, but the city population included a significant number of successful merchants. The Serbian community in Trieste numbered 300 people. Owing to the heritage of the Illyrian provinces, the Serbs in Dalmatia found themselves in a better situation, with their own schools and press. The center of the diocese had moved from Šibenik to Zadar, and the region of the Gulf of Kotor became a separate diocese. Both dioceses were placed under the Bukovina–Dalmatian metropolitanate in 1874, which was under Austrian control.

The Austrian authorities relied on the inhabitants of the former communes, where the Italian language and culture were indicators of status. The National Party, which had originally consisted of both Croats and Serbs, demanded equality, especially of language and participation in the state civil service. The Serbs supported demands for Dalmatia to be attached to Croatia and Slavonia, thus reinstating the Triune Kingdom. However, there was disagreement between the Serbs and Croats in Dalmatia, especially after 1878, when the Croats welcomed the occupation of Bosnia and advocated its annexation to Croatia.

Out of this discord emerged the Serbian National Party in 1879. It operated independently, and for a time fostered close links with the Autonomists, an urban ethnic Italian party. There was strong clerical influence on both the Serbian and Croatian sides. The Serbian party in Dalmatia only overcame clerical resistance in 1903, and its political agenda recognized the "Serbian nation of three confessions." Identifying Serbdom exclusively with the Orthodox faith carried weight in Dalmatia because it alienated influential Catholic Serbs in the southern regions of Dubrovnik and the Gulf of Kotor. Cooperation between Croats and Serbs in Dalmatia occurred simultaneously with Serbo-Croat rapprochement in Croatia at the beginning of the twentieth century.

The territory of Bosnia and Herzegovina was the last to come under the Habsburgs' control. It was officially ruled by the sultan until the Annexation of 1908 and was situated like a colony between the Austrian and Hungarian parts of the monarchy, under the joint Ministry of Finance. It had a Territorial Administration and governor, who commanded the army and police. According to the 1879 census, there were 485,496 Serbs living there, comprising 42.88 percent of the population. Toward the end of Austrian rule in 1910, 87.92 percent of the Serbian population were still peasants. Their situation was desperate because the new rulers retained the serfdom system, with the aga receiving one-third of the crop and the state its tithe. Almost three-quarters (73.2 percent) of the serfs were Serbian.

The three religious groups within the population sought support and aid from Croatia, Serbia, and the Ottoman Empire, respectively, while Austrian authorities sought to prevent these links. They chose to rely on Muslim nobles to try to overcome a newly acquired sense of ethnicity by developing a sense of belonging to the country. In the administration, the economy, and colonization policies, the Catholic element was systematically favored. The Austrian authorities' course of action was doubly dangerous for the Serbs: on the one hand it inhibited the liberation of the serfs, and on the other it undermined the processes of national cultural development and free communication with other Serb-inhabited regions that had already been initiated. The Austrian government avoided radically unseating the Muslim begs, as did the Serbian upper class in an attempt to woo influential Muslims to their side. Serfs were freed by the payment of a ransom and compensation to their former masters. Even though credit and other assistance helped, liberation advanced slowly and not all serfs had been freed by the time war erupted in 1914. Serbian peasants benefited little from the processes of modernization and Europeanization that were being carried out by the authorities.

The Orthodox congregation in Bosnia and Herzegovina remained under the Constantinopolitan patriarchate even after 1878, and in 1880 a convention was signed which granted the Austrian emperor the right to appoint a bishop by choosing one of three candidates. The territory had three bishops, who were traditionally ranked as metropolitans, and in 1900 a fourth bishopric of Banja Luka and Bihać was founded. Priests were educated at a theological school near Sarajevo. There were 231 Orthodox churches at the time of the occupation, and by 1906 there were an additional 201 new churches.

Merchants were an important component of the urban Serbian population and were financially the best off. They energetically spearheaded the struggle to preserve the language, the Cyrillic alphabet, and independent education for Orthodox Christian youth. The government sought to suppress confessional education and enforce the state education system. In the late nineteenth century there were 309 schools headed by Orthodox priests. Teachers were trained in schools in Sarajevo (the location of the department for female teachers) and in Mostar.

Local church parishes, where priests were supported by a council of laymen, were organized and became influential in Bosnia and Herzegovina, as was the case with the Serbs in Hungary. Friction sometimes arose, usually over the appointment of teachers. As in Hungary, radical nationalists criticized the church for being lenient and servile to the state authorities. Initiatives to found reading rooms and clubs as well as charitable, assistance (the precursor to social security), temperance, and choral associations, and later athletic associations, mostly originated from the parishes and towns, shaping the Serbian element of civic society. There were 330 local volunteer associations by 1912; political organizations were prohibited until the beginning of the twentieth century. The most important as regards its scope and program was *Prosvjeta* (enlightenment), founded in 1902, which by 1911 had 74 subcommittees. After 1903 there was more freedom for political activity, which led to associations on a national basis. A Serbian national organization was founded in 1907. It joined the Muslims in fierce resistance to the Annexation of 1908, attempting to prevent it and gain autonomy for "Serbian lands" under the sultan's rule.

The emperor approved the Constitution of Bosnia and Herzegovina in 1910, introducing a people's assembly divided into *curiae*, based on land ownership, religion, and profession, together with a very complicated electoral process. The modern regulations failed to bring stability because social and national tensions were on the increase, with new generations advocating revolutionary methods and violence as a means of political struggle. In the early twentieth century it became clear that the policy of imposing a special "Bosnian" consciousness was not working, but it was also evident that neither of the two expanding nationalisms, Serbian and Croatian, had absorbed the local Muslims. They were consolidated into a large group during the 40 years of Habsburg rule and resisted both assimilation and categorization into the usual models of ethnic classification.

In 1910 central Hungary, excluding Croatia and Transylvania, included a Serb population of 461,000 (it took 20 years for the population to recover from the losses of the 1848–9 struggle), on a territory exceeding that of present-day Vojvodina. Until the end of the nineteenth century, this highly urbanized group played a prominent role among their Serbian compatriots in the monarchy; their newspapers reached every region inhabited by Serbs, and the voices of their leaders were heard far and wide. In the early twentieth century, the leading role was assumed by the economically stronger and politically more important Serbs in Croatia, which became the center of opposition to the Habsburg regime.

After the Compromise of 1867, the Serbs' position was defined by the Nationalities Law, adopted in 1868, which suited neither those to whom it applied nor those who implemented it, and much was left to the discretionary powers of the competent authorities. The position of Serbian "nationality" was strengthened by an ecclesiastical and educational autonomy dating back 150 years and the traditional use of the Serbian language in Serbian towns. The Hungarian authorities respected the independence of educational establishments, but found ways of limiting it by setting higher requirements for school founders and imposing municipal instead of church schools.

The authorities changed the situation in mixed communities after the Compromise: only the symbols of the ruling nation were allowed, embodied in the language used for public signs, the names of streets, squares, monuments, and institutions, the uniforms worn by public servants, and so on. This created resistance, which led to even greater enforcement of the Hungarian language. Hungarian was introduced as a compulsory subject in elementary schools, regardless of who had founded them, and was imposed in secondary schools where very high requirements were set. A large number of state schools were opened whose task was to teach Hungarian to the population included in compulsory education. Prior to World War I, only a third of schools were not state-run.

The struggle for survival was carried on at two levels: in Parliament and in the regions populated by Serbs. The significance of their efforts is inversely proportional to the role they are accorded by historians. Energetic speeches in Parliament were futile given the balance of power, but their effect was psychological and reinforced the consciousness of ethnic unity. Ordinary people and those without the right to vote found support and courage in Serbian political parties. In daily life resistance to denationalization was exhibited by people from the state and municipal apparatus, by church and independent educational bodies, clergymen and teachers, prominent private patrons, and an increasing number of cultural societies.

The civil liberal movement emerged as an alternative to the church hierarchy and developed into the Serbian National Liberal Party, which fought for the votes of the tiny electorate comprising about 2 percent of the total population. At its best it had three or four members in the Hungarian Parliament, who left visible traces through their parliamentary work, unlike the Serbian members of Parliament who were elected from the list of the ruling Hungarian party. The patriarch and metropolitans sat in the Upper House.

The early retirement of the party's leader Svetozar Miletić, who suffered from poor health, had a great impact on the political life of the Serbs in Hungary. One wing of the Serbian National Liberal Party consisting of wealthy and notable politicians, the so-called notabilities, stood up against irrevocable rejection of the 1867 Compromise and modified the party platform in 1884 (the Kikinda platform). On the other side, a radical faction emerged out of the socialist element under the influence of partisan life in Serbia. It evolved into the Radical Party between 1902 and 1914 and was active in Hungary and Croatia. It was concerned with the rights of the lower class and fought for the general right to vote, women's equality, and democratic reforms. The leader of the Radicals was the controversial Jaša Tomić (1856–1922), who had a powerful influence on the political situation in Vojvodina and Croatia for three decades and displayed few scruples when it came to demagogy, chauvinism, and anti-Semitism.

In the early twentieth century Serb parties in Hungary clashed in elections for members of the Assembly Committee and other independent church and educational bodies which controlled church property and funds from numerous pious foundations. There were scandals and friction between politicians and the church hierarchy, which felt threatened in its management of church affairs. Lay influence along Protestant lines was contrary to the traditions of the Orthodox Church. Parties started interfering in the appointment of the patriarch, as did the state authorities, who insisted in the 1907 election that candidates spoke Hungarian. The work of the patriarch and metropolitans was graded according to party criteria; thus the archpriests of the late nineteenth century, especially patriarchs German Andjelić (1881–8) and Georgije Branković (1890–1907), were branded servants of the regime, despite their indisputable merits in improving church life. The most serious consequence of these conflicts was the suspension of decisions made by the independent church and educational bodies in 1912.

In the second half of the nineteenth century, Serbian groups under national dynasties and those under Habsburg authority were separated by state borders but were not isolated from one another. During the period of greater Serbian dependence on Austria-Hungary, following the Congress of Berlin, communication was facilitated among Serbs who had had occasional close contacts earlier on, such as in 1848–9 or during the period of the United Serbian Youth organization. While links between intellectual elites remained strong, the masses remained closed within their territorial frameworks and developed under distinctive conditions that left traces in their habits and mentality.

The common attribute of the divided Serbian population was their language; they were linked by the same church, even though the practices of religious life differed somewhat from region to region. They shared the same historical traditions, those from epics and legends, as well as those taught briefly at school. However, the structure of society differed significantly. In Hungary the population of peasants and townspeople had nobility above them, a situation that did not develop in Serbia and Montenegro. However, the nobility did not set the tone in Serbian society in Hungary since they were not numerous among the landowners. The exceptions were barons Fedor and Mihajlo Nikolić, owning 6,260 and 4,630 acres[4] of land, respectively, and Baron Miloš Bajić with 1,708 acres. However, middle-class families such as the Dundjerski, Manojlović, Kaćanski, and Gavanski had more than 1,000 acres of land apiece, and in the late nineteenth century there were three landowners in Serbia with more than 300 hectares (427 acres).

Differences were noticeable within the peasant populations as well. Statistics for Serbia from 1889 were given in hectares, while the land owned by Serbs in Hungary in the 1910 land registry was expressed in acres (0.575 of a hectare). The category of small properties (smaller than 5 hectares) was predominant in Serbia (72.6 percent), while it represented only 24 percent of the estates owned by Hungarian Serbs. There

---

4   The Austro-Hungarian acre was 57.5 ares (5,750 m²).

was a sizable amount of Serb-owned land in Hungary in the category of 20 to 50 acres (between 11 and 28.7 hectares), which accounted for 9.2 percent, while in Serbia only 7.08 percent of estates were larger than 10 hectares. The concentration of land ownership in the north was accompanied by a large number of landless peasants and significant emigration. There was no such emigration in the south, but overpopulation was frequent on land divided into small parcels, and was accompanied inevitably by chronic poverty.

Serb society in Hungary had a strong middle class of landowners, as well as a relatively high degree of urbanization. According to the 1910 census, 18.4 percent of Serbs lived in cities (17.5 percent in 1900), while city dwellers accounted for 13.2 percent of the population in Serbia. Towns were also significantly different. The dozen cities in southern Hungary, where Serbs represented a majority or were a sizable portion of the population, were cities typical of Central Europe with standard institutions and offices. Towns in Serbia gradually discarded their oriental heritage and became less isolated, with the capital setting the model for Europeanization.

The degree of illiteracy reflected socioeconomic differences and the results of previous cultural development. More than half the men and women among Serbs in Hungary were literate by the beginning of the twentieth century (41.66 percent of the women were illiterate). In Serbia, however, 78.97 percent of the population was illiterate, including over 90 percent of the women.

The region of the clan society still differed from urbanized regions. Part had come under Austro-Hungarian rule in Herzegovina, another part developed on an autochthonous basis in Montenegro, and the remaining part fought for liberation from Ottoman rule. Clans in all three areas were caught up in the process of modernization, some by state intervention, but even more through people migrating to towns to work or study and remaining there. Fostering family solidarity and maintaining domestic customs mitigated the severe effects of the market and monetary economy introduced by capitalism. The clan region stood out from the surrounding areas with its cult of ancestors, burial ceremonies, and heroic epics, even when modernization had made great advances and given cities a veneer of uniformity.

Living environments varied from Szentendre to Montenegro – town layouts, the shapes of houses and spatial organization, availability of electricity and running water. All Serbs came under the strong and enduring influence of Europe from both the north and the west, which would ultimately bury ethnic and regional differences. But these differences persisted for some time, since Europe's influence was unevenly accepted.

Plate 7.5   The beginnings of modern industry: textile factory in Paraćin, 1880. Drawing by Felix Kanitz. (From F. Kanitz, *Das Königtum Serbien und das Serbenvolk*, vol. 1, Leipzig, 1904)

In contrast to diverging developmental paths in the socioeconomic sphere, the cultural domain with its new elite was blended into a single entity that was passed on to subsequent generations. By the end of the nineteenth century, connections between the cultural elite formed a cultural space similar to that which had existed at the end of the eighteenth century, albeit a far greater and richer one.

The main medium was the press, which was dominated by local and regional newspapers. A small number of specialized publications reached all parts of Serbian society (publications of the Serbian Royal Academy, Matica Srpska, and the Serbian Literary Cooperative starting in 1892). By the beginning of the twentieth century, literary and cultural centers were created in all regions in which Serbs lived, each with their own writers. Sarajevo and Mostar followed in the footsteps of Montenegro and Dalmatia. Books, newspapers, and magazines circulated across borders, and traveling authors faced few barriers. Biographies of prominent intellectuals and writers indicate there was movement from one region to another and that important works were popular everywhere. Many were moving to Serbia and remaining there. There was no cultural gradient as in the first half of the nineteenth century. Both Serbia and Vojvodina were on an equal footing, and by the 1880s the newly proclaimed Kingdom of Serbia had taken over leadership of the cultural domain. The work of the Royal Serbian Academy, founded in 1886, was symbolic in this respect, as it brought together eminent scientists and artists from throughout Serbian lands. Belgrade's cultural leadership became undisputed after 1903, when a significant number of writers and cultural personalities from the South Slav region gathered there.

This multitude of cultural centers facilitated links with important European cultures and provided a counterweight to foreign influences. They enabled Serbs from Šumadija, for example, to become acquainted with their distant compatriots through the works of writers from Montenegro, Dalmatia, and Herzegovina. Just as Serbian literature had developed thematically in the late eighteenth century, in the late nineteenth century it ventured into previously unknown genres and styles. All the great literary movements from Romanticism to Modernism echoed in Serbian literature written before World War I. Cultural unity at the turn of the century seemed as natural and inevitable as the realistic division into states and regions with different regimes. The significance of both these aspects would become apparent when the Serbs were finally united in a single state.

Constitution and Parliament Put to the Test

The declaration of independence at the Congress of Berlin formally introduced Serbia and Montenegro as equal members of the community of European states. As such, they were faced with the task of truly bringing their systems and political development in line with the society of states that they had joined. Structural weaknesses and general backwardness could not be eliminated overnight, but an institutional foundation could be created and a political culture could be developed that were necessary for swifter modernization.

However, both new states encountered obstacles, not only in their heritage, which was difficult to change, but also in the personnel in charge of making decisions. Both countries had reached a degree of complexity that could no longer be ruled from a single throne and with a single will. Reliance on a group of individuals was inevitable, as were the numerous experts and the wide-ranging network of bodies through which the state authorities reached all areas of life and every corner of state territory. Both states at this period had absolutist rulers. Montenegro's Prince Nikola upheld an anti-modern ideology which judged a constitution unnecessary, since the people themselves and clan tradition provided the best possible models of organization. In Serbia Prince Milan Obrenović did not advocate unlimited power in principle, but applied it in practice through totalitarian behavior and by violating laws and institutions.

The much-desired territorial expansion of 1878 brought the problem of integrating new territories within the existing state. The situation was especially dramatic in Montenegro, which now had cities and urban populations. Both states were obliged to maintain previous ownership rights, while Serbia had the additional obligation of building its portion of the railway linking Europe and Istanbul. Peasants were offered the opportunity to rid themselves of their lords and take over the land they worked. The authorities compelled them to purchase the land from the owners, which gave rise to numerous disputes over prices. The matter was finally regulated in 1884 through a general purchase price that was covered by the state budget.

The change of authority was followed by the emigration of some and the immigration of others. Muslims left, including Turks, local Muslims, and islamized Albanians. Theirs was undoubtedly a voluntary departure, arising from an unwillingness to submit to Christian rule, but they also received some encouragement. At the time of Serbian expansion, Muslims accounted for 38 percent of the population in the four districts, but by 1890 the non-Serb population had dropped to 20 percent. Symbols of the Orient quickly disappeared from towns: minarets as well as other Turkish buildings were destroyed, although oriental influence remained visible in residential architecture well into the twentieth century.

Political parties formed in Serbia in the first years after the country's independence were to have a profound influence on future political events. Two new political parties of opposing orientations were created in 1881, in addition to the Liberal Party, which gained popularity after the death of Prince Mihailo and played a role in the adoption of the 1869 Constitution. The Progressive Party was founded by prominent intellectuals who shared the ruler's view that uneducated people were not ready to take part in state affairs. The Progressives were advocates of modernization, convinced that they could implement reforms from the top down, with the help of the ruler.

The other political party that was formed at the same time was genuinely new, with a large membership throughout the country. This was the People's Radical Party, founded by socialists who did not adhere to an exclusively socialist program. The Radicals were critical of government bureaucracy and favored self-government, which was popular among the peasant masses who despised the authorities, bureaucracy, and intellectuals. Since voting requirements in Serbia were very lenient (one only had to pay taxes), the electorate was broad and included almost all adult men. The Radical Party was able to politicize the peasant population and thus win elections. In the beginning party activities resembled rough meetings, but later the party became more sophisticated when it was joined by intellectuals. It characteristically placed party interests ahead of everything else and attacked any government proposal, regardless of its individual merits.

The two parties differed greatly in their foreign policies. Since Prince Milan was oriented toward Austria, the Progressives followed him. Their government (1881–7) signed a trade treaty with Austria-Hungary, as stipulated by the Berlin Congress, but it also agreed to a secret convention which required the Serbian ruler to seek Austro-Hungarian approval before concluding treaties with third countries. On the strength of this, the prince gained approval to pronounce himself king. Parliament proclaimed the kingdom in 1882 with great pomp, placing the act in historical perspective as the restoration of the medieval kingdom that had ceased to exist five centuries earlier. However, the restoration of the monarchy revealed the depth of the discontinuity: aside from the church, not a single institution, insignia, or symbol linked the Obrenović monarchy to the medieval state.

The unilateral foreign policy was unpopular and cast a shadow over legislation adopted by the Progressive government in 1881 and 1882 which made great strides toward modernization: laws on the press, on people's assemblies and associations, on judges, on making elementary education mandatory, on the National Bank, on money, and on the reorganization of the army. This legislation completed a series of modernization-oriented laws that were initiated during the regency: the adoption of the metric system (1873), joining the Latin Monetary Union, and minting money.

The implementation of the army legislation had drastic consequences. Arms remaining from the national militia were to be turned in, but the Radicals opposed this measure and urged the people not to surrender their weapons. The Radical Party's executive did not become directly involved, but the party's lower-level organizations in Timok, Zaječar, and Knjaževac in eastern Serbia organized a rebellion, the *Timočka buna*, which was suppressed by the king. Many of the rebels were imprisoned and some were executed. The party leadership fled to Bulgaria, leaving the party in disarray and without influence for some time.

A fresh crisis broke out in 1885 when the king dragged the country into a war that had no one's approval. In an attempt to obtain compensation for Serbia after the unification of Bulgaria with Eastern Rumelia, he attacked Bulgaria. However, the disheartened army, weak command, and fierce Bulgarian defense transformed the mission into a catastrophe, and Austria-Hungary once again had to come to the Serbian king's rescue. Peace was signed in Bulgaria in 1885, restoring positions before the war. Disgraced, King Milan considered abdicating in favor of his underage son. His behavior became increasingly unstable. He quarreled with the queen and fought for a divorce, and in 1887 made a dramatic political about-turn when he invited the Radicals to take power after the party leadership had returned from abroad. The Radicals joined the government and there were reprisals against members of the former state administration. About 140 people were killed, and a large number were hounded out of office.

The new government drafted a constitution with the assistance of experts from all parties. This democratic constitution was adopted in 1888, but was later rescinded. The king abdicated in 1888, and the coronation of his successor Alexander on June 27, 1889 was linked with the commemoration of the 500th anniversary of the battle of Kosovo. The anniversary celebration echoed throughout Serbdom, even though it was limited and suppressed in Austria-Hungary.

The new ruler was still a minor when he dismissed the regency, suspended the constitution on several occasions, and dismissed governments. Former King Milan returned to the country and became commander of the army. The young king also conducted a pro-Austrian foreign policy. His authority was most severely damaged by his marriage to widow Draga Mašin, his mother's lady-in-waiting, and the disgrace surrounding the queen's fabricated pregnancy. King Alexander and Queen Draga were assassinated in 1903 in a conspiracy hatched by officers and politicians, who planned to enthrone Karadjordje's descendant Petar, son of the former Prince Alexander. After his conditions were accepted and the 1888 Constitution reinstated, the Assembly proclaimed him king. The coronation took place in 1904 and was linked with the centennial celebration of the First Serbian Uprising. With the new king came a change in domestic and foreign policy, and Austria-Hungary was brushed aside in favor of Russia. Relations with western states, especially England, were in crisis because of the royal assassination, and demands to punish and remove the conspirators caused tensions in relations with the officers' corps, creating another center of power aside from the Assembly, government and king.

During three decades in which four kings from two dynasties occupied the Serbian throne, the Montenegrin ruler, Prince Nikola Petrović Njegoš, was nearing his golden anniversary. Even though he had long resisted the idea of a constitution, he did bring about changes, some of them inevitable after the Berlin Congress. With some difficulty the state borders had been set and customs taxes introduced, as was a state monopoly in the tobacco, salt, and petroleum trades. This did not help state finances; one-third of the state budget was covered by foreign aid, primarily from Russia. Loans were also taken out, which Montenegro did not repay during the period of its independence. Austria helped build roads during the last two decades of the nineteenth century, helping to link vital towns. There were also significant changes in the army. It received modern armaments and was placed under the full command of the Russian Army in 1910. In the central state administration the former

Plate 7.6 Secular iconography: idealized portraits of (a) Djordje Petrović Karadjordje and (b) Miloš Obrenović, founders of the two modern Serbian ruling dynasties. Both posthumous portraits from the nineteenth century are reproduced in textbooks, pictures, even postcards. (Supplied by the author)

Senate gave place to the High Court, State Council, and ministries, initially six in number. Having gained independence, Montenegro established diplomatic relations with the most important states, but, for financial reasons, did not have representations in all of them. From 1902 foreign diplomats resided permanently in Cetinje.

A form of political grouping took place in Montenegro at the same time that political parties were being formed in Serbia. A constitution was demanded in 1880–1, but met great resistance from the prince. The members of this group thought of themselves as the National Party and were organized as a club, but they were quickly repressed. The autocratic rule of Prince Nikola relied heavily on Russia, and when struggles for a constitution took place there, the prince finally adopted a constitution in 1905, which was modeled after the Serbian constitution of 1869. The Assembly gained in importance and all men who were of age had the right to vote, but power remained with the prince.

The next important step was the proclamation of the kingdom on the fiftieth anniversary of the prince's reign in 1910. The Great Powers consented to this change, and the celebrations were attended by the heir to the Serbian throne, but the Serbian public condemned this act as the partitioning of the Serbian people. Both the prince and the opposition were

Plate 7.7   The court of King Nikola of Montenegro in Cetinje. (Photograph by B. Strugar)

pro-Serbian in their orientation, and the prince even hoped that he might gain the Serbian throne and unite the two countries. Relations between Serbia and Montenegro experienced a succession of crises; however, this did not prevent them from joining forces when faced with the prospect of war with Turkey.

Times of War

After the territorial expansion of 1878, few Serbs remained within the Ottoman Empire, but there was still territory they really cared about. When the 1833 border was finally moved in 1878 to include the "four districts," the medieval capitals of Prizren and Skopje remained outside the Serbian state; the Peć patriarchate was not included, and Kosovo, with its central position in Serbian historical tradition, had not been freed. Just as the Serbs from southern Hungary worked toward liberating their fatherland, Serbia, in the late eighteenth century, so toward the end of the nineteenth century Serbs from the kingdom longed for the Old Serbia, which they perceived as their cradle.

The path of Serbian expansion toward its historical heart (Kosovo and Metohija, the Novi Pazar region, and northern Macedonia) was blocked not only by the sultan's rule but also by rival claims to Macedonia by Bulgaria and Greece, and by the local Albanian population in Kosovo. Everyone had historical claims to Macedonia: the Greeks according to ancient and Byzantine heritage from the eleventh and twelfth centuries, the Bulgarians according to Bulgarian rule in the ninth, tenth, and thirteenth centuries, the Serbs based on their rule in the fourteenth century, and the Turks as rulers in the last 500 years. No one considered the local population's opinion; indeed, it would have been difficult to obtain a unanimous answer, since the towns' populations consisted of Greeks, Turks, and Slavs. The Slavic people's consciousness lay dormant, and they primarily maintained Bulgarian traditions, but in some areas there was an awareness of being Serb even before the rival Serbian–Bulgarian educational propaganda of the late nineteenth century. In time the notion of their own Macedonian individuality grew and became established among sections of the elite. The political expression of this conviction that the Slavic population was neither Bulgarian nor Serbian was the energetic struggle for Macedonian autonomy. There were some who understood and acknowledged the special features of being Macedonian, but it was believed that the "floating population" would bow to whomever established lasting rule over them.

While the Greek border was slowly advancing from the south and the Serbian from the north, from 1870–2, before the Bulgarian principality was liberated, the Bulgarians contrived to establish a Bulgarian exarchate within the jurisdiction of the ecumenical patriarch. Its territory was to have a Bulgarian bishop with Bulgarian as the official church language, and there were to be Bulgarian schools and education in the Bulgarian spirit. The Serbian–Bulgarian partnership dating from the period of Prince Michael was soon replaced by mounting antagonism. Serbian involvement in the church and schools in Ottoman territory increased after 1885, but the results would not become apparent until 1896–7, when Serbian bishops were finally appointed heads of the Prizren and Skopje eparchies. Serbian schools were opened, parishes were organized, and priests and teachers became the mainstays of the Serbs' education. However, in the early twentieth century, the rivalry in Macedonia took on the form of a struggle between *komiti* and *chetniks*, Bulgarian and Serbian armed bands, who raided towns and spread fear by assassinating public figures of the opposing nationality.

In Kosovo there were visible signs of ethnic change which had accumulated since the Middle Ages with the immigration of Albanian cattle farmers. In addition to the continual flow of settlers and the islamization of urban centers, changes in the population were also caused by political events: the great Serbian migrations of 1689 and 1737, and the establishment of the border in 1878, when Albanians and other Muslims abandoned Serbian territory and Serbs left territories that remained under the sultan's control.

Faced with the prospect of the demise of the Ottoman Empire and the expansion of the Balkan states, the Albanians started seeking autonomy within the Ottoman Empire or a state on its ruins (the Prizren League) following the Berlin Congress. Since islamized Albanians represented a significant portion of the Ottoman armed forces and administration, they did not give up the Empire easily. Catholic Albanians were supported by Austria-Hungary and Italy, and certain factions were even helped by Montenegro during times of internal turmoil.

Rivalry over Macedonia hampered joint efforts against the Ottoman Empire. It was only when international crises intensified, especially during the war between Italy and Turkey in 1911 and the great Albanian uprising, that the Serbian and Bulgarian governments were able to overcome their mutual antagonism. They began secret negotiations on partitioning Macedonia, fearing the involvement of the Great Powers but supported by Russia. The plan was for an irrefutable Bulgarian area and an irrefutable Serbian area, with a disputed center, which was to receive autonomy or be divided with the arbitration of the Russian tsar. In May 1912 a Serbian–Bulgarian military alliance was forged, which continued into a chain of alliances: Bulgaria with Greece, and Serbia with Montenegro.

The allies entered war in October 1912. The Serbian army campaigned in Macedonia and toward the Novi Pazar sanjak, while the Montenegrin army moved on Skadar. After the victory at Kumanovo on October 23–4, 1912, the Serbian army entered Skopje on October 26 and proceeded toward Bitola. Serbia and Montenegro now had a common border. Since the other allies were also successful, Turkey asked for mediation by the Great Powers in early November. A truce was negotiated, but fresh hostilities erupted in early 1913. After Macedonia, the Serbian army occupied a substantial part of present-day Albania, which was torn apart by internal strife. Serbia took over the towns of Lezhë and Durrës, Tirana, and Elbasan. After a long and difficult combat, the Montenegrin army seized Skadar.

The Albanian state was proclaimed at an ambassadorial conference in London in December 1912, and Serbia was asked to withdraw its troops. Under threat of war from Austria-Hungary and pressure from the Great Powers, the Serbian army retreated, but military circles and government did not agree to the negotiated division of Macedonia. The emphasis was on securing a border with Greece at any cost and preventing Serbia from being encircled by Bulgaria and Albania.

The peace treaty had just been signed in London in May 1913, leaving Turkey with only a small area of land on the European mainland around Istanbul, when Bulgaria attacked the Serbian and Greek armies on June 30, launching a new Balkan war aimed at redistributing the former Turkish territories. Bulgaria suffered a defeat at Bregalnica between June 30 and July 8, and then came under attack from Romania and Turkey, forcing the country to negotiate a peace. Serbia held onto the Macedonian territories, but the border problems with Albania remained.

During the Balkan Wars two pillars of Serbian policy were rocked: the principle of ethnicity and the ideal of parliamentary democracy. The conquests of Albania and Macedonia demonstrated that Serbia had overstepped the aim of liberating the Serbian people, which had been its claim for decades. The coming showdown with Turkey strengthened the role of military factors in Serbia, which had in any case grown in importance since the coup of 1903. In addition to the constitutional elements of king, government, and Parliament, policies were influenced by a group of officers headed by Colonel Dragutin Dimitrijević Apis (1876–1917). This "Unification or Death" group of officers (the "Black Hand") advocated an aggressive foreign policy, maintaining contacts with Serb organizations under foreign rule and carrying out intelligence activities. They formed a center of power that contested parliamentary democracy, believing that strong military rule would achieve national goals more quickly.

Friction between the military and civilian authorities arose in the new territories where the Constitution of Serbia had not been applied. Support was sought among priests and teachers who declared themselves Serbs, and those who did not were sacked. A crisis emerged over whether priority should be given to civilian or military bodies; it then moved to Parliament, where King Petar I was forced to abdicate because of his support for the officers. He passed royal authority to his son Alexander, who became regent. Tension between the constitutional elements, the regent, the government, and a section of the officers continued until 1917 and the confrontation at Thessalonika.

The Serbian victory in both Balkan Wars reverberated among the Slav populations in the Habsburg monarchy, where public manifestations of joy caused the authorities to intervene. A state of emergency was introduced and local authorities were suspended. Austria-Hungary had shown aggressive intentions toward Serbia during the Balkan Wars, imposing ultimatums and seeking grounds for conflict. The exultation expressed by its subjects at Serbian successes added another link to a long chain of hostile acts by Austria-Hungary, including the Pig War (1906–11), prohibiting livestock imports from Serbia, and the crisis over the Annexation (1908–9). On the Serbian side, tension was heightened not by the government and responsible politicians but by sections of the press and national and secret revolutionary societies.

A young generation was emerging at this time whose experience of national and social struggles had taught them the efficacy of violence as a means to achieve goals. It was a generation that demanded action and sacrifice instead of words and political wisdom. Opposition to the Austrian regime in Bosnia was concentrated in the Young Bosnia organization, whose members were not averse to assassination. With the example before them of a comrade who had attempted to assassinate the Bosnian governor in 1910, a few members of Young Bosnia organized the murder of Archduke Francis Ferdinand, heir to the Austro-Hungarian throne, who was visiting Sarajevo to attend military exercises on St. Vitus's Day, June 28, 1914. The assassination of the heir to the throne and his consort had great repercussions worldwide, with repression of the Serb population in the monarchy and a 10-item ultimatum to Serbia, one of which was the demand that Austrian authorities take part in the investigation of the assassins' links with Serbia.

Since this incident was the first in a series of events that led to the outbreak of World War I, it has been the subject of judiciary investigations, war propaganda, and, with the passing of time, objective scientific research. It is indisputable that the accomplices received weapons from Serbian officers, and in a 1917 report Colonel Dragutin Dimitrijević Apis took responsibility for organizing the assassination. However, researchers who have investigated the case in detail wonder who precisely took advantage of whom: the Serbian officers of the young revolutionaries, or vice versa.

The Serbian Radical government, headed by Nikola Pašić, accepted all the ultimatum's demands except for one that violated state sovereignty, but it was prepared to find a way to accommodate even that. Warmongering groups in Austria, however, were reluctant to miss a favorable opportunity, and war was declared on Serbia on July 28. Montenegro declared war on Austria-Hungary on August 6, and on Germany on August 11. Russia sided with Serbia, and, based on previous alliances, Germany sided with Austria-Hungary and declared war on Russia, France, and Belgium. Austria-Hungary declared war on Russia, and France and Great Britain on Austria-Hungary. The war became worldwide when Japan joined the Entente and the Turkish Empire sided with the Central Powers.

Although its public and military circles were belligerent, officially Serbia condemned the assassination and tried everything it could to avoid war, especially since the wars of 1912–13 had left it in a state of human and financial exhaustion. Another factor was the division of the people. When war broke out there were close to 2 million Serbs living in the Habsburg monarchy. They were forcibly included in the war machinery

Plate 7.8 Victims of war: "hospital train" of the Serbian army. (From *Veliki rat Srbije za oslobodjenje i ujedinjenje*, Belgrade, 1924)

of Serbia's and Montenegro's enemies and had no other choice. Serb soldiers were mostly used on other fronts, but Croats and Muslims comprised a significant portion of the troops operating in Serbia. Unlike the previous wars, which were fought outside the state territory, this time the country was open to attack from a superior enemy on the long frontier from the Djerdap Gorge to the Montenegrin border. Austria-Hungary had a population of 50 million, while Serbia's was only 4.5 million strong after the expansion of 1912.

Serbia's fighting and suffering in World War I can be divided into several phases. In the second half of 1914, the Serbian army drove back Austrian troops who had crossed the Drina and Sava rivers during the battle of Cer on August 12–20, 1914. Having repelled a new attack by the enemy, the Serbian army crossed the Drina and campaigned on enemy territory, but was forced to retreat by November 9. This was followed by a new and fiercer attack by the enemy in which Belgrade fell, as did the territory between the Sava and Drina. The poorly supplied Serbian army was showing signs of breaking up when a shipment of arms and ammunition via Greece and reorganization of the command provided a change of fortune during the battle of the Kolubara, November 17 to December 15, 1914. Belgrade was reclaimed and the enemy was pushed back across the Drina and Sava. By the end of 1914, there were no enemy soldiers in Serbia, aside from prisoners. However, typhus, typhoid, and cholera epidemics devastated the country and caused many fatalities, adding to the number of victims of the war. A few months of tranquility followed, during which both blocs sought allies. The forces of the Entente were especially focused on Italy and Bulgaria. Italy was promised a large piece of the eastern Adriatic coast (Treaty of London, June 26, 1915) and joined the Entente, but Bulgaria joined the Central Powers since Pašić was not prepared to make concessions in Macedonia.

In the new attack on Serbia in the fall of 1915, Germany, Austria-Hungary, and Bulgaria joined forces, with Bulgaria attacking from the east and severing links with Greece. The Serbian army, followed by a great number of civilians, retreated through Kosovo and was forced to move on toward Montenegro and Albania. This is when the Montenegrin front demonstrated its importance as it protected the routes taken by the retreating Serbian army and people. The only other route went through mountains without roads, in the depths of winter and surrounded by hostile forces, an ordeal the Serbs termed the Albanian Golgotha. From northern Albania, which was controlled by the Italians, the Serbian army and refugees had to make the long voyage south to Vlorë and Corfu, and only some of them were transported by allied boats.

Exhausted and ailing soldiers perished here, after suffering the horrors of the retreat. The surviving sections of the army were refreshed and transferred by boat to the Thessalonika hinterland. Following the unsuccessful allied landing at Dardanelle, a front was established on the territory of Greece, then neutral, and later became a great theater of battle in the war. The first breakthrough came in late 1916 and focused on the Kajmakčalan mountain range. The Bulgarian army was driven back in a fiercely contested battle and Bitola was seized, marking the beginning of the reclamation of lost territories. Civilians were sheltered in camps in Greece, France, Italy, Switzerland, and North Africa, with the help and skill of the Serbian government. Special attention was given to young people of school age, who were primarily sent to continue their studies in France.

By late 1915 the entire territory of Serbia was occupied by the enemy. Macedonia, Kosovo, and Serbia south of Kruševac were under Bulgarian control, while the rest of the territory was ruled by a military government under Austria. The administration in occupied Montenegro was organized along the same lines, but there was also an attempt to establish a government. The Bulgarian administration used a whole range of methods to assimilate the population, from prohibiting other languages and names to establishing schools aimed at changing children's consciousness. In addition to the cruel regime of the victors, who arrested or interned many of the remaining Serbs or put them in work camps, the population also suffered from deprivation and famine.

Since the war's outcome could not be perceived from changes at the fronts, the loss of territory was understood as a great defeat, which intensified differences in the leadership. On the one hand, the government and Parliament were in Corfu, while the regent and his loyal officers, including the officers of the "Black Hand," were on the Thessalonika front, where they had been deployed to auxiliary positions. Relations were so tense that Colonel Dimitrijević Apis and his comrades were court-martialed for attempting to assassinate Alexander. The case, which was reviewed and annulled in 1953, "proved" their guilt and a number of prison sentences were handed down, along with some death sentences. Three were executed, including Apis.

After the Kajmakčalan crossing, the Thessalonika front remained a trench war, as was the case with certain western battlefronts. Diplomatic activities were intense, not only those of the Serbian government, but also those of Southern Slav political actors. At the beginning of the war, the Serbian Parliament stated its war objectives in the Niš Declaration of December 14, 1914; these included the unification of the Serbs, Croats, and Slovenes, which implied toppling the Habsburg monarchy. Distinguished Southern Slav intellectuals and scholars, along with Serbian diplomatic representatives, were active in the prominent states of the Entente, disseminating information on Serbian and Yugoslav aims.

The Yugoslav Committee, consisting of notable politicians from the Habsburg monarchy such as Ante Trumbić, Franjo Supilo, and Ivan Meštrović, acted similarly and had fled to allied countries on the outbreak of war. In Corfu in the summer of 1917, members of the Yugoslav Committee held negotiations with the Serbian government (and opposition) on the constitution of the future state. The Corfu Declaration was issued on July 20, 1917, stating that the union of the Southern Slavs would be a democratic and parliamentary monarchy under the Karadjordjević dynasty, with equality of names, languages, alphabets, religions, and calendars of the peoples constituting the union.

Somewhat earlier, in the spring of 1917, when parliamentary life was restored in the Habsburg monarchy, Southern Slav deputies in the Austrian Parliament issued their so-called "May Declaration," demanding the establishment of a true Southern Slav state within the monarchy based on the principle of ethnicity and the Croats' right to statehood. In time this declaration was accepted by an increasing number of Croatian municipalities as the situation changed at the fronts. It became the foundation for the creation of local "national councils," which would abandon the framework of the Habsburg monarchy and play an important role in the creation of the Yugoslav state.

Certain general incidents during the war affected the position of Serbia and its future prospects. In 1916 the allies promised the entire territory of Banat as far as the Tisa River to Romania, in the aim of winning its support. This would give Serbia a new neighbor and the portion of the population who lived there would have a new ruler. The outbreak of the Russian Revolution and Russia's withdrawal from the war upset the situation on the front and left Serbia without an important protector in diplomatic wrangling. Some compensation arrived when the United States of America joined the war. The United States later proved less committed to preserving the old European order and the Habsburg monarchy.

Preparations to penetrate the Thessalonika front began in 1918. Serbian troops, with reinforcements mostly consisting of ethnic Yugoslavs captured as Austrian soldiers in Russia, comprised almost a quarter of the allied troops. Soon after the arduous and fierce breakthrough on September 29, 1918, Bulgaria withdrew from the war. After liberating Macedonia, the allied forces were joined by Serbs in Serbia who took up arms. Belgrade was liberated by November 1, 1918, and parts of the Serbian army continued to advance into what had been enemy territory.

Parallel with this, the National Council of Slovenes, Croats, and Serbs was formed on October 6 in Zagreb, as was the National Council of Bosnia and Herzegovina in Sarajevo on October 26. A series of decrees was passed, breaking off relations with the Habsburg monarchy and merging into a new state of Slovenes, Croats, and Serbs. This newly proclaimed state was not only without international recognition; it was also threatened by Italian advances aimed at seizing Dalmatia, as well as by internal rebellions and disorder caused by revolutionary elements and deserters comprising the Green Bands. The Serbian army was thus summoned from several quarters to restore order.

Unification was focused around two centers: the National Council in Zagreb and the Serbian government, which sought to put as many regions as possible directly under its control. On November 13, 1918, at an ad hoc Grand National Assembly in Podgorica, Montenegro decided to unite with Serbia, under the Karadjordjević family. With Italian backing, the ousted Petrović dynasty and its supporters became bitter opponents of the new state. The Great National Assembly in Novi Sad on November 25 declared unification with Serbia, as did some of the municipalities in Bosnia and Herzegovina, while the National Council in Sarajevo remained with Zagreb. Both threats, from the Italians seeking to seize Slovenian land and menace Croatia and from revolutionary elements who jeopardized state order, forced the National Council in Zagreb to rely on the Serbian army and hasten unification. Negotiations in Geneva on some kind of power sharing between the National Council and Serbian government failed when Pašić's government was toppled.

In late November the National Council in Zagreb passed a decision on unification and appointed a delegation to attend the declaration of unification in Belgrade on December 1, 1918. The Paris Peace Conference, which relied only on the Serbian government, was already under way. Ante Trumbić was appointed Minister of Foreign Affairs and was the main negotiator alongside Pašić in Paris. The common state was gradually recognized by mid-1919.

8
All the Serbs in One State

Between Unitarian Ideal and Pluralist Reality

The declaration of unification on December 1, 1918 fulfilled an ideal that must have seemed unattainable only a few years earlier: for all Serbs to be in one state.[1] It seemed that the conditions had been met for the different parts of the divided Serb nation to link together and develop harmoniously. The creation of the Kingdom of the Serbs, Croats, and Slovenes established a single framework, but it was unable quickly or efficiently to eradicate the consequences of the long historical separation. In any case, the Serbs and their interests were not, and could not be, the main concern of the newly created state. Its aim was the liberation and unification of a single people with three designations, although representatives of the three peoples participated in every step of its realization through their individuality, history, and tradition.

The complex and eventful history of this joint state, which, according to its creators, had to be both a national and supranational state, cannot be the subject of this discussion. Instead, the focus must be limited to the Serbian component, primarily the influence that this state, as well as cohabitation with other Yugoslav peoples, had on Serbian integration.

It was an exceptionally difficult task to provide the means for stability and successful development of this hastily assembled state, one that had been created out of six different legal regimes, areas with no significant economic ties and with uneven social structures and levels of development, whose populations had little knowledge of each other, and

---

1 An unknown number of Serbs remained as minorities in neighboring countries. There were estimated to be about 50,000 in Romania. In Hungary, where there was the possibility of free migration, there were about 80,000 Slavs, but it is impossible to judge the percentage of Serbs. A similar situation applies to Albania, where the few thousand Slavs were primarily Montenegrins and Macedonians.

Map 8.1   Serbia and Montenegro in the Kingdom of Slovenes, Croats, and Serbs.

whose communications were tailored to their former political and economic centers. It would have been difficult to achieve even for teams of international experts; it greatly exceeded the capacity of local politicians whose views were limited and who were motivated by partisan interests. The leadership of the new state was forced to resolve many serious problems right from the outset: obtaining international recognition, attaining favorable borders, preparing elections for the Constituent Assembly, and suppressing social unrest that had built up during the period of anarchy and been radicalized by internal and external factors (on March 21, 1919, a Soviet Republic was declared in neighboring Hungary).

The Paris Peace Conference began in January 1919 and was chaired by the triumphant Great Powers, including Italy – a great opponent of Yugoslav unification. The existing Serbian border with Greece was preserved, the border with Bulgaria was slightly shifted, and the border with

Plate 8.1 Dynastic continuity: Church of St. George in Oplenac, mausoleum of the royal Karadjordjević family, built 1912, the endowment of King Petar I. (Photograph by B. Strugar)

Albania remained disputed (until 1925). It was much more difficult to draw the borders in the north, where the population had been mixed for two centuries. Romania laid claim to the entire Banat as far as the Tisa River and offered the Serbs the opportunity to move out. However, since both states were among the allies, they were forced to split Banat. In establishing the border with Hungary, a line was sought that divided settlements with a majority of Hungarians from those with a majority of Slavs. The Baranya region was most debated, and the army of the new state and local revolutionary authorities remained in Pécs and its vicinity until 1921, when it was handed over to Hungary. In Banat and Bačka significant minorities remained on both sides of the border.

It was most difficult to set the border with Italy, which had taken Trieste, Istria, Zadar and the surrounding area, the islands of Cres,

Lošinj, Vis, and later Rijeka. In Koroška (Carinthia or Kärnten), the population decided by plebiscite to remain in Austria. The unfavorable solutions on this side were no detriment to the Serb population of the new state, but made things difficult for the government of which Serbs were in control.

Numerous old political parties and some new ones, which were mostly limited to regions or ethnicities, took part in the renewed political life. One exception was the Yugoslav Democratic Party, created in Belgrade from blocs of the Independent Radical Party and the remains of the former Croatian–Serbian Coalition led by Svetozar Pribićević; another was the Yugoslav Communist Party (from 1920), created by unifying revolutionary factions of the social democratic parties from all parts of the new country.

The provisional National Assembly, consisting of representatives of political parties from throughout the country, handled state affairs until the adoption of the constitution. One deputy was appointed to the Constituent Assembly for every 30,000 people, and all males over the age of 21 (except soldiers and officers) had the right to vote. This was some-

Plate 8.2 Symbol of unity: the Parliament building in Belgrade, designed for the Serbian *Skupština*, which served as the Yugoslav Parliament until 2003. (Photograph by B. Strugar)

thing new for Croatia, Slovenia, and Vojvodina, and the electorates that elected representatives to the national councils (before 1918) were very different from those that elected deputies to the Yugoslav Parliament. The greatest gains were made by parties who solicited support from among the militant peasant masses.

In the elections for the Constituent Assembly held on November 28, 1920, the Yugoslav Democratic Party won the most votes (92 seats), followed by the National Radical Party (91 seats), which had expanded to areas inhabited by Serbs. The Communists came third with 56 seats. They had branch organizations throughout the country and strong support in regions dissatisfied with the unification, i.e., Macedonia and Montenegro. The parties that were joined in the Agrarian Union (39 seats) covered all ethnic groups and regions.

The Croatian populist Peasant Party, whose leader Stjepan Radić (1871–1928) opposed the National Council delegation's traveling to Belgrade, was the first among the Croatian parties with 50 seats. It later changed its name (Republican, later Peasant) and its programs, but remained the leading Croatian party and main representative of the people. The leading Slovene party and the pivot of Slovene policies in the kingdom was the Slovene People's Party, which held 27 seats and remained under the leadership of Anton Korošec (1872–1940). Two faith-based organizations represented Muslims: the Yugoslav Muslim Organization from Bosnia and Herzegovina held 24 seats, and the Xemijet (Association) from Kosovo and Macedonia held eight seats in the Constituent Assembly. Of the 40 registered parties, 16 were represented in the Assembly.

Unification and adoption of the constitution passed with procedural maneuvering aimed at the immediate gain of certain parties rather than the accomplishment of consensus and stability. The government's rules of procedure provided for deputies to pledge allegiance to the king, presupposing that a monarchy would be established by the constitution, which led a number of parties to boycott the Assembly. Unitary and federal concepts clashed in negotiations on preparing the constitution, as they had done when the state was created. Most parties rejected the centralist design, so the Radical government, led by Pašić, and leading Serbian parties had difficulty securing a simple majority (during unification it had been promised that the constitution would be adopted by a two-thirds majority). Promises of "just compensation" for property lost in the abolition of serfdom and agrarian reform won over the two Muslim parties, and 223 of the 258 deputies present voted in favor (35 voted against and 158 boycotted the vote).

The St. Vitus's Day Constitution, named after the historic day of its adoption (June 28, 1921), proved to be a stumbling block rather than providing stability in the new state; it was even not recognized by the leading Croatian party until 1924. In the mechanism of central authority, the monarch assumed the leading role and the government depended on him. The Assembly was marginalized and became a forum for partisan and national recriminations and confrontations. It radiated an intolerance that gradually spread to the entire country.

The political climate in the new state quickly degenerated. The Yugoslav "tribes" who had until recently been united in the struggle against Vienna and Budapest now turned against one another. Slovenes and Croats resisted Belgrade, which they perceived as a potential source of domination and exploitation. Those who urged the preservation of national traditions and autonomy were branded separatists and anti-state elements and were consistently reminded of the great sacrifices that Serbia had suffered to liberate them. The fact that the government was often changed testifies to this instability. There were 24 different cabinets during a 10-year period, and only two were ousted by Parliament – the rest were forced to resign by the king, who also chose them.[2] The monarch ruled through orders and ministerial decrees. Important measures such as the prohibition of the Communist Party were introduced through government declarations (*Obznana*, December 28, 1920). It took 12 years to implement agrarian reform, the only act that influenced changes in the socioeconomic structure, while three years were required to put into effect the constitutional provision on dividing the state into 33 regions.

Parts of the state lived according to old laws, so the country was divided into regions with mandatory church or civil marriage, regions with public records and title deeds, regions where schools operated according to the regulations of the Kingdom of Serbia and those where they operated according to regulations from the Habsburg era, and so on. Serbia's penal code extended to the entire country and military regulations in Serbia and former Austro-Hungarian lands were brought in line with each other. Tax systems were not equal, however, and remained so for a decade. Territories that were once under Habsburg rule paid higher taxes and were obliged to assume a larger share of budget contributions. Substantial differences existed between the relatively developed northwest and the backward southeast. Regions inhabited by Serbs also differed greatly. Serbs in Croatia and Vojvodina, especially those in cities, were comparatively advanced, while those who had been under Turkish rule until 1878 or 1912 were poor and underdeveloped.

---

2   Alexander I Karadjordjević, regent from 1914 to 1921, became monarch with supreme authority on the death of his father, Petar I, in August 1921.

The Serbs remained geographically dispersed and more or less mixed with the other nations in the new state. Colonization by "volunteers" in Macedonia, Kosovo, and Vojvodina was relatively insignificant and did not influence ethnic proportions. The elimination of impediments to free communication between the various components of the Serb population and its core was highly significant for developing Serbian integration. There were other problems, of course, but they went unheeded, over-shadowed as they were by the difficulties arising from Yugoslav inte-gration and the efforts to bring in line with reality the utopian and unrealistic proclamation that the Yugoslavs were a single people with three names, consisting of three tribes.

Old problems originating from a long existence apart under different conditions were joined by new ones stemming from the division of the Balkans in 1912–13 and the manner in which unification came about in 1918. Montenegro suffered in particular. At the end of the war there was considerable enthusiasm for unification in Montenegro, which was opposed only by King Nikola and a small circle of supporters of the Petrović dynasty. However, not all were in favor of unconditional unifi-cation. During elections for the Constituent Assembly in Podgorica in November 1918, advocates of unconditional unification voted using white ballot slips, while their opponents used green slips. This is the origin of the division into *bjelaši* (Whites) and *zelenaši* (Greens) that later characterized political life in Montenegro.

The manner in which the Montenegrin state was abolished and the dynasty removed created resistance, which cannot solely be attributed to Italy's involvement. The Greens and the federalist party that emerged from them did not detach themselves from the Serbian people. However, in the years following the war, the idea was spawned among a small group that the Montenegrins were a separate nation. Just as Prince Nikola had in his time derived his state from the medieval state of Duklja-Zeta, the Montenegrin separatists now distinguished Montene-grins not only from the Serbs, but also from the other Southern Slav nations. In later crises and separations this idea gained greater signifi-cance, especially with regard to the restoration of the Montenegrin state in the period of socialism. An extreme form was a faction in the late twentieth century that paradoxically denied any links between Mon-tenegrins and Serbs. Montenegro did not hold a special position in any respect, but maintained its entirety in the administrative demarcations, first as the Zeta region, later as the Zeta banovina, which included a sig-nificant part of Herzegovina and Dubrovnik.

The Kingdom of Serbia brought territories acquired in 1912–13 to the state of the Serbs, Croats, and Slovenes. Serbian administration had existed there for only slightly over two years and was discontinued during the period of Bulgarian rule (1915–18). Even though part of Macedonia was officially called Southern Serbia and the people considered to be Serbs, the population was not integrated into the Serbian nation anywhere near as much as in the other areas, such as those who had joined in 1878. A strong Bulgarian substrate remained, as well as a considerable portion of the population who felt a strong sense of Macedonian individuality. Those who identified with the Serbs constituted a minority grouped in the northern areas. Turmoil and insecurity were caused by infiltrations of Bulgarian *komiti* (armed bands). Self-government could not be relied on, and civil servants and teachers were brought in from other parts of the country.

The position of the Serbs in the lands united in 1918 had changed fundamentally. From an oppressed minority they became the ruling nation, identifying themselves with the common state; it was their dynasty and their triumphant army; they supported the policies of the state leadership. The Serbs were linked firmly to the state center; ties with the center became more important than those with the surroundings where they lived and where their material interests lay. This was manifested in different ways since the Serbs' presence in Slovenia was symbolic, while it was predominant in Vojvodina. In Vojvodina the minority groups were either small in number or had no rights (Hungarians and Germans were denied the vote in the first elections). The Serbs fostered strong links with Belgrade and Serbia (from 1929 they were in the same administrative unit as Šumadija).

The situation in Croatia and Bosnia and Herzegovina was more complex. The Serbs remained mixed with the Croats and Muslims, who were critical of the new state and its center. They demanded rights for their groups, but also regional self-government. As confrontation increased between Serbian and Croatian political parties, the Serbs in Croatia and Dalmatia were caught in the middle. They had to choose between identifying with the Serb center or with the non-Serb environment in which they lived. Political leaders were inclined toward the opinion of Svetozar Pribićević, expressed at the beginning of the twentieth century during a dispute between the independent Serbian parties in Zagreb and the Novi Sad-based Radicals: "Serbia is the most authoritative factor in judging the interests of the Serbian people." Pribićević remained true to this opinion for years and advocated rigid centralism before joining Radić in 1927 to create the Peasant–Democratic Coalition.

Ruling circles in the kingdom showed scant interest in the problems of incomplete Serbian national integration. They avoided a federal organization, among other things to avoid dividing the Serbian people, stressing that the Serbian state had disappeared. They did not seek privileges for the Serbs, but regarded the new Kingdom of the Serbs, Croats, and Slovenes as if it were an extended Serbia and governed it accordingly. The implication was that in a stable and strong common state, the Serbian element was safe in every respect. However, the state was not stable, and persistent internal struggles led members of the other nations to establish stronger ties on the grounds of ethnicity, while the Serbs were disunited. In time the Slovenes, Croats, and even the Muslims acted consistently through their large parties, while the Serbs acted pluralistically through several parties and came up with alternative designs for the state constitution.

The Serbs' integration was not aided by the ideological orientation of the regime, which was dictated by the monarch, military circles, and party leaders. Their ideology made a direct contrast between the winners and the defeated in the war, the deserving fighters and the passive beneficiaries. The objective was to increase the authority of the army, state, and dynasty, but it only created divisions among the Serbs. Idealizing the past had the same effect, where history began with wars of liberation and the "independent states" of Serbia and Montenegro, and the role of the state was exaggerated and glorified.

Unification required the Serbian Orthodox Church to adapt to the new state framework. It had played a crucial role throughout the earlier development of the Serbian people. Before unification it had been active under six different jurisdictions. After December 1918, it was gradually joined together through bishops' conferences. The bishops from Bosnia and Herzegovina and the Karlovci metropolitan first expressed the desire to unite with the Belgrade metropolitanate, since it was the church of the Kingdom of Serbia. In 1919 the Montenegrin metropolitanate followed suit. A central conference of archpriests was established with the task of obtaining the approval of foreign church bodies for unification: in Bucharest for the Dalmatian bishopric, and in Constantinople for the others. All the dioceses that were in the Kingdom of the Serbs, Croats, and Slovenes according to the peace treaties were taken over from the Constantinopolitan patriarchate in 1920, following canonical procedure. Ceremonial unification in the Serbian patriarchate took place in September 1920. State authorities did not consent to the Belgrade metropolitan being enthroned as patriarch and insisted on an election,[3] which was won by Belgrade metropolitan Dimitrije Pavlović, who was confirmed by the king. The ceremonial enthronement of the

---

3 The procedure that was applied at the time was legalized in 1930: the archpriests' council nominated three candidates, from whom the king chose one to be ordained patriarch.

patriarch took place in Peć in 1924, after the Albanian rebellion had subsided.

Considerable differences in organization of the former parishes, assemblies, and assembly committees, as well as in the role of lay men and women in general, were gradually evened out with the adoption of the Constitution of the Serbian Orthodox Church in 1931. It was immediately obvious that the church's operating regime had changed fundamentally: it now had a monastic core and monarchical rule of the bishops over the dioceses. The former highly successful forms of congregational participation in church life withered. The Serbian Orthodox Church as a whole was controlled by a regime that had been developed in Serbia from the time of Prince Miloš until the Radical governments, with little influence outside the purely religious domain. The church did not emerge a winner from the unification of 1918: the part in the Kingdom of Serbia lost the role of state church (in 1931 the new state's population was 48.7 percent Orthodox Christian), while the Karlovci metropolitan and other dioceses from the Habsburg monarchy lost their status, wealth, influence, and monastic lands, which were included in the agrarian reform. This contributed to a changeable view of Yugoslavia, which was later to make itself felt on several occasions.

Yugoslavia Decreed

When the Croatian populist Peasant Party turned away from the republican program and accepted the 1921 constitution, there was a turning point in the political life of the kingdom. The return of the Croatian Peasant Party (as it was called after 1925) to parliamentary life and its participation in government between 1925 and 1927 improved the situation in the country by eliminating the possibility of "separation" as threatened by Croatia or "amputation" as threatened by the state center. The situation deteriorated, however, and the government and National Assembly, i.e., Parliament, became the stage of violent confrontations. Guns were even pulled, as happened on June 20, 1928, when a Radical deputy from Montenegro shot Stjepan Radić and his close assistants from the speaker's podium. Two were killed on the spot, two were injured, and Radić himself died as a result of his injuries. The murder in Parliament brought the state crisis to a climax.

Anton Korošec, the only non-Serb to become prime minister, helped ease tensions for a while, but a few months later King Alexander I took more decisive measures: the *Manifest* of January 6, 1929 (the Orthodox Church Christmas Eve) abolished the constitution, dissolved Parliament, which was blamed for the failure of previous policies, and banned political parties. Thus he eliminated the mediator between king and populace. King Alexander packed the government with politicians who were more loyal to the court than to their own banned parties, and appointed General Petar Živković, head of the Royal Guard, as the new prime minister. The most prominent among the new ministers was Slovene political leader Anton Korošec. Municipal elected bodies were also dissolved.

Leading political individuals, such as Svetozar Pribićević and Ante Pavelić, came under supervision, were persecuted, or emigrated. Pavelić later organized the assassination of the king. On the other hand, the king was supported not only by the military, the state apparatus, and Yugoslav nationalists in Serbia, but also by the Freemasons and numerous individuals from Slovenia and Croatia whose positions or business interests required stability and security. Integral Yugoslavism was supported by idealist intellectuals, who based their conviction that a Yugoslav nation could be formed on the examples of Italian and German unification.

The October 1929 law on the name of the state and its territorial division was in accordance with radical unitarianism. The state was named the Kingdom of Yugoslavia, "tribal" names were suppressed, and instead of 33 state regions, the country was divided into nine administrative units called banovinas. Each banovina was headed by a ban (governor), who was appointed by the king and was later backed by a ban council having an advisory function. Even though banovinas had existed in the history of almost all areas of the country, including Bosnia and northern Serbia, they were believed to be part of the Croatian tradition, where the ban had been the executive authority until 1918. The banovinas were all named after rivers, except for Dalmatia, which was called the Coastal banovina (*Primorska banovina*). The intention was for the banovinas to replace and suppress the historical "tribal" provinces, but the opposite happened – some of them were used as a framework for national integration.

The Drava banovina included Slovene lands in Yugoslavia; the Sava banovina consisted of Croatia and Slavonia; the Coastal banovina consisted of the Yugoslav part of Dalmatia; Zeta included Montenegro, part of Metohija, and Herzegovina and Dubrovnik. The Vardar banovina covered the Yugoslav part of Macedonia with southern Serbia and Kosovo. The middle part, which was considered Serb-dominated, was divided into four banovinas, Vrbas, Drina, Morava, and Danube, which included most of the Muslims and other ethnic minorities.

Yugoslavia, consisting of banovinas, headed by integrative forces, and where the "tribes" were suppressed, was to be a melting pot that would produce the new Yugoslav nation. Political measures that had radicalized national unitarianism were accompanied by intensive propaganda in favor of integral Yugoslavism. In principle, the unitarian orientation affected Serbian as much as Slovene and Croatian traditions. Organizations and parties with Serbian names were smothered and eliminated, along with all the others. However, in what became the core of the ideology of integral Yugoslavism, the Serbian element held a privileged position, not only because of its significance in the nineteenth and twentieth centuries and its sacrifices and triumphs, playing the role of Piedmont, but also because it represented the mainstay of fundamental values. In the unstoppable progress toward unification, the Serbs embodied the idea of statehood, they were freedom-loving and were the guardians of Slavism. Unlike others who were dominated by Rome, they supported free thinking and opposed clericalism.

Romanticist and critical-scientific examinations into the past were characterized by the search for the individual origins of each nation. This is why perspectives on the development of Southern Slavs as a whole did not appear after the humanist and Enlightenment period. The ideology of integral Yugoslavism badly needed the vision of a common history leading toward unification. Thus a large number of different texts arose. The *History of Yugoslavia* (1933), by Belgrade-based historian Vladimir Ćorović (1885–1941), can be singled out for its balance, abundance of documentation, and the influence it exerted. It was noted at the time, however, and confirmed by later developments, that the ideology of integral Yugoslavism failed to achieve its goal: it did not satisfy the Serbs, let alone the other Yugoslav nations. Yet it was disseminated through schools, built into the literature and culture of the 1930s, and also had its effect later, at the time when everyone renounced it. It indirectly contributed to the reestablishment of Yugoslavia after the collapse of 1941.

The king's personal authority was used effectively to restore order in the country. A supreme legislative body consisting of legal experts brought the civic and penal codes into line and passed numerous laws on administration, on the Serbian Orthodox Church, and on education, enabling schools to become a means of indoctrination in the spirit of integral Yugoslavism. Faced with the consequences of the Great Depression, which severely affected the farmers, the state increasingly interfered in economic life. The agrarian reform was completed and peasants became the owners of the land they had received. The state introduced a moratorium on farmers' debts as well as its own.

The imposed constitution of September 3, 1931 brought the king's dictatorship to an end, but its achievements remained. The Parliament became bicameral: in addition to the Assembly, it now included the Senate, half of whose delegates were appointed by the king. Only parties that were represented throughout the country could take part in elections. In the elections of 1931, which had public and open balloting, the only party to participate was the one created by the government, the

Yugoslav Radical-Peasant Party (the Yugoslav National Party, YNP, from 1933). Yugoslavia functioned according to this constitution and many of the laws adopted during this period until its collapse in 1941. It is impossible to assess the efficiency of the king's regime since it was terminated prematurely by his assassination in Marseille on October 9, 1934, backed by Croatian and Macedonian extremists. Judging by the manner in which the king was mourned in all parts of the country, his autocratic rule was not disliked by the masses.

The heir to the throne, Peter II (1923–70, ruled 1941–5), was a minor and the state was administered by a regency, with the late king's cousin, Prince Paul Karadjordjević (1893–1976), playing the leading role. The regime did not abandon King Alexander's policies, but neither did it implement them energetically. Old problems, primarily that of Croatia's position, gradually emerged with the restoration of party political life. The Serbian opposition had now sided with the Croatian Peasant Party (CPP), since regulations requiring political parties to field candidates from throughout the country forced them to merge. The issues of autonomy and state reorganization were also the focus of Serbian parties, and especially politicians from Vojvodina.

Regular elections in 1935 tested the comparative strength of the government's party (YNP) and that of the united opposition, headed by Vladko Maček, leader of the CPP. The Serbian parties (Democratic Party, Agrarian Union) and the previously formed Peasant–Democratic Coalition took part without a common program. Even though the elections were public and the government put pressure on the voters, the opposition gained 1.1 million votes compared to the government's 1.7 million.

Milan Stojadinović (1888–1961), a financial expert and Radical politician, was appointed the task of forming a government. Its duration (1935–9) and influence on state affairs singled it out from all the others. Stojadinović continued fostering ties with Germany, which had begun under King Alexander, and repaired relations with Italy in 1937. He minimized the effects of the Great Depression by directing agrarian exports to Germany. Stojadinović won over the main Slovene and Muslim parties to the side of the new ruling party, the Yugoslav Radical Union, and placed himself as its leader, provoking the ire of the Serbian Orthodox Church in 1937 when he attempted to ratify a concordat with the Vatican.

Despite unfavorable conditions, the Croatian opposition combined with the Serbian had greater success in the 1938 elections than in previous ones. This gave Prince Paul the opportunity to appoint Dragiša Cvetković (1893–1969) as prime minister, a man who was prepared to give priority to settling relations with the Croatian opposition. After months of negotiations, the Cvetković–Maček Agreement was signed on

August 26, 1939. The previous Sava and Coastal banovinas, including districts from the neighboring banovinas of Vrbas and Zeta, constituted the Croatian banovina. It was to have a ban, an assembly, and complete jurisdiction over its administration, economy, education, and social policies. The issue of the final demarcation and separation of competencies for the expected fundamental reorganization of the state remained open.[4] After this Maček and the Croatian politicians joined the government. The Serbian opposition and public in general disapproved of the agreement. Since the Drava banovina already enveloped the Slovene area and now autonomy had fenced off Croatian territory, the issue of the formation of a Serbian unit remained, leading to comparisons and the question of whether the remaining part of the state could be Serbian territory.

The disparities that existed among the Serbs owing to the different conditions of their development had diminished over the previous two decades of life within a single state. The social structure was more balanced, nobility and serfs no longer existed, and the nation consisted of individuals equal before the law, but they nevertheless remained divided into rich and poor. The gap between the relatively developed north and underdeveloped south had not narrowed. Peasants accounted for four-fifths of the nation, most of whom lived on small plots of land scarcely large enough to feed a family. Living in Yugoslavia allowed the Serbian people to get to know one another better, even though free movement and travel were privileges of the educated and better-off. Differences in the mentality and traditional culture had not disappeared and were only slightly diminished. The Serbian people still spoke their dialects, *ekavian* in eastern and *jekavian* in western and southern areas of Serbdom.

Living in Yugoslavia offered an opportunity to reexamine the fundamental ideas of the nation itself. Were the Serbs of Orthodox Christian denomination only, as preached by the church, or were they of all "three laws" (Catholic, Muslim, Orthodox), as referred to by liberals since the mid-nineteenth century? It is indisputable that during the period between the two World Wars there were Muslims, among them prominent individuals, who identified with the Serbs. They were probably slightly greater in number than before 1918, but the core mass did not identify with the Serbs or with the Croats during this period. There were Serbs of Catholic faith, perhaps more than before, but they were not influential enough to prove through their actions that a modern society must overcome ancient confessional borders.

---

4   The constitution could not be amended until the king came of age in September 1941.

The Serbs faced a new dilemma in Yugoslav unitarianism: should they strive to preserve their traditions and marks of individuality, as did the Croats and Slovenes, or should they cede to the "Yugoslav synthesis," as directed by the state ideology, hoping that the Serbs' characteristics would prevail? Discussions on the position and prospects of the Serbs in Yugoslavia were initiated not by the government or by party leaders but by independent intellectuals assembled around the Serbian Cultural Club, headed by the lawyer and historian Slobodan Jovanović (1869–1958). The Serbian Cultural Club addressed the center of the Serbian political spectrum at a time when the extremist left and right were gaining momentum.

New European movements spread to Serbia after 1918, primarily Modernism with its dispute between academism and traditionalism. Serbian literature was especially influenced by Surrealism and had strong ties to the Paris nucleus. As with other national cultures in Yugoslavia, Serbian culture expanded to include new genres, styles, trends, and ideas, above all those that were universal. The national component of the culture that had been so important in earlier processes of integration did not develop to the same extent or with the same speed, and the official ideology of integral Yugoslavism hampered its development by suppressing "tribal" symbols and motifs.

Expanding from the margins, representatives of extreme ideologies took root: the right was inspired by fascism and National Socialism, and the left listened to Stalin or Trotsky as they had once listened to Marx and Bakunin. The driving force behind the expansion of a more persuasive version of leftist radicalism was the banned Communist Party. The traditional dislike of Germany and the assertion of German superiority prevented the growth of Nazi branches, except among the Vojvodina Germans. Nazism's guiding principles, however, such as anti-Semitism, racism, and hatred of democracy, were appended onto local traditions. From the beginning of the twentieth century the notion of race was linked increasingly to that of nation, and a racial substratum of the people with three names was postulated. An anti-European orientation and aversion to progress and worldly culture lingered from the time of the Russian Slavophiles, and was especially present in church circles. Skillful orator Bishop Nikolai Velimirović (1880–1956) had considerable success in spreading these revitalized ideas.

The extreme right found greatest expression in the *Zbor* movement led by Dimitrije Ljotić, which sought to link fascist ideals with national, even Orthodox Christian, ideals. The *Zbor* did not have any members in Parliament, since it lacked widespread support, but it did have some influence on intellectuals, youth, and even church circles. Communists were banned from active work in 1921, so they acted through so-called "legal organizations" and prominent intellectuals. The spread of leftist radicalism was facilitated by strong criticism of the official ideology and found fertile soil in the dissatisfaction of the poverty-stricken masses. The main arena where left-wing and right-wing ideologies confronted each other was the University of Belgrade.

Here, at the only university in the eastern part of the country (with one school in Subotica and one in Skopje), a vast and diverse student population came together. Even though the country was poor, families made great sacrifices to send their children to school, for higher education enabled social promotion. Poorer students from the provinces accounted for a large share of the student population. Their living conditions were difficult: they had to work to support their studies, felt despised, and were deeply unsatisfied with the ruling system. Instead of joining the large political parties, students were active within their ideologically colored organizations, which clashed among themselves. The university was a hotbed of discontent, the focal point of demonstrations and confrontations with the police, and the lives that were lost in turn strengthened solidarity among members of the same ideology. Events during the next decade (after 1941) revealed that the University of Belgrade was more important as a cradle of revolution than factories and labor unions.

Excitement over the Cvetković–Maček Agreement had not yet subsided when the attention of both politicians and the public turned to foreign political events. When war was declared in September 1939, the battlegrounds were far away, although the warring sides were near at hand. With the *Anschluss* of Austria, the Reich had become Yugoslavia's neighbor, while Italy brought the battlegrounds closer to Yugoslav borders by occupying Albania and attacking Greece. After Hungary and Romania joined the Axis Powers in late 1940, and Bulgaria in early March 1941, Yugoslavia was surrounded, and the state leadership faced a serious dilemma. On the one hand, joining Hitler's system of alliance was highly unpopular, especially in the Serbian part of Yugoslavia where preservation of the state was important for safeguarding the numerous Serbs outside of Serbia. On the other hand, there was no realistic chance of the country challenging Hitler's war machine. In March 1941 there were no Allied troops on the European continent and the USSR was bound by the Ribbentrop–Molotov Nonaggression Pact (1939).

The regency and the Cvetković–Maček government bowed before force. A pact was signed in Vienna on March 25, 1941 and included certain concessions to Yugoslavia (its territory would not be used for the transport of German troops, Thessalonika was promised). Widespread discontent, first in Belgrade and later in towns throughout the Serbian part of the country, erupted 48 hours later, on March 27, 1941, when it was announced that the government had been overthrown. The regency was also abolished and the heir acceded to the throne, five months before he was due to come of age. A group of military officers played a key role in organizing a coup, while university and secondary school students were the main organizers of street demonstrations. Later, the Communists took the opportunity of portraying the demonstrations as their achievement.

A new government was formed headed by Air Force General Dušan Simović (1882–1962), with ministers from the larger political parties. The government did not annul the pact of March 25. This detail was forgotten after 1945, when the mythology of March 27 was created. Hitler, however, decided to take revenge for the insult. Belgrade was heavily bombed on April 6, 1941, without a declaration of war, and German troops entered Yugoslavia from different directions. There was scattered resistance, but many military units were in chaos. Armed militias were active in Croatia, and on April 10 the Independent State of Croatia was proclaimed in Zagreb. The next day Maček, the deputy prime minister of the king's government, called upon the Croats to accept the new authorities. The capitulation was signed on April 17 after less than two weeks of war.

Plate 8.3   The ruined capital of a ruined state: part of Belgrade after the German bombing of April 6, 1941. (German aerial photograph, courtesy of the Muzej grada Beograda)

Death and Resurrection

The events that followed the "April war" (April 6–18, 1941) demonstrate that Hitler's actions against Yugoslavia were primarily directed against the Serbs. Yugoslavia was broken up in accordance with the wishes of those who sought a revision of the outcome of World War I. Hungary took control of Bačka, Baranya, and Medjumurje, Bulgaria gained Macedonia and southeastern Serbia, while Italy controlled Kosovo and Metohija through vassal Albania and occupied Montenegro. Slovene lands, the former Drava banovina, were divided between the Reich and Italy.

The vassal Independent State of Croatia (NDH) covered a large area of Yugoslav territory and was left in the hands of the Ustasha movement, headed by Ante Pavelić (1889–1959), the leader (poglavnik) of the NDH. It acquired the borders that corresponded to its greatest ambitions, the whole of Bosnia-Herzegovina to the Drina River and the area of Srem to Zemun,[5] but lost territory in Dalmatia, where Italy had taken the coast from Split to Nin and most of the islands. Merging local traditions of extreme nationalism with fascist racism, the Ustasha regime openly carried out a program to eliminate the Serbs, who accounted for 30 percent of the population of the NDH. One of the Ustasha leaders publicly declared that some Serbs would be killed, others deported, and the rest converted to Catholicism and turned into Croats.

All of these threats were carried out with persistent brutality. In the first months of the Ustasha rule of terror, mass slaughter was perpetrated throughout the country, especially in Croatia and Herzegovina. Serbs were deported to concentration camps and annihilated during the war, along with Jews, Gypsies, and Croatian opponents of the regime. The most notorious camps were in Jasenovac, Stara Gradiška, and Jadovno. About 200,000 Serbs were deported and found sanctuary in Serbia. The Serbian name and Cyrillic alphabet were banned; Serbs were marked with armbands, as were the Jews, and their movements were restricted. Many Serbian Orthodox clergymen who refused to leave their congregations were killed, including three bishops. Several churches were destroyed and desecrated. Throughout the country wholesale conversions took place, with no regard to the canonical regulations of the Catholic Church. The so-called Croatian Orthodox Church, headed by a Russian emigrant monk, was established in order to neutralize the influence of Serbian traditions.

---

5   Today a suburb of Belgrade, the capital of Serbia, and a border town until 1918.

What remained of Serbia was under German military command, which relied on local civilian authorities, first the Commissariat administration and, after August 1941, the "Serbian government" headed by General Milan Nedić (1877–1946). Education and church issues regarding the Serbs in Banat were handled by the government in Belgrade, while local government was in the hands of local Germans. Armed forces were also created by the quisling government, with the blessing of the occupying forces: the Serbian Volunteer Corps and Serbian State Guard, primarily consisting of the supporters of Dimitrije Ljotić and the *Zbor* movement. Thus the nationalist right wing from the prewar period became part of the enemy occupation system. Captured soldiers and officers were taken to camps in Germany. Those from Serbia remained there, while those from the territories of the German allies were released. Italy released prisoners from Montenegro. Occupied Serbia became a shelter for refugees from Croatia, Macedonia, Kosovo, and other regions. Even Slovenes (7,000) were deported to Serbia.

The continuity of the destroyed Yugoslav state was maintained by the king and government in exile, first in Cairo and then in London. Except for a group of pilots and officers, the king's government had no armed forces. The "Yugoslav Army in the Fatherland" was created later, when regular connections were established with detachments of undefeated officers, headed by Colonel Dragoljub Draža Mihajlović (1893–1946). Mihajlović's troops had a military organization and many officers, but over time they adopted the traditional attire and appearance of the irregular Chetniks: black clothes, decorated bandoleers, fur caps, and long beards.

The Communists also appeared as defenders of Yugoslav continuity, but only after the German assault on the Soviet Union on June 22, 1941. They too organized detachments at a number of locations and began attacking the occupying forces and local quisling authorities. The Russian term *partizani* (Partisans) was used to describe them, a designation they accepted. Although they did not stress their revolutionary orientation, they adopted the familiar Communist insignia of the red star and red flag. Their opponents branded them Communists, which suited the core leadership but not the Partisan mass.

Most of the armed detachments of the spring and summer of 1941 arose out of self-defense, as people fled the Ustasha slaughter and the violence of the authorities. They were led by military officers or experienced soldiers; on the Partisan side, where there were few officers, those who had fought in the Spanish Civil War played an important role. In time differences were accentuated between these rebels and they adopted the symbols of one or the other side. Despite their common objective in combating the occupying forces, the leaders of the Partisans and Chetniks were aware from the very beginning that their programs were different. Confronting each other in the small area of Serbia, they tried to agree on cooperation. In the fall of 1941, two meetings were held between Colonel Mihajlović and a then unknown Communist leader nicknamed Tito (Josip Broz, 1892–1980), but they came to nothing. By November 1941, fighters of the two rival movements were already shooting at each other.

The Partisans advanced more aggressively in their attacks against the German forces, who retaliated brutally. It was announced that for every German killed, 100 Serbs would be executed, and 50 for every wounded German. This threat was carried out in massive raids in Kraljevo and Kragujevac, when even children were taken out of schools and shot. For a while the Partisans controlled a large territory around the town of Užice in western Serbia (Užice Republic, September–November 1941). A German offensive drove them into Bosnia, and from that time until the summer of 1944, the Partisans had no significant strongholds in Serbia, with the exception of local detachments in the southern part of the country. Having left Serbia in the winter of 1941, the Partisans started organizing mobile units, brigades, and, later, divisions. Coordination was provided between the units and companies, and the strict party hierarchy maintained discipline.

The Chetnik movement had been organized along military lines from the very beginning, but it was dispersed across a large area. Connections between units were inefficient, and communication and subordination were lost among the commands. Several of the commanders acted independently, making armistices or cooperating with the occupying forces as they saw fit, especially in the Italian zone. There were also Chetnik movements that were against Draža Mihajlović, such as the Chetniks of Kosta Pećanac, who moved freely about Serbian towns. Throughout the country Chetniks took revenge against the Croat and Muslim populations for the slaughter and persecution of the Serbs.

Colonel Mihajlović's authority was elevated by the king's government. He received officers from Cairo, was promoted to the rank of general and appointed war minister, and was provided with Allied assistance. For a time even Moscow popularized Mihajlović and his struggle. Under war conditions, the importance of the radio as a means of communication, whose influence the occupier could not sever, grew among the troops and the civilian population. Radio Free Yugoslavia broadcast from Moscow, while influential stations from Britain and the United States supported Mihajlović and his troops.

Aside from the increasingly intensified and irreconcilable confrontations in the field between Partisans and Chetniks, they were also fighting for primacy in the antifascist resistance. Pointing out commanders and Chetniks who were associated with the occupiers, the Partisans accused all Chetniks of collaboration, even those who were persecuted and imprisoned by the Germans in 1944. The Chetniks' opponents made no effort, either then or later, to recognize the difference. After the war, a long-kept secret was revealed: in 1943, faced with plans for an Allied landing and pressured from all sides, the Partisans went beyond exchanging prisoners; they had attempted to negotiate a truce with the Germans and offered cooperation against the Chetniks. Some degree of supervision and arbitration between the two rival forces was provided by Allied missions, which originally contacted only the king's army, and later, after 1943, the Partisans as well. Their reports influenced the distribution of Allied assistance, and later important political decisions.

The expected Allied landing in the Balkan Peninsula affected the intensity of the fighting, with both the Partisans and Chetniks trying to secure more favorable positions. However, Italy's withdrawal from the war in the fall of 1943 brought a significant change. Germany could not supply equal forces to replace the Italian troops, who either became prisoners or changed sides and joined the Partisans. Suddenly the number of Partisan troops and units increased, partly because of an influx from the ranks of mobilized Croatian Home Guard (*Domobrani*).

In the fall of 1943 the Partisan movement began to establish a parallel government, not only locally through people's liberation committees, but also at the country level. In late 1942, the Antifascist Council for the National Liberation of Yugoslavia (AVNOJ) was created as a political body consisting of different political parties and movements. In November 1943, at its second session, the Council assumed the functions of a state body: it suspended the king's government, prohibited the king from returning to the country, introduced a federal system, and promoted Tito to the rank of marshal. From that moment the struggle for international recognition became a burning issue, with efforts for the legal position to be brought in line with the situation in the field, where the Partisans had the upper hand. These efforts proceeded in parallel with inter-Allied negotiations on organizing Europe after the war, in which Great Britain looked out for its protégés while Moscow sought to install Communist regimes. At one meeting between Churchill and Stalin in Moscow in 1944, Yugoslavia and Hungary were placed in the group of countries where each side maintained a 50 percent influence.

General Mihajlović had lost his advantage as minister and commander of the king's army. Influenced by the actual situation in the battlefield, as well as by the negotiations between the Allies, British Prime Minister Churchill tried to unite the two movements. He asked for a joint government and the assurance of democratic development after the war, just as with Poland. In June 1944 on the island of Vis, the Yugoslav government in London and the Partisan leadership reached an agreement on forming a government with democratic elements, which would unite all forces in the struggle against Germany. The state system would be dealt with after the war. At the Yalta Conference in February 1945, it was decided that AVNOJ should be expanded to include deputies from the Yugoslav Parliament elected in 1938. Draža Mihajlović was left to fend for himself when the king called on the army to join the Partisans. Even this did not bring about unification of the armies whose battles against each other yielded heavier casualties than those waged against the enemy. The restoration of Yugoslavia, however, had become a natural and indisputable goal for both the local people and the Great Powers.

In the summer of 1944 Partisan forces entered Serbia, breaking through the Chetniks' resistance, while the Germans were focused on defending the route for their troops to withdraw from Greece. When the Soviet army reached the Yugoslav border in its foray through Romania, Stalin asked the Partisan leadership for permission to operate on Yugoslav territory, which greatly increased the Partisans' authority. The Red Army took part in the campaign to liberate Vojvodina, eastern and northern Serbia, and Belgrade between October 15 and 20, 1944. Mobilization was carried out in liberated Serbia and huge numbers of young men were sent without training or preparation to the Srem front, bitterly defended by the Germans. Conscripts from Vojvodina found themselves in a similar situation, and many perished in the drive to cross the Danube in Baranya. The Partisan leadership wanted to increase their role in the Allied fight.

Six months elapsed from the liberation of Belgrade on October 20, 1944 to the end of the war on May 9, 1945, during which time the new government gained strength by establishing continuity between the kingdom and AVNOJ. In early March 1945, based on previous agreements between Tito and the king's envoy, Dr. Ivan Šubašić, a joint provisional government of Democratic Federal Yugoslavia was formed. A Provisional Assembly was created with the deputies elected in December 1938 joining AVNOJ. In the eastern part of the country populated primarily by Serbs, where greater resistance to the Communists was expected, the new authorities were introduced under the auspices of bodies of the restored Yugoslavia. Those who had taken part in the occupation regime were dealt with brutally; in most towns people were shot without trial, sometimes publicly, but more often without publicity. In the final stages of the war, the remnants of different enemies who were retreating with the German troops were destroyed in the region along the Austrian border, among them many Serbs.

The political pluralism introduced with the joint government and extended Parliament did not develop because the necessary conditions were lacking. During the second half of 1945, what remained of the five prewar political parties was marginalized by the Communist Party of Yugoslavia (KPJ) and the National Front, which was ruled by the KPJ. Outvoted and ignored, the prewar politicians withdrew from the government, protesting its undemocratic methods. They boycotted Parliament and the elections for the Constituent Assembly scheduled for November 11, 1945, and tried in vain to internationalize internal conflicts.

Some revolutionary measures were introduced even before the constitution was changed: assets and property were seized from real or alleged war profiteers and speculators, judiciary bodies were replaced, and a law was passed on agrarian reform. The electoral law was revolutionary since it extended the right to vote to women and shifted the voting age from 21 to 18. In an effort to parry the opposition's boycott, the authorities introduced a ballot box without a list of nominations ("blind boxes") as an alternative to the list of the National Front. The turnout in the elections was 88.66 percent of registered voters, and 90 percent of the votes were for the Front's list. One-fifth of the electorate distanced itself, through absenteeism and voting, from the one-party system that had started to take root.

The Republic was declared on November 29, 1945, and the constitution, modeled after the constitution of the Soviet Union, was promulgated on January 30, 1946. The state was named the Federative People's Republic of Yugoslavia; the earlier partition into republics was legalized: Slovenia, Croatia, Bosnia-Herzegovina, Serbia, Montenegro, and Macedonia each had their own government, assembly, and constitution. Serbia also had an autonomous province, Vojvodina, and an autonomous region, Kosovo and Metohija,[6] set up because of their mixed ethnic population.

Reconstruction and Development

The Serbs were the most dissatisfied with the reorganization of the state along federal lines, even though Serbs from Bosnia-Herzegovina and Croatia had been the predominant force in the Partisan army that brought about these changes. The army had indeed operated mostly outside Serbia, whose population did not come under the direct influence and ideology of the Partisans until 1944. The opposing side of Chetniks and the Volunteer Corps consisted almost solely of Serbs. The families and descendants of the "national forces," as well as the sizable

---

6 In 1968 both were called socialist autonomous provinces.

Serbian emigrant community, refused the new regime and its ideal of *bratstvo i jedinstvo* (brotherhood and unity). The absence of widespread reprisals for the 1941 treason in Croatia and crimes against the Serbs left many people embittered.

The prevailing feeling was that the federation had harmed the Serbs in a number of ways: through the ostensible invention of new nations, such as the Macedonians, and through the separation of the Montenegrins and their declaration as a new nation.[7] Later the Bosnian Muslims, who had been traditionally claimed by both Serbs and Croats, were added to the list. Another great source of dissatisfaction was the asymmetry: only Serbia had autonomous units. It was observed that Dalmatia was a natural province in Croatia, where the Serbs were present in greater numbers and more compact groups than any of the ethnic minorities in Vojvodina. In the beginning, while there was strict centralism, the autonomous provinces were not a practical problem. However, when the republics started to transform themselves into national states, provincial autonomy became one of the central issues.

During the initial period the republics and provinces served as a facade; they were a framework for the creation of national party bureaucracies whose role increased over time. The system of administration was extremely simple: "transmission belts" (Stalin's favorite metaphor) extended from the top of the leadership, which was the "driving force," and relayed directives downward to the subordinate party and state bodies, and horizontally through mass organizations and a network of institutions. The provinces were only one more rung in the hierarchy of authority.

The new authorities needed a great deal of time and propaganda to quell the Serbs' dissatisfaction, push it into the background, discipline it, and restrict it to the private sphere. Resistance to the USSR after the con-

---

7   The categorization of Montenegrins as a separate nation surprised a large percentage of the population of Montenegro. The term "Montenegrin" was not contested, since it had always been freely used; the dispute concerned what was attributed to the name. Originally it denoted a regional connection, i.e., the Serbs in Montenegro; this is how part of the population of Montenegro interprets the term today, as do most of the Montenegrins in Serbia. When the "national" Montenegrins emerged, some believed that they were created from the Serbs, while others refused these origins and traced their individuality back to the time of the Slav migration. In Montenegro itself there is no consensus, but it is clear that in recent times the Republic of Montenegro, as a national state, has strengthened the sense of individuality through education and other forms of influence. The Serbs remained primarily in Herzegovina and regions later attached to Montenegro. The complexity of the relationship is reflected in individual and family fortunes. Two leaders of Serbian extreme nationalism, Slobodan Milošević and Radovan Karadžić, are the sons of Montenegro.

flict of 1948 undoubtedly contributed to the consolidation, but the discontent did not vanish, as events following 1986 were to prove. The other republics welcomed the federal system: some were given their very first opportunity to show their individuality, such as the Macedonians; others renewed their lost statehood, such as the Montenegrins, or received essential space to complete their national integrations, such as the Slovenes and the Croats.

Regardless of whether they were in Serbia or in one of the other federal units, the Serbs, like members of all the other nations, had to endeavor to restore the war-damaged country and heal the terrible injuries they had sustained. The country was devastated and the population scattered: more than 450,000 displaced persons, prisoners, and exiles needed to return. Serbian refugees were able to return to Croatia, where forced conversions to Catholicism were annulled, but there was no return for Serbian colonists in Kosovo and Metohija and Macedonia (15,770 families), because the new regime had distanced itself from the monarchy's colonization schemes.

Aid received from the United Nations Relief and Rehabilitation Administration (UNRRA), with 3,500,000 tons of provisions ranging from clothes and medicine to locomotives, greatly helped to restore the situation. The policy of favoring the most damaged regions benefited the Serbs because the main battles had been fought in regions outside Serbia where they lived.

The new government's most far-reaching revolutionary commitment was nationalization and the unexpected extension of state regulation. Within a short period of time, all of public life had been placed under the administration and supervision of the state. The autonomous sphere where economic life and sociability were maintained disappeared completely.

The first wave of property seizures, when the assets of those who had collaborated with the occupying forces were confiscated and the capital of foreign companies sequestered, was followed by nationalization, first of larger companies in 1946, and then smaller ones in 1948. Half of the land included in the agrarian reform was reserved for the state and for machine-tractor stations. The state not only guided but also directly managed economic activities. A move away from the excessive influence of the state would emerge later, in relation to the propagation of self-management and reforming ideas. At first planned development was considered the ideal. The law on the first five-year plan (1947–51) was adopted but could not be implemented because of the country's isolation in mid-1948.

State policies with regard to the agrarian sector were of vital importance to the Serbs, since most of them were still peasant farmers after the war. The great migration to the cities would not come until later. Since the Communists in Yugoslavia followed in the footsteps of their Soviet teachers, all their energies were focused on heavy industry and the infrastructure. Very little was invested in agriculture and efforts were made to extract as much as possible from it. There was a desperate need to supply the cities, the military, and public works. Since market mechanisms were disabled, compulsory delivery quotas (*otkup*) were introduced, in other words, the collection of grain from peasants at low fixed prices. Since voluntary sales were unable to meet requirements, regulations were imposed stating the quantities that were to be delivered, under threat of imprisonment and violence. The victims were primarily farmers from grain-bearing regions, especially Vojvodina and northern Serbia.

While foreign-owned estates had constituted the primary land fund for redistribution after 1918, during the socialist agrarian reform of 1945–8 it consisted mainly of land confiscated in late 1944 from Vojvodina Germans. The owners had been moved out by the German authorities before the arrival of the Soviet troops, and those who remained were deported by the Partisans to camps, where many of them perished. Land was also seized from foundations, banks, companies, church institutions, and peasants who had more than 25–35 hectares of arable land.

The 1945 agrarian reform was followed by colonization, but only in the direction of Vojvodina. A total of 37,544 families were relocated, with Serbs and Montenegrins comprising 90 percent of this figure. Most were from land-deficient regions of Bosnia-Herzegovina, Montenegro, Croatia, and Serbia. About 10 percent returned to their native regions, even though the sale of allocated land was prohibited. This was the organized continuation of the centuries-old migrations from the mountain cattle-breeding areas to agricultural regions in the plains. Along with the disappearance of the Germans, colonization affected the national composition of Vojvodina, with Serbs constituting 54.87 percent, according to the 1961 census.

The agrarian reform provided land for tens of thousands of families, practically eliminating the group of landless peasants, but it failed to increase agricultural production, which declined for many years. Yields only reached their pre-reform level during the 1960s. Approximately the same amount of land that was distributed to the colonists was reserved for state agricultural estates that were expected to improve production.

Adhering to Soviet models, the Yugoslav Communist leadership did not rely on traditional land cooperatives (*zadruge*), which had been one of the bases of nineteenth-century socialism. The new farming cooperatives, modeled after the Soviet *kolkhoz* (collective farm), were enterprises where not only land and equipment were invested in the collective, but also labor; peasants were transformed into workers who were paid the *trudodan* (daily wage). Participation in these cooperatives was forced, just as with collectivization in the USSR, in order to prove that the Yugoslav Communist Party was fighting against capitalism. The dismal performance of these cooperatives, which canceled out the positive effects of the agrarian reform, as well as the peasants' discontent, led the state leadership to allow the reorganization and liquidation of peasant cooperatives in 1953.

The conflict between the Yugoslav Communist Party leadership and Stalin that became public in late June 1948 affected the development and position of all nations and parts of Yugoslavia. Party leaders responded to these attacks, and to the expulsion from the Information Bureau of the Communist and Workers' Parties and increasing disqualifications, by denying the serious accusation that they had abandoned the socialist way. They suppressed even the smallest weakening of purpose and imprisoned and deported anyone who concurred with the Soviet leadership's criticism. More than 16,000 people were imprisoned during this period of great tension with the USSR and the socialist countries surrounding Yugoslavia. Most were put in camps, including the infamous Goli Otok, an uninhabited island in the northern Adriatic.

In mid-1948 the rigorous political supervision and repression struck not only at those who had sympathies for democracy, but also at zealous Communists and admirers of the USSR. It was believed that this development had the greatest impact on the Serbs, who included a proportionally higher number of Communists and Russophiles. According to statistics, however, the percentage of Serb prisoners was only slightly higher than the percentage of Serbs in the Yugoslav population, although one-fifth of the prisoners were Montenegrins. From 1949 relations with neighboring states became tense. There were thousands of border incidents, and an invasion by Soviet troops was feared. All this brought about a certain homogenization of the population. Some of those who had been against the regime began to accept the authorities, fearing what might happen would be far worse.

Socialist policies also helped in the process of coming to terms with the regime, and their results were felt during the difficult postwar years in the form of labor legislation, the provision of social and health insurance, and free education. Supporting the equality of women and young people also had an impact, and poor townsfolk and the large mass of peasants who moved to the cities proved especially sensitive. The population's view of the regime was also reflected in the level of repression used: while there were more than 10,000 convictions on political charges in 1947 and 1948, this number was down to 145 in 1964.

Under the influence of the conflict with the USSR, the regime gradually changed, stressing that its aims were for a different socialism from that practiced in the USSR and neighboring countries. The emphasis shifted to self-management and community autonomy, even though the party (renamed the Yugoslav League of Communists in 1952) continued to be the absolute ruler on all levels. An attempt by Milovan Djilas (1911–95), one of the four historical members of the Politburo, to create a space for genuine democracy ended in early 1954 in a confrontation with the majority. He was banished from the party and later served several prison terms.

Reconciliation with Stalin's successors in 1955 ended the isolation of the country, which in the meantime had opened its doors to the West. Aid started to arrive from the United States, along with loans and trade. By that time great success had been achieved in developing the infrastructure and industry, creating the possibility of a better life and less deprivation. As was proclaimed at the time, one generation alone cannot bear the burden of long-term development.

Modernization through Socialism

The manner in which the Communists took power in Yugoslavia greatly predetermined the methods that would be used to change the previous system. Since there had been no real revolution to destroy the mechanisms of the bourgeois state, it remained intact and the new authorities were forced to manage it when they took over the levers of power. Changes were not designed with general philosophical principles in mind, but came about by following the concrete examples of building socialism in the Soviet Union. As fate would have it, the Soviet and Yugoslav leaderships collided relatively quickly, before the widespread transfer of Soviet models began, and this led Yugoslav Communists to abandon their reproduction. In many spheres the new Yugoslav authorities were forced to maintain the previous system and practices of old institutions.

The course of Yugoslav development differed from that of other socialist countries owing to the factors that contributed to its evolution and continuity. Its development was not directed solely by the will and decisions of the party leadership, but was molded by the forces of the past that were present in the previous system and institutions, and even more forcefully by the influence of developed countries, which were in a phase of previously unseen dynamic growth. Comprehensive economic and technical advances spread relentlessly from Northern America and the countries of Western Europe which Yugoslavia did not oppose, since progress was a core component of the new authorities' ideology. The country gradually opened up in the 1950s and started an international dialogue, although it avoided anything that might undermine party ideology and contest the party's monopoly of power.

Links with the developed world were one of the preconditions for modernization that fundamentally changed Yugoslavia and all the nations within it in the second half of the twentieth century. Another requirement was the willingness to change, the adaptability of people who had left their age-old homes and traditional crafts and were willing to be educated and trained. The immediate postwar years were marked by widespread migrations from rural to urban areas, and the expansion of all forms of education.

Accelerated industrial development continued after the period of reconstruction with a large amount of volunteer or unpaid forced labor, collective undertakings, and labor competitions. These achievements are symbolized by the great public works of the youth brigades, who built railroads – Brčko–Banovići (90 km, 1946), Šamac–Sarajevo (242 km, 1947), Nikšić–Titograd (56 km, 1948) – the Belgrade–Zagreb highway, and many other industrial facilities, such as the Ivo–Lola Ribar machine tool factory near Belgrade (1948). The construction of large industrial

Plate 8.4 Socialist industrialization and electrification: hydroelectric power station, Djerdap, one of the giants in the building of socialism. (Photograph by B. Strugar)

and power plants continued even when the emphasis shifted toward light industry and consumer goods. The largest and most costly projects were carried out later, for example, the Djerdap hydroelectric power plant, the Belgrade–Bar railway, and the Danube–Tisa–Danube canal. Towns and regions fought for the capital and credit needed to develop local industry which would spur the entire region forward. Factories or business facilities were built in every region and town, representing a turning point in development.

The state was in expansion along with the economy. The great increase in the state's jurisdiction required human resources for the administrative apparatus and various bureaucracies. The centuries-old rural overpopulation was quickly replaced by urban overpopulation. In the postwar years half the population changed their place of residence. According to the 1961 census in Serbia, 38.4 percent of the population had migrated. Serbia constantly had a positive migration balance with people arriving from other republics, with the wide strip along the Sava and Danube rivers proving especially popular. The emphasis, however, was still on migrations from rural to urban environments and the decline of the farming population. In the 1948 census, 72.3 percent of the population was rural; by 1961, this had decreased to 56.1 percent, and in 1975 only one-third of the population lived off the land.

Towns that had gained industrial or general economic facilities grew particularly fast. A workers' colony would grow on the outskirts of the old town center, while administrative buildings were constructed in the center. The colony would gradually acquire running water and a sewerage system, a development plan, and municipal services. Old historic towns expanded and were joined by a number of smaller towns and compact villages, which became urbanized. As in the early nineteenth century, scattered villages remained backward for a considerable time, the achievements of modern civilization reaching them last – even electricity and paved roads. Uniformly modern architecture covered up the Balkan or Pannonian traits that the towns had developed during earlier periods. In 1953 only 22.5 percent of Serbia's total population lived in towns with a population exceeding 10,000. By 1971 the urban population was approaching one-half (40.6 percent), and by 1981 it reached 58 percent. Large towns grew the fastest, with the capital of Belgrade at the forefront. It was the home of one in ten people in Serbia. The dark side of rapid urbanization was reflected in the change in mentality of the urban population, in architectural chaos and the destruction of the environment.

When rapid industrial development came to an end, starting in 1965, the demand for labor dropped and unemployment appeared. Migration from the villages continued, but was directed abroad. *Gastarbeiters* (guest workers) from Serbia joined other Yugoslavs abroad somewhat later and found work where there was a need for manpower (France, Austria, Switzerland), although a considerable number also reached Germany. Of the 800,000 Yugoslavs working abroad temporarily, the Serbs constituted 300,000. The outflow of workers, which proved to be short-lived in most cases, was criticized by orthodox Communists and nationalists as "a disgrace for a socialist country." However, over time the benefits were recognized: the influx of foreign currency money orders and the transfer of cultural influences, especially regarding living standards and environmental design.

Technical advances that prompted hundreds of thousands of rural residents to move required higher qualifications than those possessed by the peasants. The advocates of industrialization and electrification were aware of this fact, but they also had old socialist program goals in mind: free schooling, equal opportunity, and wide-scale education. Elementary four-year education was already mandatory according to the laws of the old regime, but could not be completely fulfilled. The socialist authorities extended mandatory education first to seven years and later to eight. What had earlier been the first half of secondary education was now available to everyone. The number of schools increased so rapidly that there was a shortage of teaching staff, and in 1954–5 qualified personnel from other services and vocations were transferred to schools. What was now the four years of secondary education no longer served as a preparation for university studies (the traditional gymnasium), but was modified to suit the needs of the economy as a training ground for different professions.

The network of higher education was the slowest to develop. Belgrade had inherited a university and its development and expansion were the center of attention. It expanded by opening new schools and making generous scholarships available to a large number of people, thus changing its social makeup. Since the only other universities in addition to Belgrade were in Zagreb and Ljubljana, the republics that did not have institutions of higher learning were the first to get them. The universities in Sarajevo and Titograd (Podgorica) were of importance to Serbian students. Individual faculties and later universities were also opened in the capitals of Serbia's provinces, Novi Sad (faculty 1954, university 1960) and Priština (1970), and later in Niš and Kragujevac. A large number of individual university departments were also founded in smaller cities. Setting up a faculty in town was a matter of prestige for the local authorities. However, the rapid expansion of the academic network had a negative effect on the quality of the studies, especially in the new schools.

Preserving the traditional link between university studies and scientific scholarly work was even more important than increasing the number of students. There were no research institutions outside of Belgrade University. There was an Academy of Science in Zagreb (1866) and one in Belgrade (1886), which were transformed into a kind of ministry of science, following the Soviet model, with the core of old academics having no influence on the new organization. Research institutes were formed within the academies, with the number of institutes in Belgrade increasing to 24. When the Soviet model was abandoned, the institutes either became independent or were placed under university management. The founding of the Vinča Institute for Nuclear Sciences (1948) was symbolic of these high objectives.

The expansion of the university and scientific institutes coincided with a period when the state was open to the world and it was possible to become acquainted with new scientific achievements in the places where they were made. Young scientists were trained in large numbers to follow and adopt innovations not only in industrial production but also in science, technology, and medicine. The ability to welcome innovations on the broadening front of scientific and technical progress was one of the most noteworthy achievements of the second half of the twentieth century and was a precondition for all later development.

Developing the pyramid of the academic system with its base in widespread mandatory education and its apex in highly specialized research institutes carried a hefty price. However, the Communist leadership could afford it since all revenues were collected in one pile, just as the absolutist rulers had done, and redistributed from there. The method was applied even when the state could no longer finance itself and was living off foreign aid and loans, and when the treasuries in the republics became increasingly important alongside the central treasury. With the development of local autonomy, some of the proceeds remained with the local authorities, which allowed for local needs to gain priority, but it also made it harder to maintain a rational balance between the investments that were made and what was received in return.

The endless series of ceremonies marking the completion of factories, railroads, roads, bridges, and health, education, and cultural institutions was accompanied by another equally long, but barely noticeable, history of struggling to be included in plans and budgets, subventions and loans. The final result was that the country became the largest debtor in Europe. The cause of the continual negative balance was primarily to be found in the political factories that operated at a loss and the immoderate ambitions of the state, which had taken everything under its control but failed to realize that everything carried a price.

The great investments without appropriate returns made it necessary to support the vast sphere of the media, publishing, and culture in general, as well as entertainment and sports. The one-party state increased its general influence in this way, but burdened itself with costs and expenditure. Publishing books and newspapers, which had previously been the business of private publishers with the exception of official publications, was now in the hands of state companies and massive organizations. A few traditional publishers, such as the Academy of Science, Matica Srpska, and Srpska Književna Zadruga (Serbian Literary Cooperative), remained as institutions, but their programs were included in the system. Only a small number of religious publications were not included in the system and were barely noticeable in public until the 1970s.

The press in Serbia expanded enormously compared to the period before World War II, with five times the number of newspapers enjoying three times the circulation. Serbia stood out favorably from the Yugoslav average, but it was still among the last countries in Europe in the number of issues sold per capita. The greatest expansion in newspapers took place between 1949 and 1953, when there was the greatest need for officially controlled information. However, when costs were settled by both the producers and the buyers, in some years circulation dropped as low as half of the earlier maximum. A similar trend was apparent in book publishing: the number of titles increased, and the number of copies dropped, which was a sign of adjusting to the needs of the public and market demands. Even though books were widely available during the first decades of the socialist period, it was the libraries founded in all larger towns, along with museums and archives, that played an important role in their dissemination.

As elsewhere in the world, the press lost its dominant position in the Yugoslav media. Radio stations had existed in Zagreb and Belgrade since 1929, and the power of the radio became apparent during World War II since its message could not be stopped by either borders or battlefields. Its influence was long limited by the price and scarcity of radio receivers, until 1950 when local industry began producing them. Transmitters spread to the republican capitals, and then to larger towns, but radio stations were not privately owned until the transition in the 1990s.

Television joined the radio (Zagreb 1956, Belgrade 1958, color broadcast 1973), and quickly became the most influential medium. When television was introduced, an attempt was made to create common programs; however, later on, coverage was adjusted to suit the transmitters and broadcasting methods of the republics and provinces. Television became an important expression of national individuality and a powerful means of integration.

Films had been around since the beginning of the twentieth century and were widespread in towns in the kingdom. Ultimately, the shift was made from passively showing foreign movies to actively producing

Plate 8.5 Symbol of modernity and advanced communications: TV tower on the top of Mt. Avala, built 1965, destroyed 1999. (Photograph by B. Strugar)

domestic films. The first film studios, were founded in Belgrade, Zagreb, and Ljubljana, and later in other republican capitals. Film was favored as a popular art whose influence had previously been tested under totalitarian regimes. The film industry was developed with state funding and contributed to international developments through participation in international film festivals.

Viewed over the long term, what was relayed and disseminated by means of the new media and through literary and artistic creations showed visible signs of a shift from the strict dogmatism and imitation of Soviet models toward a more liberal expression, building on local traditions and accepting modern trends. Starting in the 1950s there was infighting among artistic tendencies, but the crucial stance was that of the party leadership, which sought to show that socialism in Yugoslavia had a different face. The existence of modern tendencies in art, the avant-garde, and more liberal expression with elements criticizing the state of society ("film noir" in cinematography) were noticed and attributed to greater political liberties under the regime than truly existed.

The great wave of state patronage included the sphere of health and social welfare. Free health care was a popular item in the socialist programs, as was free education, and social welfare included providing assistance to the elderly and underprivileged. In its efforts to carry out these programs, the Communist leadership dealt with the heritage of the previous regime in an unequal fashion. It rejected almost everything that was private, and preserved and developed the institutional foundation created during the Kingdom of Yugoslavia. Aside from the Red Cross (Crescent) and charity activities within church organizations, private initiative ceased, and numerous associations and organizations that tended to the needs of the frail declined and died out. The 1963 law prohibiting private medical practice ended private enterprise in the domain of health care.

The inherited institutional network (Medical Faculty, Central Health Institute, health centers, outpatient clinics, polyclinics) was extended to provide basic health care to villages, factories, and schools. The network was also built upward by developing clinics, specialist hospitals, and institutes as part of medical schools. Over time the health service became qualified to accept the achievements of modern medicine and to support the development of the pharmaceutical industry, which was nonexistent until 1941. There was no shortage of results, just as in other countries with a capable medical staff and wide-ranging medical services. Contagious diseases such as malaria, syphilis, and goiter were eradicated, as were those with epidemic characteristics such as typhus. Common diseases such as trachoma and smallpox were also eliminated. Scarlet fever and diphtheria, and the previously incurable tuberculosis, no longer presented a threat. Infant mortality dropped, while life expectancy increased.

Modernization in the second half of the twentieth century brought about so many innovations in different areas that the general conditions of daily life were transformed. Fear of hunger, which had caused great loss of life during the two World Wars, was eliminated. Concerns about unemployment and poverty were substantially alleviated by the introduction of mandatory social and health insurance. A feeling of security unknown to previous generations was accompanied by the belief that burdens had been reduced thanks to limited working hours (with the exception of agricultural and domestic work), decent working conditions, and the reliance on machines that facilitated work.

There had been sudden and substantial changes in previous periods, primarily during the eighteenth century among the Serbs in Hungary, and later during the reign of Prince Miloš, and after 1880 in the Kingdom of Serbia, but they had only applied to a small section of society, those who were educated, well-off or living in urban areas. During the second half of the twentieth century, changes were widespread and included the greater part of the Serbian nation, changing its profile. The Serbs ceased to be a nation of peasants. They abandoned their villages, peasant parents and ancestors, moved to the city, and began forming a primarily urban society. At the same time they became generally more educated. Illiteracy was completely eradicated among the new generations, but returned among the elderly. Even though the entire population had been included in mandatory education for decades, in 1981 there was still 11.1 percent illiteracy among the population of Serbia, with characteristic differences: in the central areas it was 4.1 percent of the men and 17.9 percent of the women, while in Vojvodina 3.1 percent of the men and 8.3 percent of the women were illiterate. According to the 1981 census, in the entire country of Yugoslavia half the population (49.7 percent) had completed at least eight years of elementary school or secondary school, while 5.6 percent had received a higher education (10.3 percent in urban areas). These proportions surely applied to the Serbs, who comprised 36.3 percent of the Yugoslav population at the time.

The society of exclusive male domination had made great progress toward equality of the sexes. Women had come out of the shadows; they ceased to be the invisible companions of men, who were the only protagonists in historical events. The formal equality of rights and gaining the right to vote were followed by changing conditions in education, access to many professions, and the acceptance of women in public services and high-ranking state offices. These innovations were mostly made possible by general changes within the family which eased the burden of women's domestic drudgery.

The nation became healthier as a result of many factors, primarily improved health care and favorable living conditions. As was the case with many other nations, the Serbs were living longer. Life expectancy after World War II was 45 years, while in 1981 it was 74 years for women and 72 years for men. The nation had increased in size despite the heavy casualties of both World Wars, but its share in the total population of Yugoslavia declined. It was greatest in 1961, at 42.8 percent; in 1971 it had already dropped to 39.68 percent, and represented 36.30 percent in 1981. Part of the missing population was undoubtedly to be found among the 5.44 percent of people who declared themselves as members of the Yugoslav nation that year. This belated wave of grass-roots national unitarism included mostly Serbs and Croats, which caused alarm among the guardians of the individual nations and contributed to the deepening crisis in the federation in later years.

The second half of the twentieth century saw a dynamic transformation of the Serbian nation. Changes were sudden, simultaneous, and to a large extent incomplete. Just as mandatory education had not eradicated illiteracy, migrations to urban areas did not create a civic society, nor did the principles of equality of the sexes achieve true and complete parity.

Epilogue: Breakup of the Federation and the Struggle for a National State

All the Serbs did not remain in one state.

There was a crisis in relations within the Yugoslav federation, leading to breakup and wars characterized by heavy casualties, persecution, exile, the flight of millions of people, and immeasurable destruction. Instability spread throughout southeast Europe. The dramatic and tragic events have been described by many authors, some even published while the fighting was still under way. It has rarely happened elsewhere that history as knowledge and account has so quickly caught up with current events.

It is impossible to include this history within the covers of this book, not only because of its complexity and extent, but also because it is not over yet, and because neither the author nor the reader can view it from a distance, a necessary precondition for objectivity. The events of the 1990s in the former Yugoslavia are currently the topic of historical interest and research, as well as judiciary investigations, which are not even close to being concluded. Instead of recounting these tragic events, it seems more appropriate to raise certain questions about how previous Serbian history – both as an objective process and as awareness and knowledge of this process – influenced the Serbs' orientation and inadequate reaction to the challenges of the Yugoslav crisis. This inadequacy may be judged and discussed, bearing in mind the tragic consequences for the Serbian people.

The single framework within which the integration of the Serbian people had taken place since 1918 was lost with the breakup of the federative Yugoslavia. Significant parts of the Serbian people were eradicated from territories where they had existed for centuries (parts of Croatia, Dalmatia, Bosnia, Kosovo and Metohija). Serbia was flooded with hundreds of thousands of refugees, only a very small portion of whom have returned home to date. Yugoslavia and Serbia lost influence over the development of Kosovo and Metohija, even though United Nations Security Council Resolution 1244 addressing the situation in Kosovo and Metohija, adopted on June 10, 1999, did not formally separate it and declare it independent, as the ethnic Albanian majority would have liked. A rift occurred among the Serbs themselves owing to differences in perceptions and opinions of neighboring nations and minorities. The fact that the populations in certain regions with large ethnic minorities (Sandžak, Vojvodina) strongly resisted state policies added weight to this situation.

In addition to losing its natural connection and influence on fellow Serbs in other states, Serbia also struggled with hardships brought about by war: financial exhaustion and general impoverishment aggravated and increased by UN sanctions and international isolation. The isolation was broader than the formal embargo and led to the country losing its ability to keep up with international developments in science and technology. Finally, there was a great moral loss stemming from the general condemnation of the policies of the Serbian state and the actions of Serb military and civilian authorities in war-torn regions, where many grave war crimes were committed.

The Serbs were the ones to suffer the greatest direct and long-term losses in the breakup of Yugoslavia, so the question arises as to why an anti-Yugoslav option prevailed among them. There were undoubtedly many Serbs who were displeased with the changes introduced in 1945, but it is also certain that 20 years later it was precisely the Serbs who became the fiercest defenders of Yugoslavia, both among the people and among political leaders. A contributing factor to this change of view was the adoption of the part of Yugoslav ideology incorporated in socialist patriotism, which included the memory of Serb victims and the Serbs' merits in creating and restoring the joint state. The experience of life in the Yugoslav federation certainly had an impact, but as this life changed and negative impulses from reality grew stronger, historical memory was reversed, and both victims and merits seemed pointless.

In order to understand this evolution, it is necessary to reflect on the Yugoslav federation's distinct course of development. The federative organization imposed by the Communists put into effect one of the projects that had been designed and recommended by political parties and individuals during the period between the two World Wars; in some of the projects the number and makeup of the units was similar to what was established in 1945. Compared to the previous 1918–41 organization, the advantages were that the state organization was more in line with genuine ethnic relations and that it allowed for the reduction of friction and tension. This was especially apparent in the case of the Macedonians, who had been the bone of contention between the Bulgarians and Serbs, and the Muslims, who had been claimed by both Croats and Serbs. The Communist leadership, however, had an extremely simplified perception of the entire ethnic complex as a "national question," which was to be "resolved" through proper policies, good organizational schemes, and the distribution of power, and thus obscured the true gravity and complexity of the problem.

The dissemination of national, racial, and religious hatred was prohibited and fervently prosecuted, and mechanisms of egalitarian participation in government were constructed. There was a genuine effort to protect minorities, and high standards were set in this respect. Endeavors were also made toward economic equality, but it was very difficult to achieve. At the same time, a guise of harmonization was imposed through propaganda: all nations and republics were symmetrically attributed wartime merits, all were attributed equal sacrifices, all those who opposed the Partisans during the war were equally labeled servants of the occupying forces, without any understanding of the differences and concrete circumstances. The Serbian side had a difficult time accepting the symmetrical treatment of Hitler's pawn Pavelić and Draža Mihajlović, who had fought against the Germans for the restoration of Yugoslavia. Instead of critically discussing the events in the light of the facts, actual circumstances, and a background of general European development, the party version of history was dictated, and beyond that there was silence. Questions that troubled the nations, that should have been answered so as to "overcome the past," were forced underground, where they continued to arouse curiosity and foment dissatisfaction.

The attitude toward the state as a whole and other nations was formed both under the influence of official propaganda and from the experiences of life in the Yugoslav federation, which was dynamically developing. For more than a decade it was a strictly centralized state that was actually ruled by the Politburo of the Communist Party, and bodies in the federal units carried out directives and passed down regulations according to the model that was received from above. The regimes in the republics did not differ significantly.

Under the pressure of daily practice, going beyond theoretical preoccupations, when the long-term perspective was considered and workers' councils were introduced in an effort to create "self-management socialism," the question arose as to whether the Yugoslav socialist state would develop as an "association of communes" or whether the focus would be shifted from the federation to the republics, which would become the mainstays of development. The characteristic conservatism of the Yugoslav party leadership became apparent at this turning point. Just as the efforts of Milovan Djilas to radically democratize society were condemned in 1954, avant-gardism was rejected and it was decided to foster and develop nations through the republics as national states.

This fatal decision was not announced as a turnabout in "resolving the national question," but was formulated in the self-management jargon as representing the right of the working class of each individual republic to dispose of the created "surplus value," or as the right of the people to dispose of the fruits of their labor. Nations no longer felt threatened by external dangers; they were more fearful of a spontaneous slide toward centralism and unitarism. Such suspicions were motivated by certain federal institutions and services, especially the army and security authorities. There was continued boasting that the "national question" had been resolved, and "brotherhood and unity" were still considered among the highest values.

All later constitutional reforms increased the jurisdiction of the republics and reduced the significance and role of the federal state. Increasing the responsibility and independence of the republics did not by itself threaten the federation: the threat came from the unilateral orientation, the complete rejection of the balance between the whole and its parts, the federal state and its republic members. Instead, clashes increased between party oligarchies in the republics. Through them all power was drained from the federation, until it became the public image behind which the republican party leaders ruled after 1980, similar to what happened around 1950 when it was a facade that concealed the rule of the Central Committee's Politburo. One of the leaders said at the time, "Yugoslavia is what we agree it will be."

A significant step in this respect was the 1974 Constitution, which was passed only six years before the death of president-for-life Josip Broz Tito, who had been some sort of guarantor of state unity. This constitution transferred all the main competencies to the republics and raised the provinces to the same level as the republics in all respects except their name and number of representatives in federal bodies. The mechanism established in the 1974 Constitution did not carry the same consequences for all members of the federation. It primarily suited the new nations, the Macedonians and Montenegrins, who were protected by the framework of their national states, within which they completed their integration and were able to marginalize minorities. The system also suited the Slovenes quite well, whose leaders were most persistent in advocating the sovereignty of the republics. The remaining three republics,

Croatia, Bosnia-Herzegovina, and Serbia, were affected by the changes to a greater or lesser degree. The Croats used their republic to complete their own integration, and it also facilitated the silent assimilation of ethnic minorities (the Serbs made up 14 percent of the population, and were disproportionately influential as party cadres). However, a sizable part of Croats remained outside the republic, in Bosnia-Herzegovina and somewhat less in Vojvodina and Montenegro. Having assessed what was to be gained and lost, Croatia's leaders opted for increasing the independence of the republics.

In Bosnia-Herzegovina both the Serbs and the Croats felt limited in communication with their home states. All three nations in Bosnia-Herzegovina included true defenders of Yugoslavia, but from the time that the Muslims were recognized as a nation, a strong faction emerged among the Muslims advocating that Bosnia be the national state of the Yugoslav Muslims, who also existed in Macedonia, Kosovo, and in Serbia (Sandžak). Later, during the war in Bosnia (1992–5), the predominance of this faction manifested itself in assuming the historical name Bošnjak, which laid claims to the entire population and historical heritage of the land dating back to the medieval state. The ethnic Albanians were also divided, with large populations in Macedonia, Montenegro, and Kosovo. However, they had full autonomy only in the province of Kosovo and Metohija, where the largest segment of the Albanian population was located. Demands by Albanian nationalist circles for Kosovo to become a republic were never seriously considered, nor were they accepted even by Albanians within the ruling apparatus.

The changes to the 1974 Constitution had the greatest effect on Serbia. Contemporaries were less aware of the threat of losing the single framework of Serbian integration than they were of the fact that the provinces had gained complete independence, and that Serbia had become a complex state consisting of Kosovo, Vojvodina, and the remaining part called "Serbia proper." Serbia had become federalized at a time when all other republics were completing their sovereignty. The situation was made that much worse by the provincial party leadership, which constantly confronted the Serbian leadership, sought allies among the leaders of the other republics, and voted against their home republic in federal bodies.

Even though Serbia had problems with both provinces, there was still a visible difference between Vojvodina, a region with a culture of tolerance and a history of coexistence of different nations, and Kosovo, where the side that was in power had always wanted to see real and symbolic advances, but otherwise felt oppressed. Living together during the period of socialism and all the efforts made to bring things into harmony were unable to change that mentality.

In the meantime, internal bickering between the republics over the distribution of funding, loans, and the influx and outflow of revenues became public and overlapped with numerous other disputes regarding the use of language, equality in the military, and so on. The developed republics complained that the revenue they created was being centralized, transferred to underdeveloped regions, and irrationally spent, while the underdeveloped republics complained of being exploited by the developed republics. During the 1980s public sessions of central party committees were the scenes of fierce conflicts, especially between the representatives of Serbia and its provinces. The belief that national tension was introduced into the Yugoslav nations by a handful of literati is wrong – it was generated by the reality of poorly directed politics.

The gaping asymmetry, Serbia's unequal position compared to the other republics, could not remain unnoticed and without any effect on the mood of the Serbian masses, especially since the political events that took place against the background of constitutional transformations were perceived by contemporaries as having anti-Serb tendencies. The 1966 ousting and condemnation of Alexander Ranković (1909–83), for many years the second man in the Politburo, head of the federal police and state security, and Tito's potential heir, had great reverberations. Ranković was accused of acting against party interests after the 8th Congress of the Yugoslav League of Communists (SKJ) in 1964, of abusing his position, and opposing the development of "direct democracy." Ranković's fall was followed by the dismissal and forced retirement of a large number of his people in internal affairs, which was seen as a coup against "Serb personnel." Many influential defenders of the system joined the ranks of the dissatisfied at that time.

The opposition camp increased again in 1968 in connection with the large student demonstrations and the condemnation of writer Dobrica Ćosić (b. 1921) and historian Jovan Marjanović (1922–80), who were expelled from the Serbian Communist Party's Central Committee for daring to question the soundness of national policies. Among other things, they pointed out the repression of the Serb population in Kosovo and Metohija. This led to a significant number of intellectuals quitting the Communist Party in protest. Pointing out the unilateral and problematic sides of the constitutional amendments that paved the way for the 1974 Constitution in a public discussion at the Belgrade University Law School in 1971 cost a number of teachers their jobs, and one was even sentenced to a prison term.

While the previous events led to an increase in the opposition's ranks, the party's positions were weakened by the dismissal of the party leadership in Serbia, Marko Nikezić (1921–90) and Latinka Perović (b. 1933), which was carried out by Tito himself in 1972 without consideration for the voting in the Central Committee. The fall of the leadership led to the dismissal of a large number of their associates with liberal views who spoke out for more decisive democratization. Each of these events marked a drop in the influence of official party ideology and a weakening of the position of the party apparatus in Serbia. The consequences were only fully understood after 1980.

The Yugoslav party leadership and the intelligentsia that it relied upon proved to be no match for the mounting national tensions and increasingly numerous challenges to "brotherhood and unity." Its policies boiled down to prohibiting, punishing, repeating general slogans, and attempting to harmonize the situation, which was counterproductive under the changed circumstances. The defenders of official party policies, which included preserving the state as a whole, brought on themselves the myth of being conservative even during Tito's lifetime (prior to 1980), while the opposition, which was increasingly nationalistically oriented, opted for democracy. It soon transpired that the opponents of Tito's regime were not all advocates of democracy – neither in theory nor in practice. Within all nations and Yugoslav republics the opposition attracted masses through their nonconformist ideas and the boldness of their views, but showed no signs of being true alternatives to the ruling policies in resolving Yugoslavia's problems. This was very clear in the case of the Serbs.

Without a strong intellectual leadership, and without extensive knowledge of what was happening in Europe with regard to overcoming inherited national differences, what had changed in the ideas and relations between cultures, the leaders of the Serbian opposition were forced to choose their course based on history, to revive the ideas and views from earlier stages of Serbian nationalism. To this effect, they noted the similarities and analogies with situations and events from the past, and remained numb to the great changes that had occurred in the meantime which made references from the past inadequate.

In addition, the messages from the past were ambiguous. Aside from the tradition of fighting for a national state and its policies, the heritage of Serbian nationalism included the unitarian variant, which was developed during the period of integral Yugoslavism, and understood and implemented as spreading Serbdom to the other Yugoslav nations. When Yugoslavia was toppled in 1941, occupied Serbia was engulfed by a strong wave of disappointment with Yugoslavia, and Yugoslav illusions were pushed into the background by a powerful movement of returning to Serbian roots. Under German occupation there could be no turning to victories and war glories, but one could turn to the church, Orthodoxy, St. Sava's cult as consecrated nationalism, patriarchal ideas, family values, suppressing everything foreign. Values that were encouraged by the occupier were imposed, but also assimilated: racism, hatred for democracy, anti-Semitism. It is indisputable that during the war years the Serbian movement led by General Mihajlović was confronted by two traditions and fluctuated between maintaining the continuity of the Kingdom of Yugoslavia and allowing the non-Serb citizens of this state to be persecuted and eliminated.

These two traditions from the past influenced Serbian political and intellectual elites at the time when the Yugoslav crisis was approaching its climax in the 1990s. This period coincided with the collapse of the Communist system in the states of the socialist bloc, which shook the single-party regime even more and urged free elections and the reestablishment of a parliamentary and multiparty system. A power struggle was imminent and in the heated atmosphere only extreme national programs had any chance of gaining widespread support.

Slobodan Milošević (b. 1941), having become the leader of the Serbian Communist Party in an internal coup in 1987, tried to maintain the continuity of authority by merging the party with the Socialist Alliance, an inactive and insignificant organization. The Communist Party was transformed overnight into the Socialist Party of Serbia, presenting its leader with the opportunity to critically strike at Tito's regime while maintaining Partisan traditions and the achievements of socialism.

Milošević portrayed himself and his party as the protector of Yugoslavia. He condemned the leaders of the other Yugoslav republics and foreign powers for breaking up the country, while ruling the remaining rump Yugoslavia, consisting only of Serbia and Montenegro, as though it was the Serbs' national state. Resistance in Montenegro increased, and starting in 1997 the Montenegrin authorities failed to uphold the decisions of federal authorities, with only common defense and foreign policies remaining. Separating from Serbia and attaining full state independence became the core of the platforms of very influential Montenegrin political powers, and the views on Serbdom became the dividing line between political parties and coalitions. Following the other Yugoslav republics, the example of Montenegro demonstrated the fatal consequences of accepting the program of the Serbian nationalist opposition urging either a federation tailored to suit Serbia and the Serbs, or Serbia as a national state consisting of all territories inhabited by Serbs.

While the Socialist Party of Serbia and its leader tried to blend the Yugoslav and narrowly Serbian components, the former in official state policies and the latter in creating an ideological and cultural climate, the Serbs who remained in other republics following the breakup of former Yugoslavia had no strong socialist tendencies, nor did they foster the Yugoslav heritage. The main role was played by nationalist, nominally democratic parties, which focused on the national state. They fought for this by creating autonomous territories that would eventually unite with Serbia. Messages from the recent and distant past had a more direct effect in this regard. Methods of fighting for the national state were revived: authority was imposed, followed by the persecution of other nations, removing their symbols and traces, and the commission of serious crimes. The fate of the Serbs who were minorities in other republics and could suffer or perish from the same methods was not considered.

It is often claimed, and rightly so, that after the breakup of Yugoslavia the Serbs' development returned to where it had been in the early twentieth century. This similarity should be supplemented by the differences, since the general situation in the early twenty-first century is quite unlike the situation in 1903 or 1908, and therefore the consequences of the breakup of Yugoslavia are not as severe. Serbia and its neighbors are not part of a divided and feuding Europe, but part of a Europe that is uniting, where the formally united members of the European Union are expecting the other states to join them. This Europe is part of a world where principles of organization and international relations are becoming uniform, and where respect for human and minority rights is mandatory. Serbia and the states where the Serbs represent significant minorities have the same long-term objectives and are voluntarily submitting to the principles of the contemporary world order. State borders are neither as impregnable nor as significant as those that existed a century ago. Means of communication that do not stop at state borders are increasing in number. There is no "struggle for liberation and unification" awaiting the divided parts of the Serb people. Their objective is to renew severed ties with their neighbors, the European and international community, and restore the capacity to welcome what the modern world has to offer for the good and progress of humankind.

Select Bibliography

Adanir, F., *Die Makedonische Frage, Ihre Entstehung und Entwicklung* (Wiesbaden, 1979).

Banac, I., *The National Question in Yugoslavia: Origins, History, Politics* (New York, 1984).

Banac, I., *With Stalin against Tito: Cominformist Splits in Yugoslav Communism* (New York, 1989).

Beschnit, W. D., *Nationalismus bei Serben und Kroaten 1830–1914: Analyse und Typologie der nationalen Ideologie* (Munich, 1980).

Birnbaum, H. and Vryonis, S., eds., *Aspects of Balkans: Continuity and Change* (Los Angeles, 1972).

Bojović, B., *L'Idéologie monarchique dans les hagio-biographies dynastiques du Moyen-Age Serbe* (Rome, 1995).

Calic, M.-J., *Sozialgeschichte Serbiens 1815–1941* (Munich, 1994).

Castellan, G., *La Vie quotidienne en Serbie au seuil de l'indépendance, 1815–1839* (Paris, 1967).

Castellan, G., *Histoire des Balkans (XIVᵉ–XXᵉ siècle)* (Paris, 1991).

Ćirković, S., *I Serbi nel medioevo* (Milan, 1992).

Dedijer, V., *Road to Sarajevo* (London, 1967).

Dedijer, V., Božić, I., Ćirković, S., and Ekmečić, M., *History of Yugoslavia* (New York, 1974).

Dimić, Lj., *Srbija u Jugoslaviji* (Novi Sad, 2001).

Di Vitorio, A. (ed.), *Ragusa e il Mediterraneo: ruolo e funzioni di una repubblica marinara tra medioevo ed eta moderna* (Bari, 1990).

Dölger, F., *Byzanz und die europäische Staatenwelt: Ausgewählte Aufsätze* (Darmstadt, 1964).

Đorđević, D., *Révolutions nationales des peuples balcaniques* (Belgrade, 1965).

Đorđević, D. (ed.), *The Creation of Yugoslavia, 1914–1918* (Santa Barbara, 1980).

Đorđević, D., *Die Serben, Die Völker des Reiches, Die Habsburgermonarchie 1848–1918* (Vienna, 1980), pp. 734–74.

Dragović-Soso, J., *"Saviours of the Nation": Serbia's Intellectual Opposition and the Revival of Nationalism* (London, 2002).

Ducellier, A., *Byzance et le monde orthodoxe* (Paris, 1986).

Đurić, V., *Die byzantinische Fresken* (Munich, 1976).

Džaja, S., *Konfessionalität und Nationalität Bosniens und der Herzegowina: voremanzipatorische Phase, 1463–1804* (Munich, 1984).

Džaja, S., *Bosnien-Herzegowina in der österreichisch-ungarischen Epoche (1878–1918)* (Munich, 1994).

Ekmečić, M., *Stvaranje Jugoslavije 1790–1918*, 2 vols. (Belgrade, 1989).

Emmert, Th. A., *Serbian Golgotha Kosovo, 1389* (New York, 1990).

Ferluga, J., *Byzantium on the Balkans: Studies on the Byzantine Administration and the Southern Slavs from the VIIth to the XIIIth Centuries* (Amsterdam, 1976).

Ferluga, J., *L'amministrazione bizantina in Dalmazia* (Venice, 1978).

Ferluga, J., *Untersuchungen zur byzantinischen Provinzialverwaltung, VII–XIII Jahrhundert* (Amsterdam, 1992).

Fine, J. V., Jr., *Early Medieval Balkans* (Ann Arbor, 1983).

Fine, J. V., Jr., *Late Medieval Balkans* (Ann Arbor, 1987).

Fonseca, C. D. (ed.), *Le aree omogenee della civiltà rupestre nell'ambito dell'impero bizantino: la Serbia* (Galatina, 1979).

Garde, P., *Vie et mort de la Yougoslavie* (Paris, 1992).

Glenny, M., *The Fall of Yugoslavia*, 2nd ed.. (New York, 1993).

Gli Slavi occidentali e meridionali nell'Alto Medioevo, 2 vols. (Spoleto, 1983).

Hadrovics, L., *Le Peuple serbe et son église sous la domination turque* (Paris, 1947).

Hamman-MacLean, R., *Grundlegung zu einer Geschichte der mittelalterlichen Monumentalmalerei in Serbien und Makedonien* (Giesen, 1976).

Haselsteiner, H., *Bosnien-Hercegowina, Orientkrise und Südslavische Frage* (Vienna, 1996).

Haumant, E., *Karageorges – son armée, ses adversaires* (Paris, 1916).

Haumant, E., *La Formation de la Yougoslavie* (Paris, 1930).

Hoptner, J. B., *Yugoslavia in Crisis, 1934–1941* (New York, 1962).

Hösch, E., *The Balkans: A Short History from Greek Times to the Present Day* (London, 1972).

Inalcik, H., *An Economic and Social History of the Ottoman Empire*, vol. 1, *1300–1600* (Cambridge, 1997).

Istorija srpskog naroda (History of the Serbian People), 10 vols. (1980–1993).

Jakšić, G., *L'Europe et la résurrection de la Serbie (1804–1834)* (Paris, 1917).

Jelavich, B., *History of the Balkans*, 2 vols. (Cambridge, 1983).

Jelavich, B. and Jelavich, Ch., *The Establishment of the Balkan National States, 1804–1920* (Seattle and London, 1977).

Jelavich, Ch., *South Slav Nationalism: Textbooks and Yugoslav Union before 1914* (Columbus, OH, 1990).

Jireček, C., *Geschichte der Serben*, 2 vols. (Gotha, 1911–18).

Jireček, C., *Staat und Gesellschaft im mittelalterlichen Serbien: Studien zur Kulturgeschichte des 13.–15. Jahrhunderts*. Denkschriften der Kaiserlichen Akademie der Wissenschaften in Wien, Phil. hist. Klasse Bd. 56, 58, 64 (Vienna, 1912–19).

Kanitz, F., *Das Königtum Serbien und das Serbenvolk*, 3 vols. (Leipzig, 1904–14).

Kaser, K., *Hirten, Kämpfer, Stammeshelden: Ursprünge und Gegenwart der balkanischen Patriarchalität* (Vienna and Cologne, 1992).

Krekić, B., *Dubrovnik in the 14th and 15th Centuries: A City between East and West* (Norman, OK, 1972).

Krekić, B., *Dubrovnik, Italy and the Balkans in the Late Middle Ages* (London, 1980).

Krekić, B. (ed.), *Urban Society of Eastern Europe in Premodern Times* (Berkeley, Los Angeles, and London, 1987).

Krekić, B., *Dubrovnik: A Mediterranean Urban Society, 1300–1600* (Aldershot, 1997).

Laiou, A. E., *The Economic History of Byzantium*, 3 vols. (Dumbarton Oaks, 2002).

Lampe, J. R., *Yugoslavia as History: Twice there was a Country*, 2nd ed. (Cambridge, 2000).

Lampe, J. R. and Jackson, M. R., *Balkan Economic History, 1555–1950: From Imperial Borderlands to Developing Nations* (Bloomington, 1982).

Lederer, I., *Yugoslavia at the Paris Peace Conference* (New Haven, 1963).

Ljušić, R., *Kneževina Srbija (1830–1839)* (Belgrade, 1986).

Ljušić, R., *Istorija srpske državnosti: Srbija i Crna Gora* (Belgrade and Novi Sad, 2001).

MacKenzie, D., *The Serbs and Russian Pan-Slavism 1875–1878* (New York, 1967).

MacKenzie, D., *Ilija Garašanin, Balkan Bismarck* (New York, 1985).

MacKenzie, D., *Apis: The Congenial Conspirator* (New York, 1989).

Malcolm, N., *Bosnia: A Short History* (New York, 1994).

Mavromatis, L., *La Fondation de l'empire serbe: Le kralj Milutin* (Thessalonika, 1978).

Melčić, D. (ed.), *Der Jugoslawien-Krieg: Handbuch zur Vorgeschichte, Verlauf und Konsequenzen* (Wiesbaden, 1999).

Mihaljčić, R., *The Battle of Kosovo in History and in Popular Tradition* (Belgrade, 1989).

Mousset, J., *La Serbie et son Eglise 1830–1904* (Paris, 1938).

Obolensky, D., *The Byzantine Commonwealth: Eastern Europe, 500–1453* (London, 1971).

Obolensky, D., *Byzantium and the Slavs: Collected Studies* (London, 1971).

Obolensky, D., *The Byzantine Inheritance of Eastern Europe* (London, 1982).

Oikonomidis, N. (ed.), *Byzantium and Serbia in the 14th Century*. International Symposium (Athens, 1995).

Ostrogorsky, G., *History of the Byzantine State* (Oxford, 1968).

Pavlowitch, S. K., *Yugoslavia: The Improbable Survivor* (Columbus, OH, 1988).

Pavlowitch, S. K., *A History of the Balkans, 1804–1945* (London and New York, 1999).

Pavlowitch, S. K., *Serbia: The History behind the Name* (London, 2002).

Petrovich, M. B., *A History of Modern Serbia, 1804–1918* (New York and London, 1976).

Popov, N. (ed.), *The Road to War in Serbia* (Budapest, 1999).

Ramet, S., *Nationalism and Federalism in Yugoslavia, 1962–1991*, 2nd ed. (Bloomington, 1992).

Ramet, S., *Balkan Babel*, 3rd ed. (Boulder, CO, 1999).

Rothenberg, G. E., *The Austrian Military Border in Croatia, 1522–1747* (Chicago, 1960).

Rothenberg, G. E., *The Military Border in Croatia, 1740–1881* (Chicago, 1966).

Rusinov, D., *The Yugoslav Experiment, 1948–1974* (Berkeley, 1977).

Schmitt, J. O., *Das venezianische Albanien (1392–1479)* (Munich, 2001).

Shugar, P. F., *Southeastern Europe under Ottoman Rule* (Seattle, 1977).

Stavrianos, L. S., *The Balkans since 1453* (New York, 1958).

Steindorf, L., *Die dalmatinischen Städte im 12. Jahrhundert: Studien zur ihrer politischen Stellung* (Cologne and Vienna, 1984).

Stojanovich, T., *Between East and West: The Balkan and Mediterranean Worlds*, 4 vols. (New York, 1992–5).

Stojanovich, T., *Balkan Worlds: The First and Last Europe* (New York, 1994).

Stokes, G., *Legitimacy through Liberalism: Vladimir Jovanović and the Transformation of Serbian Politics* (Seattle, 1975).

Sundhausen, H., *Geschichte Jugoslawiens 1918–1980* (Stuttgart, 1982).

Sundhausen, H., *Historische Statistik Serbiens 1834–1914: Mit europäischen Vergleichsdaten* (Munich, 1989).

Sundhausen, H., *Experiment Jugoslawien: Von der Staatsgründung bis zum Staatszerfall 1918–1991* (Mannheim, 1993).

Soulis, G. Ch., *The Serbs and Byzantium: During the Reign of Tsar Stephen Dušan (1331–1355) and his Successors*, 2nd ed. (Athens, 1995).

Temperley, H., *History of Serbia* (London, 1917).

Tomašević, J., *Peasants, Politics, and Economic Change in Yugoslavia* (Stanford, 1955).

Tomašević, J., *The Chetniks* (Stanford, 1975).

Tomašević, J., *Occupation and Collaboration* (Stanford, 2001).

Vucinich, W., *Serbia between East and West: The Events of 1903–08* (Stanford, 1954).

Vucinich, W. and Emmert, Th., *Kosovo: Legacy of a Medieval Battle* (Minneapolis, 1991).

Wendel, H., *Der Kampf der Südslawen um Freiheit und Einheit* (Frankfurt, 1925).

Wheeler, M. C., *Britain and the War for Yugoslavia, 1940–1943* (New York, 1980).

Wilson, D., *The Life and Times of Vuk Stefanović Karadžić, 1787–1864* (Oxford, 1970).

Winnifrith, T. J., *The Vlachs: The History of a Balkan People* (London, 1987).

Woodward, S. L., *Balkan Tragedy: Chaos and Dissolution after the Cold War* (Washington, DC, 1995).

Index

Page numbers in *italic* refer to an illustration or map.

Academy of Sciences, 284
administrative systems
  under Austrians, 151–3, 156–7, 158–9
  Bosnia-Herzegovina, 232
  under Dušan, 70–4
  under French, 187–8
  Kingdom of Serbs, Croats, and
    Slovenes, 256–7, 259–60
  under Miloš, 190, 194–6
  Montenegro, 190, 240–2
  under Ottoman restoration in Serbia,
    176–7, 177–8, 180–1, 182, 183
  under Ottomans, 111–13, 120–1,
    221–2, 223
  Voivodstvo, 218
  Yugoslav Republic, 275, 279, 289–92
  Yugoslavia, 262, 263
agrarian reform, *see* feudalism; land
    ownership
Agrarian Union (Yugoslavia), 256, 264
agriculture
  Alliance of Serbian Agricultural
    Cooperatives, 229
  under Austrians, 157–8, 160
  corn growing, 127
  cotton growing, 127
  medieval, 53–4
  under Miloš, 193, 194
  under Ottomans, 113, 126–7, 129
  rice growing, 126
  Venetian territories, 184
  Yugoslav Republic cooperatives, 276–8
  Yugoslavia, 263
Alaça Hissar, *see* Kruševac
Alba Iulia, *see* Gyulafehérvar
Albania
  7th century, 9
  9th century, 14

13th century, 37, 50
14th century, 63, 67, 76
15th century, 108
  under Romans, xxv
  Slavs in, 252
  state proclaimed (1912), 245
  World War II, 267, 269
Albanians
  7th century, 9
  11th century, 27
  15th century, 105
  under Austrians, 154
  and Illyrians, 2
  in Kosovo, xxix, 243, 244, 289, 292
  in Montenegro, 225
  under Ottomans, 129–30
  search for autonomy, 244
  in Yugoslav Republic, 292
Albrecht, king of Hungary, 104
Aleksinac, battle of (1806), 179
Alemanni, 31
Alexander I Karadjordjević, king of
    Yugoslavia, 246, 249, 257, 261–2,
    264
Alexander Karadjordjević, Prince, 196,
    207, 211–13
Alexander Obrenović, king of Serbia, 240
Alexander, Prince, ruler of Wallachia, 76
Alexius I Comnenus, Byzantine emperor,
    27–8
Alexius III Angelus, Byzantine emperor, 33
Alfonso of Aragon, 106
Alliance of Serbian Agricultural
    Cooperatives, 229
Anagastum, *see* Nikšić
Andjelić, German, patriarch, 234
Andjelković, Koča, 177
Andrew II, king of Hungary, 38

Andrija, prince of Hum, 37
Andrijas, King, 79, 80
Andronicus II Palaeologus, Byzantine
    emperor, 49–50, 61, 62, 64
Andronicus III Palaeologus, 62, 63, 64
Angelina, Despotess, 101
Angora, battle of (1402), 88
Anjous, 49
Anna Dandolo, 38
Annunciation Assembly (1861), 219
Antae, 10
Antifascist Council for the National
    Liberation of Yugoslavia (AVNOJ),
    272, 273
Apis, Colonel, see Dimitrijević, Dragutin
Arad, 159
Arbanon (Raban), 37
architecture, 61, 98–9, 119, 168–70
Arilje monastery, 60
Armenians, xxvii, 53, 128, 160
armies
    Montenegro, 240
    Serbia, 239, 247
    see also military service
Aromani, see Tzintzars
Aromanians, 211
Arsenije, Archbishop, 46
Arsenije II, Patriarch, 134
Arsenije III Ćarnojević, Patriarch, prince
    of Albania, 143, 144, 147, 148–50
Arsenije IV Jovanović, Patriarch, 153,
    154, 156, 177
art, see painting
Austria and Austrian Empire: events
    Serbian resettlement, 117–18
    War of the Holy League (1683–99),
        140, 143–5, 146
    war against Ottomans (1593–1606),
        141–2
    Serbia under, xxiv, xxvii, 143–5,
        146–75
    Hungary liberated from Ottomans
        (1699), 146–51
    Hungarian rebellion (1703–), 148–50
    Serbian War (1714–18), 151
    Austro-Turkish War (1736–9), 153–4
    Austro-Turkish War (1788–91), 177
    Venetian territories ceded to Napoleon,
        187
    extension of Balkan territories, 188
    reclamation of Dalmatia, 188
    19th-century relations with
        Montenegro, 189
    Serbian rule, 196–203
    1848 unrest, 200–3
    temporary dethronement of Habsburgs
        (1849), 203

    proclamation of Dual Monarchy, 210,
        219
    Serbian rule, 217–21
    establishment and abolition of
        Voivodstvo, 218–19
    Anschluss, 267
Austria-Hungary: events
    proclamation of Dual Monarchy, 210,
        219
    Great Eastern Crisis (1875–8), 223, 224
    occupation and rule of Bosnia-
        Herzegovina, 225–6, 230–2
    Annexation of Bosnia-Herzegovina
        (1908), 230, 231
    trade treaty with Serbia, 239
    aids Serbia in war against Bulgaria
        (1885), 239
    helps Montenegrin development, 240
    Balkan Wars (1912–13) and effects, 246
    assassination of Francis Ferdinand and
        consequences, 246–7
    World War I, 247–51
Austro-Turkish War (1736–9), 153–4
Austro-Turkish War (1788–91), 177
Autonomists, 230
Avars, 8, 11, 13
AVNOJ, see Antifascist Council for the
    National Liberation of Yugoslavia

Bačka
    19th century, 201, 203
    20th century, 254, 269
    under Austrians, 158, 160, 166
    and Great Migration (1690), 144
    under Ottomans, 119–20
Baja, 197
Balkan Wars (1912–13), xxviii, 244–5
Balša III Balšić, 91, 92
Balšić brothers, 76, 77, 78, 80, 81
Banat, 119
    1848–9 unrest, 201, 203
    under Austrians, 151, 155, 158,
        159–60
    under Ottomans, 141–2
    schools, 165–6
    split with Romania, 254
Banjska monastery, 60, 154
banking, 229
Bar
    12th century, 31
    14th century, 71
    15th century, 92
    16th century, 123
    under Ottomans, 185, 224
Bar archbishopric
    11th-century status, 26, 28
    12th-century status, 38

conflict with Dubrovnik for
  ecclesiastical jurisdiction, 40, 47–8
under Ottomans, 125
synod of 1199, 41–2
Baranja (Baranya), 144, 147, 201, 269
Basil I, Byzantine emperor, 16
Basil II, Byzantine emperor, 20–1, 21–2,
  24
Bassiana, 3
Bayazid, Ottoman sultan, 82, 84, 85, 86,
  87–8
Bayazid II, Ottoman sultan, 140
Bayle, Pierre, 174
Bečej, 200
Bečkerek, 159, 200
Bela IV, king of Hungary, 46–7, 48–9
Bela Crkva, 159
Bela Palanka (Remesiana), 3, 224
Bela Stena, 107
Belasica, 125
Belgrade
  buildings, 121, 152, 206, 255
  education, 164
  Great School, 181, 181, 198, 207,
    209
  hospitals, 194
  population, 281
  printing presses, 139, 198
  steamboats, 205
  trade, 128
Belgrade: events
  under Bulgarians, 34
  under Byzantines, 52
  handed over to Serbia (1403), 89
  as despots' seat, 99, 107
  seized by Hungary (15th century), 103
  Ottoman conquest (1521), 115
  as Ottomans' seat, 111, 112
  Austrian capture (1688), 143
  Ottomans retake (1690), 144
  Austrian capture (1717), 151
  as Austrians' seat, 153, 160
  Ottomans retake (1739), 153
  Belgrade pashalik, 176–83, 190–203
  temporary Austrian takeover (1789),
    177
  and janissaries' war, 178
  First Serbian Uprising (1804–13), 179,
    180
  cultural leadership, 236–7
  World War I, 248, 250
  World War II, 268, 268, 273
  see also Singidunum
Belgrade, Treaty of (1739), 154
Belgrade, University of, 267, 282, 293
Belgrade metropolitanate, 193, 260–1
Belgrade pashalik, 176–83, 190–203

Belin, 83, 85
Belje estate, 157
Beloš, 30, 31
Beogradske ilustrovane novine (Belgrade
  Illustrated Newspaper), 210
Berlin, Congress of (1878), 225
Bezdin monastery, 120
Bihor, 107
"Black Hand," 245, 249
Blaznavac, Milivoje, 214
Bodin, Constantine, prince of Duklja, 26,
  27, 28–9
Bodjani monastery, 120
Boka, 185, 187, 188
books
  18th century, 166, 173–4
  19th century, 197, 198
  20th century, 284
  early printed, 109, 110, 138–9
  see also literature
Borač (Gruža), 85–6, 103
Boril, tsar of Bulgaria, 37
Boris (later Michael), khan of Bulgaria,
  15
Bosnia, Kingdom of
  13th-century territories, 39
  14th-century territories, 62
  15th-century territories, 93
  first use of name, 111
  monasteries, 118
  origins, 12–13
Bosnia, Kingdom of: events
  status (1138), 23, 29
  13th-century church, 28, 41, 45, 47
  and Nemanja, 32
  14th century, 78
  partial takeover of Serbia, 80–1
  Ottoman raids, 86
  Hungarian conquest, 86, 87
  becomes Ottoman vassal, 102–3, 105
  disputes with Serbia, 106
  Ottoman conquest, 108
  Serb refugees from Ottomans, 117
  and Austrians, 151, 154
  19th century, 179–80
  Serb plans for expansion, 212, 214
  under Ottomans, 222
  Nevesinje rebellion (1875), 223
  Austrian occupation, 226
Bosnia-Herzegovina
  church, 260
  ethnicity, xxix, 256
  Muslims in, 256
Bosnia-Herzegovina: events
  joining, xxiii
  Austro-Hungarian occupation, xxviii,
    230–2

Bosnia-Herzegovina: *events cont.*
  Austro-Hungarian Annexation (1908),
    230, 231
  Constitution approved (1910), 232
  opposition to Habsburgs, 246
  World War II, 269
  status in Yugoslav Republic, 274, 292
  war in (1992–5), 292
Božidar Vuković, 139, 140–1
Brajići, 186, 187
Braničevo, 34, 52, 103
Branivojević brothers, 62
Branko Mladenović, 67
Branković, Georgije, Patriarch, 234
Brda, 187
Breza, 7
Britain, 212, 240, 272
  see also England
Broquière, Bertrandon de la, 52
Bucharest, Treaty of (1812), 182
Buda
  16th century, 119
  17th century, 143, 144
  under Austrians, 159, 169, 197
Budva
  14th century, 71
  15th century, 92, 93, 123
  18th century, 187
  19th century, 188
Bukovina–Dalmatian metropolitanate, 229
Bulgaria and Bulgarian Empire: *events*
  tribes in, xxii–xxiii
  Proto-Bulgarians and Serbs, 13–15
  Proto-Bulgarians and Byzantines, 14,
    17–18, 20
  Christianization, 15
  and Serbia, 18, 20
  collapse, 20
  11th century, 25–6
  Serb incursions, 32
  12th-century regrowth in power, 34
  involvement in Serbian power struggles,
    35
  internal power struggles, 37
  defeat of Theodore I, 46
  Mongol incursions, 47
  links with Dubrovnik, 48
  conflict with Serbia, 50
  Serbia takes temporary control, 62–3
  involvement in Byzantine struggles, 66
  emperor becomes Ottoman vassal, 79
  Ottoman conquest, 86, 87
  Ottomans driven out, 90
  Berlin Congress outcomes, 225
  rebellions against Ottomans (1875,
    1876), 223
  Serbian war with (1885), 239

  ambitions to own Macedonia, 243–4
  Balkan Wars (1912–13), 244–5
  World War I, 248–9, 250
  influence in Macedonia, 259
  World War II, 267, 269
Bulgars, 160
Bushatli family, 186–7
Byzantine Empire
  influence, xix
  joint rule practice, 64
  and missions, 15–16, 17
Byzantine Empire: *events*
  7th century, 8–9
  early relations with Slavs, 11–12, 14,
    15, 16
  early relations with Bulgarians, 14,
    17–18, 20
  early relations with Serbs, 18
  Balkan territories, 20–1, 24
  schism from Rome, 22
  struggles with Hungary, 22–3
  Balkan uprisings, 24–6, 29
  Norman Balkan incursion, 27–8
  Byzantine–Hungarian wars, 29–31
  temporary overthrow (1204), 34
  restoration by Nicaean Greeks (1261),
    47
  13th-century relations with Serbia,
    49–50
  internal struggles, 62, 64–5, 66
  14th-century conflict with Serbia, 62–3
  links with Serbia, 63–4
  Ottoman incursions, 79, 86
  15th-century relations with Serbs, 88–9
  fall to Ottomans (1453), 106–7
  see also Constantinople
Byzantines, 9

Čačak, 96, 112, 143
calendars, 172
Campo Formio, Treaty of, 187
Cantacuzina, Empress Mara's sister, 114
Cantacuzinus, Toma, 114
Capistrano, Giovanni, 107
Carentani, 12
Caričin Grad, *see* Justiniana Prima
Carinthia, 255
Čarnojević, Petar, count, 202
Časlav Klonimirović, prince of Serbia,
  18–19
Catholicism
  13th-century Serbia, 40–5
  in Bosnia-Herzegovina, 230
  Byzantine schism, 22
  under Byzantines, 22
  Dušan's banning of conversion to, 69
  and German miners, 55

in Habsburg Empire, 147, 162–3
under Ottomans, 125, 137
in Yugoslavia, 264, 265
censuses, Ottoman, 113
Čestin (Šumadija), 86
Cetinje, 110, 185, 242
Chalcocondyles, 84
Charles of Durazzo, king of Hungary, 83
Charles Robert, king of Hungary, 52
Chetniks, 270–4
Chilandar monastery, 33, 74, 98, 138
cholera, 194
Chomatenos, Demetrios, 43–4
Christianization, xviii–xix, 15–17
Chronograph, 139
churches and church building
under Austrians, 168–70, *169*
under Ottomans, 119, 120, 133–4,
137–8
cinema, 284–5, 286
Civil Code (1844), 196
clans and clan society, 129–33
18th century, 185
19th century, 216, 235
Austro-Turkish war (1736–9), 153–4
Karadjordje's rebellion, 179, 181–2
Clement III (antipope), 28
coal mining, 193
Codex Justinianus, 68
coins and minting
medieval Serbian state, 55–7, *56*, 93–4,
100, *100*
under Milan, 239
under Ottomans, 129
Coloman, king of Hungary, 22
colonization, under Austrians, 153, 159–61
communism, 209, 266–7, 270–4
Communist Party of Yugoslavia (KPJ;
later Yugoslav League of
Communists), 274–9
Compromise (1867), 219, 227
Constantine (missionary), 16
Constantine, son of Milutin, 62
Constantine VII Porphyrogenitus,
Byzantine emperor, xviii, 11, 12
Constantine the Philosopher, 101
Constantinople
first name change, 6
foundation, 5
Ottoman resettlement of peoples there,
115
Ottoman siege (1394), 86
Ottoman siege (1453), 106–7, 134
Ottoman treatment of Catholics, 137
Slav and Persian siege (626), 8
see also Byzantine Empire
Corfu Declaration (1917), 250

Ćorović, Vladimir, 263
Ćosić, Dobrica, 293
Court Chamber, 157, 158, 159–60
courts of law, 71–3
craftsmen, 122, 159, 212, 229
Crimean War (1853–6), 211–12, 216
Crna Reka, 182
Croatia
10th-century territories, 12
11th-century territories, 22, 24
ethnicity, xxix
monasteries, 119
Croatia: *events*
encounters with Franks, 14–15
and Byzantine authority, 16
Bulgarian attacks on, 18
struggles with Hungary, 83–4, 86
migrations from Ottoman lands, 117
temporary French rule, 187
19th-century resistance to Hungary, 202
status of Serbs in 19th century, 227–9
calls for statehood (1917), 250
post-unification politics, 256, 257, 259,
261
post-unification reorganization, 264–5
World War II, 268, 270
Independent State of Croatia (NDH),
269
status in Yugoslav Republic, 274, 292
see also Triune Kingdom
Croatian Orthodox Church, 269
Croatian Peasant Party (CPP), 256, 261,
264
Croats
in Bosnia-Herzegovina, 292
difference from Serbs, xix
migrations, 11, 117
origins, xviii, 10, 11
tribal territories, xxii
Crusades
to Holy Land, 28–9, 32, 34, 36
against Ottomans, 86, 104
Cukić, Pavle, 190
culture
19th century, 198, 236–7
under Austrians, 170–4, 197
Dalmatia, 188
despot period, 100–1
Dušan's reign, 65
folk culture, 132–3
icons, *74*, 98
Montenegro, 190
under Ottomans, 119
Yugoslav Republic, 283–6
Yugoslavia, 266
see also books; periodicals and
newspapers

Ćuprija (Horreum Margi), 3, 177
Cvetković, Dragiša, 264
Cvetković–Maček Agreement (1939),
  264–5

Dabiša, see Stefan Dabiša, king of Bosnia
Dalj, 148
Dalmatia
  monasteries, 118
  Serbs in, 188, 229–30
Dalmatia: events
  under Romans, 2, 5
  Goths in, 7
  Bulgarian subjugation, 20
  under Byzantines, 24
  14th-century Bosnian subjugation, 83
  14th-century Hungarian subjugation, 86
  under Venetians, 92
  under Ottomans, 117
  partial liberation from Ottomans, 143
  17th-century decline, 183–4
  temporary French takeover (1797), 187
  retaken by Austrians (1814), 188
  post-unification, 259, 260
  World War II, 269
  see also Triune Kingdom
Dalmatia and Diocletia, Kingdom of, 32
Daničić, Djura, 200
Danilo, Metropolitan, 185
Danilo I, prince of Montenegro and Brda,
  215–16
Danilo II, Archbishop, 97, 101
Dardania, 2
Davidovica monastery, 60
Davidović, Dimitrije, 195
debt and credit, 95, 114
Dečani monastery, 53, 59
Declatoria, 197
Defenders of the Constitution, 195, 196,
  212, 213
Dejan, Dušan's brother-in-law, 67, 76
Dekatera, see Kotor
Deligrad, 179, 182
Demetrius, panhypersebastos, 37
Demir Kapija, see Prosek
Democratic Party (Yugoslavia), 264
despots
  Byzantine award of title, 88–9
  definition, 88
Dessa, grand župan, 31
Didymoteichos, battle of (1352), 66
Dimitrije, župan, 48, 60
Dimitrijević, Dragutin (Colonel Apis),
  245, 246, 249
Dinaric Alps, xxi, 9
Diocletian, Roman emperor, 5
Djaković, Isaija, metropolitan, 143, 150

Djerdap hydroelectric power station, 280
Djilas, Milovan, 279, 291
Djordje, ruler of Zeta, 47, 48
Djordje Branković, Despot, 101, 116
Djordje II Branković, Despot, 144
Djordje of Kratovo, 139
Djunis, 224
Djuradj Balsić, 78, 82
Djuradj Branković, Despot
  coins of, 56
  folk epic about, 117
  monetary reform, 95
  reign, 101, 102, 103–4, 106, 107
  seat, 99–100
  succession, 88–9, 91
Djuradj Crnojević, 110, 138
Djuradj Stracimirović, 82
Djuradj II Stracimirović Balšić, 89, 92
Djurdevi Stupovi monastery, 60
Dobrovski, J., 208
Dobrnjac, Petar, 181
Domavia, 3
Domentian, 42
Dračevica, 80
Draga, queen of Serbia, 240
Dragaš, Constantine, 80, 81, 86
Dragaš, John, 80, 81
Dragaš brothers, 79
Dragović monastery, 118
Dragoviči, see Druguviti
Dragutin, king of Serbia, 45, 48–9, 50–2,
  60
Drivast, 92
Drman, ruler of Kučevo, 50
Drstar, see Durostorum
Druguviti (Dragoviči), xxii, 10, 11, 12
Društvo srpske slovenosti (Society of
  Serbian Letters), 198
Dubočica, 103
Dubravica, see Margum
Dubravnica, battle of (1381), 83
Dubrovnik (Ragusion)
  trade and industry, 94, 95, 96, 128
Dubrovnik: events
  Byzantine reliance on, 22, 24
  promoted in Mihajlo's church reforms,
    25, 26–7
  captured by Normans and retaken by
    Byzantines, 28
  Serbia signs truce with (1186), 31–2
  conflict with Bar for ecclesiastical
    jurisdiction, 40, 47–8
  relations settled with Serbia, 49
  13th-century prosperity, 58
  settles conflict between Dušan and
    father, 63
  buys Ston from Serbia, 63

14th-century relations with Serbia, 67
comes under Hungarian rule (1358), 76
war with Serbia (1361–2), 77–8
war with Nikola Altomanović, 78–9, 80
political status in 15th century, 104
Stefan Vukčić Kosača's attack on
    (1451), 106
Ottoman encirclement, 108
fall to France (1806), 187
Dukagjin, 131, 142
Duklja, 16, 20, 22, 25–9, 32
Dukljani, 12
Duljebi, 10, 12
Dunaszekcsö, 148, 169
Durostorum (Drstar), 22
Durres, see Dyrrachium
Dušan, Stefan, Emperor of the Serbs and
    Greeks
14th-century view of, 97
childhood, 61
coins of, 56
crowned as young king, 62
reign, xxiii, 63, 64–75
title, 10
Dušan's Code (1349), 53, 65, 68–71, 69,
    73
Dyrrachium (Durres): events
briefly held by Bulgaria, 20
Byzantine reliance on, 22, 24, 25
Norman attack on (1081), 27
Byzantines regain, 28
temporary Serbian control, 50
Venetians procure (1392), 92

economic development
under Austrians, 159
Great Depression, effects of, 263, 264
medieval, 52–8, 93–6
under Miloš, 193
under Ottoman restoration, 178
under Ottomans, 113–14, 125, 126–9
Yugoslav Republic, 276–8, 280–1, 283
Edirne, Treaty of (1878), 224, 225
education
18th century, 163–7, 168
19th century, 181, 188, 198, 209–10,
    239
Bosnia-Herzegovina, 231
Croatia, 228
Hungary, 220–1, 232–3
Montenegro, 217
study abroad, 207
Yugoslav Republic, 278, 282–3, 287
Yugoslavia, 263, 267
Eger, 197
electricity, 205
hydroelectric power station, 280

Emeric, king of Hungary, 38
England
19th-century Balkan involvement,
    188
see also Britain
Enlightenment, in Serbia, 174
Epirus, 65
Esztregom, 197
Eugene of Savoy, Prince, 157

factories, 236, 280–1, 283
famine, 193, 286
fascism, Yugoslav support for, 266–7
Felix Romuliana, 5, 6
"Felling of Knezes," 178
Fenek monastery, 119
feudalism
abolition, xx, 218
under Austrians, 157–8
medieval Serbian state, 53–4
serfs, 74, 231, 256
films, 284–5, 286
finance, national, 283
see also taxation
First Serbian Uprising (1804–13), xxviii,
    178–82
Fiume (Rijeka), 184
Florence, 84
folklore, 208
France
in Balkans, 187–8
French Revolution (1789), influence of,
    174, 204
influence in Montenegro, 189
rise in Balkan influence, 212
takeover of Venetian Republic (1797),
    187
Francis Ferdinand, Archduke, 246–7
Franks, 13, 14, 15–16
Frederick Barbarossa, Holy Roman
    Emperor, 31, 32
Freemasons, 262
Fruška Gora monasteries, 119, 138
Fundina, battle of (1876), 224

Galerius, Roman emperor, 5
Galič, 30
Gamzigrad, 5, 6
Gara, Nicolas de, the Elder, 83
Gara, Nicolas de, the Younger, 80, 82,
    85
Garašanin, Ilija, xiv, 212
Gavril Radomir, tsar of Bulgaria, 20
Gavrilović, Jovan, 214
Gennadios Scholarios, Patriarch, 134
George, king of Duklja, 29
Gepids, 7

Germans
  in Banat, 159–60
  in Voivodstvo, 218
  in Vojvodina, 277
Germany
  relations with Yugoslavia, 264, 266
  World War I, 248
  World War II, 267–73
Gnjilane, 225
Gojnik, Prince, 15
Golemović, Oliver, 114
Goli Otok, 278
Golubac, 103, 107
Gomionica monastery, 118
Goražde monastery, 139
Gornji Kotari, 184
Gostović monastery, 118
Goths, 6–7
Gračanica monastery, 60, 60, 61, 83, 139
Gradac monastery, 60
Grahovo, battle of (1858), 216
Grbalj, 131, 186
Grdan of Nikšić, 142
Great Court of the Land, 180
Great Depression, effects of, 263, 264
Great Migration (1690), 144, 146, 147
Great Moravia, 15–16
Great School, Belgrade, 181, 181, 198,
    207, 209
Great Vlachia, 9
Greece
  alliance with Serbia (1867), 214
  ambitions to own Macedonia, 243
  Balkan Wars (1912–13), 244–5
  World War I, 249
  World War II, 267
Greeks
  13th century: Balkan incursions, 47
  in 19th-century Serbia, 211
  in medieval Serbian state, xxvi, xxvii
  in Ottoman Empire, 128
Gregory VII, Pope, 26–7
Grgur Branković, son of Despot Djuradj,
    104, 114
Gruža, see Borač
guilds, 122, 159, 212
Gulf of Kotor (Boka) diocese, 229
Gusinje, 225
Győr, 197
Gyulafehérvar (Alba Iulia), 119
Gyulhane hatt-i sherif (1839), 221–2

Habsburg Empire, see Austria and
    Austrian Empire; Austria-Hungary
Haçi-Prodan, 182
Hadžic, Jovan, 196
Hamartolos, George, 65

hatt-i Hümayun (1856), 223
Helen, Queen, wife of Uroš I, 49, 58–60,
    61
Heraclius, Byzantine emperor, 9, 11
heraldic arms
  19th century, 226
  medieval, 100, 100, 132, 133
  metropolitanate, 171
Herceg Novi, see Novi
Herder, Siegmund, baron, 193
Herzegovina
  16th century, 136
  17th century, 141
  19th century, 179
  Austro-Hungarian occupation, 226
  ethnic mix, 130
  first use of name, 111
  Great Eastern Crisis (1875–8), 223, 224
  monasteries, 118
  Nevesinje rebellion (1875), 223
  uprisings against Ottomans, 215, 216
  see also Bosnia-Herzegovina
Hodges, George Lloyd, 195
Hodoš monastery, 120
Holy Roman Empire, 31, 32
Honorius III, Pope, 38
Horreum Margi, see Ćuprija
Horvat, Ivaniš, 83, 85
Horvat, Pavao, 83
Hrmanj monastery, see Rmanj monastery
Hrvoje Vukčić Hrvatinić, 87, 91
Hum
  12th century, 32
  13th century, 37, 40, 48
  14th century, 62, 63, 65
Hungarians, in Voivodstvo, 218
Hungary, Kingdom of
  mining, 94
  Serbs in, 143–75, 196–203, 217–21,
      232–5
  Slavs in, 252
Hungary, Kingdom of: events
  early expansion, xxi
  land struggles with Serbs, xxiii
  rise, 22
  struggles with Byzantines, 22–3, 29–31
  struggles with Bulgaria, 34
  involvement in Serbian power struggles
      in 13th century, 35, 48–9
  overlordship of Serbia, 38–9
  conquest by Mongols and restoration,
      46–7
  disintegration, 50
  involvement in Serbian affairs in 14th
      century, 52, 66, 76, 80, 85–6
  internal struggles, 83–4
  Crusade against Ottomans, 86

conquest of Bosnia, 86, 87
internal struggles, 89, 107
links with Serbia, 91, 101, 102, 107
conflict with Serbia, 103
Balkan Crusade against Ottomans, 104
power balance with Ottomans, 104–5
attacks on Ottomans, 106, 107, 108
Serbian migrations to, 115
conflict with Ottomans, 115–16, 140
trade with Ottomans, 128
liberation from Ottomans (1699),
    146–51
incorporation of Military Border,
    154–5
Serb jurisdiction, 154–6, 196–203
Hungarian colonization, 160–1
1848 unrest, 200–3
independence declared (1849), 203
declaration of Dual Monarchy, 210,
    219
Serbian rule, 217–21
establishment and abolition of
    Voivodstvo, 218–19
Soviet Republic declared (1919), 253
post-World War I boundaries, 254
World War II, 267, 269
see also Austria-Hungary
Huns, 7
Hunyadi, Janos, 104, 105, 106, 107, 117

Ičko, Petar, 180
icons, 74, 98, 119, 170
Ignjatović, Jakov, 209
Illyrian Court Commission (later
    Deputation), 156–7, 166, 174
Illyrian Provinces, 187–8
Illyrians, 2
Illyricum, 1–7
Ilok estate, 157
Independent State of Croatia (NDH),
    269
industry, 96, 193, 204–5, 280–1, 283
Innocent III, Pope, 38
Irene Palaeologue, Byzantine empress, 61
Irig, 159
Isaac II Angelus, Byzantine emperor, 32–3,
    34
Islam
    islamization of Balkans, 122–3, 125–6
    see also Muslims
Italy
    boundaries post-World War I, 254–5
    relations with Yugoslavia, 264
    resettlement of Serb refugees, 117
    World War I, 248, 251
    World War II, 267, 269, 270, 272
Ivan Alexander, tsar of Bulgaria, 63

Ivan Crnojević, 108–10
Ivan Frankopan, Count, 117
Ivan Stefan, tsar of Bulgaria, 63
Ivankovac, battle of (1805), 179

Jadar, 179
Jadovno, 269
Jagodina, 177
Jakšić, Dmitar, 116
Jakšić, Jovan, 116
janissaries, 176, 178–9
Janjevo, 125
Jasenovac, 269
Jašunje monasteries, 138
Jefrem, Patriarch, 101
Jelačić, Josif, ban, 202–3
Jelena, queen of Hungary, 30
Jelena, Empress Mara's niece, 114
Jelena, queen of Bosnia, 87
Jelena, sister of Dušan, 65–6
Jelena, wife of Dušan, 75, 76
Jelena Lazarević, 92
Jews
    in 19th-century Serbia, 225
    anti-Semitism, 266, 295
    under Austrians, 160
    under Ottomans, xxvii, 114, 128
John V Palaeologus, Byzantine emperor,
    64, 65, 66
John VI Cantacuzenus, Byzantine emperor,
    64, 65, 66, 75
John VII Palaeologus, Byzantine emperor,
    88, 101–2
John Asen II, tsar of Bulgaria, 46
John Comnenus Asen, Dušan's brother-in-
    law, 67, 76
John Ducas, 28
John Uglješa, Despot, 79
John Uroš Palaeologue (Ioasaph), ruler of
    Thessaly, 75
John Vladimir, prince of Duklja, 20
John Vladislav, tsar of Bulgaria, 20
Joseph I, ruler of Austria, 150
Joseph II, ruler of Austria, 163, 174, 177
Jovan II, Patriarch, 141
Jovan Branković, Despot, 101, 116, 140
Jovan Monasterlija, 144
Jovanović, Petar, metropolitan, 193
Jovanović, Slobodan, 266
Jovanović, Vićentije, metropolitan, 163,
    165
Jovanović, Vladimir, 208
Jovanović Batut, Milan, 210
Julinac, Pavle, 171
Justinian I, Roman emperor, 5, 7
Justinian II, Byzantine emperor, 14
Justiniana Prima (Caričin Grad), 5, 7

Kabužić brothers, 94
Kačanik, battle of (1690), 143
Kačići, 24
Kallinikos I, Patriarch, 150
Kalocsa archbishopric, 22, 45, 157
Kalojan, tsar of Bulgaria, 35, 36–7, 38
Kamengrad, 125
Karadjordje, *see* Petrović, Djordje
Karadžić, Vuk Stefanović, 199, 208
Karanovac, 177
Karlovci (Karlowitz), 159, 164, 201, 228
Karlovci Assembly (1848), 201
Karlovci metropolitanate: *events*
  established, 150
  assumes jurisdiction over Belgrade
    metropolitanate, 153
  18th-century status, 177
  eastern bishoprics moved to Sibiu
    metropolitanate (1864), 220
  unites with Belgrade metropolitanate
    (1918), 260
  post-unification status, 261
Karlowitz, Treaty of (1699), 146
Karlstadt (Karlovac), 119
Kärnten, 255
Kastoria, 75, 85
kefalija system, 70–1
Kekaumenos, 25
Keve, *see* Kovin
Khuen-Hédervary, Karoly, ban, 228
Kikinda, 200
Kinnamos, John, 29
Klimente, 154
knighthood, 100
Kocelj, prince of Lower Pannonia, 16
Kolašin, 225
Kolovrat, 3
Kolubara, battle of the (1914), 248
Komarom, 197
Konavli (Konavle), 16, 24, 80
Kopaonik mining complex, 124
Kopitar, Bartholomeus, 199, 208
Korčula, 31, 187
Korošec, Anton, 256, 261, 262
Koroška (Carinthia or Kärnten), 255
Kosovo
  11th century, 23
  17th century, 143
  18th century, 154
  20th century, xxix, 274
  breakup of Yugoslav Republic, 289,
    292
  ethnicity, 244
  importance to Serbs, 243
  status in Yugoslav Republic, xxiv, 274
  World War I, 249
  World War II, 269, 270

Kosovo, battle of (1389), 84–5
Kossuth, Lajos, 200
Kotor (Dekatera)
  13th-century prosperity, 58
  14th-century decline, 76–7, 94
  14th- and 15th-century military crises,
    92
  17th century, 143
  British capture (1814), 188
  laws, 71
  as Mihajlo's court, 26
  Mongol raids, 47
  under Venetians, 92, 185
Kovin (Keve), 115
Kozachinsky, Emanuel, 164, 165, 173
Kragujevac, 195, 205, 209, 271
Krajina, 24, 117, 179, 182
Kraljevo, 271
Kratovo, 123, 125
Krka monastery, 118
Krupa monastery, 118
Krušedol monastery, 119, 150
Kruševac (Alaça Hissar), 99, 103, 111,
  177
Kučajna, 124
Kudelin, ruler of Braničevo, 50
Kulin, ban of Bosnia, 35, 45
Kumanovo, battle of (1912), 245
Kumans, 53
Kupinik, 116
Kuršumlija, 179, 224
Kurtzbeck, Joseph, 166
Kyustendil, *see* Velbužd

labor
  conditions in Yugoslav Republic, 287
  migration overseas, 281–2
Ladislas, king of Hungary, 22
Ladislas of Naples, 83, 84, 89, 92
land ownership
  19th century, 191, 212, 234–5, 238
  under Austrians, 157–8
  Kingdom of Serbs, Croats, and
    Slovenes, 256, 257, 261
  Montenegro, 216
  under Ottomans, 176, 222, 223
  Yugoslav Republic, 276, 277
  Yugoslavia, 263
language reforms, 19th century, 198–200
law and order
  under Dušan, 70–3
  under Ottomans, 129, 131
Lazar, Despot, 106, 107
Lazar Branković, 88, 91
Lazar Hrebeljanović, Prince
  at battle of Kosovo (1389), 83–4, 85
  and church, 97–8

coins of, 56
lineage, 97
part in internal conflicts, 80
power base, 78
seat, 99
title and position, 81–2
and Vuk Branković, 79
legal system and legislature
19th century, 196, 212
under Dušan, 67–73
Hungary, 197
Kingdom of Serbs, Croats, and
  Slovenes, 257
Montenegro, 187
under Ottomans, 120, 131
Yugoslavia, 263
Leskovac, 180, 225
"Letovnik" (Hamartolos), 65
Letopis, 197
Liberal Party (Serbia), 238
linguistic studies, Slavic, 208–9
Lipljan (Ulpiana), 3, 47
literacy
20th century, 235, 287
Montenegro, 217
under Ottomans, 131, 139
see also education
literature
19th century, 198, 237
under Austrians, 171–4
early printed books, 109, 110, 138–9
hagiographies, 35, 101
novels, 173
under Ottomans, 139
Serb historiography, 171
Yugoslavia, 266
livestock farming
medieval Serbian state, 54
under Ottoman restoration, 177
under Ottomans, 113, 116, 126, 129
Ljotić, Dimitrije, 270
Ljudevit Posavski, prince of Croatia,
  14–15
Lombards, 7
Lomnica monastery, 118
Louis I Anjou, king of Hungary, 83
Ludwig, King, 16
Lukarević, Miho, 95
Luštica, 92

Macedonia
7th century, 9
13th century, 49–50, 52
14th century, 63, 66, 79, 81
19th- and 20th-century struggles over,
  243–4
attitude to unification, 258–9

Balkan Wars (1912–13), 245
communism in, 256
Muslims in, 256
under Ottomans, 126, 143
status in Yugoslav Republic, 274, 290,
  291
World War I, 249, 250
World War II, 269, 270
Maček, Vladko, 264, 265, 268
Mačva
13th century, 48, 49, 50
14th century, 83, 85
15th century, 103
under Ottomans, 126, 143
Magyars, 19, 22
see also Hungary, Kingdom of
Mahmud pasha, 186
Maine, 186, 187
Majdanpek, 124, 125, 153
Makarije, Patriarch, 134
Maksim Branković, 139
Manasija, see Resava
Manifest (1929), 261–2
Manuel I Comnenus, Byzantine emperor,
  30–1
Manuel II, Byzantine emperor, 88
manuscript copying, 100–1, 139
Mara, Empress, 114
Marashli Ali-Pasha, 183
Margaret (Maria), Hungarian princess, 34
Margum (Dubravica), 3
Maria, queen of Hungary, 83
Maria Theresa, Austrian empress, 154,
  155–6
Marjanović, Jovan, 293
Marko, Bishop, 100
Marko, King, 78, 79, 80, 81, 86
Marković, Sima, 190
Marković, Svetozar, 220
Martinići, battle of (1796), 186
Marx, Karl, 217
Mary Palaeologina, 62
Mathew Cantacuzenus, 76
Matica Dalmatinska cultural society, 188
Matica Srpska, 197, 219, 236, 284
Matija Ninoslav, ban of Bosnia, 45
Matthias Corvinus, king of Hungary, 108,
  115–16, 140
Mauricius, Roman emperor, 8
May Declaration (1917), 250
media, 284–5
see also periodicals and newspapers
Medjumurje, 269
Medun, 185
Mehmed I, Ottoman sultan, 91, 102
Mehmed II the Conqueror, Ottoman
  sultan, 106, 120, 134

Mesić monastery, 120
Meštrović, Ivan, 250
Metéora, 98
Methodius (missionary), 16
Metohija, 269, 274, 289
Michael (formerly Boris), khan of
    Bulgaria, 15
Michael I Angelus, despot of Epirus, 37
Michael VIII Palaeologus, Byzantine
    emperor, 49
Michael Asen, tsar of Bulgaria, 48
Michael Shishman, tsar of Bulgaria, 62
migrations, xxi–xxiv
    18th century, 160
    19th century, 189, 197
    under Austrians, 159–60
    early migrations, 11
    Great Migration (1690), 144, 146, 147
    under Ottomans, 115–20, 154
    overseas labor, 281–2
    to Russia and Banat, 155
Mihailo, Prince, 196, 207, 213–14, 215
Mihajlo, Grand Prince of Duklja, 31
Mihajlo Andjelović, 107
Mihajlo Višević, prince of Zahumlje, 17,
    18
Mihajlo Vojisavljević, prince of Duklja,
    25–6, 26–7, 28
Mihajlović, Dragoljub Draža, colonel,
    270, 271, 272, 273, 290
Milan Obrenović, king of Serbia, 196,
    214–15, 237, 239, 240
Mileševa monastery, 58, 80, 131, 139,
    141
Miletić, Svetozar, 219, 233
Milica, Princess, 89, 90
Military Border (Vojna Krajina)
    16th century, 119
    17th century, 148
    19th century, 196, 197, 218
    Croatian takeover, 228
    education, 220–1
    French partial takeover, 187
    incorporation in Hungary (1741),
        154–5, 159
    life on, 161–2, 165
    towns in, 159
military service
    19th century, 210, 213
    under Germans, 270
    Kingdom of Serbs, Croats, and
        Slovenes, 257
    Montenegro, 216, 217
    under Ottomans, 113–14, 178, 222,
        223
    under Venetians, 184
Miloradović, Mihailo, 185

Miloš Belmužević, 116
Miloš Obrenović, Prince, xiv, 182–3,
    190–6, 213, 241
Milošević, Slobodan, 295
Milutin, Stefan Uroš II, king of Serbia,
    49–52, 58, 60, 61–2
    coins of, 56
Milutinović-Sarajlija, Sima, 198
mining and mineral deposits, xxii
    19th century, 205
    coal mining, 193
    medieval Serbian state, 54–5, 57, 71,
        93–5, 96
    silver, 93–4, 114
    under Ottomans, 114, 123–5, 124
    under Romans, 3
Mirijevski, Teodor Janković, 166
Miroslav, prince of Hum, 31, 32
Mišar, battle of (1806), 179–80
Mitrovica, 157, 159
Mladen III Bribirski, 65
Moesia, 2
Mohaćs, 197
Moldavia, 138, 180
Moldavian Campaign (1710–11), 185
Moler, Petar, 190
monasteries
    under Austrians, 170
    Dušan's Code on, 69
    under Ottomans, 118–19, 120, 137–8
    royal and noble endowments, 58–61,
        98–9
    way of life, 53
    see also individual monasteries by name
money, see coins and minting; debt and
        credit; finance, national
Mongols, 46–7, 87–8
Montenegro
    communism in, 256
    printing, 190
    territories, 227, 253
Montenegro: events
    under Romans, 6
    fall to Ottomans, 108–10
    clan society, 131, 185
    under Ottomans, 142–3
    18th century, 185–7
    19th century, 179, 189–90
    merger with Boka (1814), 188, 189–90
    relations with French, 188
    development of nationalistic feelings,
        210
    alliance with Serbia against Ottomans
        (1866), 214
    move to secular rulers, 215–17
    Ottoman attacks (1853, 1858, and
        1862), 215–17

Great Eastern Crisis (1875–8), 223–4
    Berlin Congress outcome, 225, 227
    early days of independence, xxiv,
        237–8, 240–3
    Constitution established (1905), 242
    kingdom proclaimed (1910), 242–3
    support for Albanians, 244
    Balkan Wars (1912–13), 244–5
    World War I, 248, 249
    unites with Serbia (1918), xxiii, 251
    effects of unification, 258, 260
    World War II, 269
    status in Yugoslav Republic, xxviii,
        274–5, 291
    and breakup of Yugoslav Republic, 295
Morača monastery, 48, 60
Morovlachs, 9, 184
Moštanica monastery, 118
Mostar, 231, 236
Mt. Athos, 43, 82, 101
Mt. Avala TV tower, 285
Mrazović, Avram, 166
Mrkalj, Sava, 199
Mrkšina Crkva monastery, 139
Municipium Dardanorum (Sočanica), 3
Municipium Malvesatium (Skelani), 3
Murad I, Ottoman sultan, 79, 83, 84–5
Murad II, Ottoman sultan, 103, 104, 106
Musa, brother of Suleyman, 91, 102
Muškatirović, Jovan, 174
Muslims
    in Bosnia-Herzegovina, 230–1, 256,
        292
    in Macedonia, 256
    in Serbia, 225, 238
    in Yugoslavia, xxix, 265
    in Yugoslav Republic, 290
Mutimir, Prince, 15, 18

Načertanije, 212
Naissus, see Niš
Napoleon Bonaparte, 182, 187
Narentanoi, 12
National Council of Bosnia and
        Herzegovina, 250–1
National Council of Slovenes, Croats, and
        Serbs, 250–1
National Front, 274
National Party (Dalmatia), 230
National Party (Montenegro), 242
National Radical Party, 256
National Socialism, Yugoslav support for,
        266
Nationalities Law (1868), 220–1, 232
nationhood and nationalism
    19th-century ideas of, 208–9
    20th-century ideas of, 294–5

royal family and church, 58–61, 59,
        97–8
    Serb notions of, 265–6
    Serb sense of tradition, xiv, 170–1
    Serbs as chosen people, xi, 35–6, 46
    Yugoslav attempts at integration,
        262–3
NDH, see Independent State of Croatia
Nedić, Milan, General, 270
Nemanja, Stefan (St. Simeon the
        Myrrhoblete), grand župan, xix,
        31–3, 35–6, 41, 98
Nemanjić, Rastko, see Sava I, Archbishop
Nenadović, Pavle, metropolitan, 165
Neoplanta, see Novi Sad
Neretljani, xxv, 16, 18, 24
Neusatz, see Novi Sad
Nevesinje rebellion (1875), 223
Nicaea, 42, 47
Nicephorus II, 75
Nicopolis, battle of (1396), 86, 115
Nikezić, Marko, 293–4
Nikola Altomanović, 78–9, 80
Nikola Petrović Njegoš, prince of
        Montenegro, 216–17, 223, 237,
        240–3, 258
    court of, 242
Nikola Zojić, 87
Nikolaus Ujlaki, king of Bosnia, 108
Nikolić, Atanasije, 198
Nikolić, Fedor, baron, 234
Nikolić, Mihajlo, baron, 234
Nikoljac monastery, 118
Nikšić (Anagastum), 7, 185, 224, 225
Nikšić, Melentije, 190
Niš (Naissus), 3
    16th century, 112, 126
    17th century, 143
    18th century, 153, 154, 177
    19th century, 180, 224, 225
nobility
    19th century, 191–2
    under Austrians, 158, 234
    medieval Serbian state, 73–4
    under Ottomans, 114
Nomocanon, 68
Normans, 27–8, 30, 31
Nova Srbija (New Serbia), 155
Nova Varoš, 179
Novak Belocrkvić, 87
Novi (Herceg Novi)
    under Bosnians, 93
    and Ottomans, 108, 110
    Spanish capture (1537–8), 141
    textile industry, 96
    under Venetians, 185
Novi Pazar, see Ras

Novi Sad (Neoplanta, Neusatz, Ujvidek)
    1848–9 unrest, 200, 203
    cultural role, 219
    destruction (1849), 203
    education, 167
    foundation, 154, 159
    industry, 205
    printing, 197
    uprising (1779), 166
    see also Petrovaradin
Novo Brdo
    14th century, 78, 94
    15th century, 95, 104, 107, 115
    16th century, 123, 125

Obeda monastery, 119
Obodrites, 10
Obradović, Dositej, 164, 174, 181
Octoechos, 109
Odescalchi, Livius, 157
Ohrid, 63, 67, 115
Ohrid archbishopric, 20–1, 40, 41, 134
Omer Pasha Latas, 216, 222
Oplenac, Church of St. George, 254
Orfelin, Zaharije, 170, 173, 174
Orhan, Ottoman emir, 66
Orthodox Church
    11th century, 26–7, 28
    13th century, 40–6
    Balkan organization, 17, 18, 22
    buildings, 21
    Ohrid archbishopric, 20–1
    schism from Rome, 22
    Slavonic Gospels, 19, 41
    see also Croatian Orthodox Church;
        Serbian Orthodox Church
Ostrovica, 103
Ottoman Empire
    army system, 105
    effects of rule, xx, xxvi–xxvii
Ottoman Empire: events
    conquest of Pannonian Basin, xxi
    first strongholds in Europe, 66
    14th-century expansion, 79, 82–3, 86–7
    battle of Kosovo (1389), 84–5
    Mongol threat, 87–8
    struggles between rulers, 90–1
    conflict with Balšić family, 92
    and Serbs, 102–4
    Balkan Crusade against (1443–4), 104
    15th-century relations with Hungary,
        104–5, 115–16
    capture of Constantinople (1453),
        106–7
    final Balkan onslaught, 107–10
    Serbian rule, 111–45
    treatment of captured peoples, 115

Serb rebellions against, 140–5
war against Habsburg Empire
    (1593–1606), 141–2
war against Venetians (1645–69), 142–3
War of the Holy League (1683–99),
    140, 143–5, 146
Moldavian Campaign (1710–11), 185
Serbian War (1714–18), 151, 185–6
Austro-Turkish War (1736–9), 153–4
invasion of Habsburg Empire (1739),
    153
state weakness, 176
Belgrade pashalik, 176–83, 190–203
janissary regime, 176, 178–9
Austro-Turkish War (1788–91), 177
Karadjordje's rebellion (1805–13),
    178–82
Russo-Turkish War (1806–12), 180,
    181–2
Miloš's rebellion (1815), 182–3
Serbian move to autonomy, 191, 195–6
Crimean War (1853–6), 211–12, 216
continued interference in Serbia, 213–14
Serbian attempts to rid self of vassalage,
    214–15
attacks on Montenegro (1853, 1858,
    1862), 215–17
Balkan rule, 221–3, 243–5
Great Eastern Crisis (1875–8), 223–5
Balkan Wars (1912–13), 244–5
World War I, 247
Ovčar-Kablar monasteries, 138
Ozren monastery, 118

painting, 74, 98, 119, 170
Pajsije, Patriarch, 137, 139
Pakrac, 157
PLižna, Ivan, 83
Pančevo, 159, 200, 205
Pannonia, 2, 7
papacy
    Byzantine schism from Rome, 22
    11th century, 26–7, 28
    12th century, 38
    13th century, 40–2, 47–8
    14th century, 66
Papraća monastery, 118
Paraćin, 96, 236
Paris Peace Conference (1919), 253–5
Partisans, 270–4
Partoš monastery, 120
Pašić, Nikola, 247, 248, 251, 256
Passarowitz, Treaty of (1718), 186
Paštrovići, 131
Pasvanoglu, 178
Patarins, 45
Paul Karadjordjević, Prince, 264

Pavelić, Ante, 262, 269, 290
Pavle, metropolitan of Smederovo, 134–5
Pavle Branović, prince of Serbia, 18
Pavle Radenović, Prince, 87
Pavlović, Dimitrije, metropolitan, 260–1
Pavlović, Milentije, metropolitan, 193
Peasant–Democratic Coalition
    (Yugoslavia), 259, 264
Peasant Law, 68
Peć, xxiii, 107
Peć patriarchate, *135*
    abolition (1766), 177
    commencement, 50
    under Ottomans, 134, 150
    restoration (1557), xxvii, 135–7, *136*
Pécs, 159
People's Radical Party (Serbia), 238,
    239–40
periodicals and newspapers
    18th century, 172
    19th century, 198, 210, 236
    Dalmatia, 188
    Hungary, 197
    Montenegro, 190, 217
    Voivodstvo, 219
    Yugoslav Republic, 283
Perović, Latinka, 293–4
Persians, 8
Pest, 197, 198, 200
Petar I Karadjordjević, king of Serbia,
    240, 246, 257
Petar II, king of Yugoslavia, 264, 268,
    270, 272, 273
Petar I Petrović Njegoš, Metropolitan,
    179, 187, 189
Petar II Njegoš, Metropolitan, 189–90,
    215
Petar Odeljan, 25
Peter, tsar of Bulgaria, 18
Peter I the Great, tsar of Russia, 164, 185
Peter Gojniković, prince of Serbia, 15, 18
Petronijević, Avram, 196
Petrovaradin (Novi Sad), 148, *149*,
    158–9, 160
    see also Novi Sad
Petrović, Djordje (Karadjordje; Black
    George), 179, 180–1, 181–2, 190,
    241
Petrović, Mojsije, metropolitan, 163
Petrović, Sava, metropolitan, 186
Petrović, Vasilije, metropolitan, 186
Petrović-Knićanin, Stevan, 211
Phocas, Roman emperor, 8
Pig War (1906–11), 246
Pirot, 224, 225
Piva monastery, 118
plague, 194

Plav, 225
Pljevlja, Holy Trinity monastery, 118
Pobori, 186, 187
Podgorica, 185, 225
Polit-Desančić, Mihailo, 219
Popović, Jovan Sterija, 198
Popović, Vicentije, metropolitan, 151, 153
Popovo Polje, 37, 48
population
    19th century, 194, 197
    Voivodstvo, 218
Poreč, 179
Požarevac, 177, 179, 194
Praevalitana, 6
Prapratna, 26
Praviteljstvujušči sovjet, 180
Predislav, *see* Sava II, Archbishop
Preljub, Caesar, governor of Thessaly, 65
Pressburg, Treaty of (1805), 187
Pribićević, Svetozar, 229, 255, 259, 262
Pribislav, prince of Serbia, 18
Priboj, 180
Prilep, 63
Primislav, *grand župan*, 31
Priština, 91
Privrednik association, 229
Prizren (Prizdriana), 21
    14th century, 77, 79
    15th century, 107
    under Ottomans, 111
    Virgin of Ljeviška monastery, 61
Procherion, 68
Procopius, 16–17
Progressive Party (Serbia), 238–9
Prohor, Archbishop, 134–5
Prokuplije, 179, 225
Prosek (Demir Kapija), 37, 50
Prosvjeta, 231
public health, 194, 210, 278, 286

Raban, *see* Arbanon
Radić, Stjepan, 256, 261
Radič Branković, 80, 81, 114
Radič Crnojević, 92
Radical Party (Hungary), 233
Radical Party (Yugoslavia), 264
Radičević, Branko, 200
Radjevina, 179
Radojković, Mileta, 195
Radoslav, king of Serbia, 38, 46, 55
Radoslav, *župan*, son of Prince Andrija,
    48
Ragusion, *see* Dubrovnik
Rajačić, Josif, patriarch, 201, 202
Rajić, Jovan, 167, 171, 173, 174
Rákóczy, Ferenc II, 148, 149–50
Ranke, Leopold von, 183

Ranković, Alexander, 293
Ras (Novi Pazar), 153, 179
  13th-century decline, 50
  churches, 17, *21*
  geographical position, 12–13, 21
  as medieval trade route, 23
  Serbian capture (12th century), 29–30
  as Serbian political center, xxiii
Ras bishopric, 40
Raška land, 30
Ratislav, prince of Great Moravia, 15–16
Ravanica monastery, 99, 103
Regulamentum (1770, 1777), 166–7
religion
  as differentiating factor, xix
  under Ottomans, xxvii, 131
  Serbian Christianization, xviii–xix,
    15–17
  and Serbian nationhood, xx, 265
  Slavic, xviii, 16–17
  see also Catholicism; Croatian
    Orthodox Church; Orthodox Church;
    papacy; Serbian Orthodox Church
Remesiana, *see* Bela Palanka
Resava (Manasija) monastery, 89, *90*, 99,
  107
Riječki Grad, 185
Rijeka Crnojevića, *see* Žabljak
Ristić, Jovan, 214
Rmanj (Hrmanj) monastery, 118
Roman Empire
  in Balkans, xxv, 1–7
  rise of eastern, 6–7
Romania
  Balkan Wars (1912–13), 245
  and Banat, 254
  Serbs in, 252
  World War I, 250
  World War II, 267
Romanians, 160, 201, 218
Roma (Gypsies), xxvii, 211
Rostislav Mihajlović, 47
Rovine, battle of (1395), 86
Rudnik, 80, 123, 125, 179
Rudo, 180
Rujno monastery, 139
Russia: *events*
  acts as Serbian church patron, 138
  18th-century migration to, 155
  help for Serbian education, 164–5, 166
  19th-century involvement in Serbian
    affairs, 179, 180, 182
  Moldavian Campaign (1710–11), 185
  and Montenegro, 185, 186, 189–90
  attempts to take over Venetian
    territories, 187
  and Miloš, 195

and Hungary, 203
Balkan role diminished, 212
Great Eastern Crisis (1875–8), 223,
  224, 225
Peter I makes alliances with, 240
Montenegrin dependence, 240, 242
Russian Revolution (1917), 250
see also USSR
Russo-Turkish War (1806–12), 180,
  181–2
Ruthenians, 160

Šabac (Zaslon), 96, 179, 180, 194
Šabac bishopric, 193
Sabor, 151, 153, 155
Sabov, Dimitrije Anastasijević, 167
Šafarik, P. J., 208
St. Luke monastery, 119
St. Sava, *see* Sava I, Archbishop
St. Sergius Marketplace, 92
St. Vitus's Day Constitution (1921), 256–7
Salona (Solin), 8
Salonae (Aspalaton), *see* Split
Samokov, 125
Samuel, tsar of Bulgaria, 20
San Stefano, Treaty of (1878), 225
Sandalj Hranić, 87, 92
Sandžak, 289
Sarajevo, 118, 231, 236, 246
Sase, 124
Sava I, Archbishop (St. Sava), *98*
  as archbishop, 38, 42–4
  burning of remains, 142
  church building, 17
  death and cult, xix, 45–6
  as diplomat, 37, 38, 39
  hagiography of father, 35
  ordination, 33
Sava II, Archbishop, 38, 48
Sava III, Patriarch, 97
Saxons, xxvi, 54–5, 71
Šćepan the Little, 186
"Sclavinias," 10–15
Selim II, Ottoman sultan, 137–8
Selim III, Ottoman sultan, 177–8
Seljuks, Byzantine war against (1071), 25
Šemljug monastery, 120
Serbia
  "Baptized Serbia," 12, *13*
  10th-century territories, *13*
  12th-century territories, *32*
  13th-century territories, *39*, *51*
  15th-century territories, 91–3, 101,
    102
  19th-century territories, *192*, *227*
  royal family and church, 58–61, *59*,
    97–8

Serbia: *events*
  early threats, 13–15
  early rulers, 14–15, 17–19
  Bulgarian subjugation, 18, 20
  11th century, 20–4
  uprisings against Byzantines, 24–5
  involvement in Byzantine–Hungarian
    wars, 29–31
  campaigns against Byzantines, 31–2
  Nemanja's legacy, 34–7
  Nemanyid period, xxiii
  power struggles, 35–7
  kingship inaugurated, 38–40
  church made autocephalous, 40–6
  Mongol incursions, 47
  local struggles, 47–9
  two kingdoms period, 49–52
  internecine strife, 61–3
  Dušan's expansionism, 64–6
  involvement in Byzantine struggles, 66
  conflict on Dušan's death, 75–80
  end of Nemanjids, 79–80
  partial Bosnian takeover, 80–1
  battle of Kosovo (1389), 84–5
  rulers made Byzantine despots, 88–9
  struggles with Ottomans, 90–1, 102–4,
    106, 107–10
  vassalage, 101–2
  fall to Ottomans, 103–4, 107–10
  state restored (1444), 105
  Ottoman rule, 111–45
  partial liberation, 146–51
  rebellions against, 140–5
  Ottoman restoration (Belgrade
    pashalik), 176–83, 190–6
  janissary regime, 176, 178–9
  First Serbian Uprising (1804–13), xxviii,
    178–82
  Miloš's rebellion (1815), 182–3
  Miloš's rule, 190–6
  autonomy gained (1829–33), 191
  constitutional period, 195–6
  spread of liberalism, 207–8, 219–20
  help given to Serbs in 1848, 211
  plans for expansionism, 212
  Ottoman interference, 213–14
  1869 constitution, 214–15
  and Montenegro, 217, 219–20
  Great Eastern Crisis (1875–8), 224–5
  independence gained (1878), 225
  Berlin Congress outcomes, 225, 227
  early days of independence, 237–40
  monarchy restored (1882), 239
  war against Bulgaria (1885), 239
  reaction to Montenegro's kingdom
    proclamation (1910), 242–3
  expansion ambitions, 243

  Balkan Wars (1912–13) and effects,
    244–5
  involvement in Francis Ferdinand's
    assassination, 246–8
  World War I, 248–51
  declaration of unification (1918), 251,
    252
  role in unified kingdom, 252–3
  effect of Paris Peace Conference (1919),
    253–5
  World War II, 270
  status in Yugoslav Republic, 274, 278,
    292, 293–4
  Yugoslavian breakup, 288–96
  20th-century growth in nationalism,
    294–5
Serbian Bank, 229
Serbian Cultural Club, 266
Serbian Law (1887), 228
Serbian Literary Cooperative, *see* Srpska
    Književna Zadruga
Serbian National Liberal Party (Hungary),
    233
Serbian National Party (Dalmatia), 230
Serbian Orthodox Church
  administrative centers, xxiii
  under Austrians, 147–51, 153, 155–6,
    157, 166–7
  book printing, 138–9, 171
  in Bosnia-Herzegovina, 231
  in Croatia, 228
  in Dalmatia, 230
  and education, 162–5
  Justinian's influence, 7
  in Kingdom of Serbs, Croats, and
    Slovenes, 260–1
  and law, 68–9, 71
  and nobility, 98
  under Ottomans, xx, 114, 118, 125,
    133–9
  place in social hierarchy, 73
  and rulers, 58–61, 59, 97–8
  and tradition, 35–6, 46, 171
  in Venetian territories, 184–5
Serbian Orthodox Church: *events*
  early days, xix
  foundation of autocephalous church,
    40–6
  struggles, 47–8
  14th-century split, 97
  monastery building, 118, 138
  struggles for patriarchate, 134–7
  Peć patriarchate restored (1557), xxvii
  property confiscations, 137–8
  role in Great Migration (1690), 144,
    147
  Habsburgs hamper unification, 147–8

Serbian Orthodox Church: *events cont.*
  and Rákóczy uprising (1703), 148–9
  struggles for autonomy, 150–1, 153,
    155–6
  Regulamentum (1770, 1777), 166–7
  Peć patriarchate abolished (1766), 177
  Declatoria (1779), 196–7
  Ottomans grant religious freedom
    (1829–33), 191
  French legalize religious tolerance
    (1808), 188
  19th-century autocephaly, 192–3
  19th-century position, 207
  19th-century Austrian reforms, 220
  interference from Austrian regime,
    233–4
  Constitution (1931), 261
  see also churches and church building
Serbian Royal Academy, 236
Serbian War (1714–18), 151, 185–6
Serbs
  9th-century campaign against Arabs, 16
  10th-century territories, 12, *13*, 15
  19th-century cross-border links, 234–7
  administrative centers, xxiii
  in Austria-Hungary, 226–35, 247–8
  in Bosnia-Herzegovina, 292
  as chosen people, xi, 35–6, 46
  differentiation from neighbors, xiii, xix
  early German and Polish, xvii
  early religion, xviii, 16–17
  early uses of name, 10, 11
  ethnicity of medieval state, xxvi
  in Hungary, 143–75, 196–203, 217–21;
    see also separate entry
  identity, *see* nationhood and nationalism
  in Kingdom of Serbs, Croats, and
    Slovenes, 258, 259–61
  NDH program against, 269
  origins, xvii–xix
  under Ottomans, xx, 221–3
  relations with other peoples, xxiv–xxix
  role in Partisans and Chetniks, 274
  in Roman Empire, 1, 3, 6
  sense of tradition, 170–1
  and Slavs, xvii–xviii
  and statehood, xiv
  in Venetian territories, 183–5
  World War I, 247–8
  in Yugoslav Republic, 274–6, 287–8
  after Yugoslav Republic breakup,
    295–6
  in Yugoslavia, 262–3
Serbs in Hungary: *events*
  Serbian War (1714–18), 151
  Ottoman invasion and territories lost
    (1739), 153–4

Hungarian jurisdiction, 154–6, 196–203
Military Border incorporated in
  Hungary, 154–5
18th-century calls for reform, 174
"privileges," 196–7
help given to Serbia, 197–8
1848–9 unrest, 200–3, 218
Vojvodina proclaimed, 201–3
Duchy of Serbia set up, 203
Magyarization, 210
establishment and abolition of
  Voivodstvo, 218–19
Serbs, Croats, and Slovenes, Kingdom of
  the (later Yugoslavia), xxiv,
  xxviii–xxix, 252–3, 255–62
Serres, 76, 78, 82, 86
Severci (Severjani), xxii, 10, 12, 14
Sheperus, Cornelius Duplicius, 141
Shishman, Prince, 50
Shkoder, *see* Skadar
Šibenik, 184
Šibenik metropolitanate, 188, 229
Sibiu metropolitanate, 220
Siderokapsa, 124
Sigismund of Luxemburg, king of
    Hungary
  death, 103
  and Djuradj, 103
  reign, 85–6, 87, 89
  struggle for Hungarian throne, 83, 84
Simeon, St., *see* Nemanja, Stefan
Simeon, tsar of Bulgaria, 18
Simeon Uroš Palaeologue, governor of
    Epirus and ruler of Thessaly, 65, 67,
    75, 98
Simović, Dušan, 268
Singidunum (Belgrade), 3, 8
Sirač, 148
Sirmium (Sremska Mitrovica,
    Szavaszentdemeter), 115
  11th century, 21, 22
  13th century, 50, 52
  under Romans, 3, 5, 8
Skadar (Shkoder)
  Balkan Wars (1912–13), 245
  Balša III's siege, 92–3
  capture by Michael I Angelus, 37
  Ottoman capture (1479), 108
  Simeon's attack (1358), 75
  Venetian takeover (1395), 92
Skanderbeg, George Castriota, 105, 108
Skelani, *see* Municipium Malvesatium
Skopje
  Austrian capture (17th century), 143
  Bulgarian uprising (1072), 25–6
  under Byzantines, 22
  Ottoman capture (1392), 86, 92

Serbian attacks on, 23, 47, 49, 66
Serbian capture (1912), 245
Slaveno-serbskija vjedomosti, 172, *172*
slaves, Ottoman, 115
Slavjanoserbija, 155
Slavonia
  11th century, 22
  under Austrians, 147
  education, 166
  Ottoman conquest (1536), 118
  Ottomans driven out, 143
  monasteries, 119
  see also Triune Kingdom
Slavs
  Balkan settlement, 9–15
  branches, 10
  early religion, xviii, 16–17
  migrations, xvii, 7–10, 11, 14
  and Proto-Bulgarians, 13–14
  relations with other peoples, xxiv–xxv
  in Roman Empire, 1, 3, 6, 7–8
  and Serbs, xvii–xviii
Slobozia, Treaty of (1807), 180
Slovaks, 160
Slovene People's Party, 256
Slovenia
  French temporary rule, 187
  post-unification politics, 256, 257
  status in Yugoslav Republic, 274, 291
Smederevo
  Austrian capture (18th century), 177
  coins of, 56
  First Serbian Uprising (1804–13), 179
  Ottoman siege (1439), 104
  Ottoman siege (1459), 107–8
  under Ottomans, 111, 112
  rebuilding (1427–30), 99
Sočanica, *see* Municipium Dardanorum
social organization
  13th and 14th centuries, 73–4
  19th century, xx
  under Austrians, 158
  and Christianization, xviii–xix
  under Ottomans, 114, 119
  see also clans and clan society
social welfare, 286–7
socialism, 209, 215, 220
Socialist Party of Serbia, 295
Society of Serbian Letters, 198
Sofronije of Podgorica, Metropolitan, 150
Solin, *see* Salona
Sombor, 159, 167
Sopoćani monastery, 58
Spain, war against Ottomans, 141, 142
Split (Aspalaton, Salonae), 8, 83, 184
Split archbishopric, 17, 26–7, 40, 41
Spuž, 185, 225

Srebrenica
  Bosnia and Serbia quarrel over (1448),
    106
  under Hungarians, 117
  under Ottomans, 111, 123, 125
  Serbia takes over (1411), 91
Srem
  16th century, 118
  17th century, 144, 147
  18th century, 151, 160, 166
  19th century, 201
  monasteries, 118–19
Srem diocese, 22
Sremska Mitrovica, *see* Sirmium
Sremski Karlovci, 165, *169*
Sretenje Ustav, 195
Srpska Književna Zadruga (Serbian
  Literary Cooperative), 236, 284
Stalin, Joseph, 275, 278
Stanjević monastery, 186
Stara Gradiška, 269
Starčević, Ante, 228
Staro Nagoričino monastery, 61
Stefan, Prince, son of Vukan, 48, 60
Stefan Branković, Despot, 104, 107
Stefan Crnojević, 107, 110
Stefan Dabiša, king of Bosnia, 86, 87
Stefan Dušan, Emperor, *see* Dušan,
  Emperor of the Serbs and Greeks
Stefan Lazarević, Despot
  alliance with Ottomans, 85, 87
  at battle of Nicopolis (1396), 86
  biography, 101
  reign, 88–91, 92–3, 101–3
  relations with Hungary, 101
  seat, 99
Stefan Nemanjić (Prvovenčani), *grand
  župan* and king of Serbia, 32–3,
    34–5, 37–40, 42, 46
Stefan Ostoja, king of Bosnia, 87
Stefan Tomašević, 107–8
Stefan Uroš, Emperor, *see* Uroš, Emperor
  of the Serbs and Greeks
Stefan Uroš I, king of Serbia, *see* Uroš I
Stefan Uroš II Milutin, king of Serbia, *see*
  Milutin
Stefan Uroš III Dečanski, king of Serbia,
  61, 62, 63
Stefan Vojislav, *see* Vojislav, prince of
  Duklja
Stefan Vukčić Kosača, 96, 104, 106
Stejić, Jovan, 198
Stephen I, king of Hungary, 22
Stevan of Metohija, 150
Stjepan II, ban of Bosnia, 45, 80
Stojadinović, Milan, 264
Stojković, Atanasije, 174

Stojković, Milenko, 181
Ston, 25, 63, 76
Stracimir, 31
Stratimirović, Djordje, 202
Stratimirović, Stefan, metropolitan, 167, 171
Strez, Lord, 37
Strojimir, Prince, 15
Strumica, 63
Strymonioi (Strumljani), 12, 14
Studenica monastery, 33, 36, 58
Šubašić, Ivan, 273
Subotica, 159
Suleyman, Ottoman sultan, Bayazid's son, 89, 90–1, 92, 101–2
Suleyman I the Magnificent, Ottoman sultan, 120
Šumadija, see Čestin
Supilo, Franjo, 229, 250
Šupljikac, Stevan, voivoda, 201, 203
Svyatoslav, prince of Russia, 20
Syrgiannes Palaeologus, 63
Szavaszentdemeter, see Sirmium
Szeged, 159, 169, 197
Székesfehérvár, 197
Szentendre, 144, 159, 167, 169, 197

Tamerlane, 87–8
Tamiš River, 159
Tatars, see Mongols
Tavna monastery, 118
taxation
    under Austrians, 157–8
    Kingdom of Serbs, Croats, and Slovenes, 257
    mining, 55
    under Miloš, 191
    Montenegro, 190, 240
    Ottoman Bosnia, 222, 223
    under Ottomans, 113, 120–2, 178
technology
    19th century, 204–7
    medieval, 96
Theodore I Lascaris (Angelus), Byzantine emperor, 44, 46
Thessalonika, 8, 12, 46, 249, 250
Thessaly, 9, 65, 75, 86
Tičar, battle of (1810), 182
Tihomir, grand župan, 31
Tilsit, Treaty of (1807), 180
Timişoara, 159, 167, 201, 218
Timočka buna, 239
Timok bishopric, 193
Timur, 87–8
Tirol, Dimitrije, 198
Tito (Josip Broz), 271, 272, 273, 291, 293–4

Tomić, Jaša, 233
Toplica, 103
towns and cities
    19th century, 235
    20th-century urbanization, 280, 281
    under Austrians, 158–9
    medieval development, 99–100
    under Ottomans, 122–6
    Roman Empire, 3–4
    trgs, 96
    urbanization under Miloš, 193–4
trade
    19th century, 212
    under Austrians, 159
    Bosnia-Herzegovina, 231
    medieval, 54, 57–8, 93–6
    under Ottomans, 127–9, 178
    Pig War (1906–11), 246
    salt, 92–3
transport and communications
    19th century, 204–5
    Ottoman Empire, 128
    railways, 238, 280
    roads, 4, 240
Transylvania, 119, 141–2
Travunia, 16, 17, 24, 28, 32
Travunians, xxv, 12
Trebinje, 79, 80
Trepča, 91, 94, 123, 125
Triballi, 2
Trieste, 184, 229, 254
Triune Kingdom (Croatia, Slavonia, and Dalmatia), 155, 158
Trogir, 184
Trumbić, Ante, 229, 250, 251
Tvrdoš monastery, 118
Tvrtko, ban of Bosnia and king of Serbia, 80–1, 83–5, 92, 97
Tzintzars (Aromani), xxv, xxvii, 128, 160

Ujvidek, see Novi Sad
Ulcinj
    14th century, 71
    15th century, 92, 93
    16th century, 123
    under Ottomans, 185, 224
Ulpiana, see Lipljan
Ulrich of Cilli, Count, 103, 106
United Nations Relief and Rehabilitation Administration (UNRRA), 276
United Serbian Youth organization, 214, 219–20
United States, 250, 279
universities and research institutes, 267, 282–3
urbaria, 158

Uroš, Emperor of the Serbs and Greeks, 64, 75–8, 79, 139
  coat of arms, *132*
Uroš I, *grand župan*, 30
Uroš II, *grand župan*, 30
Uroš I, king of Serbia, 38, 47, 48–9, 55, 58
  coins of, *56*
Usora, 13
USSR
  and Partisans, 271, 272, 273
  World War II, 267
  and Yugoslav Republic, 275–6, 278–9
  see also Russia
Ustasha movement, 269
Užice, 96, 112, 143, 179, 271
Užice bishopric, 192, 193

Vaiuniti, 14
Valjevo, 96, 179
Valjevo bishopric, 192, 193
Varaždin, 119
Varvarin, battle of (1810), 182
Velbužd (Kyustendil), 80, 112
Velbužd, battle of (1330), 62
Velimirović, Nikolai, Bishop, 266
Venedi, 10
Venetian Republic: *events*
  fights against Normans, 27
  Nemanja allied with, 31
  takeover of Dubrovnik and Dyrrachium, 37
  conflict over Dubrovnik, 48
  treaties with Dušan, 65, 67
  attacks on Croatian territories, 66
  ousted from Adriatic cities (1358), 76
  links with Ottomans, 82
  support for Sigismund of Luxembourg, 84
  regains Adriatic cities, 92
  disputes with Despot Stefan, 92–3
  conflicts with Bosnia, 104
  takes over Zetan territories, 107
  alliance with Hungary, 108
  war against Ottomans (1537–8), 141
  Venetian–Turkish war over Crete (1645–69), 142–3
  War of the Holy League (1683–99), 143
  war with Ottomans (1714–18), 151
  support for Montenegro, 185
  17th-century Serb migrations to, 183–5
  Serbian War (1714–18), 185–6
  fall to France (1797), 187
Venetian–Turkish war over Crete (1645–69), 142–3
Vezilić, Aleksije, 174
Vidin, 178

Vienna, siege of (1683), 143
Viminacium, 3
Vinča Institute for Nuclear Sciences, 283
Vinkovci, 159
Visconti, duke of Milan, 84
Višegrad, 179, 180
Višeslav, 103, 107
Visibabe, 3
Vlachs, xxv–xxvi
  13th century, 53
  14th century, 71
  15th century, 105
  absorption, xxvii
  as herdsmen, 54
  initial encounters with, 9
  in Ottoman Empire, 116, 117, 118, 129–30
  as warriors, 105, 113, 130
Vladislav, king of Serbia, 38, 46, 47, 48
Vladislav II, 62
Vladislavić, Sava, 185
Vlastimir, Prince, 15, 16
Vlatko Vuković, 87
Voihna, *kesar*, 76
Voivodstvo, 218–19
Vojislav (Stefan Vojislav), prince of Duklja, 24–5
Vojislav Vojinović, Prince, 76, 77
Vojlovica monastery, 120
Vojna Krajina, *see* Military Border
Vojvodina, xxiv
  20th century, xxix, 259
  and breakup of Yugoslav Republic, 289
  proclaimed (1848), 201–3
  World War II, 273
  Yugoslav Republic, 274, 277
Vozuća monastery, 118
Vranje, 23, 225
Vršac, 159, 166, 200
Vučić-Perišić, Toma, 196, 211
Vučiji Dol, battle of (1876), 224
Vučitrn, 111
Vujanovski, Stefan, 166
Vujić, Joakim, 198
Vuk Branković, 79, 80, 82, 84, 86, 87
Vuk Grgurević, Despot, 116, 140
Vuk Lazarević, Prince, 88, 89, 90–1
Vukan, *grand župan*, 23–4, 28
Vukan Nemanjić, *grand župan*, 32, 33, 34, 38, 42, 45
Vukašin, king of Serbia, 77–8, 79
Vukovar, 157, 159

Wallachia, 138, 180, 214
War of the Holy League (1683–99), 140, 143–5, 146
Wladyslaw III Warnenczyk, Prince, 104

women
    under Austrians, 162
    in clan society, 131
    education, 188
    equality, 233, 278, 287
    literacy, 235, 287
    right to vote, 274
World War I (1914–18), xxviii, 246–51
    Paris Peace Conference (1919), 253–5
World War II (1939–45), 267–73

Xemijet (Association), 256

Yalta Conference (1945), 273
Young Bosnia organization, 246
Yugoslav Committee, 250
Yugoslav Communist Party, 255, 256, 257
Yugoslav Democratic Party, 255, 256
Yugoslav League of Communists, *see*
    Communist Party of Yugoslavia
Yugoslav Muslim Organization, 256
Yugoslav National Party (YNP; formerly
    Yugoslav Radical-Peasant Party),
    263–4
Yugoslav Radical Union, 264
Yugoslavia, Kingdom of (later Republic
    of)
    ethnic frictions, xxviii–xxix
    foundation, xxiv, 262
    integration propaganda, 262–3
    member countries' attitudes to, 274–6
    nationalization, 276–8
    state organization, 289–92
Yugoslavia: *events*
    Constitution (1931), 263
    World War II, 267–75
    collapse and breakup (1941), 268–9
    restoration as republic (1945), 273–4
    postwar reconstruction, 276

conflict with USSR, 275–6, 278–9
Constitution (1974), 291–2
breakup of republic, 288–96

Žabljak (Rijeka Crnojevića), 110, 185,
    225
Zadar, 184, 254
Zadar, Treaty of (1358), 92
Zadar diocese, 229
Zagreb, 22
Zaharije Pribisavljević, prince of Serbia,
    18
Zahumljani, xxv, 12
Zahumlje
    10th century, 17, 18
    11th century, 24, 25, 28
    12th century, 32
    and Byzantine authority, 16
Zakonik, *see* Dušan's Code
Zaplana, 125
Zaslon, *see* Šabac
Zavala monastery, 118
Zbor movement, 266, 270
Ždrelo, 103
Žefarović, Hristifor, 170
Zemun, 157, 159, 200
Zeta
    10th century, 25
    Balšic takeover, 76
    Bosnian capture (15th century), 104
    Mongol raids on, 47
    and Nemanja, 32
    as territory of heirs, 49, 61, 63
    Turks cut off from Serbia, 107
    and Venice, 92
Žiča archbishopric, 50
Žiča monastery, 43, 44
Žitomislić monastery, 118
Živković, Petar, 262

CPSIA information can be obtained at www.ICGtesting.com
Printed in the USA
BVOW041851050812

297060BV00007B/51/P